The social history of Canada

MICHAEL BLISS, GENERAL EDITOR

THE EXPULSION OF ITS PROTESTANT FARMERS

The tragedy of Quebec

ROBERT SELLAR

WITH AN INTRODUCTION BY ROBERT HILL

UNIVERSITY OF TORONTO PRESS

© University of Toronto Press 1974

Toronto and Buffalo

Printed in Canada

Reprinted in 2018

ISBN (clothbound) 0-8020-2068-2

ISBN 978-0-8020-6195-9 (paper)

LC 73-90925

The original edition of this work appeared in 1907

An introduction

BY ROBERT HILL

Introduction

In the summer of 1907 Robert Sellar, a veteran rural newspaperman entering the sixty-seventh year of his life,[1] printed one thousand copies of a modest 120-page book in the office of his newspaper, the *Canadian Gleaner*, located at Huntingdon in the heart of the Chateauguay valley farmlands of southwestern Quebec. He entertained no illusions about making any money from the sale of this book: bitter experience in the past had taught him otherwise. His *Gleaner Tales*, a commendable contribution to early Canadian letters in more sanguine younger days, had had a disappointing sale. And even as he laboured on his latest venture, thousands of unbound pages of his formidable *History of Huntingdon County*, published at his own expense in 1888 to chronicle the heroism of the Chateauguay valley's old-country pioneers, lay mouldering in the cellar for occasional use as mail wrapping. After a threadbare career of forty-four troubled years in country journalism, Sellar was, in fact, well inured to hardship and quite resigned to financial loss. For he was a man who had always prided himself on his firm adherence to strong and outspoken principles – a man who felt himself actuated in the publication of this particular volume by a compelling sense of duty.

The book was entitled *The Tragedy of Quebec*, and its subtitle, *The Expulsion of Its Protestant Farmers*, tells much of the preoccupations that brought it into being. Published in four editions between 1907 and 1916, it remains to this day one of the most controversial politico-religious tracts ever circulated in Canada. To its detractors it represented (and still does) the quintessence of Anglo-Saxon francophobia and Protestant bigotry. Its adherents saw it as a timely warning of the threat to Canada's British integrity inherent in the power of the French-Catholic ecclesiastical establishment of Quebec. 'Possibly,' cautioned the Montreal *Herald* as the controversy over the book mounted, 'it should be read only by those who have the balanced judgement necessary to resist being carried away, whether into enthusiastic acceptance or into violent hostility, by the picture presented.' It was not the sort of book about which one could easily remain neutral.

However explosive its contents when dropped upon an unsuspecting Canadian reading public in 1907, Sellar's *Tragedy of Quebec* contained little that was new for anyone familiar with the lifelong political and editorial proclivities of its author. Identifying himself as a 'Scotch radical,' he espoused from the beginning to the end of his days a liberalism firmly rooted in nineteenth-century maxims of free trade and separation of church and state. His first employment in Canada, in 1857, was as a typesetter at the Toronto *Globe*, then in the vanguard of Upper Canada's struggle against everything that was held to be iniquitous in the union of church and state in the neighbouring French-Catholic section of the province. The George Brown of the 1850s was the incarnation of Sellar's ideals, and in 1863 the youth was recruited to found the *Canadian Gleaner* for his erstwhile employer's supporters in Huntingdon, Canada East. Settled mainly by Scots, Huntingdon County was in many ways more typical of Ontario than Quebec, and its elected member, Robert Brown Somerville, had acquired a certain notoriety in becoming the sole Lower-Canadian parliamentarian to cast his vote in favour of representation by population. Sellar threw his struggling new weekly zealously into the fray; the 'Principles on which the *Gleaner* is to be Conducted' which he inscribed in his private diary[2] in October 1864 reveal the extent of his objectives:

1 It shall always be uncompromisingly Protestant.
2 Recognizing the truth that Lower Canada can never be permanently quiet, or prosperous, or every man in it have equal rights, until the Popish organization in it has been thoroughly destroyed, the *Gleaner* shall advocate the abolition of tithes and all compulsory taxes, the incorporation of religious institutions of any nature, the holding of lands in mortmain, and all other exclusive privileges, not resting still until the Papacy in Lower Canada is placed on the same footing as the Protestant denominations.
3 It shall do its utmost to prevent the two Provinces from being separated.
4 Its end to be attained, is to have every man in Lower Canada possessed of the same rights and privileges, secular schools and voluntarily supported churches, the Government confined strictly to its administrative and legislative capacities, and the most utter and entire separation between Church and State. Nothing short of this to be ever accepted.

To this unequivocal statement of principle he appended a set of rules for his personal conduct to which he remained equally consistent for the remainder of his long life:

1 Rather to offend half a dozen friends, than insert anything personal or uninteresting to my readers.
2 To consider whether I am right in forming a decision, and then to stick to it no matter how unpopular or offensive it may be.
3 Never to seek any office whatever.
4 Never to accept a single sixpence as a gratuity from any man, but to be most scrupulous in preserving my independence.

To a youthful militant like Sellar the disillusionment inherent in Brown's sudden coalition with his enemies for the purpose of achieving Confederation was shattering. Had Ontario despaired of its efforts to ultimately assimilate Quebec? Was it now only intent on ridding itself of French and papal influences through a federal system that would virtually abandon its sister province to a French-Canadian majority as yet unemancipated from the sway of an ominous ecclesiastical establishment? Kicking over party traces, Sellar rallied his readers against the Confederation movement in what was destined to be the first of many lost crusades. 'The Upper Canadian, the French Canadian, the New Brunswicker or the Nova Scotian may accept it,' lamented the *Gleaner* on the eve of Confederation, 'but the old-country residents of Lower Canada can only submit to it.' Time alone would demonstrate Ontario's folly in allowing the 'virus' of Quebec sectarianism to infect the constitution of the new Dominion.

The march of events subsequent to 1867 did little to convince Sellar that he had been in any way mistaken in his dire forebodings of trouble to come. It soon became obvious that the segregation of Quebec from Ontario had indeed rendered its people, French Catholics and British Protestants alike, particularly vulnerable to clerical aggression in the heightening world struggle currently being waged against liberalism by the forces of ultramontane reaction within the Roman Catholic Church. The *Syllabus of Errors* and the Dogma of Papal Infallibility were well known to Sellar's readers, and the *Gleaner* was acutely sensitive to what it took to be local manifestations of the new initiatives from Rome.

The Quebec bishops, Sellar believed, were attempting to forge a French-Canadian equivalent to the successful Catholic party of Germany, and the fruits of their endeavours were becoming patent in many areas. In 1871 a clerical political programme instructed

Catholics to vote only for candidates who accepted a platform of unqualified obedience to the Church. In 1875 Quebec's education ministry was abolished by provincial legislation placing the bishops in effective control of the schooling of Roman Catholic children. Freedom of the press was being systematically throttled by unrestrained exercise of the clerical ban. Campaigns of intimidation and proscription against free thinkers, exemplified by the Guibord case, were being carried to new extremes. In the Eastern Townships, 'free' soil was being enveloped by a network of canonical parishes endowed with municipal powers by bishop's decree. Church-sponsored 'colonization' societies were fast making a mockery of Galt's celebrated guarantees to the 'English' electoral ridings by filling them with French Canadians at public expense. In Quebec's courts, where civil law compelled the payment of ecclesiastical tithes, neither judge nor jury was exempt from priestly influence. Perhaps most appalling to Sellar was the spectacle of a 'British' legislature compliantly surrendering civil responsibility for the maintenance of schools, hospitals, reformatories, and even lunatic asylums, together with appropriate grants of public money and land, special charters, and tax privileges to a growing host of ecclesiastical corporations.

To make matters worse, clerical intrigue was beginning to rear its head even beyond the borders of Quebec, in the Métis troubles and the agitations for tax-supported parochial schools in New Brunswick, Ontario, and the Northwest. Sellar found it grimly ironical that Alexander Galt, Lower Canada's renowned Father of Confederation, should feel constrained to publish pamphlets attacking ultramontane aggression as inimical to the civil liberties of Canadians within ten years of the consummation of the great event. Ontario's 'deluded notion' that Confederation would confine clericalism to Quebec was palpably exploded, and well might the *Gleaner* lament George Brown's abandonment of the great old doctrine of representation by population.

It is beyond the scope of this brief commentary to enter into a prolonged account of Sellar's tribulations as he pursued his solitary destiny in the unrewarding environment of rural Quebec, but it would be fair to say that his life was not uneventful. Threatened frequently with bodily harm and subjected on at least one occasion to physical violence, burned out by Fenians, arrested on trumped-up criminal charges, burned in effigy, evicted more than once by irate landlords (invariably Conservatives or Catholics), his struggling paper placed under ecclesiastical ban by the local priests and subjected to ruinous competition in its limited English-language field by the establishment of subsidized party newspapers, he adhered through thick and thin to his hallowed ideal of separation of church and state. Hated by the Bleus, he also failed to endear himself to Quebec's so-called Liberals, who shrank from the politically-suicidal anticlericalism (and even the party name) of their martyred Rouge predecessors, and who solicited clerical support as openly as their opponents. The aims of Garibaldi, lamented the *Gleaner*, were not descernible in such innocuous Liberals as Luther Holton, Chateauguay's member of parliament and a key party organizer, whose boast that he had never offended French-speaking Catholics in over twenty years of public service was all too well founded. Repeatedly Sellar worked for the reconstruction of the Liberal party on the basis of pure liberal principles, but without success. In 1876, for example, he succeeded in obtaining the commitment of a county convention of Huntingdon Liberals to an anticlerical platform of his own design, but the withdrawal of local French-Canadian support and the reluctance of public men to endorse unequivocal principles blighted his hopes for a grass-roots regeneration of the party throughout the province.

National politicians were another source of constant irritation and disappointment. Macdonald's opportunism was held beneath contempt, while Brown's departure from Grit principles was followed by the pandering of Mackenzie and Blake to the Quebec vote. Dalton McCarthy, the maverick Conservative seen by the *Gleaner* as the brightest hope of 'young Canada' in the late 1880s, retired from public life with his mission incomplete. Wilfrid Laurier's unexpected political heroism in the Manitoba schools settlement fired Sellar's enthusiasm and started the *Gleaner* talking about a 'silent revolution' in Quebec, but disillusionment set in with the prime minister's surrender to clerical pressure for sectarian education in the new provinces of Saskatchewan and Alberta in 1905. Provincial leaders, especially Mercier's 'Castor' (ultramontane) cohorts, were generally written off as a flock of clerical toadies – the sole exceptions being the ineffectual Joly and the well-meaning Marchand, who tried unsuccessfully in the wake of the Manitoba settlement to restore government control of Quebec education. Thus, throughout the better part of his active lifetime, Robert Sellar found himself in bitter opposition to the established order of things in his adopted province.

However distressing Sellar found the hostility of Quebec's Roman Catholics to his determined efforts to deliver them from alleged clerical bondage, what filled his cup of woes to overflowing was the congenital reluctance of his own people, the English-speaking Protestant minority, to take a firm public stand in accordance with their innermost convictions on church and state issues. 'There is nothing disheartens me more than the coldness shown by so many Protestants towards every effort to overthrow the Papacy,' he once confessed to his diary. 'How many of them have shook their heads when the *Gleaner* has taken a stand against it; how many have tried to dissuade me from interfering with it.' Indeed, to a sizeable segment of Quebec's cautious minority the outspoken *Gleaner* had become something of a social and political pariah. Nor did its demanding editor appease his co-religionists with his scrupulous application of the same rigorous principles in criticism of Protestant causes and institutions. Protestant clergymen, prone to indulge in pulpit fulminations about the state endowment of Romanism in Quebec, were charged with hypocrisy in their ready acceptance of tax-exempt privileges and public grants for their own denominational institutions. Quebec's Protestant Committee of Public Instruction was another prime target for its neglect of rural schools, its attempts to graft religious trappings onto the secular curriculum, and its craven acceptance of $60,000 of 'hush money' from Mercier's 'iniquitous' Jesuit Estates settlement. Montreal's well-to-do Protestant congregations were berated for their chronic neglect of the 'great work' of French evangelization, through which devout souls like Sellar hoped to solve a multitude of problems by converting the French Canadians to Protestantism. Leaders of the Orange order elicited snorts of disgust from the *Gleaner* for their political apostasy in supporting the Conservative party, accepting cabinet portfolios alongside the most rabid upholders of ultramontane pretensions, and for seeking legal incorporation in Quebec in the same manner as a community of monks. Less legitimate modes of Protestant action were condemned without qualification. Better to 'let Protestantism die,' counselled the *Gleaner* on the formation of the International Protestant League after the shooting of Thomas Hackett in Montreal in 1877, than to seek to preserve it through a 'dark-lantern society.' Similarly, the Protestant Protective Association of the 1890s, which sought to exclude Catholics from public office and private employment, was denounced as 'a society of hate and selfishness' that had 'fastened a stigma on the fair name of Protestantism as the champion of civil and religious liberty which it will take years to efface.' How could Quebec be freed from clericalism, Sellar wondered, if those who knew better practised clericalism themselves? As early as 1864, in his personal diary, he had worried about the inconstancy of his compatriots. 'At the day of Judgement will God hold the Protestants of Lower Canada guiltless of the awful idolatry and superstition which enwraps it?' he had asked. 'They know what is right, and yet they will not raise even a finger to overthrow the wrong; but wink at it for the sake of a hollow peace and for lucre.' Such revealing sentiments might serve as a prologue for the dread reckoning he described nearly a half-century later in *The Tragedy of Quebec.*

It will come as no surprise to any reader of *The Tragedy of Quebec* to learn that Robert Sellar was accused many times during his life of bigotry and francophobia. He was dubbed 'Fanatic Bob' by his local enemies, while the French-language press habitually responded to his brusque editorials with cries of 'orangiste.' No less a personage than Premier Honoré Mercier saw fit to denounce him publicly, in the Quebec assembly and later in print, as 'a rabid fanatic who never misses an opportunity to show his hatred against anything which is French and Catholic.' Yet it is a singular fact that Sellar considered himself no such thing. He made a firm distinction between religion and clericalism, did not discuss the former in his newspaper, but insisted on his right to comment forthrightly on the latter. He loathed violence, never advised change through any unconstitutional process, and endured innumerable aspersions against his character with remarkable calm and restraint.

The charge of francophobia, less apt than that of bigotry in Sellar's case, invariably stemmed from the close liaison in the nineteenth century between French-Canadian nationalism and the Roman Catholic Church. Sellar was, to be sure, the determined foe of anything that threatened the cherished British connection, but this did not necessarily make him antagonistic towards the French-Canadian people, the great majority of whom he respected as loyal subjects. If he did hold a grudge against French Canadians, it had to do with their galling reluctance to deliver themselves from ecclesiastical thralldom. That achieved, he did not see language and culture as constituting a serious impediment to harmonious relations between English- and French-speaking Canadians. A 'French Quebec' as opposed to a 'Papal Quebec,' he often argued, 'the Dominion could contemplate with complacency, because its people would differ from the other provinces in speech alone: in every other regard they would be in touch with their fellow-subjects.' He defended the equal status of the French language with English in the province of Quebec, called for better French courses in the Huntingdon Academy, and was even prepared to see Protestant children attend French-language schools where population warranted, provided only that the schools be state-controlled and strictly nonsectarian. But the Quebec Church, he discovered, had cleverly buttressed itself against disestablishment by anointing itself the guardian of its own special brand of French-Catholic nationalism, making it virtually impossible to assault without seeming also to attack the French-Canadian nationality. From the St Jean Baptiste Society (to which no French Protestant need apply) to the prevailing doctrine of 'providential mission,' implying the eventual erection of a French-Catholic theocratic state to the exclusion of all others, the religious nationalism of the ultramontanes was abhorrent to a dyed-in-the-wool British Protestant like Sellar. Indeed, one of the motives underlying the writing of his *History of Huntingdon County* was the desire to refute the growing notion in Mercier's time that Quebec's only true 'enfants du sol' were the French Canadians, and that all others were mere interlopers. Such claims had been intensified by census figures revealing a startling process of frenchification in many townships originally pioneered by Protestants. Sellar's controversial analysis of this phenomenon ultimately emerged as the central thesis of *The Tragedy of Quebec*.

Sellar's first detailed explanation of the alarming stagnation of Quebec's English townships was advanced in the crisis atmosphere of 1886, in a long editorial debate with the Toronto *Globe*, whose Liberal backers were sympathetic to French-Canadian unrest over the hanging of Louis Riel. The same conclusions were later elaborated in special correspondence written to feed the anti-Quebec bias of the influential Toronto *Mail* and nourish Ontario's reawakening concern about the régime of church and state in the neighbouring province. And in 1889, in a widely-circulated pamphlet attacking Mercier's Jesuit Estates settlement, published under the imprimatur of the Equal Rights Association of Ontario, the determined agitator trotted out his arguments for the third time. His motive in each instance was the same – to give the lie to the oft-repeated assertions of French-Canadian politicians and their collaborators in English Canada that Quebec's treatment of its linguistic and religious minority was a model of justice which the other provinces would do well to emulate.

To Sellar there was nothing in the plight of the declining British-Protestant minority that could possibly recommend the extension of the odious 'Quebec system' to the virgin soil of Manitoba or any other part of Canada. Did not Quebec's taxes, particularly those levied on corporations, fall most heavily on the minority? Was not the minority inadequately represented in the cabinet, in public offices, and in the courts? Had not state-supported schools, hospitals, and other institutions been relegated to exclusively sectarian control, necessitating costly and wasteful duplication by the minority? Were not bills subjected to the scrutiny of the cardinal prior to their introduction in the legislature? Did not the census figures show that the Quebec minority had languished under Confederation, that British Protestants were fast disappearing from many rural sections and had made material gains nowhere beyond the island of Montreal? Finally, was not the Roman Catholic parish system, with its compulsory tithing, the underlying cause of the townships' decline? It was about this last contention, lying at the core of Sellar's thesis, that controversy invariably raged. Denying that the tithe law, operative only against properties owned by Catholics, was of no concern to Protestants, Sellar posited the following pattern of township growth and decline in his editorial debate on the subject with the *Globe* in 1886:

We will suppose that, say, fifty or sixty years ago, a hundred families came from the North of Ireland, from England, from Scotland, and settled in the bush. With incredible toil and privation, they cleared the forest, and changed the wilderness into a smiling settlement. They became prosperous and contented; supporting good schools and a church. One morning they are startled by the information that the Catholic bishop has issued a decree constituting their township a canonical parish. They are indignant, but cannot help themselves. The few Catholic families among them are formed into a congregation, pay tithes, and a small church is built. How is the priest to live? He cannot, without outside help, unless he manages to substitute Catholic owners for the Protestant holders of the land, and to affect that change he directs his attention. When from either death or other change a farm is offered for sale, a Catholic buys it. The church authorities provide the money, which is secured by mortgage. That farm while owned by a Protestant yielded nothing to the priest; now it gives him a yearly revenue of from $20 to $50. Every farm obtained is a clear gain, and therefore more than the market value can be paid. The process goes on steadily for years, and increases in rapidity with each one bought, for when an Old Countryman has lost his neighbour and sees a French Catholic in his place, he has less inclination to remain. By-and-by it is found difficult to keep up the [Protestant] church, and unless aid is obtained from the home-mission fund of the denomination to which it belongs, regular services cease to be held in it. In the Presbytery of Montreal alone there are 16 churches now dependent upon such aid, which 20 years ago were self-sustaining. The dispersion of the Protestants goes on and the families left cannot maintain a school. For the sake of their children, they have also to sell out and go where they will obtain suitable society and educational and religious privileges. The canonical parish has become a municipal one and the victory of the Church of Rome is complete. A settlement founded and built up by Old Countrymen has been captured, and added to its tribute-paying domain.[3]

Sellar estimated that the farms remaining in English-speaking hands in Quebec would be worth a million dollars in annual revenue to the Roman Catholic Church if French Canadians could be substituted for the current owners. How long, he asked the *Globe*, would the farmers of Ontario have rested content under a system of laws that offered a material premium to French-Catholic ecclesiastics to displace them from their homesteads?

Having suggested motives and methods underlying the alleged clerical campaign to frenchify the Quebec townships, Sellar's thesis proceeded to challenge the constitutionality of the tithe on township soil and to demonstrate that its abolition lay well within the competency of the Canadian parliament. He deemed such proof necessary in view of the prevailing assumption that the tithing prerogative, the very cornerstone of the established foundation of the Quebec Church, was one of the inviolable privileges secured to it by treaty at the time of the Conquest – a misapprehension so common that even the astute Toronto *Mail* and the Presbyterian Board of French Evangelization had fallen into it. The truth, as Sellar discovered in ransacking old documents at Laval University and the newly-created Canadian archives, was that the tithe system was sanctioned by neither international treaty nor imperial legislation as far as the townships of Quebec were concerned.

The tithe question had been distinctly reserved to 'the King's pleasure' by the surrender terms of 1760, and the Treaty of Paris made no mention of either parishes or tithes. British law was affirmed by the Royal Proclamation of 1763, and for over a decade Canadian habitants did not pay tithes unless they chose to do so voluntarily. By the Quebec Act, passed by the imperial parliament in 1774, French civil law was indeed restored, but only to the eighty-two parishes already in existence and not, as commonly supposed, to the province as a whole. The vast tracts of newly-surveyed wild lands, designed for British settlement, were measured in acres and not arpents, municipal divisions were styled townships rather than parishes, and lots were granted in free and common soccage and not according to seigniorial tenure. So explicit were these stipulations that for years the habitants were discouraged by their priests from quitting the depleted and overcrowded soil of the seigniories for the new and fertile townships where they could have lived as free men beyond the mediaeval pale of the compulsory tithe. But in 1839 Sir John Colborne's council, anxious to propitiate the clergy in the wake of the rebellions, issued an ordinance authorizing the extension of the parish system beyond the old bounds. The clergy, tacitly assuming the tithing power to be inherent in the parish system, now began to promote French-Canadian settlement in the townships despite the fact that the new Canadian legislature declined to ratify Colborne's ordinance in 1841, 1843, 1846, and again in 1849. It was not until 10 August 1850, that the ordinance (which legally should have expired in 1841) was finally ratified, and by this time an expanding network of parishes was a fait accompli in the townships.

That the legal basis for the spread of the parish system onto allegedly non-fief land turned out to be of purely colonial origin struck Sellar as a 'monstrous usurpation.' Was not such legislation in clear violation of the imperial statute of 1774? British settlers had taken up their abode in the Eastern Townships and Huntingdon County under the king's guarantee of English law; was it within the constitutional jurisdiction of a Canadian assembly later to violate that compact by making land held in free and common soccage liable to the servitude of French law upon seigniorial land? Sellar claimed knowledge of dozens of original settlers 'who would never have felled a tree' had they dreamt that the Quebec priesthood would one day hold a conditional lien on lands conveyed to them under the royal manual. But there was, he insisted, a solution at hand in that 'what a Canadian parliament has granted, a Canadian parliament can take away.' Let the people of Ontario perceive the extent to which British law had been subverted in Quebec; let them beware of the tentacles of Quebec sectarianism reaching into their own province; let them heed the recent lessons of the Northwest and the threat of Mercier's autonomy cry to Canada and the British connection; let them ponder the spectacle of an established church fostering, through parochial schools that were a libel upon education, a separate nationalism of race and creed; and let them then act to abolish the cancerous 'Quebec system' altogether, preferably before the British-Protestant communities of the townships had passed out of existence. This strident appeal and the arguments upon which it rested were fundamentally unchanged when incorporated into *The Tragedy of Quebec* some twenty years later.

Reaction to Sellar's theories on the decline of the townships was typically hostile. The *Globe* thought it downright 'silly' to attribute the decline of Quebec's Protestant population to tithes paid by Roman Catholics. Ontario had no tithe law, yet the same population trends were in evidence west of the Ottawa. English-speaking people in both provinces were simply moving to better their condition elsewhere, and were fortunate that their farms were being taken by frugal French Canadians willing and able to live on less. Nobody was forcing the Quebec Protestants to leave; their immunity from tithes was to their profit in relation to the rest of the population; and what farmer would object to having always at hand a buyer willing to pay 'more than the market value' for his property?

Introduction   xix

Perhaps the Roman Catholic tithe law should be considered a 'positive advantage' to the Protestant farmers of Quebec.

Such criticism left Sellar unmoved for several reasons. The 1881 census showed 139,086 Protestants living outside Quebec's four major cities, and he considered their gain of only nine thousand in twenty years abnormally low even after general rural decline had been taken into account. Careful study of population ratios with similar Ontario counties, settled at the same time as the townships, convinced him that the Protestants of rural Quebec ought to have numbered at least 180,000 by 1881. The *Globe*'s attempted parallel between the French-Canadian invasion of the bush, barren, and exhausted lands of eastern Ontario and the displacement of English-speaking settlers from the best farms in Quebec overlooked this sizeable discrepancy. It was due, Sellar insisted, to the extraordinary pecuniary incentives afforded the Roman Catholic clergy by the tithe system. It was natural that youthful swarms should be attracted to the growing cities, the booming American midwest, and the promising Northwest, but Sellar's concern was with the shrivelling up of the original hives.

When, prior to the critical Quebec election of 1886, Sellar began to reiterate his disputatious ideas under pseudonym in the Toronto *Mail*,[4] Liberals in both provinces reacted with alarm. 'Are we to destroy Confederation,' cried the *Globe*, 'and plunge into a war of re-conquest because Protestant farmers in the Eastern Townships can always get high prices for their land?' The Montreal *Herald* agreed that it would be suicidal to attempt to despoil French Canadians of the very privileges that made them loyal, while James D. Edgar of the pro-Mercier Ontario Liberals published an open letter warning Quebec's English-speaking minority of 'great danger' should the French-Catholic majority become 'irritated and alarmed.' On the Conservative side, Sellar's agitation in the *Mail* provoked a disavowal from none other than Sir John A. Macdonald in a political speech on 17 September:

If a man be Catholic in Quebec he gives a certain portion of his crop to the priest of his parish — a certain portion of his grain only, mind you. If he raises roots or hay or cattle he pays no tithes, and if he chooses to see the error of his ways and cheat the priest of his tithes, if he chooses to turn Protestant, he need not pay tithes any more

[Laughter]. ... If a Lower Canada farmer has a large crop, why the parson is lucky — Providence has helped the parson as it has helped the farmer. And if the crops fail, why Providence has deserted the farmer and has deserted the parson too [Laughter]. That is their system, and they like it, and it is a system of which Protestants cannot complain, for they have nothing to do with it. And if these people do not complain of it why should we in another province, with different institutions, try to force our opinions upon them and get up an agitation upon a point of this kind? I disapprove of it altogether [Cheers].

This was the prime minister at his jocular best, but to Sellar the issue was not whether the habitant should support his priest, but whether he should be forced to do so by the laws and courts of a British province. A similar reaction greeted Sir Hector Langevin's more thoughtful defence of the system before an Ontario audience on 11 October. 'If the habitants are so much in love with the system as Sir Hector declares they are,' retorted the *Gleaner*, 'why does he object to allowing it to rest upon their goodwill instead of the law?' The truth was 'that there is not one habitant out of fifty who would pay tithes if he could help it, and there is all manner of jockeying used to escape paying the full quantum.' Nor was the system as equitable as had been alleged. Habitants were also liable for a compulsory building tax, and additional levies when parishes were divided. There were farms in Sellar's district that had been taxed to build no fewer than three churches, and the province was currently caught up in a church-building 'mania' whereby perfectly adequate older buildings were being replaced by magnificent stone structures standing in stark contrast to their poverty-stricken surroundings. The disestablishment of the Church of Rome, implored the *Gleaner*, implied neither despoliation of its resources nor interference with its religious teachings. The laws, language, and religion of the French Canadians did not depend upon statutes enforcing the compulsory payment of tithes. Surely religion consisted of something other than 'filling the bag by legal assessment.'

Three years later, in the midst of the furor over Mercier's sensational Jesuit Estates settlement, Sellar again brought his views on the decline of the British-Protestant minority to the forefront of public discussion. Disgusted with the minority's tame acceptance of legislation it considered outrageous, and particularly with the servile stand of its elected representatives against federal disallowance, he forwarded a letter entitled 'The Disabilities of Protestants in the Province of Quebec' to the Equal Rights Association of Ontario in December 1889. It was essentially a repetition of the now familiar theory that Protestant farmers were being squeezed out of Quebec by the working of a tithe and parish system which functioned, as far as the townships were concerned, in violation of early imperial statutes. Its circulation by the Association provoked an immediate reaction from Premier Mercier,[5] who branded its author a fanatic and endeavoured to refute its allegations in a lengthy pamphlet prepared at a cost of five thousand dollars to the taxpayers of Quebec.

Mercier's treatise, though a remarkable document in many respects, left much to be desired as a technical rebuttal of Sellar's thesis on the 'usurpation' of non-fief township soil by the parish system. The premier, complained Sellar in a letter to the Equal Rights Association 28 May 1890, 'indulges in many digressions, drags in subjects the pamphlet does not mention, and which he proceeds to gravely refute.' Mercier's claim that the Church of Rome did not own an inch of land in Quebec (since only the names of the various religious corporations and parochial fabriques actually appeared on the registry books) was a 'mere juggling with words'; his elaborate elucidation of the good works and low salaries of priests and nuns was beside the point; his argument that such ecclesiastical privileges as mortmain and tax exemption were equally available to Protestants hardly justified their existence; his assertion that Sellar, for suggesting that civil courts should not be required to enforce the payment of tithes, was an 'apostle of irreligion, apostacy, and even atheism' was ridiculous; his contention that the Quebec Act had authorized the extension of the parish system throughout the entire province, and that subsequent distinctions in the municipal code between seigniorial and non-seigniorial land had arisen solely from the majority's generous deference to the wishes of the minority, was shot through with historical and constitutional error, and he had even misquoted the act so as to leave out a clause vital to his opponent's case.

Mercier's assertion that the parish system and all its appurtenances applied to every acre of Quebec was far from reassuring to

Protestants apprehensive about finding themselves subjected to French and papal law. 'The systematic crowding out of the Protestants from the Eastern Townships with a view to bringing the lands under ecclesiastical control and taxation was an article of general belief among Protestants long before Mr Sellar wrote his pamphlet,' ventured the Montreal *Star*. 'Most people would take Mr Mercier's "reply" as a confirmation rather than as a refutation of the theory.' Perhaps the weakest aspect of Mercier's case, as the *Star* pointed out, was the 'petulance displayed every time he is under the necessity of mentioning the name of the author of the offending pamphlet.' Well might Sellar, poor 'obscure journalist' and 'ignorant writer' that he was, take what solace he could in the realization that his 'delerious fanaticism,' 'too-vivid imagination,' 'sense of honesty more than doubtful,' and other dubious qualities had never before been assailed from so elevated an office. The Equal Rights Association, although given leave to do so by Sellar, did not repudiate its connection with the controversial pamphlet, but in the end it mattered little as the movement was already on the decline.

Several factors motivated Robert Sellar to plead his case anew to a younger generation of readers through *The Tragedy of Quebec* in 1907. Not the least of these was a growing personal sense of urgency and despair. The principles to which he had dedicated his soul and his strength, and in whose ultimate triumph he had believed with religious fervour, now seemed unlikely to prevail in his lifetime if at all. Quebec's incipient 'silent revolution' of the post-Mercier era had floundered on the rocks of an unreformed school system. Sellar's optimism, engendered by Laurier's handling of the Manitoba schools crisis, had waned with the passage of time until it was finally obliterated by the insertion of clauses providing for separate schools in the autonomy bills of the new prairie provinces in 1905. The exodus of English-speaking farmers had continued apace, and the bleak census returns for 1901 revealed that Protestants (who had managed to retain a majority in six counties in 1881) now outnumbered Catholics only in Brome and had sunk to minority status for the first time in Sellar's own stronghold of Huntingdon. From the Eastern Townships came the solitary voice of Sellar's kindred spirit, W.E. Jones, also mourning 'the passing of the minority' in his Richmond *Guardian*. 'I remember expressing my doubts to Sir Alexander [Galt],' he commiserated, 'and drawing his attention to the probable result of the ecclesiastical legislation then threatening the overthrow of the free and common soccage title of the land of the townships' counties.'

The Montreal *Witness*, onetime trumpet of the Quebec minority, addressed itself to the problem of Protestant decline in the summer of 1906 by opening its columns and calling on readers to submit their views. For weeks the letters poured in, comprising a special feature entitled 'The English Exodus.'[6] Some were pessimistic, others optimistic; some boosted the Northwest at the expense of Quebec, others deprecated the prairies and extolled the townships; suggested solutions ranged from massive British immigration to consolidation of the Protestant churches. But the *Witness* was able to discern a predominant reason for the exodus in the minds of many: 'It is because parents find it impossible to send their children to other than Roman-Catholic schools and see before them the danger of their becoming Roman Catholics and forgetting even their mother tongue.' Correspondents to the *Gleaner* tended to agree. 'Twenty years ago I paid taxes in two municipalities to Protestant schools, which were good schools,' wrote one farmer. 'They have both ceased to exist, and my tax now goes towards educating Catholic children; schools to which I cannot send scholars. They notify me to pay the tax and give me a receipt in French. The only redress farmers in my position have is to leave the province. When a few leave that makes it worse for the balance, and compels them to leave also, until there is not a Protestant in the settlement.' The problem of the Protestant exodus, concluded the *Witness*, had become so closely tied to the schools problem 'that he who could solve the latter would almost solve the former.'

The Protestant exodus had become both a cause and an effect of an alarming educational crisis in the Quebec townships by the turn of the century. Rural elementary schools had been virtually abandoned by the Protestant Committee of Public Instruction since 1875, and their partial efficiency had been further impaired by the continuing drain on population. A report by John Adams, an English educationalist brought over by Sir William Macdonald in 1902 to survey the situation, confirmed what was already obvious — that the condition of the rural academies was satisfactory, that of the model schools less so, and that of the elementary schools deplorable.[7] In 1905 there were three Protestant school districts in Huntingdon in which no teachers were engaged, and sixty-six Protestant elementary schools in the province had closed that year. According to figures released by the Protestant Committee in 1906, nearly half of the nine hundred elementary schools of the Quebec minority averaged only twelve pupils, and only 170 remained open for the full academic year. But the recommendations of Adams and others, which prompted the philanthropic Macdonald to sponsor experiments in school consolidation and to found Macdonald College as a teacher-training institution, only scratched the surface as far as Sellar was concerned. The real trouble, although nobody wanted to mention it publicly, was the sectarian system which divided the scholars according to creed and necessitated the maintenance of two schools in sparsely-populated country districts where there was barely sufficient support for one. The *Gleaner* watched with interest as the federal agriculture minister, Sydney A. Fisher of Brome, organized in conjunction with John R. Dougall of the *Witness,* a 'great educational campaign' to save the rural schools.[8] Sellar attended the opening meeting in Huntingdon 14 August 1906, and concluded that the strident condemnations of public apathy and verbose disquisitions on the value of learning emanating from the highly-touted galaxy of speakers were missing the point. Only William A. Weir, the provincial member for Argenteuil, in his call for some sort of organization aimed at retaining farms in the hands of English-speaking Protestants, came remotely close to what Sellar considered the root of the difficulty. The local people appeared to have a clearer grasp of the essence of their problem than had the well-meaning pundits who had come to advise them. The only real solution, vouchsafed the chairman of the Huntingdon meeting in thanking the city speakers, was 'one school for all.'

Such were the preoccupations that induced an aging Robert Sellar to write and publish *The Tragedy of Quebec.* His immutable belief that Roman Catholic clericalism and its inevitable concomitant, the separate school, had blighted the development of the Quebec townships reinforced his congenital hostility towards their extension to other parts of Canada. The same ominous force that had threatened Manitoba with sectarian division and stifled Quebec's 'silent revolution' of the late 1890s now sought a foothold in the new provinces of the west. In Ontario, where expanding French-Canadian communities along the Ottawa were wresting control from the original

Protestant and Irish-Catholic settlers by converting their old 'union' schools into sectarian and French-speaking institutions, Sellar could see nothing but trouble in store. His *History of Huntingdon County* had been written to chronicle the rise of the British Protestant yeomanry in Quebec; his *Tragedy of Quebec* would account for their sad decline. Perhaps the death knell of the Protestant settlements of rural Quebec would arouse the rest of Canada and prevent the reenactment of their tragic history in Ontario and the west. When publishers tended to shy away from his inflammatory manuscript, Sellar dipped into his slender lifetime savings for one thousand dollars, bought a new typograph machine, and set to work printing it himself. Advertising it as 'a book with a purpose,' he called on his readers to send it 'far and near' to enable it 'to do its work.' He put it on sale for only a dollar – losing more money to maximize circulation – and put himself to the additional expense of mailing one hundred copies to newspapers throughout Canada and Britain.

The main thesis of the work, apart from the introductory chapters construing Quebec's history from a distinctly Protestant viewpoint, consisted of Sellar's traditional views concerning the 'usurpation' of township soil by the tithe system. But the book, unlike his earlier polemics, was alive with imagery designed to tear at the heartstrings of the sympathetic reader. Callous indeed was the Protestant who remained unmoved by the poignant scene in which, for the first time, 'a priest drives up the lane lined by maples which the grandfather of the disapossessed Protestant planted, and levies tithes on the yield of fields his great-grand parents redeemed from the wilderness and which four generations of Protestants have plowed.' It was a measure of Sellar's bitterness that he was prepared to expose, for the first time in print, the deep religious undercurrents that governed his personal convictions. Could not the plight of the Quebec Protestants be due to divine retribution for their having failed not only themselves, but God and the French Canadians, in s sort of providential mission of their own?

Of the hundreds of first settlers I have conversed with, not one in twenty said they crossed the Atlantic with the intention of remaining in Quebec. Was there no purpose in this? Are the settlements of Ulstermen and of Lowland Scots that rose in the midst of the all-pervading forest to be regarded in no other light than that which the economist views them? ... In no other part of the continent was there more need than in Quebec for a body of men and women to bear witness with their lives that no fellow-mortal can stand between the soul and God, teaching the twin truth of the individual responsibility and of the spiritual independence of man. The settlers, so strangely guided to Quebec, knew this great truth, but hid it in their materialism, their eager seeking after what the world can give, and the example they ought to have set was lost in their inconsistent lives, their indifference to the eternal welfare of the people whose eyes were upon them. ... Had they realized the grandeur of their opportunity, had they been faithful to their duty, would they have been abandoned to those who, from their first coming, plotted against them? The Protestants of Quebec had presented to them an opening to do a grand work. They threw it away, and as a people they have been thrown away. ... They have been sinned against, wantonly and aggressively, but they have also sinned by not living up to the knowledge they possessed.[9]

It might not be unfair to conclude that, despite Sellar's attempts to study objectively the phenomenon of Protestant decline in the townships, his *Tragedy of Quebec* was, in the final analysis, a product of theological judgement.

Unlike Sellar's earlier books, *The Tragedy of Quebec* sold well, especially in Ontario. Watson Sellar, later auditor-general of Canada under R.B. Bennett, recalled bringing home one evening a mail order from the president of the Toronto Street Railway for one hundred copies, whereupon his father put on his hat and went out in a blizzard to wrap the package that very night. Well might the *Hamilton Times* remark, in one of the early reviews, that 'whatever good or evil the volume may do, the author is terribly in earnest.' Reaction for and against the book was widespread throughout the country. 'Mr Sellar has written a book that should be as deadly an enemy to ecclesiastical privilege in Canada as "Uncle Tom's Cabin" was to slavery in the United States,' applauded the Toronto *Evening Telegram.* But the Montreal *Canada*, one of the few French-language journals to call attention to *The Tragedy of Quebec*, attributed the disappearance of Quebec's rural Protestant population to purely economic and social causes and dismissed Sellar's anti-Catholic polemic as 'les "novissima verba" d'un homme fatigué de lutter, de penser, et d'espérer.'

Perhaps the most thoughtful criticism of *The Tragedy of Quebec* was that written for the Winnipeg *Free Press* by Téleophore St Pierre, a French-Canadian journalist of Quebec origin. 'People who see evil everywhere and who are prone to accuse everybody of sordid motives are seldom safe guides in the study of such complicated and trying problems as the evolution of Quebec,' he wrote in preface to a reassuring defence of the 'Quebec system.' Priests in Quebec could not levy tithes at will; the rate was fixed by law and the full amount seldom exacted. Church property was, in fact, administered by the laity through a fabrique, or corporation, elected annually by the ratepayers of the parish in much the same manner as a New England town meeting. Quebec's courts, however obsolete, had dealt numerous setbacks to the clergy, who rarely invited their interference. School financing was entirely in the hands of the legislature. To say that the clerical hierarchy dominated legislation was easy, but the documents cited in Sellar's appendix as proof bore the antiquated dates of 1875 and 1876, since which time the Quebec people had repeatedly voted contrary to the explicit wishes of their clergy. The rural decline that had overtaken the Quebec townships was universal throughout eastern North America, and the progress of the French Canadians required no explanation apart from the prolific qualities of the race. Canadian intervention in the internal affairs of Quebec would be unconstitutional, and the Quebec Protestants themselves were asking for no such thing. In Sellar's own words, St Pierre concluded, those not taken with the emigration fever were content to enjoy 'socially agreeable' and 'commercially profitable' relations in a province whose material progress for the preceding decade was unsurpassed in eastern Canada.

Sociologists of a later day, working on the assumption that the related forces of urbanization and industrialization were responsible for population change in the Quebec townships, have largely ignored the explanations advanced by Sellar. Jean I. Hunter, for example, hints at but does not investigate the parish system as a factor underlying English decline.[10] Aileen D. Ross dismisses somewhat summarily the feeling of English-speaking residents 'that the movement of French Canadians into the Townships is a well-organized scheme to push them out completely,' stating that 'neither the French nor the English understand the underlying processes which have caused their changed positions.'[11] Sellar, for his part, would certainly have rejected any suggestion that a farmer would sell out and leave Quebec without knowing the reason why. Nor would he have accepted Dr Ross' contention that the English-speaking farmers were attracted by city life while the French were less susceptible to urban influences. When such claims were advanced in 1901 by the Montreal *Presse*, the *Gleaner* replied that nineteen out of twenty farmers who had sold their places in Huntingdon were still farmers. 'Go to Iowa, Indiana, Illinois, Michigan, Wisconsin, Minnesota, the two Dakotas, or to Manitoba,' Sellar wrote, 'and you will find the men who left Huntingdon County sowing and reaping as of yore.' The 'pretence' that the French Canadian 'turns to the soil as a child to its mother' he dismissed as 'pure bosh.' The French Canadian was no lover of farming, 'as is proved by the hundreds of families who have abandoned their farms to crowd into Montreal and into factory-towns like Valleyfield, Magog, and Cornwall.' Many New England towns were composed largely of former habitants who had spurned proposals by colonization agents to return to the soil.

But Sellar, despite his insistence that sectarian laws were primarily responsible for the decline of Quebec's English-speaking farm population, was by no means unaware of the influence of urbanization, industrialization, and other causes cited by his critics. Another major thrust to his editorial policy over the years had been his espousal of free trade, not only on the basis of his doctrinaire liberalism, but also because he sincerely believed it to be in the best interests of the farming class for whom he spoke. None of his critics appeared to notice that for decades the *Gleaner* had inveighed against the National Policy on the grounds that it was undermining the agricultural way of life in eastern Canada and driving both French- and English-speaking farmers off the land and even out of the country. The first agrarian protest against the Laurier government's virtual adoption of the National Policy was organized in 1898 by none other than Robert Sellar, and when he spoke for the Quebec delegation at the great farmers' march on Ottawa in 1910 he was dubbed 'the Grand Old Man of the farmers' movement' by the *Farmers' Sun*. The *Gleaner* reflected his familiarity with the damaging effects of farm mechanization, increasing western competition, changes in the dairy industry, and the economic unfeasibility of the hundred-acre farm on the smaller farming operations of the Quebec townships. None of this pertinent knowledge was introduced in *The Tragedy of Quebec*, however, tending to substantiate the prevailing assumption that it was a work of very special pleading.

Early in 1909 Sellar was asked by Horatio Hocken, the new proprietor of the Orange *Sentinel* of Toronto, to bring out a second edition of *The Tragedy of Quebec*. Hocken wished to circulate the book as a relevant tract in the crisis brewing between the Orangemen and the Franco-Ontarians over separate and bilingual schools. Sellar could see no reason for slackening his personal crusade against the spread of the 'Quebec system.' By 1908 the 'peasant pope,' Pius X, had succeeded in suppressing progressive elements within the Roman Catholic Church, and nowhere was the reactionary trend better exemplified than in the resurgent wave of ultramontane nationalism sweeping Quebec. New nationalist clubs, particularly the Association Catholique de la Jeunesse canadienne-française, founded in reaction to the Boer war, guided by the Jesuits, nourished in the classical colleges, and stimulated by the Northwest and Ontario schools controversies, seemed markedly more Catholic than French. Their organs, notably the new Quebec *Action sociale catholique,* were decidedly Castor in tone, and their aspirations openly those of the ultramontane separatist Jules Paul Tardivel (whose political novel *Pour la Patrie* would never have been reviewed by the *Gleaner* had not the legislature voted money for five hundred copies to be distributed as prizes among the schools).

Nor was Sellar reassured by professions of a broader nationalism on the part of Henri Bourassa and the Ligue Nationaliste, for there was nothing attractive about a Canadianism based on anti-British sentiment, separate schools, and parochial notions of racial and religious exclusiveness. Educational reforms implicit in Godefroy Langlois' call for a provincial ministry, uniform textbooks, and compulsory free schooling were being suppressed largely through Bourassa's influence, while Archbishop Bruchési had succeeded in scotching Premier Gouin's plans for a non-sectarian academy at Rawdon and a non-denominational technical school in Montreal. Another sign of the times was Archbishop Bégin's ban on the Quebec Auditorium Theatre because one of its plays (*La Tosca*) reflected on the priesthood. Yet another was Archbishop Bruchési's pastoral of 17 November, 1907, instructing Catholics to shun all association with Protestants that could conceivably give rise to the growing 'evil' of mixed marriages. The traditional claim of the Quebec Church to be impervious to civil authority where marriages involving Catholics were concerned was stirring new and vexatious controversy which reached its height, following a series of annulments of marriages contracted before Protestant ministers, with the invocation in 1909 of the papal ne temere decree declaring the only valid marriages between Catholics to be those solemnized by priests.

The intensification of sectarian antagonism did not make Sellar very receptive to French Canada's accompanying mood of linguistic assertiveness. Armand Lavergne's campaign for the legal equality of French with English on coins, stamps, and in the public services was galling in view of 'the suppression of English that is going on in the townships — the serving of legal documents in French on people who might as well have had them presented in Greek, French being declared the official language in municipalities that were settled by English and organized by them, the maintenance of a system which has the effect of closing English schools by the score, the deliberate and persistent replacing of English officials with French.' Even with regard to a bill for the better observance of Sunday, undermined by Bourassa's protests about federal invasions of provincial affairs, Quebec seemed determined to break step with her sister provinces.

Under such circumstances there was little standing in the way of agreement between Hocken and Sellar concerning republication of *The Tragedy of Quebec.* Sellar not only agreed to update the book appropriately, but to waive all royalties on condition that Hocken circulate it as widely as possible at the lowest possible price. It appeared in May 1909, selling at only half a dollar in paper cover, and succeeded in focussing national attention on its contents as the dispute over Ontario schools moved towards a crisis. Late in 1910 a third edition appeared, again enlarged to amplify the attack on canon law and separate schools, and was at once the subject of national, and even international, press and public debate. Sellar, now something of a hero in Protestant Ontario, was invited by the Orangemen to second a resolution against the ne temere decree at their mammoth celebration in Toronto that summer. He returned home from his exhilarating excursion to find that the Bishop of

Valleyfield had ordered the faithful to sever all dealings with him – a setback that prompted him to alter the name of the *Canadian Gleaner* to *Huntingdon Gleaner,* dispense with its familiar crown and Bible masthead, register the paper under the proprietorship of two of his sons, and retire temporarily, for their sake, from his editor's chair.

By this time *The Tragedy of Quebec* had transcended Canadian political arenas to become a manual for the Ulster Unionists in the critical years prior to World War I. Sir Eward Henry Carson, currently organizing a volunteer military force to oppose the implementation of home rule, entered into an extensive correspondence with Sellar, who contributed a series of articles on Quebec's experience under 'home rule' to the Presbyterian unionist Belfast *Witness* in 1912. The sad plight of the Quebec minority, he argued, would become that of the Ulster Protestants with a Roman Catholic majority in power. The articles, published in pamphlet form by the Ulster Unionist Council under the title *Ulster and Home Rule: A Canadian Parallel,* brought Sellar an invitation to move to Belfast to edit a unionist daily, but the crisis was postponed by the outbreak of the war.

With the war came renewed acrimony between French- and English-Canadians over Ontario's decision to restrict the use of French in its public schools. Sellar watched with apprehension as Premier Gouin and his legislature threw their weight behind the agitations of Cardinal Bégin and the Quebec bishops against the offending regulations. The 'boche of Ontario,' the country was asked to believe, were to blame for Quebec's inadequate response to the war effort. To Sellar the plausible cry for 'bilingual' schools was a fraud. The much-maligned regulation seventeen was not without provision for French-language instruction, but what the clerics really sought was retention of tax support for the French-language, priest-controlled, sectarian schools of Quebec that had been bodily transplanted into Ontario. It was not Premier Whitney, his ministers, or his successors who were responsible for the current crisis, 'but the French priests who deliberately planned the conquest of Ontario.' Had not the sedulous efforts of dedicated clerics over a fifty-year period gone a long way towards recreating in eastern Ontario the non-violent subjugation of the Quebec townships? How long would it be before the compact host 'recruited, led, and encamped by

French priests' would hold the balance of power in the Ontario legislature? Was not the final issue 'whether this Canada of ours is to be British, and nothing else than British, or whether it is to be a mongrel land, with two official languages and ruled by a divided authority?' Such were the queries raised in 1916 by the fourth and final edition of *The Tragedy of Quebec*.

Public reception of the fourth edition of *The Tragedy of Quebec* pushed the total circulation of Sellar's bitter tract well over fifty thousand as public opinion hardened against the French Canadians in the latter years of the war. To Sellar, now nearing the end of his days, it seemed fittingly ironic that Quebec, in the throes of the conscription crisis, should be in the incipient stages of revolution on the fiftieth anniversary of Confederation. Could there be any more eloquent justification of his views since those early days when the *Gleaner* had been established to advocate representation by population?

In a biting pamphlet entitled *George Brown: The Globe: Confederation*, Sellar sang his troubled swan-song to the people of Canada. In contrast to the prevailing tendency to canonize the Fathers of Confederation, he pronounced Canada's federal constitution a 'disastrous failure' as a remedy for the evils it had been primarily designed to overcome. Had Galt's guarantees saved the British-Protestant minority of rural Quebec? Had history borne out Brown's assurances that federal union would release Ontario from the baleful influence of French-Catholic clericalism? Had fifty years of church-controlled education in Quebec taught its youth to be loyal to the Empire? Had the pretence of the compatibility of a dual allegiance to spiritual sovereign and temporal king been justified? Most disconcerting of all to the veteran crusader had been the reluctance of his own people to sustain him. The Quebec minority, it seemed, abounded in 'Superior Beings' prone to lecture their less enlightened fellows about toleration and broad-mindedness, sometimes from a genuine desire for mutual good feeling, sometimes from cynical motives of personal advancement or material gain, but nearly always from premises that sacrificed inner conviction for temporary peace. Speaking biographically, he testified to the rewards awaiting anyone who would take up the quixotic challenge of attempting to reform conditions in Quebec:

You say you are in favour of a system of public schools; with the blackest looks they can command, you are denounced as seeking to destroy religion. You say you wish to have equal rights for every man, you are abused as a bigot. You say the government should recognize no sectarian division in our population, you are accused of persecution. Every move made to bring about the abolition of special privileges is met, not with argument, but with abusive epithets. This hinders many from taking a stand against a system they are convinced is dangerous to the peace and security of the nation, for they shrink from being classed either as bigots or persecutors.

Hoping that in the conscription crisis would come the long-awaited convulsion that would finally purge the body politic of the 'sectarian virus,' he presented yet again his list of requisite reforms – a single marriage law and uniform system of public schools for the Dominion, withdrawal of all grants of public money from sectarian institutions, abolition of tax privileges enjoyed by religious bodies and limitation of their real estate to actual needs, and the repeal of all laws authorizing ecclesiastical corporations to levy compulsory dues. He died quietly 29 November 1919, at the age of seventy-eight, his lifelong objectives unattained.

Sellar's sons, believing *The Tragedy of Quebec* to be bad for the circulation of the *Gleaner,* did their best to suppress it following their father's death. To this day it continues to pop up in second-hand bookstores and university libraries, perplexing new generations of readers perhaps unaccustomed to such combativeness in a work of Canadian history. It stands as a prime example of the ultra-Protestant interpretation – a tradition that it did much to establish. Sellar was familiar with the works of Garneau, Parkman, and Kingsford (from whom he borrowed heavily); his view of Canadian history was markedly similar to that of another Victorian liberal, Goldwin Smith, with whom he corresponded following publication of the first edition. Dissatisfaction with secondary sources led him to original documents at Laval University and the new Canadian archives, and he considered himself the first writer to set the record straight on the tithes question. His analysis of the past was primarily designed to trace clericalism in Canada to its very origins; their discovery in the roots of the French régime was a foregone conclusion.

'He who would grasp the political problems that confront the Dominion,' he reasoned, 'must ... trace the shadow of these despotic times in darkening our national life – the shadow projected over the Dominion by the descendants of people who, for five generations, were inured to implicit obedience, to absolutism in church and state, kept separate and by themselves from the rest of the world as a preserve for priest and crowned tyrant.'[12] He agreed with Kingsford and Parkman that the Conquest was of inestimable benefit to French Canada, but took pains to demonstrate his own contention that British rule had entrenched rather than terminated the hegemony of the priesthood in Quebec. His interpretation was also unique in its portrayal of Canada's history as one of racial and religious conflict – a notable departure from the efforts of other writers to prove that the harmonious functioning of British institutions comprised the ultimate solution to the country's problems. He was, in a subtle way, perhaps closer to the opposing tradition of Garneau, who had also felt impelled by threats to cultural and religious survival to employ history as a call to action rather than as an academic delight.

That *The Tragedy of Quebec* should be read anew is fitting, for there is probably no better guide to the principles, prejudices, and passions that animated British-Protestant Canada in the nineteenth and early twentieth centuries. The image of French-Canadian society that it projected has been so deeply embedded in the English-Canadian mind that traces of it still persist. To dismiss it as mere crankery, as many have preferred to do, overlooks not only its remarkable sale and obvious acceptance, but also its political impact both in Canada and abroad. To discount it as an isolated case of bigotry is to fail to understand the mentality of thousands of people who, in the circumstances of their day, upheld it as a 'handbook of civil rights for Canadians.' Its bigotry was that of the age, and requires understanding. Current relaxation of public feeling in Canada about religion and clericalism makes it difficult for many modern readers to appreciate the extent to which such a book, as recently as a half-century ago, influenced popular thinking on real socio-political issues.

Sellar's authenticity as a spokesman for grass-roots Protestant opinion is not hard to verify, particularly if one looks beyond the conciliatory careers of the English-Canadian politicians who were always contradicting him. The peculiar exigencies of the party system in a binational state encouraged political habits of moderation and compromise that Sellar found frustrating, and elected representatives of the Protestant minority of Quebec were at best reluctant spokesmen for their constituents on sensitive issues. While English-speaking legislators at Quebec meekly accepted Mercier's Jesuit Estates settlement, for example, Sellar's protests were echoed by public petitions and by the ruling court of every Protestant denomination in the province. *The Tragedy of Quebec*, similarly, was the embodiment of attitudes which may have been politically untouchable but which were by no means confined to its author. English-language historians have paid insufficient attention to Sellar, but their French-Canadian counterparts have tended to accept him, along with Lord Durham, as a hard but creditable exponent of a hostile point of view. 'Quoi qu'on puisse penser de la thèse de l'auteur,' wrote Gustave Lanctot of *The Tragedy of Quebec*, 'il faut reconnaître sa parfaite conviction, qui le porta à publier, à ses frais et contre ses intérêts, ce livre où il expose ses idées personnelles.'[13]

Some, in contemplating Sellar's work, will see only bigotry; others may discern a true tragedy of Quebec. A few, who come to know him better, may perceive a tragedy of a more personal sort – the tragedy of Robert Sellar, an honest, devout, and courageous soul embittered by the repeated shattering of uncompromising visions of the Canada that might have been.

NOTES

1 For a detailed account of Sellar's life and times, see Robert A. Hill, 'Robert Sellar and the Huntingdon *Gleaner*: The Conscience of Rural Protestant Quebec, 1863-1919' (unpublished PhD thesis, McGill University 1970).
2 Sellar's diary, and numerous other documents comprising the Robert Sellar Papers, have been deposited in the Public Archives of Canada.
3 *Canadian Gleaner* (Huntingdon), 4 Mar. 1886. See also *Gleaner*, 11, 25 Feb., 18 Mar. 1886. For the *Globe*'s side of the dispute, see *Globe* (Toronto), 2, 16, 23 Feb., 10 Mar. 1886.
4 See the letters signed 'English-Speaking Liberal' in *Mail* (Toronto), 19, 28 July, 3, 10, 17, 24 Aug., 29 Oct., 24 Dec. 1886.

5 See Equal Rights Association for the Province of Ontario, *Important Letter by a Resident of Quebec as to the Disabilities of Protestants in that Province* (Toronto 1890); see also Honoré Mercier, *Answer of the Honorable Honoré Mercier to the Pamphlet Published by the Equal Rights Association Against the Majority of the Inhabitants of the Province of Quebec* (Quebec 1890). For the complete Equal Rights correspondence, see the pamphlet *Quebec Minority* (Huntingdon 1891).
6 See *Daily Witness* (Montreal), 18, 28 Aug., 1, 5, 15, 22, 26, 29 Sept. 1906.
7 See John Adams, *The Protestant School System in Quebec* (Montreal 1902).
8 For coverage of the 'educational crusade' and the public meetings at Huntingdon, Richmond, Knowlton, Inverness, Lachute, and Ayerscliff, see *Daily Witness*, 14, 16, 17, 18, 24, 31 Aug. 1906.
9 Robert Sellar, *The Tragedy of Quebec: The Expulsion of Its Protestant Farmers* (Huntingdon 1907), 102-3
10 See Jean I. Hunter, 'The French Invasion of the Eastern Townships: A Regional Study' (unpublished master's thesis, McGill University 1939).
11 Aileen D. Ross, 'French and English Canadian Contacts and Institutional Change,' *Canadian Journal of Economics and Political Science*, XX, 3 (August 1954), 281
12 Robert Sellar, *The Tragedy of Quebec: The Expulsion of Its Protestant Farmers* (Toronto 1916), 42-3
13 Gustave Lanctot, 'Un régionaliste anglais de Québec, Robert Sellar,' *Bulletin des recherches historiques*, XLI (1935), 173-4

The tragedy of Quebec

ROBERT SELLAR

To H. C. Hocken of Toronto I dedicate this book. Unasked he held out a helping hand when other encouragement I had none.

"The conclusion is inevitable, from the nature of the means employed, that a deep-laid plan exists for the complete subjugation of Lower Canada to ecclesiastical rule, with the view of extending the same baneful influence hereafter to the whole Dominion. In this view the importance of early and stern opposition to the schemes now being gradually disclosed, becomes the duty of all good citizens, be they Catholic or Protestant."—SIR A. T. GALT in 1877.

"Are you unable to distinguish between Clericalism and Religion? I am not combating Roman Catholicism as a Christian creed; I am fighting that sinister conspiracy which uses the forms of religion to destroy human liberty and the prosperity of States."—GAMBETTA.

CONTENTS.

	Page.
CHAPTER I.—The Coming of the English-speaking Farmers	11
CHAPTER II.—Canada Under the Kings of France	21
CHAPTER III.—Canada Under British Rule...	53
CHAPTER IV.—Re-Appearance of Anti-British Feeling	89
CHAPTER V.—Quebec Thrown Open to Immigrants	123
CHAPTER VI.—Development of the Nationalist Idea	130
CHAPTER VII.—Before and After Confederation	173
CHAPTER VIII.—The Supplanting of the English-Speaking Farmers	196
CHAPTER IX.—Canon Law	225
CHAPTER X.—It is a Papal, not a French Quebec that Menaces the Dominion	256
CHAPTER XI.—Nationalism and Nationalists	280
CHAPTER XII.—The War of French Priests on Ontario's Independence	287
CHAPTER XIII.—The Peril of Clericalism	329
CHAPTER XIV.—Is Our Northwest to be British or Papal?	346

PREFACE.

The first edition of this book appeared in 1907. Its purpose was to reveal to the people of the other provinces of the Dominion the condition of the English-speaking farmers in the Province of Quebec, in the hope that they might be stirred to action to preserve a remnant and to take steps to prevent a like fate overtaking farming communities in the other provinces. The book was welcomed by few. It was described as a fire-brand production, the embodiment of bigotry. The booksellers of Montreal would not have it on their counters. The press ignored it, the few notices it received being carefully qualified so as not to be taken as endorsing either its sentiments or its statements. An exception was the Telegram, of Toronto, which heartily commended it. Not until the march of events showed its warnings as to the English-speaking provinces being in peril from the power that dominated Quebec, in the matters of language, education and marriage, did the book obtain a general circulation. A second edition was called for, and in it and in the third a wider range was taken in dealing with aspects of clerical interference outside of Quebec, and the effort made to make it a handbook of civil rights for Canadians.

The long historical introduction has been objected to as a defect. I do not see how the present day evils of priestly domination. can be successfully dealt with unless traced to their origin. The fact that no writer had treated the records of the early days of Canada critically, all having perpetuated the delusion of their being romantic and heroic, impelled me the more to go to the heart of the subject and print what the archives at Ottawa reveal.

The following extract from the preface of the first edition gives the reasons which justified the issue of the book and the standpoint of its writer:

When I came to Huntingdon, in 1863, the county, leaving out one of its municipalities, St. Anicet, was as solidly Protestant as any in Ontario. I have witnessed the decline of its Protestant population to the point of being in the minority. The same change, only in a more marked degree, has taken place in all the counties east of the Richelieu. The transformation is going on with startling rapidity. Often, when friends deplored the departure of Protestant farmers, I heard them ask, "Did the electors of the other provinces know what is happening to us in Quebec, would they not intervene?" I thought of including testimony from residents of different sections as to the extent of the change going on, but desisted, on finding reluctance to putting their names to the information they gave me. This was no reflection on these friends, for to make themselves known would be, in their several neighborhoods, to expose them to the malignity of the dominant power. The proof of the expulsion of Protestant farmers is abundant without individual evidence. It is palpable to the most unobservant. It is open to question whether this book will help the Protestant farmers. There is, however, no question as to the failure of the policy that has been pursued—the policy of fawning, of silence, of loud talk about tolerance, broad-mindedness, living in peace and harmony, —a policy most agreeable socially, in business profitable, in public life the only road to preferment, but under which the Protestant farmers have gone on disappearing. Agitation on their behalf may fail to help them, but cannot make their situation worse. Viewing the immense resources of the Church of Rome in Quebec, how its influence permeates every channel of life and bends every interest to advance its own, with no encouragement from the other provinces, no offer to help them, it is not surprising that the Protestant farmers of Quebec have hitherto made no resistance. The expression often heard among them, "What's the use of butting our heads against a stone wall?" "We don't like it, so let us get out and leave the province to them," represents their attitude. In the hope that a plain statement of the case of the Protestant farmers of Quebec will bring them help, and lead to such legal changes as will preserve those settlements that are still substantially intact, I have written this book. Doing so means to me loss of friends and loss of business, so that nothing save a sense of duty could actuate me. I could not find a publisher, even in Toronto, and the printing, poor as it is, was effected at a sacrifice.

CHAPTER I.

The Coming of the English-Speaking Farmers

The eighteenth century was nearing its end before the solitude of that vast region which lies south of the parishes that border the St. Lawrence, between the Chaudiere and the Richelieu, was disturbed by aught save the cry of the water-fowl as it winged its way over Lake Memphremagog, or the howl of the wolf from its rocky den on the slope of Mount Tom. The old world had been rent by wars; dynasties had risen, flourished, and disappeared, and yet that bewitching expanse of forest, lake, and mountain, threaded by rivers beside which the Thames and Clyde are but streamlets, continued undisturbed, its beauty and possibilities of wealth alike unknown. From a sky as clear as that of Italy the sun bathed this region of romantic beauty summer after summer, autumn dyed its mantle of forest in hues of gold and scarlet, and winter mantled it in ice and snow, but all this loveliness for uncounted centuries was unseen by man, save when some lone Indian, in search of game, strayed from his fellows. It must be a baffling thought to the dwellers of the Old World, that a stretch of country larger and fairer than that for which kings fought and armies perished remained unowned and unoccupied in the Province of Quebec down to a period almost within the memory of a few yet living.

The day, however long delayed, came at last, when the white man, intent on making a home in this long secluded land, crossed its untrod frontier. He was a scout from a host of people dissatisfied with the granite hills of New England. His rifle was his dependence for food; his axe his weapon for subduing the untamed wilderness. Selecting for his future home a spot on the bank of a glassy lake, where the growth of timber told his experienced eye the soil was rich, he woke the echoes which, for aught he knew, had slumbered since the world was new, as he felled the first tree, and with it the virgin page of an untold past was soiled and the charm of this long-hidden solitude broken. The deer, as it grazed on the spring-buds, startled by the unwonted sound, leapt into the darkest recesses of a forest whose hour had come. With the admirable skill of the American woodsman the newcomer hewed and shaped the fallen trees and rolled them together to form a rude shelter that would serve until a better house could be built. Then he left, blazing the trees as he retraced his steps, marking the first avenue of communication. Before a month has sped he returns, but not alone: his wife and children are with him. From dawn to dark the sound of the axe is heard, the felled trees are piled together, and one night the glare of their burning gilds lake and hill. The wife and mother aids the stalwart husband in rolling aside the trunks that defied the fire, and the first clearance is made. The seed, so painfully carried on the shoulder from the far-south home in Massachusetts, is committed to the virgin soil, and in its rapid growth the eager couple see food for the coming winter. But there is no cessation to their toil. The war on the forest goes on and logs are shaped for a shanty that will defy the weather. When the corn begins to tassel visitors come, relatives and old neighbors, to see for themselves this new land and how their friends are faring in it. They help to rear the modest shanty, and having seen how much better the soil is than that where they dwell, resolve to make the change when they have gathered their harvest from their

stony fields. Before the first snowflakes fly, from not
one, but half-a-dozen shanties, smoke rises above the
treetops.

Once started, the growth of the settlements was
rapid. Paths were blazed through the bush from what
is now New Hampshire and Vermont, and over them
streamed a hardy class into the recesses of the newly
opened region. Those who settled in the western section found convenient access to Montreal by way of
the Richelieu, and by opening short lines of road
northward, but those to the east were not so fortunate.
They were much farther south of the St. Lawrence,
and a broad belt of hilly country, covered with forest,
bade defiance to their efforts to reach the city of
Quebec. The settlements had grown to some importance long before even a rumor reached the ears of the
people of Montreal and Quebec of what was going on
to the south. Trappers first brought word of the incursion of New England squatters into Canada, and
lumbermen gladly found in the new settlements an
unexpected source of supplies. When the facts became
known the elder Papineau and his coterie were annoyed, they desired no increase in the number of English-speaking people, and, had it been in their power, would
have expelled the new-comers. The governor proposed a road be built from Quebec to give them access
to that city. Papineau resented the proposal; the legislative assembly would not vote a sou for such a purpose. The proposed road hung fire until, in 1810,
Governor Craig overrode the will of the legislature
by employing squads from the garrison to make it.
It was indispensable, he said, to show these strangers
they have made themselves part of Canada and to
cause them to take an interest in its government. A
channel of communication between them and Quebec
city, he went on to declare, must be opened at once.
To secure the money needed to hew a path through
the intervening forest he sold the land it crossed. The
summer of 1810 was altogether unfavorable for road

making; yet, despite rain and cold, the soldiers, earning a little extra pay, worked with a will. At no period had agriculture among the habitants been at lower ebb; from their wretchedly tilled fields they barely harvested enough to supply their own wants. High prices, paid cash down, failed to bring a sufficiency from the parishes surrounding Quebec to feed its garrison. Governor Craig saw in the new settlements a sure source of supplies, and he was not disappointed. No sooner did his road tap them than droves of cattle were driven over it. At the beginning of September the price of beef in Quebec market had fallen from 14 cents a pound to 8, and six weeks later it could be had for 6, and of better quality than the parishes supplied. It was a rough road, stretching from Quebec to Shipton, where it connected with a road the settlers had made, but it ensured the development of the new settlements by giving them a market. In summer over it went bellowing a succession of herds of beef cattle: in winter sleighs laden with grain and pork. Mr. Bouchette, the Surveyor-General, traversing the road on its opening, tells with astonishment the progress he found in the new settlements, the succession of tidily-kept homes, surrounded by gardens and freshly-planted orchards, primitive grist and saw-mills on the streams, incipient villages with workshops and asheries, churches and schools. The population he estimated at 20,000. The coming of war in 1812 increased rather than diminished the population. War against Britain was unpopular in New England, and the number who volunteered was insufficient to supply the quota of men required from each State. Conscription had to be resorted to, and to escape the draft hundreds, possibly thousands, fled across the line into the new settlements. Many in the townships to-day, who affect to be of U. E. stock, are descendants of these skedadlers. With the peace, the majority returned to the United States, but many remained. An untoward effect of the war was the closing of the

Craig road. As a possible avenue for invasion, its
bridges were destroyed and the highway blocked by
slashing the trees that grew along it. Despite that,
the settlements flourished. The British commissariat
was offering unheard of prices for supplies, and cattle
and grain by devious ways reached camp and garrison.
With the passing of the war-cloud, which to the new
settlers had a silver lining, prosperity increased. Those
stony slopes which strike the traveller to-day as barren, gave then a lot of ready money by converting the
trees that clad them into potash, and once cleared
yielded several crops of wheat. To be candid, all the
settlers were not industrious. Fugitives from justice
found in the new settlements safety from U. S. officers,
for there was no extradition treaty. Bishop Stewart,
in his experiences at Frelighsburg, has given a vivid
insight into the character of this lawless portion of
the population. Men who had fled to escape paying
their debts, forgers, thieves, clustered along the frontier and avoided defining their crimes by using the
convenient phrase that they were "line-bound."

The population was almost entirely of American
origin, the scattered communities being as intensely
New England in customs and opinions as those of Vermont, New Hampshire, and Massachusetts which they
had left, but the day came when it was to be leavened
by an infusion from the British isles. The cessation
of the Bonaparte wars was followed in the Motherland
by a collapse alike in agriculture and commerce.
Farmers were unable to pay their rents, manufacturers
could find no customers for their goods, traders were
ruined by bad debts. In the country farm laborers
were starving: in the cities the streets were thronged
by mechanics in search of work. Distress was as general as it was acute. Among the means of relief suggested was emigration. In those days the proposal was
a novelty, and, at first, was repulsive to those to whom
it was proposed. Passionate affection for the land of
their birth, dread of a dangerous sea-voyage, and of

the hardships to be met in an unknown land, had to be overcome. In 1818 a beginning was made, and the experiences of the venturesome spirits who led the way were eagerly read. Their letters were passed from family to family in the parishes they had left. They told of a good land in the West, where every man could win a farm by hard work. Repugnance to emigration wore away, and gave place to eagerness to begin life anew beyond the Atlantic. The Imperial Government assisted by setting aside warships that had lowered the flag of Napoleon to carry those disposed to leave, coupled with promises of free grants of land and some assistance in making a start in life in the bush. Each year saw the number of emigrants increase, and it was no wonder, for, save that love of native land which distinguishes the Anglo-Saxon, there was naught to keep back the working classes. The lot of the peasantry was peculiarly hard. The son of the cotter, even in those tender years when others more favored are at school, was set to work to increase the family earnings that procured only the coarsest food. His manhood was a period of hopeless toil, every penny earned needed to save those he loved from privation; cringing to the titled owner of the acres he labored, bullied by the factor of the great man to supply more money for his extravagance, taxed on everything he bought to maintain a great military establishment, and to pay interest on the national debt. Ground down in body and spirit he saw no escape from the shadow of seeking poor-relief should sickness disable him or when old age overtook him, but by facing the horrors of the Atlantic passage in the hold of a small and ill-found ship and of braving the toils and privations of the backwoods. For over thirty-six summers there was a constant stream of sailing-ships, leaving the ports of England, Ireland, and Scotland, whose course is, to this day, marked in ocean depths by the bones of those who perished from disease or hunger while seeking refuge from the conditions they were fleeing from. Then was the opportunity of peopling the Eastern Townships with settlers who would have averted the fate that has overtaken them, but it was missed. A few runlets from the great tide of immigration that was sweeping up the St. Lawrence were indeed turned into the townships of the Province of Quebec, but they were trifling compared with what they might have been. The cause was the selfishness of individuals, the fatuity of the provincial government. Instead of holding the land to bestow on whoever undertook to clear it, the government presented it to political favorites. When the poor immigrant, whose wealth lay in his sturdy limbs, sought land in the townships, he found it had been conceded by the government, and that the owner wanted a price he could not pay. Turned aside, he sought the free grants in Ontario. Great blocks of land were everywhere thus held, whose owners neither made roads nor paid taxes, yet whose property was growing in value from the improvements made by the settlers around them. Tens of thousands of immigrants, who would have gladly filled the vacant lands that lay between the parishes bordering on the St. Lawrence and the United States, were turned away, and the last opportunity of making Quebec essentially British was lost. Isolated parties of immigrants, however, did find a footing. Scattered over the wide territory that stretches between the head-waters of the Chaudiere and the majestic Richelieu, settlements sprung up of Irish, both from the South and North, of Lowlanders and Highlanders, and of English, showing what might have been with a just land policy. The influx from the United Kingdom, small as it was, modified the character of the American element. West of the Richelieu there was along the frontier an expanse of land still in a state of nature. Here immigrants found it easier to get a foothold, and Lacolle, Napierville, Chateauguay and Huntingdon gave promise of becoming English-speaking counties.

These settlers from the Old Land started under different conditions from the Americans, who could regain their birthplace by a few days' journey along forest paths, who were in their native element in bush-life, and who knew how to meet the vicissitudes of the climate. The Lowland Scot, rejoicing with his family to be released from shipboard with its horrors of dirt, disease, and lack of food and water, eagerly sought a lot in the bush of which he had heard so much, and found one on the bank of a river. When landed on the lot he had secured, and the cadence of the paddles of the canoe that had conveyed the family was lost in the distance, he had time to survey his new estate. His wife, seated on the chest that held their chief wealth, overcome by the sense of perfect isolation, realizing the completeness of their separation from kindred and fearful of the future in this lonesome wilderness, unable to stifle her emotions, silently wept, while the children around her, unable to comprehend her regrets for the past or her fears for the future, were lost in wonder and admiration of the novel sights which surrounded them, and Colley, whom they could not bear to leave behind when they left their home amid Scotland's hills, barked in delight at the squirrels who, darting from tree to tree, eyed the new-comers with daring curiosity. The father, as he scanned the overshadowing trees, which opened in endless vistas wherever he turned his gaze, realized the gigantic task he had assumed in conquering these giants of the forest and wringing from the soil, cumbered with the litter of centuries, the food to feed his dear ones. The feeling of despair that hovered near was driven back by the proud thought that the land on which he stood was his own, and that, for the first time in his life, what he wrought for would be his. Grasping the axe he had bought at Quebec he, unused to handling it, awkwardly attacked the saplings around him to form a covering from the cold of the fast-coming night, while his wife, suppressing her emotions, set to work to light a fire and prepare their first meal. When the placid surface of the river was reflecting the glow of the evening sky, the father ceased his labors and all gathered to partake of it, with thankful hearts. And then, before retiring beneath the booth of poles and brush the father had managed to shape, with no sound to disturb them save the chitter of some mother-bird as she gathered her nestlings under her wings, and the laving of the stream on whose bank they clustered, from that untrodden spot for the first time since Creation's dawn rose the sounds of praise and prayer. With full hearts that psalm in which the Scottish peasantry have for generations expressed alike their trust in and thankfulness to an ever-present God, the 23rd, was sung, then the father poured out his gratitude to Him who had preserved them amid the dangers of the deep, and whose kindness had followed them into the wilderness. At the petition for those they had left behind, the answering sob of wife and daughter spoke of the undying affection of the Scot for kith and kin, and for the dear old land. The help of distant neighbors having been sought, a day was fixed for a bee, when trees by the score were felled, and out of their trunks logs fashioned to build the walls of a shanty with scoops to roof it, and when the wife took possession she felt prouder of it than a duchess of her mansion. Their days were days of unceasing toil, of hardship and privation. When the nights grew long and the maples were reddening, the potatoes, hoed in amid the tree roots, were secured, and these were the chief winter's food. The patching and mending of clothes to resist the bitter cold of a Canadian winter, the unremitting warfare with the axe to enlarge the clearing, the joy of securing the first pig, the first cow, the first horse, the widening fields, the growing means, encouraged effort and deepened satisfaction, until the long-looked-for time came when the parents could rest in simple competency. All, however, in that severe ordeal were not successful. Many who tried to carve from the forest independent homes lost heart and abandoned what they had accomplished, but the majority persevered until success rewarded their efforts, and out of forbidding wildernesses of swamp and bush they created districts which have come to be ranked among the finest agricultural sections of the Dominion.

These settlers, whether American or British, dispossessed nobody. The country they occupied was in a state of nature when they went upon it. What is more important, it had never been ceded, the title being still held by the Crown. In the name of the King governors gave these settlers patents for their lots and promised them protection under the laws of England. The land, therefore, was theirs by authority of the King and by their labor in clearing and bringing it into cultivation. Yet they were treated by the representatives of the majority as intruders; as being where they had no right to be. The history of the Province of Quebec during the 19th century largely consists of attempts, under varied pretences, to drive them out; the beginning of the twentieth sees the fruition of these attempts. To trace to their source the causes of this antipathy to English-speaking occupants of the land in Quebec and follow its results to the other Provinces of the Dominion is the chief purpose of this book.

CHAPTER II.

Canada Under the Kings of France

When the feudal system was strong, when to be a soldier was considered the proper occupation of a gentleman, when war was chronic, and Europe a battlefield, there came the astounding announcement that a new world had been found beyond the Atlantic. The announcement was not welcomed as opening a way of relief for the suffering masses, for there was poverty and wretchedness among the peasantry to which there is no parallel in our day. Such an idea was not conceivable to the governing class, who regarded the common people as the Athenian looked upon his slaves, as beings different from himself. Their condition never gave a thought to those who could have helped them. Colonization is a modern conception: the transplanting of people in order to better themselves never dawned on the minds of the kings and nobles of those days, nor for a century or two succeeding the discovery made by Columbus. All they thought of was enriching themselves, and they regarded the new world as the miner looks upon the glistening rock his pick has unexpectedly uncovered. Spain was first in the field, and jealously resented intrusion into those countries where she had found the precious metals existed, so that the kings of other nations, whose cupidity was aroused by the stories of ship-loads of bullion poured into her lap, had to try the shores north of the Tropics, and successive explorations proved that neither silver nor gold was to be found in them. Disappointed in this, they cherished the idea that a passage might be found leading to China and the Ind. In those days these countries were believed to be possessed of wealth that baffled imagination. The tales of the few Europeans who had survived the perils of the journey by land merely whetted the desires of those who heard them, and the belief was universal that if a short cut could be found, they who reached the Orient would come back laden with pearls and diamonds and gold. One way by sea had been found, round the Cape of Good Hope, but that involved a voyage for which their ships were so unequal that the perils and sufferings of those who had dared it appalled those who would have liked to follow. A short route westward was sought, and the motive that incited the King of Spain to help Columbus caused Henry of England to equip the expedition of Cabot, which resulted in the discovery of what we now call Canada. Disappointed in Cabot's not finding a passage to India, Henry did not follow up the discovery, the knowledge of which, however, was given to the world together with a chart, showing the coast-line of the part of Canada which Cabot had traced. Thirty-seven years later, the King of France helped Jacques Cartier to equip an expedition to explore the land Cabot had discovered. That America was a great continent, vaster than Europe, was not conjectured by any explorer, and if one had hazarded such a surmise, it would have been treated with scorn. The land Columbus discovered, and whose coasts, north and south, were traced by his successors, they believed to be an island, a long one to be sure, but narrow, and there must be a channel across it. The spanning of the isthmus of Panama confirmed this misconception, and ship after ship was sent to find an opening in the long barrier of land through which they would sail to the Pacific and come back with their holds filled with the riches of the Ind. This was the cause of the assistance given by the French King to Jacques Cartier on his three voyages. He did not sail, as is popularly supposed, to an unknown land, for the coast-line of what we now know as Massachusetts, Maine, Nova Scotia, Newfoundland, Labrador, had been defined and laid down in maps. More than that, fishermen had discovered, years before Cartier sailed, the inexhaustible wealth of the banks that lie off Newfoundland, and ships from as far south as Portugal and north as Iceland were dropping their lines upon them each summer. It is probable Jacques Cartier came from among those fishermen, and that it was while so engaged he heard from the Indians on the shores of Labrador, where crews landed for wood and water, that the Straits of Belle Isle led to a great inland sea which ran westward. That this great sea was the long-sought break in the wall which led to the Pacific was his conclusion, and the records of his three voyages show how confident he was in this belief. Sailing through the Straits of Belle Isle he found his way into the gulf of the St. Lawrence, and, as day after day, he traced its shore-line trending southwest, he was convinced he had made the grand discovery. In this belief his second voyage confirmed him, when he penetrated still farther west, expecting each day the channel would expand into the Pacific, when he would shape his course for China and return to France in triumph. In this delusion he was only the first of a number of his countrymen, who, for the next hundred years, fruitlessly sought a passage to China by the St. Lawrence. While baffled in the object of his voyages, Cartier's visits to the St. Lawrence showed him a profitable trade could be developed with the Indians, for he was a trader from a trading-town and had an eye to the main chance. He began that barter with the Indians for furs which, long after his day, led to France renewing her connection with Canada. The popular belief, that Cartier's discovery of the St. Lawrence valley was followed by France taking possession and founding a settlement, has no foundation. When he returned from his third voyage to the St. Lawrence his attempts at settlement ceased. His associate, Roberval, made further trial, failed disastrously and also went back to France. Canada then reverted to its original condition, and the rule of the Indians was undisturbed for nigh seventy years. During that long period Canada was a No-man's land, free to whoever chose to visit its great river. Hardy fishermen from England, France, Portugal, not only filled their holds with fish caught in the gulf and its bays, but added to their profits by dickering with the Indians for furs. For nigh a century Canada bore the same relation to Europe as Patagonia did to the civilized world of our own day—a place free to whoever wished to go and seek the riches to be found in its waters, to trade with its natives, and, if regard for their scalps permitted, to spy into its land. Of the boats that thus paid summer visits to the St. Lawrence nearly all were manned and owned by French Protestants who were energetic and daring beyond their fellows. Tadousac was their chief port of call, followed in time by going as far west as Quebec, Three Rivers, and Montreal. This fact, that it was French Protestants who first developed the resources of Canada, is constantly ignored. It was the work they did during those seventy years that prepared Canada for permanent occupancy. The rivers were the highway of the Indian, and at the mouths of the Saguenay, the Maurice and the Ottawa the daring Huguenot trader each summer awaited them. The trade was dangerous and fitful. Some seasons full cargoes of furs were obtained; others not sufficient to pay expenses. This arose from the irregular habits of the Indian, whose main purpose in life was war, hunting for furs being a by-occupation. Often the trader waited at the mouth of the Maurice or Ottawa for the appearance of the string of birch-bark canoes, and waited in vain: the redmen were on the warpath.

The Huguenots would have done more for Canada than maintain its trade in furs. The persecution of them was hot and tens of thousands of them flocked, to escape flame and famine, the sword and the galleys, into Germany and England. They would gladly have carved out new homes for themselves in the forests of Canada, but the privilege was denied them, so no Mayflower landed a party of Pilgrims on the banks of the St. Lawrence. The opportunity was lost of creating a greater colony than that of New England, and for that loss France has to blame her priests, who opposed giving those whom they named heretics even the poor privilege of banishment to a distant and savage land.

Two generations of independent skippers had come and gone before the rulers of France attached to Canada the slightest importance. The weak efforts they then put forth to re-occupy Canada, showed their low estimate of its value. If any merchant or combination of merchants in St. Malo, Rochelle, or Harfleur would undertake the risk and expense of occupying Canada in the name of France, the government would give him or them a monopoly of its trade. The bait was poor enough, but towards the beginning of the seventeenth century a few snapped at it and lost money. None succeeded until Champlain appeared.

There are only two men whose names are associated with the settlement of Canada to whom the epithet distinguished can be joined. One was Champlain the other Frontenac, and both, while most dissimilar in character, were alike in this, the coming of each marked a new era in the destinies of the country. Champlain combined, like hundreds of others in the Atlantic seaports of those days, the callings of sailor and soldier, trader and explorer. With the financial aid of a Protestant, de Monts, he sailed for the St. Lawrence, intent on making money out of the concession of exclusive license to its trade which Henry of Navarre had bestowed upon his friend. The uselessness of the royal gift was shown by the disregard of the Huguenot skippers anchored at Tadousac, who flouted the King's letters-patent and pointed their cannon at the ship of its possessor. Champlain perceived that whoever wished to get ahead of the free-traders and make anything out of the country, need not rely on the King's authority, but outstrip them in their methods, and this he proceeded to do by building permanent trading-posts and, instead of brief summer visits, stay the year round among his customers. In this Champlain anticipated the policy of the Hudson Bay company, the most successful of fur corporations. He built huts at Quebec, and for the first time in seventy-three years Frenchmen again stayed over the winter, and thus France resumed her occupation of Canada, which really dates from 1608, and not from 1543, the year when Jacques Cartier and Roberval abandoned it as worthless territory. Having built a resting-place, Champlain next turned to the wandering bands of Indians, whose trade he sought. Among the means to secure their attachment he backed then in their feuds, went with the tribes he favored on the warpath, and won for them easy victories with his matchlocks. It was a disastrous move. He failed to make permanent friends of the savages he helped, while those whom he defeated became the inveterate enemies of the Frenchmen. Thenceforth the history of the French in North America is largely a record of Indian wars. Marching with his new-found friends on the war-path, revealed to Champlain the interior of the country, giving him some idea of its vastness. He saw a lake that was given his name, he penetrated far towards the sources of the Maurice and Ottawa; he stood on the shores of the great inland seas—lakes Ontario and Huron. In regard to this matter of exploration of the interior of the continent, parallels have been drawn between the settlers of New France and of New England, disparaging to the latter. Those who have done so overlook the fact that the St. Lawrence is the key to the interior of the continent, and possession of that key fell to the French. To explore the region west of Massachusetts meant journeyings on foot that were impossible from the difficulty of carrying sufficient supplies through trackless forests, the encountering of expanses of swamp, the oft recurrence of fordless rivers. Daring and enduring of fatigue and privation as the backwoodsmen of New England were, it was a physical impossibility to penetrate any great distance westward. It was far different with Champlain and his furtraders, who had settled on the banks of the great highway which Nature had provided into the interior of the continent, and on which the canoe could make as easy a passage then as to-day. It was by so simple a process as paddling up the great river by which they dwelt that the head of Lake Superior was reached and the Mississippi tapped. It is more of a reflection on the men of Quebec and Montreal that, with such ready means at their door, twenty-six years elapsed from Champlain's settling at Quebec before they discovered Lake Michigan, forty-one before they saw the waters of Lake Superior, and sixty-five years before they ascertained a great river flowed southward from the watershed of Lake Erie into the Gulf of Mexico. Had New Englanders lived on the banks of the St. Lawrence, would they have rested content two score years before they found out whence the mighty river came, and to what regions its lakes and tributaries led? Only a people made torpid by the influences under which they dwelt could have been content to gaze, day after day, for two score years on the mighty flood that flowed past their doors without seeking to discover its source.

Champlain's connection with Canada covered a period of twenty-seven years, nigh a generation, yet such trifling progress was made that at the end of these twenty-seven years his enumeration of its settlers gave Quebec a population of only 120, and his estimate of the total number of French in New

France was only 200. Champlain's attempt to settle the country was a failure, and had it not been for an unlooked for circumstance, the annals of his sojourn would have simply resembled those of a fur-trading company. That circumstance was the priesthood making Canada a mission field. Although not the first to come, the Jesuits professed to monopolize the task of bringing the Indians within their Church. The Jesuits had learned the service that can be rendered to any cause by the printing-press, and each year the parent society in France prepared selections from the reports sent by those in charge of the stations they had established in Canada, and published them, thus anticipating the modern missionary tidings. These reports are tiresome and monotonous narratives, and abound with pious inventions. The object of publishing these reports, or relations, was to induce those who read them to contribute towards carrying on the work, so a good story was always told of marvellous successes, with exaggerations of sufferings and of need for assistance. The alleged conversions are not by ones or twos, but by thousands, sealed by stories of providential interventions and miracles that only a credulous and childish generation would credit. As these reports appeared regularly during forty years, they are exceedingly voluminous and would have gone on had they not become a butt for the wits of Paris, who dissected their pious inventions and held them up to the laughter of the nation. To stop the flow of falsifications that were being used to injure the church, they were interdicted. These journals show that what the Jesuit meant by converting the Indian was baptizing him. That the savage understood the rite or gave his consent made no difference as to its efficacy. If there was no water at hand, the Jesuit, by moistening his finger at his lips, dotting the outline of a cross on the forehead of the savage, with the muttering of the prescribed formula, held that the act changed the destiny of the Indian from perdition to salvation. The church was

The Tragedy of Quebec.

the ark, baptism meant admission, and devotees in Old France were regularly regaled with reports of hundreds of conversions. The Indian might go on in his old courses, and they were abominable beyond those of any South Sea Islander, but they did not affect his new character as a convert. When he visited Quebec, if he appeared in a religious procession in the forenoon, he might engage in the torture of an Iroquois captive in the evening. The change was external: change of heart and life was not looked for. When the canopy over the host was borne in procession at Quebec by four painted savages, fresh from the warpath, with bloody scalps in their belts, the incident was related for the delectation of readers in France as proof of the victories of the church. No white could know the Indian better than Frontenac, he made companions of their chiefs, he lived in their wigwams, he wore their dress, he joined in their games, he followed them in their hunts and their wars. The Jesuits had carried on their missions for half a century when Frontenac visited their stations, one after another, and became fully acquainted with their methods and their converts. What was his verdict? In a confidential despatch to the court of France he writes: "The Jesuits "will not civilize the Indians because they wish to "keep them in perpetual wardship. They think more "of beaver skins than of souls, and their missions are "pure mockeries." The Indians had been made a source of revenue to the Order.

The nuns had no better success with the Indians. Intendant de Meulles tells the minister in France they take the Indian girls into the Ursulines convent, "where they only learn how to pray and to speak "French, all of which they soon forget, and when "they have once been married to some Indian they "hardly ever pray and never speak French."

The love of supremacy which caused the Jesuit to engage in the intrigues of the courts of Europe, led him to sit by the camp-fire in the councils of the savages, to raise his voice to recommend alliances, to engage in those negotiations with other tribes in which guile and deceit predominated, to declare war, to plan attacks. To profess zeal for souls while urging the redman to boil the captive taken from a hostile tribe, in order to make reconciliation impossible, to baptize the victims to whose torture they had consented, to send an envoy to Boston to invite the Puritans to co-operate in exterminating the Iroquois, are specimens of the spirit and acts of men who dared to assume the name of Jesus. Their missions were a travesty on Christianity, and it is no extenuation to urge their sufferings and death. There have been propagators of Mohammedanism as earnest, as full of fiery zeal, as self-denying, as exultant under torture, as ready to face death in awful form, as Goupil or Jogues. Martyrdom proves the sincerity of the victim, but it does not prove the truth of his belief. The labors of the Jesuit ended in nothingness. The tribes who came under their influence and were guided by their advice were beaten in war and became extinct. The thousands of converts they professed to have made left not a vestige behind, unless, indeed, the halfbreeds of Caughnawaga and Lorette be so considered. The fatuous nature of their labors was noted in Canada even when their missions were in their glory. Father Le Clercq drily remarks that so soon as the reports of the Jesuit missionaries disappeared the host of converts which the letters had enumerated disappeared also.

The one result of the coming of the Jesuits was that, at a critical juncture, it determined the retention of Canada by France. Its value as a region for the supply of furs had come to be recognized, but the trade was so precarious, so much of a gamble, large profits one year followed by as great losses, that France would never have decided to hold Canada on that score. The religious sentiment of France had been impressed by the narratives of the Jesuits until the

transformation of the Indians into Catholics came to
be looked on as a sort of crusade, and members of a
corrupt court endeavored to compound for their sins
by lending their influence to measures for the retention of Canada; enthusiasts of both sexes offered their
services, donations and legacies flowed into the Jesuit
treasury, and the King authorized them to collect, on
market and exchange, a contribution named "God's
penny." While this tide of sentiment was at its
height an event happened that threatened to end it.
An English privateer, Kirke, after sweeping every
French sail from the St. Lawrence, made an easy
capture of Quebec in 1629, and the red banner of St.
George floated over St. Louis castle. The British held
undisputed possession of the entire country during the
ensuing three years. That possession would have
become permanent, preventing the bloodshed, the
burnings of heart, the difficulties felt to this hour,
but for the interference of the Jesuits. Their missions
in Canada gave them distinction and renown over all
rival Orders, influence in the French court, and a
source of income they no more liked to lose than
the great grants of land they anticipated along
the St. Lawrence, and so they besought Cardinal
Richelieu to regain the country that had been lost.
England was not disposed to give back the territory
she had won by fair fighting, and rejected the over-
tures of France. The Jesuits were persistent in the
pressure they brought to bear on Richelieu, and finally,
on his offering to pay the balance of his wife's dowry,
King Charles First snapped at the money, for he was
ever needy. The Jesuits triumphed; Britain ceded
Canada back to France. The saying, that the Scots
sold their King for a groat is proof of their shrewdness; a king who could sell an undeveloped empire for
payment of an overdue debt was not worth a groat.

The records of Canada under the rule of France
naturally fall into three periods:

1st. From the voyage up the St. Lawrence of

Cartier, in 1534, to the coming of Champlain, 1608, during which time Canada was nobody's land; its waters frequented by fishing-boats of all nations, which added to their gains by buying furs: a period of 74 years.

2nd. From France taking possession by Champlain's forming a settlement at Quebec, 1608, to his death in 1635, which witnessed his persistent but futile efforts to found a colony, and the appearance in Canada of the Jesuits under the guise of missionaries to the Indians: a period of 27 years.

3rd. The resolve of Richelieu to make Canada a crown colony, the introduction of the seigniorial and parish systems and of forced emigration, ending in Wolfe's victory—embracing 120 years.

Cartier may be taken as representative of the first period, Champlain of the second, Frontenac of the third. The retrospect of the first period is that of an occasional sail stealing along the shores of the gulf, landing to salt the fish its crew had caught and to barter with wandering tribes for beaver skins. Of the second, of a bold and resourceful man endeavoring to obtain a foothold in Canada for his nationality: of black-robed priests who called rites and observances Christianity. The third is the period whose shadow still projects over Canada, which began with the closing years of Champlain, the finest figure that flits across its record. It was not his fault that his life-work ended in failure. The conditions under which he labored, a policy of monopoly and exclusion on the part of the French Government and of daily interference with his plans by narrow-minded priests, would have defeated the wisest of leaders. No wonder he left Quebec a cluster of huts huddled beneath the rocky cliff, inhabited by some 120 whites, who depended for food on the arrival of the spring fleet from France, who had not cut a single road, their only avenues of communication forest trails alone perceptible to the bush-ranger, without a plow and without a horse. One hundred years had elapsed since Cartier had wintered in the St. Charles River, and yet there were not over 200 French inhabitants, and these, the letters of visitors tell us, lived in privation, squalor, and ignorance.

Apparently it was Kirke's capture of the country that caused the French Government to bestir itself, for his deed showed if they did not take steps to occupy Canada in earnest they would lose it. Richelieu undertook the task in autocratic fashion. Ships were chartered and filled with emigrants levied as he would soldiers, and plans devised which a body of officials were appointed to carry out. Were men automatons and the wilds of Canada as easily controlled as the cantons of France, the cardinal's designs would have succeeded. The feudal system, which France was beginning to discard, he sought to graft on the free soil of the New World—the system of a nobility holding the land and renting to those who tilled it—a system that discouraged industry and independence alike, by making the toiler the slave of the aristocrat. With the introduction of seigniories came the parish system—that is, as the seignior collected from the habitant, who cleared the land of forest and brought it into cultivation, a fixed portion of his miserable earnings, the priest also was to have a share, and a larger share than the seignior, of his scanty crops. That settlement should prosper under these twin-systems was impossible, and so, during the third period we find the people often starving, dependent for supplies on the Mother Country, and looking to it for aid to make improvements which the New Englanders, with fewer natural advantages, but under a different system, were making for themselves and prospering. This period is often written about as one of Arcadian joys—when the seignior joined the priest in ruling the inhabitants with paternal benevolence, when the notary was their only man of business, when the bishop was looked up to with a simple reverence that made him almost divine, and the governor was bowed before as the embodiment of the kingly power and magnificence of Versailles. Those who speak thus conjure a picture that never existed: which the most casual reading of the despatches and correspondence of those days dissolves. With a salary of $1,800 a year it was difficult for the governors to live, much less to keep up the appearance of a court, and to make ends meet they dabbled in the fur and brandy trades. Their attempts to keep up vice-regal style on their petty resources, their squabbles with those around them as to the degree of attention that was their due, their fight over the spot where the governor's chair should be placed when he attended mass, whether he should be incensed by the deacon or an altar-boy, whether he should be the first to be presented with the brush at the blessing of holy water, have precedence in receiving blessed tapers, palms, and bread, who had the right to try cases of witchcraft, such incidents as these Cervantes would have chuckled over, and only his pen could have done justice to the seigniors strutting round their log-cabins with sword and cocked hat, while wife and daughters were chopping wood to cook his lordship's dinner or delving their clearance that there might be a supply of garlic and cabbage against the coming winter; or, at other times, in faded finery, idling in the narrow lanes of Quebec or Montreal, affecting the airs and dissipations of the distant court and engaging in intrigues for petty offices. Scrupulous in maintaining their dignity by not putting their hand to honest work, they were not above living upon the sorely-won earnings of their censitaires, whom they looked down upon as of other blood, and, so far as the changed conditions allowed, exercised over them the feudal tyrannies that lingered in France. The hated corvee compelled the tenant to leave his own clearing to cultivate the fields around the seigniorial log-hut, into his lean meal-bag his lordship was not ashamed to thrust his fist, and, if resistance was made, tried him as a criminal and inflicted humiliating punishments.

New France had been a crown colony for thirty years without making much advance. In 1666 Quebec was a village of less than 700 inhabitants, Montreal numbered a hundred less, and the total population was set down at 3,418. The stagnation that had prevailed so long was now to end, and it was broken by the coming of Frontenac, a man of restless energy and indomitable preseverance, who had an assistant equally pushing in Talon, whose plain common-sense and practical methods entitle him to be ranked as a French Benjamin Franklin. He saw that the beaver had wrought only injury to the people. To make for the woods with gun and traps was an easier way of earning a living than hewing down trees and putting in crops. Talon perceived farming must replace the fur trade. He reported to Colbert that, during the four-score years the French had occupied the country from its settlement by Champlain, only eleven thousand acres had been brought under cultivation, and that nearly everything needed was brought from France, including flour and pork. Talon encouraged the clearing of land and raising cattle, the building of grist and sawmills, of tanneries and shipyards, of foundries and asheries, and gave a new impetus to the fishing industry by securing for it a monopoly of the French market. The fur trade had been a blight to the struggling population. It bred idleness, improvidence, and the gambling spirit, for it was with hunter or trader either a feast or a famine. Many of the young men, fascinated by the freedom of the forest, threw off the duties of civilization and joined the Indians. Against these coureurs de bois, these bush-rangers, who combined the habits of the white vagabond with the morals of the Indian, the king prescribed severe penalties and Laval the terrors of the church. It is a modern discovery that these lazy vagabonds were "romantic." Regarding the attitude of these early settlers to the clergy, their rising in revolt on the imposition of tithes shows they were not to be compared in blind obedience to their descendants of our day.

While Talon was teaching the gospel of work to the sleepy, do-nothing colony, dependent on the hide of an animal whose industry reproached them, Frontenac was maturing his plans and laying down the lines of a policy which he meant should make France supreme on this continent. He marked the marvellous advances of the English colonies to the south, how New England ships traded afar, how the Albany merchants had established posts on Lake Ontario and were handling more furs than the dealers of Montreal. The English colonies had forged far ahead, but he would check them and give New France the pre-eminence. Her geographical position gave her the means, and he would use them. In those days, when the railway was undreamt of, the St. Lawrence was the sceptre of the continent; whoever held it and knew how to wield it, could sway its destiny. The first step was to prevent the English getting a foothold on the great lakes: that was essential to establishing the sovereignty of France, and he set about driving them back, built a fort at Kingston, and established a series of posts that would prevent them moving westward. The discovery of the Mississippi in his day aided him, and along it and its tributaries he built a line of log forts, forming a frontier beyond which no English trader or settler dare venture. Frontenac thought imperially, many have done likewise; what distinguished him from the herd of political dreamers was that he had the vitality and executive ability to carry his designs into effect. He had the physical strength to personally direct and the administrative faculty that secures success. His journeyings on foot and by canoe were marvellous; he examined every situation before selecting a site for fort or post, and was never daunted by unexpected obstacles. He was wofully cramped in means, yet with the little he could command he worked wonders. Left alone, he would have obtained for France a grip on the continent that could not have been unclasped. He won control of the great lakes by establishing trading-posts on Ontario, Erie, and Michigan. Westward of Huron he planned forts, and southward he designed French settlements should extend to the mouth of the Mississippi, hemming the English between the Ohio and the Atlantic. What prevented the realization of these magnificent plans? What was it, in this, her new birth of energy and enterprise, that suddenly brought New France to a halt in her onward sweep to the sovereignty of the Continent of America? There is only one answer, so apparent that even Garneau could not conceal it. The Jesuits had come to hate Frontenac, he had thwarted them, he had become master where they had ruled, the Indians took his word before theirs. His independent nature would not bend to their yoke, he sought to confine them to their religious duties, and resented their interference with the courses he shaped. Stung by his attitude towards them, by his deeds, his words, these men, to whom their church was above everything, trampled on all patriotic considerations and conspired to thwart whatever he attempted. They cast suspicion on his every act, turned his subordinates against him, misrepresented, by letters and delegates, his administration to the government of France, and prevented its giving him the aid he asked. Frontenac was for France and the colony he had come to love; the priests were for their church, and, in their eyes, the supremacy of their order and of their church was of more moment than the supremacy of France over a territory vaster than even La Salle conjectured. They exerted the potent influence they possessed at Versailles to have him deposed as governor. The King, worried by their entreaties, signed his recall, and appointed the nominee of the Jesuits his successor. Frontenac's departure, says Garneau, was a triumph for the Laval party. The bishop and the Jesuits chuckled as the great man stepped on board ship: with his departure went forever the prospect of New France becoming supreme in America. To the patriotic Frenchman, there can be no sadder reading than the official records that show how Laval and the Jesuits galled the fiery spirit of Frontenac, irritated him with petty persecutions, and baffled his far-sighted designs. When, seven years later, he was besought to return to Canada to save her from the Indians who threatened the extinction of its settlers, he was verging on seventy, unable to resume the plans of his mature manhood, even had he found conditions as he left them. The opportunity to realize them had passed forever. He did what he could. He saved its inhabitants from the tomahawk of the Iroquois: it was no fault of his that the sovereignty of North America was not also saved to New France.

The attempt to make French power predominate roused the antagonism of the English. There was room and verge enough for both, yet forbearance and regard for each other's rights were unknown on either side. The Jesuits deliberately incited the Indians to raid the frontier settlements of New England and New York, accompanying them and encouraging them with assurances their object was pious, that English and Dutch Protestants were human only in appearance. The thirst of the Indian for blood was stimulated by the governor of Quebec promising ten crowns for every scalp of the Bostonians they fetched back, and twenty crowns for each prisoner. At the distance of two centuries, the horrors of those raids still make the flesh creep. The English, in self-defence, retaliated, and in their spirit and methods they were no better than their enemies. Both peoples professed, each in their own way, to be peculiarly religious, yet, in carrying into practice the essence of Christ's teaching, love to God and man, the Puritan was no better than the Jesuit. This third and last period of the early history of Canada is written in blood: men who knew

The Tragedy of Quebec.

better, instead of clearing the forest and cultivating the soil, living in brotherly love, devoted themselves to slaying their neighbors, bribing the savages to help them in their dreadful purpose. To talk of heroism in connection with the leaders in these deeds is to pervert the meaning of the term. The red fiends who at midnight rushed the slumbering hamlet, butchering mother and babe, torturing the grey-haired sire and his stalwart sons before dealing the fatal blow; or who, stealing behind the settler, while ploughing his little clearing, buried a tomahawk in his brains; or, worse still, waiting in the bush, shot the Puritan maid while tripping her way to the church on the hill, are to be regarded with horror. Does the blare of trumpet and roll of drum, the shimmer of gold and scarlet, the waving of plume and banner, the high-sounding names of nobility, the benison of priest or bishop, the panegyric of the orator or the eulogium of the historian, place all the French soldiers, from Iberville to Montcalm, or their opponents, from Schuyler to Wolfe, on a different plane? The savage took life in his ignorance, the white against his knowledge of what was right. Of the two, the Indian was the more excusable.

The kings of France looked on the ordinary settler in two lights, as a customer for the manufactures of France, and as a unit of the garrison that held Canada for France. To ensure his being a customer for what France had to sell, governors were instructed to destroy looms, to limit tanneries, restrict the number of tradesmen, and to see that nothing was made that France could supply. Hemp and flax might be grown, but were to be shipped to France to be converted into rope and linen. No tobacco was to be raised, no mills built, and the keeping of sheep prevented, so that no cloth be woven. All raw material was to go to France, nothing was to be manufactured. Colonies, said a royal memorial to Vaudreuil, "Are settled only for "their usefulness to the country which founds them, "and never with the idea of their doing without the

"Mother Country." These orders were impossible to strictly enforce except in the neighborhood of towns, but their existence made clothing so dear that the laboring class were in rags. To keep the Canadian a soldier, no more horses were to be allowed to live than needed to work the land. "The great number of horses "has the effect of making the people effeminate," writes the minister to Quebec in 1710. Three years later he renews his injunction. "It is most important "that the settlers should be made to return to the use "of snow-shoes, and the horses and winter vehicles be "destroyed, otherwise the settlers would become "effeminate and lose their superiority." Hocquart, the last intendant except one before the conquest, and who therefore knew New France in its most developed stage, gives this sketch:

"All the inhabitants of the rural districts are "skilled in the use of the axe. They make for them-"selves nearly all their farm implements, and build "their own houses and barns. Many of them are "weavers, and make coarse linen and cloth they call "'droguet,' with which they clothe themselves and "their families. They love to be taken notice of and "caressed, and are extremely sensitive to contempt "or the smallest punishment. They are reserved, vin-"dictive, given to drunkenness, using largely of spirit-"uous liquors, and have the reputation of not being "truthful. This description is applicable to the "greater number, and more especially to the country "people. The townspeople are less vicious. They "are all attached to their religion. There are but few "criminals. They are flighty and self-conceited, and "hence they do not succeed as they might in the arts, "agriculture and trade. To this must be added idle-"ness, which is induced by the long and rigorous "winter. They are fond of hunting, sailing and travel-"ling, and have not the coarse, rustic appearance of "our French peasants. They are, generally speak-"ing, docile enough when stimulated by a sense of

"honor and justly ruled; but they are naturally re-
"fractory."

Every man was compelled to have a musket. If
they had not money, the officials were to take produce
in payment. All between 16 and 60 were required to
turn out when ordered to do military duty, or to work
on fortifications. The wall around Montreal, the batteries of Quebec, were built by enforced labor. No
householder dare refuse to billet soldiers. That the
supply of soldiers might not fail, governors were
adjured, in solemn state despatches, to insist on marriages at fifteen years of age, and governors and bishops
complacently reported on a good crop of babies. That
there might be no lack of women, they were shipped to
Canada like cattle. A despatch to Talon reads: "His
"Majesty has heard with pleasure that of the 165 girls
"sent to Canada last year, only 15 remained unmarried.
"Will send out 150 more girls this year. He did well
"to order that the volunteers should be deprived of
"the privilege of trading and hunting, if not married
"within two weeks after the arrival of the girls. Has
"given orders that the girls who are sent to Canada
"shall be strong and healthy." While the Kings of
France treated the habitants of Canada as animals to
fulfil their behest, they were no worse than the priests.
As a means of converting the Indians, the Jesuits kept
urging young men to marry squaws, offering a dowry
as an inducement. Select your brides from the wig-
wam was the advice to young men of Bishop Laval.
At first the French Government rather approved of
this, but, finally realizing what it meant, sent an order
to the governors to oppose intermarriage with the savages: if the priests had none, the administration at
Paris had some regard for the purity of the French
race. The clergy, on moral grounds, encouraged early
marriages, and finally it became part of the law that a
girl could marry when 14, and a lad when 18. Neither
the endorsation of priest nor legislator could change
the law of nature, and to this hour Quebec suffers the

consequences in its hideous mortality of the children of immature parents and the unusual proportion of survivors defective in mind or body.

The picture of Canada under France strikes the onlooker especially in one regard—the complete isolation of its people from the rest of the world. From first to last the royal orders are that there was to be no intercourse except with France. No foreign vessel was to be permitted to enter the St. Lawrence, no goods except of French manufacture to be imported. When scarlet cloth was required for the Indians by traders, it was the agents of the King who bought it for them in England. Once, during a time of war, it was necessary to ship furs by a neutral; the Dutch vessel that was chartered was not allowed to go within thirty miles of Quebec, and twenty soldiers were put on board to make sure no foreign merchandise be landed. To visit the English colonies was more severely punished than robbery. Canoes found on rivers leading southward were broken, and a lookout party maintained to see that none enter them. Woe to the hunter who was discovered to have sold his beaver hides in Albany. The penalties of the secular power were reinforced by those of the priesthood. From the pulpit repulsive stories were told of the Protestant settlers to the south of Canada and the terrors of the church threatened against whoever dared to approach them. The result of all this was, that for 150 years New France was substantially a big convent, whose inhabitants were forbidden to go beyond its bounds: kept as a preserve of feudal ideas, customs, and tyranny, and, at the same time, of priestly exclusiveness. He who would grasp the political problems that confront the Dominion must realize what this means, and trace the shadow of these despotic times in darkening our national life—the shadow projected over the Dominion by the descendants of people who, for five generations, were inured to implicit obedience, to absolutism in church and state, kept separate and by themselves from the rest of the world as a preserve for priest and crowned tyrant.

Under the rule of the French kings Canada, in the common-sense of the word, never was a colony. In our day, when we speak of a colony we mean a body of people who have left their native shore to better their condition by settling in a new country. That was never so with New France, which came into existence as a place for fur-traders and ended as a military dependency. In both states of existence it was actually a preserve of the church of Rome. The priests who came as missionaries to the Indians determined this. In 1615, when Champlain sailed with four Recollet priests, an edict forbidding Protestants to live in Canada was promulgated. Hitherto French Protestants had been the main agents in carrying on its trade, henceforth they were excluded. The charter granted the company of the hundred associates in 1627 went further, it specified the company was not only to permit no Protestant to take up his abode in Canada, but to exclude persons of all other nationalities—they must keep New France exclusively for Catholic Frenchmen. Thirty-seven years later, when the West India Company was given possession, the order was repeated—they were to permit no Protestants to settle in Canada. The enforcement of these regulations fell to the Jesuits. Not a ship cast anchor off Cape Diamond they did not board on the hunt for Protestants. The Protestants of Rochelle in those days were the sailors of France, and it was rare none were among the crew. They were kept under watch until the ship left: no worship by them on deck, no singing of hymns was allowed. If among the emigrants they discovered one tinged with Protestant views he was taken in hand to be disciplined. The search of the Jesuits was best rewarded when there were soldiers on board. Levied in different parts of France, it was not surprising stray Huguenots were found. In acting thus they were encouraged by the King. In a memorial, dated

June, 1686, he tells Governor Denonville he "is de-
"lighted to inform him that a great number of con-
"versions to the Catholic religion are taking place.
"Have revoked the Edict of Nantes. We hope that
"the example given by France will be of use in Can-
"ada. Must labor for the conversion of the heretics.
"If any of them are obstinate, place soldiers in garri-
"son among them, or cause them to be imprisoned,
"coupling the severity with the care necessary for
"their instruction, as to which you must act in concert
"with the bishop." What "instruction" meant and
how those who fell into their hands were "instructed,"
the Relations of the Jesuits tell—the means they used
to dispossess the devil who blinded the heretic, his
seeing a new light, his penitence, his adding to the
triumphs of the confessors. What was done with those
who would not recant, the Relations pass in silence.
Of their fate, however, we have a glimpse due to the
ecclesiastical and civil authorities disagreeing as to
what should be done with a Protestant who persevered
in his convictions. Among the new arrivals was Daniel
Vvil, whom the Jesuits discovered to be a Protestant.
He was taken in hand by them, what the means they
used we are not told, with the result that he agreed
to become a Catholic. With great pomp he was
received by Bishop Laval into the Catholic church.
Relieved of the pressure that had been brought to
bear upon him and which had caused him to do violence to his conscience, Vvil neglected to attend mass.
He was brought before an ecclesiastical court when
he declared his regret at abjuring the reformed faith,
and his determination to hold to it. The court found
him guilty as a contumacious heretic and doomed him
to death. He was handed over to the civil authorities to carry out the sentence. Governor Argenson
refused, and it is his refusal that caused the preservation of the facts of the case. Had he done as it is
to be presumed his predecessors did in like cases,
obeyed the order of the priests, we should never have

heard of the fate of Daniel Vvil. Awaiting a change
of governor, Vvil was kept a prisoner in the midst of
a community where none dare express to him a word
of sympathy or bestow an act of kindness. History
abounds with instances of weak men facing death with
fortitude when the sentence was carried out promptly,
but here was a man who knew death was inevitable,
yet subjected to the suspense of months, all the while
knowing he could save his life by submission to the
priests who continued to torment him with their im-
portunities. Can his constancy be otherwise explained
than that, in his prison, he had an unseen visitor who
fulfilled the promise made to whoever confessed Him
before men? The fatal hour came in the fall of 1661.
A new governor had arrived, D'Avaugour, who had
no qualms in obeying the bishop. Vvil was brought
forth from his cell, led to the public square of Quebec,
and, in presence of a crowd of spectators, faced a
platoon of soldiers. The captain uttered the word of
command, there was a volley of flame and smoke, and
Vvil lay stretched on the ground, pierced by many
bullets.

When New France had attained its height in population, it was still the boast that among their no inconsiderable number there was not a single Protestant.
"Praised be God," writes Governor Denonville in an
official report, out of the twelve thousand souls who
make up New France, "there is not a heretic here."
The children stolen in the raids on New England were
handed over to the nuns, and their baptism and first
communion made occasions of special celebration.
The extreme to which the spirit of exclusiveness was
carried is shown in the case of a visitor from New England, who, possessed with the idea that a passage to
the Pacific could be found by way of the Saguenay,
had crossed to the St. Lawrence by following the
Chaudiere. He was promptly arrested and sent away
by the first ship. A vexed question, which divided the
officials of the colony, was whether it was justifiable to

sell brandy to the Indians. The opinion of the theologians of the University of Toulouse was sought. They decided it was, their chief reason being that thereby the Indians were protected from heresy, for, if they could not buy brandy in Canada, they would go to the English settlements in New York State.

Frontenac complained that the confessional was used as an inquisition into the inner life of each family, and for every thoughtless word regarding church or clergy the offender was called to account. Frontenac was not alone in objecting to the use made of the confessional as a means of espionage on family life. La Salle, the explorer, complained that, by its means, the priests "enter as it were by force into the secrets of "families, and thus make themselves formidable." Frontenac declared their prying into the lives of the people to be worse than the Spanish Inquisition. La Motte-Cadillac, on his arrival at Quebec, was astounded at the state of society, and wrote a friend, "Nobody "can live here but simpletons and slaves of the ecclesi- "astical domination." The interference in family affairs extended to dictating dress and amusements. In a mandement, Bishop de Saint Vallier complained of the immodest head dress of the women, "appearing "both abroad and at home, and often even in the "churches, with their heads uncovered or only half "concealed under a transparent head dress, with a "collection of ribbons, laces, curls and other vanities; "and what is still more to be deplored and fills our "soul with grief is, that they do not hesitate to make "themselves the instruments of the devil, and co-oper- "ate in the loss of souls redeemed by the blood of "Jesus Christ, by laying bare their necks and shoul- "ders, scandalizing thereby, and causing the loss of "numberless persons."

The punishments for breaking the rules laid down by the clergy were generally puerile, sometimes cruel. The girl who added a geegaw to her attire, the son who failed to return to the paternal roof by nine

o'clock, the father who tarried in the tavern by the
brandy-bottle, all fell within the discipline of the
clergy. Their interference extended to what is now
called criminal law. On the ground that crimes concerned morals, they were active prosecutors. The
rack was a recognized means of discovering evidence,
the slitting of lips, mutilation of tongue, ears and
hands were ordinary punishments, and burning at the
stake was not unknown. The monastic orders to whom
grants of land had been given, used their power as
seigniors to enforce their clerical commands. The
scandal of this became so clamant that the King finally
deprived both Sulpicians and Jesuits of judicial power.
The bishops were repeatedly checked by the King for
trenching on the sphere of the courts. Bishop Saint
Vallier issued an order to his cures to refuse absolution and the Easter sacrament to those who did not
pay their tithes: he was commanded to retract. The
proscription of Protestants was continued to the end.
The commerce of the world at large, then as now, was
in the hands of Protestants, and branches in Quebec
and Montreal represented Protestant firms, who supplied the colonists with goods that were indispensable,
and which they could not possibly obtain in any other
way. At first the members of those houses were
allowed to stay during the season of navigation only—
they must go before the St. Lawrence was frozen.
This rule in later days was relaxed. The priests made
complaint to the King. May 30, 1754, he sent the
order to send away all Protestants of foreign origin,
and to confer with the bishop as to what was to be
done with those who were French. The governor replied that to drive away Protestant traders would be
an injury. "There are fourteen Protestant houses,"
he tells the King, "which carry on three-fourths of the
"trade of the country, and if they were driven out
"the colony would greatly suffer, the Canadian mer-
"chants not being numerous enough nor having the
"capital to meet all requirements." The King's

answer was to write to the bishop to look into the matter, and if it could be done without too great an injury to trade, to have the Protestant merchants sent to France. Thus, up to the last hour of French rule, Protestants were denied domicile.

It is a cant phrase of our day to speak of the French regime as "the heroic period" of Canadian history, as a season of delightful romance, of Arcadian simplicity. They who do so, know not of what they speak. The official correspondence that has come down from these days reveals the pettiness of the French court in trying to regulate details beneath the dignity of a great State; its employing its officers to act as spies on one another; the jealousies of these officers and their strivings to supersede those above them. What sense in talking of the age of explorers, when we have the despatches of the King commanding that no encouragement be given La Salle? Greed and dishonesty characterized those in office, who used their power to oppress the poor. Personal liberty there was none, for the people were under unceasing supervision. Punishments were of constant occurrence for infraction of church duty. Failure to attend mass or working on a saint's day were crimes. Owing to his having appealed to the council against his sentence, there has been preserved in the official records the case of Louis Gaboury, convicted of having eaten meat during Lent. He was to be tied to the public whipping-post for three hours, then taken to the door of his parish church where, on his knees, he was to beg pardon from God, to pay a fine of 20 francs and the milk of a cow for a year.

The control of the individual and of the family involved that of the government of the country. Frontenac remarked, "Masters in spiritual matters is "a powerful lever for moving everything else." The clergy dictated the course the governor and his subordinates were to follow, and, on refusal, there was trouble. When a governor was persistent in rejecting their advice, they used their influence at the court of France to secure his recall. No inconsiderable part of the state papers relating to New France concern contentions between the clergy and the governors. Talon, sagacious, cool, politic, did his best to secure the support of the priests in his patriotic policy of trying to make New France self-sustaining, yet, when nearing his departure, he reports to Colbert, "I should "have had less trouble and more praise if I had been "willing to leave the power of the church where I "found it. It is easy to incur the ill-will of the Jesu- "its if one does not accept all their opinions and "abandon one's self to their direction even in temporal "matters, for their encroachments extend to affairs of "police, which concern only the civil magistrate." Five years later, after prolonged experience and wide knowledge of the country, Frontenac wrote the same minister, "Nearly all the disorders in New France "arise from the ambition of the priests, who want to "join in their spiritual authority an absolute power "over things temporal, and who persecute all who do "not submit entirely to them." First under the Jesuits, then of Laval and his successor, St. Vallier, New France was governed according to the ideas of the priests, for the resistance of the governors was intermittent and, in the end, ineffective. Of Laval it was Colbert who said, "He assumes a domination beyond "that of other bishops throughout the Christian world, "and particularly in the kingdom of France."

To preserve the inhabitants of New France from heresy, it was deemed necessary by the priests to keep them in a state of tutelage. Although they could not read, no heretical book should be brought from across the sea. A French visitor, La Hontain, declares the priests "prohibit and burn all books but books of devo- "tion." The intolerance of New France was a reflex of that of the Mother Country. The first year William III. sat on the throne of England, a plan was agreed on at Versailles for the conquest of New York. The sealed instructions given to the commander of the expedition were, that on his overcoming the garrison and obtaining possession of the country, he was to confiscate the lands and all other property of the Protestants, whether Dutch or English, and send them out of the country. Untoward events prevented the sailing of the fleet.

It is the constant pretension of the priesthood that the country which submits implicitly to their rule thereby ensures both happiness and prosperity: that the only one certain means of a people becoming good and great is to place themselves under their direction. In no other part of the world was their rule ever more complete than in New France, which lay at the feet of the priests from Champlain to Vaudreuil—a period of 150 years. They had every chance to make good the pretension that their church alone has the secret of national success, yet socially, commercially, intellectually, and politically, New France was a failure. The reports of intendants are dotted with complaints of the pride and sloth of the people, necessitating public distribution of alms and providing a house of refuge. The country swarmed with beggars. Bishop de St. Vallier complained he was overwhelmed by their visits. Bishop Pontbriand, in 1743, suggested to the King that steps be taken to rid Quebec of beggars by banishing them. Charlevoix, the Jesuit historian, could not help contrasting the easy circumstances of the New England settlers with the poverty of the people of New France. Material prosperity, however, is not everything, and it is possible for great moral virtue to exist where privation prevails. On the evidence of two bishops it was not so in Canada. Bishop Duplessis asked permission from Governor Maurepas to keep the gate on the terrace at Quebec leading to his palace locked, because the lawn beneath his windows was made an idling place in the evenings. "Under my window," the bishop writes, "it is that the lower class "of people of both sexes assemble after supper; that "these people there indulge in licentious conversation;

"that drunkards come there to sleep off their potations,
"etc.; that on Sundays and fete days one's head is split
"by the noise that the people make playing at skittles
"and ball." The state of morals in Quebec and smaller
towns was a reflex of that of Versailles. To this the
last bishop under French rule bears striking evidence.
In a pastoral issued during the winter of 1760, Bishop
Briand deplores the little zeal for piety displayed
everywhere; the injurious and wicked speeches maintained against those in whom we ought to place all
our confidence; the profane diversions to which we are
addicted, the insufferable excesses of the games of
chance, the impious hypocrisy in derision or rather in
contempt of religion; the various crimes that have
multiplied in the course of this winter. Then he goes
on to ask, "Were there ever such open robberies, so
"many heinous crimes of injustice, such shameful
"rapines heard of? Who has not seen in this colony
"families devoted publicly to sins of the most odious
"nature? Who ever beheld so many abominations?"

Except in furs, New France had no trade worth mentioning; her wholesale merchants were few, with headquarters abroad. Her retailers were men of small
capital. Intellectually she was dead. There were no
schools outside the towns, and these confined their
curriculum to prayers and instruction in the
catechism. There was no printing press in the colony,
and no resident of it was allowed, without the King's
leave, to have anything printed in France. The priests
had been given every opportunity to mould New
France, and this was the result—a country without
a single element of what constitutes national greatness.
Whoever argues that clerical rule is a blessing, that it
ensures success for the government and happiness for
the people, let him explain why New France was a
failure politically and socially. There is no test so
conclusive as that of a system being put into actual
practice. For 150 years New France had tested clerical
rule under conditions so favorable that its advocates

can take no exception to them. The priests were given full opportunity to prove their claim to the secret of successful government. With the proof before us of their failure to make good their claim, are we going to submit to a fresh trial of their rule? Is not one experiment on Canada's soil, with every condition favoring the priests, enough to satisfy us that clerical rule is a blight to material progress and intellectual advancement? The long tutelage of Quebec under the priests explains many of the perplexing conditions that to-day hinder the Dominion in her onward march, for although the Conquest ended the rule of the French King, it is of vital moment to bear in mind the Conquest did not end the rule of the priests. With the coming of the British the lesser evil vanished—the greater remained. What was the blight of New France continues to be the blight of our Dominion.

Reviewing the history of New France it will be seen it resembled the history of those settlements which Spain and Portugal planted in South America save in material wealth. In the one there was gold and silver, in the other the only realizable plunder was beaver skins. The soldiers sent to rob the natives of South America of their stores of the precious metals were accompanied by members of that great organization which, under the guise of religion, seeks to rule mankind. Each and all of the dependencies in South America fell into decay. The cause was the same that stifled the energies and defeated the aspirations of a nobler race than Spanish or Portuguese in New France.

CHAPTER III.

Canada Under British Rule

That Canada should have fallen to the British by force every generation of its inhabitants since Wolfe's victory has had cause to regret, and it will be cause for regret to generations to come. Freedom of the will in the individual causes him to resent his career being shaped by the violent interference of an outsider, and the same sentiment is as strong in a collective sense. No people ever yet were overcome by foreigners who accepted the yoke of the conqueror with contented resignation. It would be a reflection on the Almighty, whose creatures we are, were it otherwise. The sense of wrong, the spirit of independence, the natural love for kith and kin, the traditions of the race, survive the lost battle, and, though they may smoulder, will flame out long after the deed of conquest. In a material sense the French-Canadians profited by the change of rulers. They had been treated by the kings of France as slaves—refused self-government even in municipal affairs—their services and property taken without compensation by the representatives of the king, who were as corrupt and worthless a lot of officials as ever cursed any country. Let him who wishes to know how New France was governed not go to Parkman, who picks out from the musty records only the details that enable him to embellish his delightful narrative, but to the royal despatches to the governors and intendants and their reports, and be will learn how, in the minutest details of daily life, its inhabitants lived under a system of mediaeval absolutism destructive alike of initiative and of self-respect. At the hands of the King's officials and at those of his seigniors, the common people knew naught save oppression and robbery. When Quebec fell they were in a pitiable condition. The habitant's horses had been seized to draw the war-supplies of Montcalm and de Levis, his oxen confiscated to feed their soldiers, his sons drafted to fill the gaps in their ranks, and to raise a crop to keep his other children alive, he had to harness his wife and daughters to the plough. The only money he had seen for years was paper promises to pay, which had become discredited. Even had the war between France and England not resulted in the capture of Quebec, in another year famine would have compelled the surrender of Canada. In the campaign of 1760 the soldiers were on short rations and the order was to give no butcher-meat to women. To the common people the coming of the British meant emancipation from oppression, and security in the enjoyment of what they earned. For the first time in his life the habitant was his own master and allowed to keep the fruits of his labor. It is interesting to read of what the expectations of the peasants were at the time of the conquest. They looked for coercion and iron-handed oppression: they expected to be treated as they had treated the settlers of the New England frontier, but, instead, were met with kindness. It is a fact, as important to bear in mind as it is undeniable, that the French in Canada never knew content and plenty until they came under British rule. No degree of material prosperity, however, can smother sentiment. The hand that gave them security and justice was the hand of a stranger, of a stranger who had taken possession of their country by force, whose creed they had been taught from infancy to abhor as an invention of Satan, and whose language they did not understand.

The reflection is a provoking one, that the brutalities of war should have substituted a forced union for the friendly approach of the two peoples that was coming. The hour of Frontenac's recall sounded the doom of the hope of New France's sovereignty on the American continent, and with the passing of that hope her drift into an alliance with the English-speaking colonies was unavoidable. These colonies were advancing by leaps and bounds into self-governing nations, increasing in population and in material resources: New France had ceased to grow and was becoming yearly more impoverished. Her people numbered less than 100,000; those of the English colonies nigh 3,000,000. The situation of the inhabitants of Canada had come to the point when they could no longer defy those colonies, and self-preservation would have forced them into a treaty of amity. New France could not continue as it was, and Wolfe's victory only precipitated the change. How great would have been the difference, however, between the French voluntarily seeking a friendly alliance with the English and their being forced into submission, we can see in comparing the spirit of the Creoles of Louisiana towards the Anglo-Saxon with that of the French-Canadian. Considering how Canada was made part of the British Empire lessens surprise that thrice fifty years has failed to wither the national aspirations of the losers. At the same time, recalling how much British rule has done for them, that it rescued them from poverty, tyranny, and an intolerable administration of affairs, that it has given them self-government and equal rights; that every avenue of honor, profit, and responsibility in the service of the Empire has been thrown open to them; that all the privileges that pertain to the native-born Briton have been made theirs; it is surprising that assimilation has made such trifling progress, and that the feeling of exclusiveness should prevail to the degree which exists. In tracing to its source why this is so, the cause of the peculiar difficulties of the Dominion is also found.

With the coming of the British the military element of New France disappeared, leaving behind the seigniors, the clergy, and the habitants. The total number speaking French who became subjects of George III. is commonly set down at 60,000. In January, 1759, a census was taken to ascertain how many were able to bear arms in the coming campaign. It showed there were 15,229 between sixteen and sixty years of age who could take the field, and the total population was reported as 85,000. Twenty months later, at the capitulation, Vaudreuil handed the British authorities an official statement that of enrolled militia there were 16,000. During those twenty months the male population suffered from the effects of war, so that to ascertain the total population a higher ratio than the usual one to five must be taken. Multiplying 16,000 by six would show the population to be nigh 100,000. There was no such exodus to France after the conquest as is generally represented. The official letters of the time show there was great difficulty in securing shipping for the surrendered regulars of Vaudreuil's army, and that the number of resident Canadians who asked to be sent to France was trifling. Instead of the native population being reduced by the change of rulers, it was increased, for General Murray reports that from British authority ensuring security to those who cultivated the soil, there was a large influx of Acadians who had been living in New England. When the treaty of Paris was signed the population must have exceeded 100,000, and only those who want to make miracles where none exist will repeat the statement of 60,000.

The Habitants.

The inhabitants, with trifling exceptions, resided on strips of land along the banks of the St. Lawrence and the Richelieu. For the first time the farmer of New France knew what security means, being safe alike from the attack of the Indian and of the domiciliary visit of an official who, in the name of the French king, forcibly requisitioned whatever the army needed, not excluding his sons. More than that, for the first time, they began to feel the ennobling sense that they were their own masters. As one English officer put it in his report, "they began to feel they are no longer slaves." Haldimand, who spoke French and freely mixed with the habitants, declares they were well pleased with the change, which put new life into them and stimulated them to make undreamt of improvements in their condition. The new rulers were a surprise to the habitants. From infancy the English had been pictured to them as monsters who professed a religion invented by the devil, and who would, if they captured New France, destroy everything that was French or Catholic. Finding them to be different was grateful to a people who were at their mercy. Knowing he would possess what he grew, the habitant applied himself as he had never done before to extending and cultivating his clearing, and from a state of living on the verge of famine he before long had a surplus to sell, and Canada became an exporter of grain.

The Seigniors.

In one respect the habitant was disappointed. He had expected under the new ruler to be freed from the demands of the seignior. Why the claims of the seignior on the land were not cancelled, is probably to be explained by the relation of tenant and landlord being the only conceivable method of holding land of which General Murray and his military successors had any conception. That the man who has redeemed the land from forest for cultivation should own it, never seems to have flashed on their minds. In the Old World the noble leased the acres and the tenant paid him rent, and that arrangement the governing class had come to look upon as part of the Divine order. For the next fifty or sixty years we find the ruling class boggling over the difficulty of settling the question of ownership of the soil, one governor after another making experiments, all of which had as a feature, in some form or another, a lord of the manor and tenants. The seigniory system was a survival of a form of feudalism no longer known in England, and which the new rulers at first did not comprehend. The seigniories had been granted by the French kings on condition that certain services be rendered him: the land was not sold or bestowed, merely the usufruct was granted by the King in compensation of specified services. The moment those services ceased to be rendered the grants reverted to the crown. In like manner, the seignior allotted portions of the land thus ceded to him to men who bound themselves to do him homage, to render certain services, to pay a prescribed rent, and a fine should they sell. The rent was small, yet large to men in their circumstances: the fine was generally prohibitive as to sale. As King George did not want the services for which King Louis had ceded the land, the seigniors could not pretend they were rendering the obligations which entitled them to hold it. The seigniors were in the position of men who hold property under a servitude: when the servitude lapses, the property goes back to the owner. As suzerain by conquest, the seigniories fell to King George. Instead of taking possession, and declaring the censitaires owners, the British authorities dilly-dallied with the system, and it was left to hinder the advancement of the country, to be a standing grievance with the habitant, and to be a troublesome question with successive administrations for nigh a century. There is still a survival of the system in the rent fixed by the Act of 1854, and which will, some day, call for legislative remedy. The seigniors who, without authority, arrogated to themselves the name noblesse, deprived after the Conquest of the petty civil positions and their pay as officers of the militia, formed a discontented class, from which the two Papineaus and like agitators were drawn.

Position of the Priests.

While the seigniors kept their rents, the priests lost their tithes. For fifteen years after British rule was established, their support came as gifts from their people, or, as Solicitor-General Wedderburn stated, of contributions under threat of excommunication. Nothing so helped to reconcile the habitants to the new rule as the abolition of tithes, for tithes had always been unpopular. The priests lost nothing else. They were left undisturbed in their pastoral work, and shared in the prosperity that British rule brought. Abbe Le l'Isle Dieu, Vicar-General of the diocese, writing to Versailles in December, 1766, tells the minister: "The "new Bishop of Quebec, who arrived on the 28th June, "was acknowledged as titular bishop, eight days after, "by the English government. . . Our religion is "professed as publicly as it was before the cession of "the country. The only restriction imposed is that "priests are not to be brought out here from France, "unless they are natives of Canada or of the Colonies, "within the jurisdiction of the diocese."

The Supremacy of the Church of Rome.

In the Province of Quebec the Church of Rome enjoys immunities and privileges unknown in any other part of the world—even in those countries which have Catholic sovereigns. Here, on British soil and under a Protestant King, that church is not only, as it is right it should be, autonomous, unrestricted by the State in its spiritual sphere, but, what is wrong, exercises many of the powers that belong to the State. It levies taxes for the building and upholding of its churches and the houses of its clergy, and a yearly tax for the support of the priest of each parish. These levies are privileged, coming before other debts, and their payment is enforced by the machinery of the secular courts. The vows of nuns and religieux are recognized by the civil law. The real estate of the church is exempted from taxation, and much of that real estate was made inalienable by mortmain. Education is placed in the hands of the bishops, who have a pledge that the legislature shall make no change in its regulations without their consent, nor interfere with their distribution of the grant of public money. While the Provincial Government is thus the servant of the priests, the hierarchy resents all appearance of supremacy of the State, and for this reason disregards Dominion proclamations, even when for fasts or thanksgivings. In a word, the Church of Rome sits as a queen in Quebec, panoplied in her assumptions by law, receiving from the State whatever she asks, dominating the Province as the first interest to be considered and served.

When it is pointed out that this supremacy is inconsistent with the rights of British subjects who do not own her sway, that the concessions made to her infringe upon their privileges, the answer comes that the Church of Rome has prescriptive rights in the Province of Quebec which cannot, by either legislature or parliament, be modified, much less taken away. The contention is that when Canada was ceded, Great Britain bound herself by the treaty of Paris to continue to the priesthood the privileges and powers they possessed during the period of the French occupation. As I will prove, in a subsequent chapter, by citations from the records of New France, these privileges and powers were exceedingly restricted. The point, however, to be considered now, is whether the treaty of Paris bound Britain to guarantee special privileges to the priesthood. Do facts support this assertion?

The first time the British came in contact with the demands of the priests for exclusive treatment was at the capitulation of Quebec after Wolfe's victory. The officer in command, among the terms he asked in consenting to surrender, included a request that there be no interference with religion. In his reply, dated September 18, 1759, General Townshend stated:

"The free exercise of the Roman Catholic religion

"is granted, likewise safeguards to all religious per-
"sons, as well as to the bishop, who shall be at liberty
"to come and exercise, freely and with decency, the
"functions of his office, whenever he shall think
"proper; until the possession of Canada shall have
"been decided between their Britannic and most
"Christian majesties."

Fearful of outrage on church and convent the French officer asked for assurance of protection, which Townshend granted. As to the bishop exercising his functions in the town he could do so, until the Kings of England and France decided what the future of Canada should be. On the standing of the Papacy the article has no bearing, it simply concedes what any humane officer would grant. The following summer General Amherst invaded Canada from the West and after driving the enemy's forces before him invested Montreal. Vaudreuil recognized the hopelessness of the struggle, that it must end in surrender, and so, while Amherst was waiting for his cannon to come from Lachine to batter down the city wall, he received a flag of truce asking for terms. Amherst was willing, and gave his beaten opponent the privilege of suggesting the terms he desired. Vaudreuil was solicitous as to the fate of his soldiers and of the citizens alone, but the priests insisted on also preferring their demands, which they did in these words:

"The free exercise of the catholic, apostolic, and
"Roman religion shall subsist entire in such manner
"that all the states and the peoples of the towns and
"countries, places and distant posts, shall continue to
"assemble in the churches and to frequent the sacra-
"ments as heretofore, without being molested in any
"manner, directly or indirectly. These people shall
"be obliged, by the English Government, to pay the
"priests the tithes and all the taxes they were used to
"pay under the government of his most gracious
"Majesty (the King of France)."

Opposite this demand General Amherst wrote:

"Granted as to the free exercise of their religion; "the obligation of paying the tithes to the priests will "depend on the King's pleasure."

Years afterwards, when clerical pretensions revived, a meaning favorable to the levying of tithes was endeavored to be given to the words, "Depends on the King's pleasure." How did priests and people understand them in the early years of British occupation? Their practice was the best interpretation of what the words meant. Fourteen years after Amherst wrote these words, Attorney-General Maseres, who had resided in Quebec, was called as a witness before the House of Commons. Standing at the bar the question was put, "Since the Conquest have habitants had "the option of refusing to pay tithes?" He answered:

"They certainly have, and sometimes make use of "it. The priests never presume to sue for tithes, "either in the court of King's Bench or Common Pleas, "knowing there is no possibility of succeeding. The "ground of that opinion of theirs, and of mine is, the "strong words of General Amherst's answer to the "demands on the part of the French General, for the "continuation of the obligation of the people to pay "their tithes and other dues, namely, 'Granted as to "the exercise of their religion, but as to the obligation "of paying tithes, that will depend upon the King's "pleasure.' That has been universally understood, "till now (1774) to have been a positive dispensing "with the obligation. It has often happened that "the habitants have not paid tithe; much oftener that "they did, from their regard to their religion."

To judge fully of the intention of Amherst with regard to the demands of the priests, it is proper to consider all the articles inserted at his instance. On reading them there is no mistaking the attitude of General Amherst. As a tolerant man he wished the people to have liberty of conscience, as a just man he wished to dispossess no one of his property. Beyond this he would not go. He would recognize none of the privileges the priests had enjoyed under the King of France, would not even allow the nomination of the bishop to the French King, or grant power to the bishop to erect new parishes.

The Treaty of Paris.

Three years later there was a meeting of representatives of Austria and Prussia, of Britain and France to draft a treaty of peace. When the article regarding religion was reached in the part of the treaty that concerned Canada, the French ministers asked that it read:

"His Britannic Majesty, on his side, agrees to grant "the liberty of the Catholic religion to the inhabitants "of Canada; he will consequently give the most effect-"ual orders that his new Catholic subjects may profess "the worship of their religion according to the rites of "the Roman Church as they have done."

The British representatives would not consent. They would grant all Amherst had agreed to at the capitulation, and nothing more. They demanded that the words, "as they have done," be struck out. The French ministers pled in vain for their retention. They were scored out. Fearful even then that the article might be construed into Britain's agreeing to allow the Church of Rome the status it had under France, they insisted on adding the words, "So far as "the laws of Great Britain permit." After some demur, the French, finding it impossible to get the Englishmen to recede, agreed, and the article as confirmed read:

"His Britannic Majesty agrees to grant the liberty "of the Catholic religion to the inhabitants of Canada: "he will, consequently, give the most effectual orders "that his new Roman Catholic subjects may profess "the worship of their religion, according to the rites "of the Roman Church, as far as the laws of Great "Britain permit."

The meaning of the article is obvious, whatever

privileges Catholics were to enjoy, were to be measured by British law and not by French law. The article is similar to the one in the treaty of Utrecht, 1713, in which France surrendered Nova Scotia to Britain, which set forth that the Acadians would be allowed "the free exercise of the Roman Catholic religion as "far as the laws of Great Britain do permit the same." Nobody pretends that this agreement gave the Acadians anything beyond toleration, and these words, repeated fifty years afterwards, conceded no more to the Catholics of New France. To the negotiators of the treaty of Paris the article was plain enough. They had been familiar with its interpretation, as applied to the government of Nova Scotia, for half a century. If the article in the treaty of Paris gives the priests the right to tithe and toll in Quebec, then the treaty of Utrecht gives the priests of Nova Scotia the same right.

The English commissioners were resolute in having it fully understood that the subjects whom France was abandoning were to come under the rule of Britain divested entirely of everything that pertained to their old status, and to that end insisted on the adoption of this additional article:

The King of France "cedes and guarantees to his "Britannic Majesty, in full right, Canada and its de- "pendencies . . . and makes over the whole . . . "in the most ample manner and form, without restric- "tion and without any liberty to depart from the said "cession and guarantee."

The conveyance of Canada was thus made without a single reservation or condition in favor of its inhabitants, the French King abandoning his late subjects to the conqueror with brutal indifference. In the entire treaty there is not a single word about the French language or French laws. For the prevailing impression, that the treaty of Paris placed the French-Canadians on a different plane from other British subjects, by preserving to them certain distinctive privileges, there is no foundation. That such a notion exists is due solely to the assertion of those whose interest it is to have it believed, but the fact is, that whatever is found exceptional in Quebec rests not upon treaty-rights, and whoever says to the contrary, asserts what he cannot prove.

King George's Proclamation.

The treaty was signed in February, 1763, and the following October George III. issued a proclamation defining the limits of the new dependency, prescribing how it was to be governed, and the conditions on which intending settlers could rely. So soon as military rule could with safety be superseded, Canada was to be created into a Province, similar to the thirteen colonies to the south of it, and have an assembly representative of the people, who would make laws and otherwise provide for its government. Until such time, the royal proclamation went on to declare:

"All persons inhabiting in, or resorting to, our "said colony, may confide in our royal protection for "the enjoyment of the benefit of the laws of our realm "of England."

The proclamation instructs the governor to constitute courts for trying cases, both civil and criminal, as near as may be agreeable to the laws of England. There is not a word in the proclamation modifying this assurance of English law to whoever should settle in Canada, and not a word of any exception in favor of the French-Canadians. This proclamation of George III. is unqualified and absolute in placing Canada under the same conditions as Massachusetts or New York. The proclamation declared Canada to be English, and nothing but English. There is not even reservation of the French tenure of land. In the direction as to selling lands to settlers and of grants to soldiers and sailors who had served in the late war, it is specified the land shall be conveyed on the same terms as exist in the other British colonies. This proclamation, issued a few months after the treaty of Paris was signed, recognizes in no way that French-Canadians were to have any privileges other than those that pertained to them as British subjects. In this there was no disappointment to the French-Canadians. Judge Hey, the first Chief Justice of Quebec under English rule, in his evidence before the House of Commons in 1774, testified that at the conquest the French-Canadians "neither expected to retain their "religion nor their laws, and looked upon themselves "as a ruined and abandoned people. The general ex-"pectation among the habitants was that King George "would be as absolute as their late royal master, and "order them to be Protestants." The lenity with which they were treated, Quebec's first Attorney-General, Maseres, confirmed in this remarkable statement, "I am of opinion," he said, "with General Am-"herst, that if the priests had been given their living "(that is, pensioned), and their places had been sup-"plied by Protestants, the Canadians would have been "satisfied." Such was the slavish reverence ingrained on the habitants for their King, that there is no cause to doubt the conclusions of these witnesses, one of whom spoke French equally with English.

Instructions to Governors.

General Murray, on becoming Canada's first civil governor, received instructions from the Secretary of State, Earl Egremont, to guide him. He was told (August 13th, 1763), to guard against attempts by the French Government through the priests to keep the habitants in expectation of restoration of the rule of King Louis. Here are the Earl's words:

"His Majesty has reason to suspect that the French "may be disposed to avail themselves of the liberty "of the Catholic religion granted to the inhabitants, "to keep up their connection with France, and to in-"duce them to join for the recovery of the country. "The priests must, therefore, be narrowly watched,

"and any who meddle in civil matters be removed.
"Whilst there is no thought of restraining the new
"subjects in the exercise of their religion according
"to the rites of the Romish Church, the condition is,
"as far as the laws of Great Britain permit, which
"can only admit of toleration, the matter being clearly
"understood in the negotiation for the definite treaty
"of peace, the French ministers proposing to insert
"the words 'comme ci devant' (as they have done),
"and did not give up the point until they were plainly
"told it would be deceiving them to insert these
"words. You are, however, to avoid everything that
"can give the least unnecessary alarm or disgust to
"the new subjects. The greatest care must be used
"against the priest Le Loutre, should he return to
"Canada, where he is not to be allowed to remain, and
"every priest coming to Canada must appear before
"the governor for examination and to take the oath
"of allegiance."

This is the evidence of a nobleman who was present while the treaty was being negotiated, and is positive proof as to what was the object in adding the clause, "As far as the laws of Great Britain per-"mit." Britain was asked to continue the status of the priests as it had been under France, and Britain said No, and added nine words to the article which decisively deprived the priests of their powers under French rule and placed them where the law of Britain placed them. Ten years after the treaty was ratified, when the Quebec Act was being contemplated, the law officer of the House, Wedderburn, afterwards Lord Chancellor, gave this written opinion on the article:

"This qualification ('as far as the laws of Great
"Britain permit') renders the article of so little effect,
"from the severity with which, though seldom
"executed, the laws of England are armed against the
"exercise of the Roman Catholic religion, that the
"Canadian must depend more upon the benignity and
"wisdom of your Majesty's Government for the pro-

"tection of his religious rights than upon the pro-
"visions of the treaty."

Canada having been made by the treaty of Paris, part and parcel of the British Empire, arrangements had to be perfected for its government. In December, 1763, General Murray received his appointment as governor of the Province of Quebec, with minute instructions as to what he was to do. The following were the directions he was to follow in ecclesiastical affairs:

"And, whereas, we have stipulated, by the late
"definite treaty of peace, concluded at Paris the 10th
"February, 1763, to grant the liberty of the Catholic
"religion to the inhabitants of Canada, and that we
"will consequently give the most precise and most
"effectual order, that our new Roman Catholic sub-
"jects in that Province may profess the worship of
"their religion, according to the rites of the Roman
"Church, as far as the laws of Great Britain permit;
"it is therefore our will and pleasure, that you do, in
"all things regarding the said inhabitants, conform
"with great exactness to the stipulations of the said
"treaty in this respect. You are not to permit of
"any ecclesiastical jurisdiction of the See of Rome,
"or any other foreign ecclesiastical jurisdiction
"whatsoever, in the Province under your government.
"And to the end that the Church of England may be
"established, both in principles and practices, and
"that the said inhabitants may, by degrees, be induced
"to embrace the Protestant religion, and their children
"be brought up in the principles of it; we do hereby
"declare it to be our intention, when the said Province
"shall have been accurately surveyed, and divided
"into townships, districts, precincts, or parishes, in
"such manner as shall be hereinafter directed, all pos-
"sible encouragement shall be given to the erecting of
"Protestant schools in the said districts, townships and
"precincts, by settling, appointing and allotting
"proper quantities of land for that purpose, and

"also for a globe and maintenance for a Protestant
"minister and Protestant schoolmasters; and you are
"to consider and report to us, by our commissioners
"for trade and plantations, by what other means the
"Protestant religion may be promoted, established and
"encouraged in our Province under your government."

In the instructions there is not a word as to the French language, while as to courts and laws General Murray is advised to copy those of the other American colonies, especially of Nova Scotia.

What These Documents Enacted.

These are the facts of the treaty: (1) The French King asked that the article of the treaty regarding religion read so as to leave the priests their old status. (2) This the British not only refused, but inserted words to make it clear the priests would only have the status allowed by the English laws then in force. (3) To make the matter more definite, an article was included in the treaty declaring the French King made over his subjects in Canada without restriction. (4) Following the treaty King George issued a proclamation declaring English law to be the law of Quebec. (5) The priests recognized they possessed no longer the status under the French regime by not exacting tithes or dues by law. (6) The instructions to the first British governor were that he was not to permit any ecclesiastical jurisdiction of Rome, and was told it was the intention to make the Church of England the Established Church of Canada.

Positive and continued assertion goes a long way with people too indolent or too careless to inquire whether such assertion has a foundation of fact. For generations the people of Canada have been listening to solemn assurances that the treaty of Paris secured to Quebec peculiar privileges, and these assurances have been accepted, although reference to the treaty, even without considering the circumstances under which it was drawn, or its interpretation by the governors and officials who had to carry it into practice, would show they are falsehoods. Yet these untruthful assertions continue to be daily made. Take one recent instance. The Montreal Bar was invited to send a representative to the annual banquet of the New York Law Association, held at Albany, in February, 1907, and their batonnier, P. B. Mignault, K.C., was deputed. In his speech Mr. Mignault said:

"It seems to me that, speaking for the Montreal "Bar, I might be permitted to refer to the system of "laws under which we practice our profession. The "Province of Quebec is an old French colony. . . . "When the fortune of arms went against its sturdy "peasantry, they stipulated, in the articles of capitu- "lation, that they should still be governed by the cus- "tom of Paris. This request was granted by the "treaty of Paris."

When an eminent lawyer thus perverts facts, small wonder the average French-Canadian believes what is exceptional in his privileges of church, language, and laws is secured by treaty. Seeing these immunities and privileges do not have any foundation in the treaty of Paris, what authority is there for them? They rest solely on legislation, and what legislation gave legislation can take away.

The Quebec Act.

The first concessions were contained in the Act of 1774, and the opening so made has been taken advantage of to obtain a succession of favors from the Quebec and Dominion Legislatures. To the Quebec Act, regarded by French-Canadians as their Magna Charta, is to be traced the origin of the evils which have befallen the English-speaking settlers, and which it is the purpose of this monograph to describe. It is consequently necessary to examine it minutely and the circumstances under which it was passed.

There never would have been trouble in the consolidation of Canada with the Empire but for the

priests and those who styled themselves the noblesse.
The latter did not number seven score, and not one in
a score had the slightest claim to the rank of nobility.
They had held militia commissions in the French army,
or had been officials in Quebec's civil service. The
change of masters had left them without employment.
The English governors would have given them positions, but could not owing to the oaths then prescribed
for admission to the King's service, so they lived in
poverty, too proud to work with their hands, but not
too proud to accept gratuities. Idle and dissatisfied
they agitated for changes that would better their
position. Under the new rulers the habitants were
prosperous and contented; the little knot of gentry
were the reverse. Had the intolerant oaths that then
barred the military and civil service been waived in
their favor they would have become valuable servants
of the British Crown: shut out by wretched regulations, proud and poor, arrogant and vain, they resented the law that debarred them from positions of profit
and honor and constituted a centre of discontent
against the government. All the petitions for changes
in law sprang from them. If, they said, Canada is
British, it ought to be ruled as part of the Empire;
self governing with representative institutions, and so
they agitated for changes which would provide opportunities for benefitting themselves. The habitants,
ignorant of constitutional government, took no part
in an agitation they could not comprehend: all the
same, the little knot who were clamoring that Quebec
be given a legislature pretended they represented the
people as a whole.

For four years after Canada had come into Britain's possession it was under martial law. To the
habitants this was nothing new: under the rule of
Louis XV. they had known no other, it was simply a
benigner form of the rule they were accustomed to.
Garneau terms it the period of military despotism.
Did New France ever know of any other form of gov-

ernment? The issuing of the royal proclamation of 1763 ended military rule by giving a governor and council to the Province. This continued until the Quebec Act came into force.

The Debate on the Quebec Act.

The beginning of May, 1774, the government, without previous notice, laid before the House of Lords a bill to provide for the better government of the Province of Quebec. It met with no opposition, and in a fortnight was adopted and sent down to the House of Commons. It was a short bill, embodying three important enactments:

Restored French law.

Repealed test oaths and invested the priesthood with authority to levy tithes and dues:

Provided that the Province be ruled by a governor and nominated council.

Who the author of the bill was cannot be stated with certainty. This is known, that it was advised by Carleton, then governor of the Province, and was strongly favored by the King. Lord North was Premier, and anything, no matter how foolish, George III. might ask, he would support, the more so, when, as this bill promised to do, he would be saved trouble in managing the new possession. Passed hurriedly by the Lords, the bill suddenly appeared in the House of Commons at the fag-end of a session, which was to be the last of that parliament, so when it came up for its second reading, out of a House of 588, only 134 were present. Believing the work of the session was ended many members had gone home; many were engrossed in preparations to ensure their re-election. The expectation that the bill would slip through the Commons as easily as it had done in the House of Lords was speedily dissipated. The ministers had offered no explanations when the bill was introduced, and the motion that it be read a second time was formal. It likely would have passed without debate but for

Thomas Townshend, who rose to oppose the motion, and to the close of the debates led the opposition. He was against making Quebec French, and foretold what would be the result of the bill. With a prescience that tells of a penetrating intellect, he pointed out the effect it would have on those English emigrants who had settled in Canada, relying on the promises of the King's proclamation of 1763. "Would it not be better "by degrees," Mr. Townshend asked, "to show the "French-Canadians the advantages of the English law, "and mix it with their own? You have done the con- "trary: you have taken from the English subject his "benefit of the law of England, and you do not offer "in exchange to the French subject that change "of the constitution, which, if introduced in a mod- "erate manner, would attach him to Britain. I am "convinced," he added, "this bill, if carried into exe- "cution, will tend more to rivet in the Canadians "prejudices in favor of French rule than it will "attach them to the Government of England." Other members took the same view. Lord Cavendish held the true policy was to assimilate the new subjects, who had been, he remarked, transferred to Britain by the French king like deer in a park. To give them, he said, their old laws and customs will ever make them a distinct people. The necessity of keeping good faith with those who had settled under the promises of the proclamation of 1763 was urged by several. The persons affected were not the few who had found homes on the St. Lawrence, but the thousands who had moved from the thirteen colonies into the valleys of the Ohio and Mississippi, for, it has to be understood, the Province of Quebec then covered the territory out of which great States were afterwards carved. The defence of the bill was purely apologetic. None of the ministers who spoke pretended they cared much for the bill, which was, they assured the House, merely experimental. Lord North was a master in big phrases and affectations of superior wisdom. He patronized the opponents of the bill, was sorry they could not understand it, or see they were misled by prejudices. In view of the interpretation placed on the bill by a certain class in our times, the Premier made two striking admissions. The bill was to be no irrevocable statute; he intended it should be changed or repealed in the near future. It was not, he told the members, to be a perpetual settlement. His Solicitor-General, afterwards Lord Chancellor Wedderburn, was more explicit. "An objection has been urged against "the measure," he said, "namely, that there is no "clause in the bill to make its operation temporary. "Now, I consider this bill, in its nature to be temporary. "A bill of this kind cannot but be temporary, because "it is a bill of experiment." Lord North's other admission was more remarkable. "The honorable "gentleman demands of us, will you extend into those "countries the free exercise of the Roman religion? "Upon my word, I do not see that this bill extends it "further than the ancient limits of Canada," that is, the priests were to only exercise their privileges in those parishes in which they had done so under the French regime. Afterwards, when speaking to the objection of a Catholic bishop in Quebec, he remarked:

"Whether it is convenient to continue or to abolish "the bishop's jurisdiction is another question. I can- "not conceive that his presence is essential to the free "exercise of religion; but I am sure that no bishop will "be there under papal authority, because he will see "that Great Britain will not permit any papal author- "ity in the country. It is expressly forbidden in the "Act of Supremacy."

Those who read so much into the Quebec Act should consider the intention of the Premier who submitted it. Charles Fox, the keenest of parliamentarians, based a point of order on the restoring of tithes and church dues. The bill proposes to restore them, said Fox, that is imposing a money-tax on the Catholics of Quebec. The bill comes to us from the House of Lords, which has no power to originate a bill to raise money, therefore the bill could not be considered. Lord North argued the bill did nothing of the kind, for it merely continued a tax that already existed. The retort was obvious. If tithes and dues already exist, what need for mentioning them in the bill? If they did not exist, the bill must be thrown out on the point of order. This threw on the ministers the necessity of proving tithes were being levied, and their attempting to do so brought out evidence of the highest value as to the status of the priest since the conquest. Mr. Dunning, afterwards Lord Ashburton, declared he had it on the best authority that the priests had not been since the cession in possession of tithes and dues, nor will they unless this bill becomes law. Mr. Townshend said he also had it on the best authority that the priests never dared to sue for tithes. Sergeant Glynn, an eminent lawyer, scouted the drawing of any distinction between a tithe and a tax. The right to the tithe had ceased to exist, but would be restored if the bill passed. The right to the tithe, in future, he declared, is founded not on anything in the past, but upon this Act of Parliament, and will be an entirely new right. The ministers finally had to acknowledge tithes and dues were not in existence in Canada, the Solicitor-General admitting the priests had not since the conquest sued in the courts, but had adopted the method of enforcing payment by threats of excommunication. Fox had justified his point of order, but the government overruled it by a vote. They pressed the bill to its second reading, and it passed by 105 to 29. This showed its defeat was hopeless, but the opposition continued their efforts in the expectation of introducing amendments. Of these amendments two excite surprise in our times—their strenuous efforts to graft in the bill trial by jury in civil cases, and the right of habeas corpus. Daily experience in England was showing that only trial by jury stood between the people and the tyranny of the Crown, and that removal of habeas corpus might mean at Quebec lettres de cachet, then a real terror in Paris. To understand the force of arguments on these two points we must place ourselves in the position in which the people of England then stood, with the Crown stretching its prerogative to the utmost and believed to be ready to use, if it dared, the despotic methods of the French court.

When the House went into committee on the bill, a new figure appeared, that of Edmund Burke, who at once lifted the debate to a higher plane. Pointing out that the House was asked to impose a code of laws with which no member was conversant, he demanded evidence as to the need of the bill, and of the nature of the French laws and customs it proposed to restore. It was monstrous to enact laws of which the members had no knowledge. There were, he understood, reports on the subject; he asked that these reports be laid on the table for the information of members. He was answered the reports were too voluminous to copy in time for use. Baffled in this direction, he demanded that witnesses be examined. The ministers say the bill is a necessity, and until such proof is adduced I, for one, will never give my vote for establishing French law in Canada. Shamed from forcing the bill into law without some proof of its need, witnesses were called. Of these only three were material, namely, the late governor, Sir Guy Carleton, afterwards made a peer with the title of Lord Dorchester, his Attorney-General at Quebec, Maseres, and his Chief Justice, Hey. It was well known Carleton was humoring the King in his desire to have the bill passed, yet, to pointed questions, he had to acknowledge there was no dissatisfaction among the body of the people in Quebec, that the habitants were prosperous and contented, that they did not want self-government, that they feared any change would lead to trouble and expense, and that the agitation for change was confined to the seigniors, who wanted admission to places of trust and honor equally with the English. The courts that had been in existence since the proclamation did not give satisfaction, and, in that regard, the desire to return to old customs and usages was general. The evidence of the other two witnesses went to confirm the belief that there was no urgent need for the bill. When asked how it would affect the English inhabitants, Hey cautiously answered it would disincline them to remain in Canada. "My idea," he said, "is that a country conquered from France is, if "possible, to be made a British province." He favored adopting the French laws regarding land and personality, but all else, commercial and criminal, should be English. The unexpected lenity with which the French had been treated, had caused the agitators to rise in their demands, and they now asked nothing short of entire restoration of their laws and customs.

The calling of General Murray was demanded, but the ministers evaded the request. His testimony would have been of highest value, and would have been against the bill. One member said he especially wanted Murray called in order to explain the difference in estimates of the population of Canada. The statement of the bill that it was 65,000 at the time of the conquest, and was now 150,000, was incredible; and so it was.

Before entering into the principle of the bill, Burke raised a point concerning the status of English-speaking settlers. The bill, as introduced, conceded to Quebec the angle of land westward from the edge of Lake Champlain. On behalf of New York he objected to this, because it would bring within the frontier of Quebec a number of settlers who believed they were on land belonging to New York. "Unless the line is rectified," urged Burke, "you reduce British "free subjects to French slaves." He went on to say the line proposed was not a line of geographical distinction merely, for it was not a line between New York and some other English settlement, but a line which would separate men from the right of an Englishman, by placing them under laws which are not the laws of England. Compared with English law and rule, the eloquent Irishman exclaimed, the law and rule of France is slavery. You cannot deprive the forty or fifty thousand settlers on the New York frontier of the benefit of the laws of England, yet this is what the bill proposes. I would have English liberty carried into the French colony, but I would not have French slavery carried into the English colonies. The case thus made out by Burke was so clear to the majority of the members, that Lord North yielded and accepted Burke's amendment that the boundary of Quebec from Lake Champlain to the St. Lawrence be the 45th parallel of latitude, which continues to this day.

If English-speaking settlers drawn into Quebec by a change of boundary would be slaves, what of those then residing in Quebec or who hereafter might go there? This was also spoken of, and by those on the ministerial benches with a superciliousness and ignorance that was shocking in legislators engaged in shaping the destinies of a future empire. They held that the settlers then in Quebec were not worth considering. They were few, less than 360 men, apart from women and children; nearly all were disbanded soldiers, who, having the privilege of selling liquor without license, were keeping taverns and grog-shops. The better class, the military and civil officials, and the merchants doing business in the ports, were merely sojourners, who expected to return to Britain. What of future English-speaking settlers? The ministerialists declared there would be none. Mr. Dunning, opposing the bill, asked: "Ought you not, upon the "principle of strict justice, to make some provision for "persons coming to Canada upon the promise of Eng- "lish laws, and who will find, should this bill pass, "they have got into a country governed by a despot- "ism—that they have got into a country where the "religion they carried with them has no establish-

"ment?" Solicitor-General Wedderburn replied that the government did not wish to see Canada draw from Britain any considerable number of her inhabitants. The number of English who have settled in Canada is very few, and "it is one object of this bill that these "people should not settle in Canada," and went on to declare the policy of the government to be to prevent settlements of English beyond its southern boundary, or westward of the Ohio, to say to intending settlers, "this is the border, beyond which, for the advantage "of the whole empire you shall not extend your-"selves." This was the view taken by his colleagues, that English-speaking people should not be allowed to take up land in Canada, and, therefore, all they had to consider was the 150,000 French-Canadians. The gentlemen on the government benches looked on Canada as an inhospitable land of ice and snow, with a fringe of Frenchmen dwelling on the banks of the great river that had its source in an unexplored wilderness, whose vastness baffled imagination.

The ignorance that led them to denounce emigration was matched by their ignorance regarding religion. This parliament, in which no member who would not take the oaths of the test act, and was, therefore, composed almost exclusively of Episcopalians, had no conception of religion existing without an establishment. The proof of the contrary, furnished by the Nonconformists of Britain and by the Puritans across the Atlantic, they totally ignored. There must be tithes and dues, appointments of bishops and other dignitaries by the King, state authority for rubric and liturgy, or there could be no church. This pretension was used by those who, in supporting the bill, yet held they were sound Protestants. Even Burke was unable to take the larger view, that with the maintenance of religion the State should have nothing to do—that the existence of religion depends not upon the breath of kings or parliaments, and that State assistance smothers the Divine spark. The acute legal mind of

Mr. Dunning saw the absurdity of what the government was proposing, that a Protestant King be head of an established Roman Catholic Church in Quebec, and the greater absurdity, which the Premier suggested, co-ordinate establishment of that church and the Church of England, and argued for simple toleration of both. He contended that to establish was to encourage, and pointed out the difficulties that would arise from establishing a church which did not recognize King George as its head. The Premier scouted the fear thus raised, for, he declared, he had it from the law officers of the Crown, that the Catholic bishop of Quebec was subject to the King's supremacy. As the debate proceeded and members realized all the bill would do, those who were military men feared one result would be the reviving of that militia which had ceased with the surrender of Vaudreuil. Binding the priests to King George by privileges dependent upon his will they thought secured to him the services of their parishioners as soldiers. This was an impression which experience at the outbreak of the American revolution showed was erroneous, when the habitants refused to turn out as militiamen for priest or seignior. The reverse was taken for granted, however, and the belief prevailed that the bill would give the King an army irresponsible to parliament. Col. Barre, who had served under Wolfe, and whose figure appears in West's picture as one of those surrounding the dying soldier, with Irish frankness declared the object of the bill was to secure to the King "a Popish army to "serve in the colonies, destroying all hope of peace "with them, for the Americans will look on the "French-Canadians as their task-masters, and, in the "end, their executioners. That is the plan of the "government, not a man of them denies it; I wash my "hands of the bill, I declare my solemn aversion to it." William Burke, the friend, but not a relative of Edmund, denounced the bill as the worst that ever engaged the attention of parliament, for its object was to establish the Popish religion and French despotism in a conquered province. All the efforts of the opponents of the bill to make it consonant with the principles of the British constitution, have been defeated. "There will come an hour," he foretold, "when it will be necessary to testify there was some "opposition entered against this mad proceeding." The objections of the few who realized the grave results that would flow from the bill were finely expressed by Sergeant Glynn and Burke in the closing debate.

The ministry showed no concern over the opposition the bill evoked. Secure in his servile following Lord North, when blocked by the Opposition, called for a division, and the Opposition was easily outvoted. Even when the attendance was barely a seventh of the total, he was secure in a two-third majority. So lightly did the Premier think of the bill, that he once adjourned the debate in order that he might attend a private entertainment. The bill passed the Commons substantially as introduced. When it came before the Lords for concurrence in the amendments, Pitt, who had been unable to attend when the bill was being considered, arose from a sick-bed to enter a protest against it as subversive of liberty and opening the door to fresh dangers. It will shake the affections of the King's subjects on this side of the Atlantic, he declared, and lose to him the hearts of those on the other side. The warning of the statesman who had won Canada, who had rescued England from danger and disgrace, and led her, wherever her flag floated, triumphant over the forces of the combined Catholic Powers of Europe, was unheeded. Only six peers voted with him, and the bill was declared carried by the votes of 26. On hearing of the progress of the bill the trade guilds of the city of London took alarm at the abolition of civil actions, as likely to affect their collection of debts in Canada, and the Mayor, heading the council, went to wait on the King to ask that he refuse assent to the bill. That the measure was of his own suggestion, the King proved by delaying to receive the deputation on a quibble until he had declared it law. When news of the adoption of the bill reached the American colonies there was an outcry of indignation. Their people saw the hurt done them by passing the Act, and resented it. Their State legislatures adopted resolutions denouncing it in language their descendants care not to acknowledge. Instead of allaying the spirit of disaffection, by reviving fear of French domination, it intensified discontent. For a King who would set Catholic against Protestant, French against English, the Americans had less regard than ever. In the declaration of independence the passage of the Quebec Act is made one of the offences of King George's government that justified casting off his rule.

The Provisions of the Quebec Act.

What were the changes made by this Act which caused so much discussion in parliament and dissatisfaction abroad? The first and second sections define boundaries, the third confirms titles granted for lands, the fourth repeals any provisions in previous ordinances, and the proclamation of 1763, in so far as they may conflict with the Act, the fifth is the vital section, and reads:

"And for the more perfect security and ease of the "minds of the inhabitants of the said Province, it is "hereby declared, That His Majesty's subjects, pro-"fessing the religion of the Church of Rome, of and "in the said Province of Quebec, may have, hold and "enjoy the free exercise of the religion of the Church "of Rome, subject to the King's supremacy, declared "and established by an Act made in the first year of "the reign of Queen Elizabeth, over all the dominions "and countries which then did, or thereafter should "belong, to the Imperial Crown of this realm; and that "the clergy of the said Church may hold, receive, and "enjoy, their accustomed dues and rights, with respect "to such persons only as shall profess the said re- "ligion."

The sixth section provides for the establishment and maintenance of a Protestant clergy, the seventh dispenses with the oath of the days of Elizabeth, in which the claims of the Papacy are renounced, and substitutes one which simply promises true allegiance. The eighth runs thus:

"That all His Majesty's Canadian subjects within "the Province of Quebec, the religious orders and com- "munities only excepted, may also hold and enjoy "their property and possessions, together with all cus- "toms and usages thereto, and all other civil rights ". . . as may consist with their allegiance to His "Majesty, and subjection to the Crown and parliament "of Great Britain; and that in the matters of contro- "versy, relative to property and civil rights, resort "shall be had to the laws of Canada, as the rule for "the decision of the same."

Section ten extends this by including all moveables which may be given or bequeathed either according to the laws of Canada or of England. Section eleven establishes English criminal law. The remaining sections provide for the constituting of a council to assist in governing the province, levying taxes, and other executive matters.

The two important sections are five and eight. On analyzing five, it will be seen it gives the power to the priests to compel their people to pay tithes and taxes to build and maintain churches, and nothing more. The section does not recognize the Catholic church as an established church, nor confer upon it any of the attributes of an established church, beyond giving priests the help of the law to secure support from their parishioners. Section eight is peculiar in its wording. Literally interpreted, it placed the province under the laws then in existence in Canada, which were those of England. The phrase "laws of

"Canada" was dictated by pride, to avoid specifying the laws of France. The intention of the framer of the Act was the guide to those who administered it. It was made clear, however, that the restoration of French law was not to extend to all the province, but to be confined to the seigniories. Section nine reads:

"Provided, always, that nothing in this Act contained shall extend, or be construed to extend to any lands that have been granted by His Majesty, or shall hereafter be granted by His Majesty, his heirs and successors, to be holden in free and common soccage."

The importance has not been attached to this section that it deserves, for it confines the application of sections 5 and 8 to an extremely limited area. When the Act was passed the only land in the province not held in free and common soccage was the seigniories, which formed a fringe along the St. Lawrence and the Richelieu, some ten miles deep. Outside that narrow fringe, sections 5 and 8 had no force. The Act of 1774 amounted then to this, that in the seigniories, and in the seigniories only, French civil law was restored and the priests could collect tithes and dues. Outside the seigniories the law remained as fixed by the proclamation of 1763. The Act is invariably spoken of by French commentators as applying to the entire Province of Quebec. Section 9 places beyond controversy that the re-enactment of French law was confined solely to the parishes then in existence, an insignificant portion of the province.

Of the practical effect of the changes made we have an official and authentic estimate of the meaning of its provisions by the ministry who submitted the Quebec Act. It received the royal sanction on June 22nd 1774. Six months afterwards Sir Guy Carleton was appointed governor of Quebec. The royal instructions he received as a guide for himself and the council that was to be formed were unusually voluminous. After pointing out the discrimination to be exercised in allowing the French "the benefit and use of their "own laws, usages and customs" in regard to real estate and descent, the new council is admonished to consider well in framing its ordinances "whether the "laws of England may not be, if not altogether, at "least in part, the rule for decision in all cases" of a commercial nature. The instructions as to religion shatter into dust the pretence that the Quebec Act made the Catholic church an established church. Governor Carleton is enjoined to recognize no such pretension, but to keep the bishop and priests under his control, and to prevent them exercising their clerical functions until licensed by him. The value of the Act of 1774 to the priests lies not so much in what it conceded, as in making an opening for further demands. Once granted that they should have exceptional privileges in the seigniories, demand was piled upon demand as opportunity presented itself, each demand as conceded forming an excuse for asking more and urged as a reason for legislators giving what was asked. It is the old fable of first a finger, then an arm, ending in the whole body.

Quebec Has No Treaty Rights.

This chapter has been unduly extended by giving the text of quotations instead of summarizing them. This was necessary in view of the fact that when any proposal is made to assimilate Quebec with the other provinces of the Dominion in law and administration, it is met with the declaration that the proposal conflicts with the "guaranteed rights" of Quebec. In daily conversation, from the platform, on the floor of parliament, from the judicial bench, from the pulpit, changes have been declared as utterly impossible on this score, and the idea has been propagated that the French language, French laws, and the plenitude of power enjoyed by the priests were pledged by a solemn treaty, with which parliament dare not interfere. In examining into whether this is really so, it was necessary to quote literally. And what has been the result? First, that neither the treaty nor any of the imperial documents has a single word about the French language. The assertion that its official use was guaranteed has not a tittle of evidence to rest upon: it is a pure fabrication. Nowhere in the treaty or the documents it is based upon is the French language even mentioned. Second, this is also true as to French laws. **The treaty** not only makes no reference, however indirectly, to such laws, but by the fourth article transferred the inhabitants of Quebec to the British Crown without restriction. Third, as to religion. The treaty merely guaranteed that degree of toleration which Catholics would have received without specification. That is not all. Following the treaty, King George issued a proclamation, in which he assured all who went to Quebec "may confide in our royal protection "for the enjoyment of the benefit of the laws of our "realm of England." In instructing Murray, its first governor, how he was to rule the province, the King **enjoins him** that, while giving such scope as the laws of England allowed to his Roman Catholic subjects, he was not to admit the jurisdiction of Rome. This measure of mere toleration was recognized as all that could be expected under the treaty, and no complaint was made by those affected or by the French Government that Article Four was not observed.

Privileges granted by legislation stand upon a different base from those secured by an international treaty. When by treaty, they can only be withdrawn with the consent of the contracting nation. If granted by legislation, they can be dealt with like any other statute. Were the consent of France needed to strip the priests in Quebec of the immunities and powers they enjoy, that government, which is strongly anti-clerical, would exultingly give it. That consent is not **required, for those** immunities and powers are not of treaty but of legislation, and what legislation gave legislation can take away. The Dominion Parliament is competent to deal with the Quebec Act, or any other statute that affects the interests of the people. To the priests the Act of Parliament of 1774 gave them power to collect tithes and fabrique taxes in the eighty-two parishes then in existence, and nothing more. Outside those parishes the priests had no such right. The instructions to the governor who was to administer the Act, inform him the concession does not imply the Church of Rome in Quebec is an established church, and he is forbidden to recognize its episcopal powers. Finally, the Act, while restoring French law and usage, does not do so in the province at large, but only in that small portion of it held under seigniorial tenure, and that only for a time, for the council is admonished by the King to bring that law, as opportunity presented, into harmony with English law.

The French-Canadian has no treaty rights, but he has what is higher than any the king of his forefathers could have demanded for him—the rights of a British subject and these alone. The priests have not a shred of treaty rights. The immunities they enjoy have no higher authority than legislative Acts passed since the Conquest. Their peculiar privileges, so injurious to those who repudiate their rule, so threatening to the peace of the Dominion, were obtained piecemeal, and at wide intervals, by legislation. At any time, by the will of the majority of the electors of the Dominion, whatever is contrary to the public weal in the laws of the Province of Quebec, can be annulled by act of parliament.

Why the advisers of George III. did not continue Canada as a Crown colony has not been satisfactorily explained. Probably some one, who has access to the state papers of the period, may think it worth his while to unveil the causes that led to giving Canada constitutional government long before it had a population fitted for self-government. The explanation, repeated parrot-like in so many histories, that it was done to secure the goodwill of the French-Canadians, in the impending struggle with the American colonies, is absurd on the face of it. When the Quebec Act was submitted, the Imperial Government was blind to the coming danger across the Atlantic, and was resting in full security. In the long debate in the House of Commons, there is not a single sentence, either from the Ministerial or Opposition benches, to indicate that the bill was of a precautionary nature—a prudent step to take on the eve of a struggle. That is neither the tone nor the language of the debaters. There was neither foresight nor wisdom in the passing of the Quebec Act, for it failed to make friends of the French-Canadians, it disgusted the handful of English who had settled in Quebec, and formed a new cause of complaint to those of the Americans who were discontented with British rule.

CHAPTER IV.

Re-appearance of Anti-British Feeling

War being the greatest of all violations of natural law, it follows that the penalty which befalls nations who have crossed swords must be in proportion. Earthquake and volcanic irruption, flood and drouth, famine and epidemic, are each of terrifying significance to mankind, yet the consequences of all these combined are not comparable to the woes that war lets loose. And there is this peculiarity about them, that long after the cause, indeed, often when the war from which they arose has passed from memory, the woes remain. The loss of Canada to France is directly traceable to the bloodthirsty spirit of its founders. They aimed at a military colony, with every man a soldier, and it was by flourishing the sword in the face of their neighbors New France provoked its fate. Had they kept by spade and plough the colony would have lived. The overthrow of the power of France in America is referred to by those of English speech with exultation, and Wolfe's victory is quoted as something inspiring. Yet it is writ plain on the page of history that the conquest of Canada was a blunder—a presage to the greatest disaster that ever befell the British nation and the Anglo-Saxon race. Had the consequences of the battle of the Plains of Abraham been foretold by one of the Highlanders who won it, claiming second sight, the news of the victory would have been received wherever English is spoken with lamentation. It was the conquest of Canada that made the American revolution possible. Had there been no Conquest, a peaceable separation of the thirteen colonies from the Mother Country would have come in time. There was disaffection among the inhabitants of the thirteen American colonies, a number of them had become restless under the interference of the Westminster parliament and wanted to be rid of it. The one influence that kept them in check was the existence of French power on the continent, for they knew it was only with the aid of the Imperial army and navy they could defend themselves. It was to the British fleet along the Atlantic coast and the British regiments north of the Hudson and west of the Ohio to which they owed the safety of their homes, so while the French peril existed they put up with their grievances and clung to British connection. The Conquest of Canada brought a change; France had disappeared from the continent, the danger of their seaports being bombarded by the fleets of Louis XV. or of their settlements being ravaged by his soldiers had gone forever. Disaffected Americans could now safely shake their fists at King George and pursue their plans for independence. The winning of Canada removed the obstacle to their pushing for separation, and, at the same time, strange to say, it was the immediate cause of hastening separation. The Conquest of Canada had exhausted the Mother Country, and the demand by King George's ministers that the Americans should help to pay the cost of a war waged at their request and in their interest set the colonies in a flame. The Boston tea party to some is funny, yet it and other like acts was a refusal to pay an honorable debt. The overthrow of the power of the French Kings in America was clearly of more importance to the people of the thirteen colonies than to the artisans and farmers of Great Britain, yet the colonists refused to pay a dollar of what it cost to haul down the French flag

and thereby secure the integrity of their country. It
was the Conquest that precipitated the war of the
Revolution, and that war gave birth to a spirit of
hatred and jealousy on the part of the Americans which
has often thwarted Britain's purposes and helped her
enemies. Worse than that, it ranged those who speak
the same language and profess the same faith in open
antagonism. The false patriotism of militarism glories
over Wolfe's crowning achievement; true patriotism,
the offspring of the love of humanity, cannot. The
Canadian patriot sees in that victory the origin of the
dangers that threaten his country—the continuance of
institutions irreconcilable with freedom. The progress
of events would have decided the destiny of Canada
without wager of battle. A generation later its separation from France would have been inevitable. How
differently would Quebec have entered into an English
alliance had the step been taken after the downfall
of the Bourbons? In that case the Church of Rome
would have been disestablished by her own members,
the effete institutions which France had fastened upon
Canada would have been flung aside by those who
suffered from them. The people, aroused from the
torpor of absolutism, would have welcomed partnership with their English neighbors as co-equals, as allies
and brothers in the cause of freedom. Let it be set
down as a self-apparent fact, that Wolfe's victory preserved in the New World what the Old World soon
afterwards destroyed—the clerical and temporal institutions of feudal France. The France that died at
the taking of the Bastile, and which disappeared from
the banks of the Seine, was spared on the Plains of
Abraham and survives to-day on the banks of the
St. Lawrence.

British Authorities Neglect to Colonize Quebec.

Under any circumstances the conquest of a country
is the greatest misfortune that can befall the conqueror.
The world is so ordered, that each nationality can only

be content when self-governed. Rule by **outsiders** arouses a spirit of antagonism that appeals to every man who has felt the glow of patriotism. That the rule of the stranger is better than that it superseded does not change the attitude of the beaten people. They are foreign laws imposed by force. To the French-Canadians the rule of the English was the more obnoxious that it was that of new-comers who differed from them in language and creed. In General Murray and his officers they saw not only their hereditary enemies, but men whom they had been taught from infancy to regard as heretics. That Murray was considerate of their needs and tolerant of their prejudices, that he had changed their government for the better, given them a security they had never known, released them from burdens of taxation and service that had ground them to the dust, went for little. The exhaustion of a long war compelled them to submit, but there was nothing to evoke their love. That they would yet see the stranger driven forth by France was their hope. Remarkable to relate, there was not the slightest move by the British towards assimilation, no effort made to induce settlers either from the American colonies or from the Mother Land, and the habitants, prospering as they never had done, went on increasing, forming a solid body of people impervious to British ideas of civil and religious liberty. Had the Government of George III. said plainly, that, as by the treaty of peace, France had relinquished all claim to Canada, they would treat it as a part of Britain and endeavor to make it British in deed as well as name, the likelihood is that each succeeding generation would have become more and more attached to Britain. Instead, the Canadians from the first were treated with distrust, the attitude of the governing class being that we witness to-day in Egypt and India. The possibility of their rising in revolt was the spectre that haunted each successive governor, and caused the maintenance of garrisons obnoxious to the inhabitants and burdensome to the British taxpayer. Canada was rich in natural resources, yet instead of developing them by encouraging emigration from the United Kingdom, where hundreds of thousands lived in penury, the government forbade the settlement of the wilderness that awaited the hand of man to burst into abundance. The policy of conquerors in all ages, to plant in the countries they subdued settlements of people upon whose allegiance they could rely, the British rulers ignored. But they went further. With a fatuity past comprehension, they not only took pains to prevent English settlers coming to Quebec, but restored to the people whom they guarded against such intrusion, the distinctive features of the French regime. By a sweep of his pen George III. wiped out English jurisprudence and restored the laws of the Kings of France, and fastened anew on the people the parish system. The latter was restored under conditions the French Kings would not have listened to. When they gave the priest power to tax and tithe, he was held accountable to the Crown for the way in which he used those privileges, there was appeal by the parishioners to intendant and governor. It was extraordinary powers exercised by priests at the will of an arbitrary monarch, who, as he saw fit, curbed and suspended. Under the French regime the parish system, resting upon the will of an arbitrary ruler, could be modified or repealed at his whim; under British rule it was given the authority of a statute and was re-established in a way that left the priest irresponsible to the courts. It is important to grasp all that is here implied. The Imperial Parliament, by the Quebec Act, gave the priest power to levy taxes to build and maintain church and parsonage, and to provide his living. It did not stop there, it also gave him authority to use the King's courts to collect these taxes, yet exempted him from accountability to the government or to the courts. On a select body of men was bestowed the privilege of using the law courts, which means the authority of the Crown, to collect taxes without responsibility either to Crown or judge. What Bishop Laval sought, but could not get from Louis XIV., an ecclesiastical system independent of the state, yet using the state as its servant, George III., while pluming himself on his Protestantism, was the cause of enabling the priests to get in his new domain. What was the gratitude of the priests towards King George? For a quarter of a century after the battle of the Plains of Abraham the expectation was strong that France would speedily recapture Canada: that it was only a matter of a few years when the Union Jack would be hauled down. Possessed of this conviction the priests exerted themselves to keep their people from learning the speech of their new rulers, by declaring English to be a Protestant language, and exhorted them to live apart from those who spoke it. The methods of that time to keep the French habitants a separate people are still in use.

The American Revolution.

When the last regiment that wore the uniform of Louis XV. marched on board a transport at Quebec to be conveyed to France, the brake was snapped that had kept the discontented portion of the inhabitants of the American colonies from going to extremes in their disputes with Britain. No longer afraid of French assaults on their borders, no longer in need of the help of King George's soldiers and ships to protect them from French invasions by land or sea, they rapidly developed their design of separating from the Motherland. Tidings of what was going on to the south of them filtered slowly into the settlements on the St. Lawrence. Getting his news by way of Halifax the governor, Carleton, knew in the fall of 1774 a congress, sitting at Boston, had decided on sending to England an ultimatum that meant war. Carleton, like all other military men, scouted the idea of the colonists making good their threat, believing their first brush with the King's troops would bring them to their senses. This belief was so strong that the danger of war was not taken seriously until the battle of Bunker Hill. Before adjourning, the Boston Congress adopted an address to the inhabitants of Quebec inviting their co-operation. Of this address 2,000 copies were printed, and during the winter agents crossed from Massachusetts and New York State, circulating copies and trying by house-to-house canvass to win adherents. Not one in a thousand of the Canadians could read the address, and those who might have spelt it out were repelled by its length and involved sentences. More effective were the personal visits, helped by the presence in Montreal of a knot of American traders. The report was set afoot among the habitants that the Quebec Act, instead of being in their favor, was really designed to put them back under their seigniors as in the days of New France, and that they would have to respond to their call to serve in the militia. Carleton appealed to Bishop Briand to counteract the intrigue. The bishop, as the correspondence in his biography shows, was convinced the Americans would be beaten, but he saw how his church might profit from the existing condition of affairs and new concessions obtained from Britain for the priests. The bishop, therefore, complied with Carleton's request and issued a letter to the priests to refuse the sacraments to sympathizers with the American rebels. The letter, before the summer of 1775 was over, was proved to be blank cartridge. The priests remained neutral, watchful alone of their own interests.

The United States Invasion of Canada.

United States historians pass lightly over the attempt to get possession of Canada, treating it as an incidental episode in the war, which it was not, for it was a serious movement, planned by Washington and earnestly backed by Congress. It was not alone the immediate danger of invasion from the north they sought to prevent, but to make sure that they would not have again on their frontier a hostile power. They would prevent that, by making Canada part of the Republic they had organized. The passing of the Quebec Act seemed to the leaders of the revolution to restore the situation that had existed from the days of Champlain. They declared they foresaw in the restoration of the French power under the protectorate of the British Crown, a revival of the contest for the possession of the continent, with savage raids on their settlements, such as Frontenac and Montcalm planned. The winning of Canada looked to them essential to the existence of the new Republic. Washington declared the annexation of Canada to be of the utmost importance, and that this view was also that of those who with him were directing affairs, was shown by their detaching, at a critical period, so important a personage as Benjamin Franklin to try and conciliate the French.

The easiest way for the Americans to invade the province was by Lake Champlain. The sentinel forts that guarded its southern end, Ticonderoga and Crown Point, were captured without difficulty, for their garrisons were mere corporal guards—old men left to preserve these old French fortifications from decay. Having obtained command of the lake, the Americans speedily appeared in the parishes at its head. Carleton hastened from Quebec with what troops he could gather to cover Montreal. His forces were ridiculously inadequate. To guard all Canada he had only battalions of two regiments, little over 800 men. If the habitants sided with the invaders he foresaw disaster, but, confident in their siding with him, he issued the call for the enrollment of the militia and had 6,000 muskets ready to arm them.

It is remarkable that although the history of Canada goes back only three centuries, and is therefore modern, and that of every decade, whether under French or English rule, we have voluminous official records, it should abound in myths. Perhaps the myth which is the most glaring perversion of fact is that which represents the saving of Canada to the British Crown during the American revolution as due to the devotion of the priests and the loyalty of the habitants. Hundreds of orators, amid thunders of applause, have drawn the picture of Canada cruelly abandoned by France and dominated by a British garrison, yet, when threatened by American invaders, the habitants, persuaded by their beloved pastors, rallied for the defence of their new master. What are the facts as presented in the despatches of Governor-General Carleton, his successor, Haldimand, and other officials? They reveal a peasantry who loved neither the Republican nor the Loyalist, and who, on being asked to join the militia, were seized with dread that the old absolutism of the priest and the hated rule of the seignior under the French regime were to be restored. The call to arms they would not listen to, and where a seignior attempted to drag them into the ranks they resisted with force, and gave him to understand they were no longer vassals. The feudal duties of corvee and military service had vanished before the roll of Wolfe's drums. The effort to raise the militia was in vain. Carleton then turned to the Indians, and was again disappointed. Seeing the habitants refused to fight, the Indians would not go on the warpath alone. The governor buoyed himself with the hope that if the habitants would not fight the Americans, they would not help them. Without the assistance of the habitants they could not cross the St. Lawrence, and therefore he considered his position on the north shore secure. He was speedily undeceived. In September, 1775, St. Johns was taken. The invaders then divided, one column descending the Richelieu to Sorel: the main body struck for Montreal. The habitants, impulsive and excitable, were carried away by the imposing strength of the Americans, and the fine speeches of compatriots who accompanied the strangers. From a state of indifference they went to the other extreme, were seized by a frenzy of excitement, welcomed the invaders, sold them provisions, supplied them with guides, brought them intelligence of what the British were doing.

The British Abandon Montreal.

Carleton tried to make a stand at Longueuil, was discomfited, and escaped with his little army to Montreal. He cherished the hope that the Americans would not be able to cross the river for lack of boats. There was delay, and he thought he was correct in his surmise. The delay was in collecting boats. In an agony of disappointment Carleton saw the habitants ferry the Americans over to besiege him. Montreal was still surrounded by the wall of the French period, and although he had only sixty soldiers, eighty sailors, and a handful of English-speaking militiamen, Carleton resolved to hold it, for he had cannon, while the enemy so far had only rifles. He soon realized his position was untenable from what he termed the treachery of the French, who cut off the parties he sent out to gather supplies and captured his messengers. He complained bitterly. The disobedience of the people increased, they everywhere helped the Americans, while the King's representatives were betrayed. A messenger, who had eluded the enemy, brought word Sorel was in the hands of the Americans, and that a thousand Frenchmen had joined their ranks. The language in which Carleton speaks of the habitants is that of a man cruelly deceived. He had been instrumental in carrying the Quebec Act in the belief its concessions would reconcile them to British rule, and was now mortified to find this very Act used by the Americans as a reason why the French should join them. In his despatches to England Carleton refers to the baseness of the habitants, their ingratitude for all the favors shown them; as a wretched people blind to honor. He had his eyes opened on another point. He saw the habitants really hated the seigniors, and regretted he

The Tragedy of Quebec.

had not asked them to enlist in regular regiments instead of using the old militia machinery of France. While waiting to be attacked by the Americans, an alarming despatch reached him. An American army had threaded the wilds of Maine, and unexpectedly appeared on the shore opposite Quebec. Carleton realized that prompt action was needed. With traitors within and without its walls, to defend Montreal was going to be difficult, but of what use would it be to hold Montreal should Quebec be lost? Quebec was the key of Canada, and must be saved. On the night of the 11th of November he embarked his little garrison in boats and abandoned Montreal. Its inhabitants threw open its gates and welcomed the Americans the following day.

The Siege of Quebec.

Running the gauntlet of batteries at Berthier and Sorel, Carleton reached Quebec in a rowboat on the 19th, and none too soon. His experience at Montreal was repeated, for he was told the Americans had been given every assistance by the habitants, and had been ferried by them across the St. Lawrence.

They were now in camp, within striking distance of the walls, awaiting the reinforcements they knew were on the way. Carleton used the breathing spell to complete his defences. On the 4th of December, the American army being now in full strength, he was summoned to surrender. Carleton's reply was he would not parley with rebels, and the siege began. The Americans had two advantages, that of numbers and in having the people of the country with them. Carleton's sole advantage lay in the fortifications, which he had barely enough men to cover. Assaults by day and night were made and stoutly repulsed; worse than these attacks, which were open and could be met, were the machinations of traitors within the walls to betray the garrison. On New Year's Eve the Americans had arranged for a midnight attack, which resulted in their disastrous repulse. The spot where one of their generals, Montgomery, paid his life for his temerity, is recorded on the cliff at the foot of which he fell. This disaster to the Americans had an immediate effect on the habitants, shaking their belief that they were going to win, and hastened the revulsion of feeling that was already working in their minds. For a month their enthusiasm for their American visitors had been waning, and this British victory hastened the change. The continental army was leavened with ruffians, who repeated on whoever was suspected to favor the British the outrages they had practised on the loyalists of New England, while between the United States commissary officer who cleaned out his barnyard and handed in payment paper scrip, and the British official who always paid in coin, the habitant drew comparisons, and began to edge back to the side of the British.

To the besieged garrison the winter crept wearily on, and during five months the only spot in Canada where the Union Jack floated was from Cape Diamond. Both sides of the river were in the undisputed possession of the Americans. At their headquarters in Montreal they raised a regiment of French-Canadians. Arnold enlisted another regiment of them at Quebec, and reported he would have taken more had he been able to equip them. A third regiment was embodied at Sorel. General Schuyler wrote from Montreal to his chief: "I can have as many Canadians as I know "how to maintain." At Three Rivers there was no difficulty in raising 500 rank and file and in getting thirty of the better class to accept the commissions of Congress to command them. During that winter of 1775-76, when the Province of Quebec was practically a State of the Union, we hear not a word of the promise made by Bishop Briand to Governor Carleton that the priests would refuse the sacraments to whoever aided the invaders. All the Americans needed to complete their conquest of Canada was the capture of the citadel of Quebec. Each week increased the difficulties of the Americans to win that little spot. The Canadians who had so effusively welcomed them were cooling in their ardor as they foresaw the possibility of Quebec holding out until the British fleet came, which would be the doom of the invasion. The Americans were quick to note the change of tone. Reporting to Congress as to how matters stood, General Wooster wrote: "There is little confidence to be placed in the "Canadians, they are fond of being of the strongest "party." When the St. Lawrence at last cast its coat of ice the little garrison was faced with a prospect of famine, for they had exhausted their supplies, and Carleton foresaw that unless ships speedily arrived from England Canada was lost to Britain. The Americans redoubled their efforts. Their batteries were planted nearer, occasionally throwing hot shot in order to set fire to the barracks of the little garrison, who responded shot for shot. Perched on the point of the cliff, where the St. Lawrence suddenly expands from a river into an ever-widening sea, sentinelled on either bank by forest-clad mountains, the defenders, from earliest dawn turned eager eyes down the vistas of the two channels formed by the Isle of Orleans for the long-delayed relief, and day after day sought repose when darkness came with the sickness of deferred hope. On the morning of the 6th of May a shout went up that three sail were in sight, and when, on drawing nearer, the red flag of their country was discerned flying from the foremast of the leading ship, strong men broke down from the reaction of the suspense of five months, and with tears and shouts of joy grasped each others hands. No sooner had the ships cast anchor than boats were lowered and the landing of troops began. The hour of remaining on the defensive had passed. Ordering the long-closed gates to be thrown open, at the head of the garrison and of the newly-arrived soldiers, Carleton at noon marched out to give battle to the Americans. It was too late.

They, too, had spied the ships and instantly began their retreat, abandoning cannons and stores. All Carleton could do was to convert their retreat into a rout, pursuing them until they crossed the St. Lawrence.

Why the Americans Did Not Keep Canada.

For nigh a year the Americans had been on Canadian soil; six months in undisputed possession of every part except the few acres enclosed within the fortifications of Quebec. Why, then, did Canada not continue to be part of the American Republic? Because it had a governor with the head to plan and the hand to carry out his plans. Had Carleton surrendered when surrounded at Montreal, the Stars and Stripes would be floating to-day over Canada. It is to his daring flight to Quebec, to his placing its fortifications in a posture of defence, to his dogged courage in defending them under every form of discouragement for five cold, dreary months, that the maintenance of Britain's hold is due. It may be said, it was the arrival of the British fleet in the spring that saved Canada. It is true, had not help come when it did, the Americans would have triumphed, but it is equally true that had Carleton not kept a foothold on Cape Diamond, the one spot in a vast territory that had not surrendered to the enemy, the coming of British reinforcements in the spring of 1776 would have been of no avail. With the fortifications of Quebec in his possession, General Thomas could have prevented the British fleet passing the Cape and the landing of the troops it carried. It was Carleton who saved Canada in 1776, and whoever says otherwise denies the honor that is his due. Priest, seignior, and habitant had knuckled to the American Republicans; it was Carleton and his little garrison who defeated their plans.

The end was not yet, however. At their headquarters in Montreal, the Americans had been busy all winter in trying to strengthen their foothold. Congress sent a delegation, which included Benjamin Franklin, to win over the Canadians. The very men who two years before formally protested against the Quebec Act in language so outrageous that their descendants ignore it, the Congress that had been unable to suppress "astonishment that a British parliament should "ever consent to establish in Canada a religion that "has deluged its island with blood, and dispersed im- "piety, bigotry, persecution, murder, and rebellion "through every part of the world," now sent a Jesuit, Father John Carroll, whose special duty was to win over the priests, promising that the American Congress would do more for them than Britain had done! He could not get the priests to declare themselves. They discriminated in a way we do not now realize between the British across the Atlantic and the Bostonians. Under the latter name they classed the settlers of the colonies south of Canada, and hated them with a perfect hatred, the Dutchman equally with the Puritan. For generations they had encouraged war being waged upon them, and had held them up to their people as frightful examples of heresy. Were they now going to exchange the rule of the British Government, little as it was to their mind, for that of the new Republic created by their inveterate enemies? They temporized with both sides, waiting to see who was going to win.

On hearing frigates were on the way to Montreal, the Americans withdrew to above the Lachine rapids, which prolonged their stay a few months. With their final departure the danger of Britain losing Quebec did not end, for when France, in 1778, espoused the cause of the revolutionists, sending an army and a fleet to assist, the peril to Canada took another shape. The French-Canadians became excited on hearing their Mother Country had taken the side of the Americans. Haldimand, who was now governor, apprehended the worst, especially when he heard of the false report that the Pope had absolved the Canadians from the oath of allegiance they had taken to King George. "If," Haldimand writes to England, "the "Americans invade the province with a few hundred "French soldiers, the Canadians will take up arms in "their favor, will serve as guides and furnish pro- "visions." Detecting one priest communicating with the enemy he deported all who were natives of France, and asked the home government to replace them by priests from Savoy. In June, 1779, when it was known a second invasion of Canada was planned, he wrote that any misfortune to the British defenders would raise the whole country for the Americans. In September he again deplores the leaning not only of the habitants but of the priests towards France, and declared that, at the appearance of French soldiers with the Americans, they would throw themselves into their arms. The ingratitude of the seigniors was a grief to him. In 1781 he reports to the Imperial authorities that the success of the French fleet and the surrender of Cornwallis had made the Canadians bold. To the suggestion that he enlist them, he replies, "I "cannot trust them with arms for the defence of the "province, as it would be dangerous." Difficulty in dealing with the priests again plagued him. Two he shipped to France. Even the conduct of the superior of the Seminary was unsatisfactory, and the Governor's conviction was, that "the attachment of the priests to "France will engage them in the interests of the "rebels." What need of quoting more from the despatches of the men who guided Canada's destinies during that critical time? The assertion that it was the priests who preserved our country to the British Empire during the American revolution, is a deliberate and flat perversion of the truth. Had the French fleet steered from Yorktown for Quebec the figment that it was the priests who kept Canada to Britain during the American revolution would have been exploded.

False Pretences.

During a debate at Ottawa in the Commons, on the 30th of April, 1908, the Hon. L. P. Brodeur, then Minister of Marine, and now a judge of the Supreme Court, in extolling his compatriots, said:

"We are glad to serve under the British Crown to "which we are devoted. And when at different times "in our history British connection was in danger it "was the French-Canadians who were there to defend "the British Crown. Who in 1775 stood up in defence "of the British Crown if not the French-Canadians? "Who in 1812 fought the battle of Chateauguay and "repulsed the American troops, if not the French-"Canadians?"

Of such are the fictions by which the priests' claims for special privileges are supported. The evidence is beyond controversy that the French-Canadians in 1775 rose in revolt when it was attempted to enroll them to fight the Americans, that when, in 1776, the Americans came they fraternized with them, gave them the help and supplies without which they could not have come to the gates of Quebec and Montreal, and finally, several thousand of them took the oath of allegiance to the new Republic, and were enrolled as soldiers under its flag. A year after his sore experience in repulsing the American invasion, when he had time to deliberately review the past, Governor Carleton wrote the Colonial Secretary in London: "As to my opinion of the Canadians, I think there is "nothing to fear from them while we (the British), "are in a state of prosperity, and nothing to hope for "when in distress."

Touching Mr. Brodeur's reference to Chateauguay, it is open to question whether it is correct to call it a battle, seeing the killed and wounded on both sides counted less than fifty. It was a mere skirmish. The facts are these: The Americans had planned an invasion of Canada to capture Montreal. The Grand

Army of the North, as it was named, was divided into two columns. One, under Wilkinson, was to build flat-boats at Sackett's Harbor, and, embarking in them, sail down the St. Lawrence to Isle Perrot. At some point on the south bank, facing that island, they were to find the other part of the army, under General Hampton, whom they were to ferry over in their boats and then cross to the Island of Montreal. The success of the plan depended on the two divisions meeting at the right time. Wilkinson bungled his part, frittering away the season, always about to leave with his flotilla of boats down the St. Lawrence, and then postponing. At the beginning of October Hampton was ordered to break camp and march to the St. Lawrence. At the point where the river Chateauguay flows into the St. Lawrence he was advised he would find Wilkinson with the boats. Hampton crossed the line into Canada, and, capturing outlying posts, reached a point within fifteen miles of where he had been told Wilkinson would be waiting for him. His way was here blocked by rude barriers thrown up on the north bank of six successive ravines which crossed the road he must follow. These breastworks, formed of trees that had been felled, were defended by militia, Indians, and a battery of artillery, the whole under command of General de Watteville. Spies had brought Hampton complete information of the nature and strength of the obstructions, and he had guides, both French-Canadian and American. On the afternoon of the 26th of October he began his advance. At the first breastwork he halted, waiting for the appearance of a column on the east bank of the river which he had sent to make a flank attack. During this waiting a few harmless vollies were exchanged. Through the promptitude of Major Macdonell, that flank movement had failed, a fact of which Hampton was ignorant until the day, cloudy and gloomy, was nigh spent. Darkness setting in, he ordered the army to return to their tents, intending to resume operations next morning by bringing up his artillery to shatter the obstructing breastworks. On reaching camp he found a messenger with a despatch from Ogdensburg, reporting that Wilkinson had not moved. He was astounded, for he supposed if not at, he must be near, Chateauguay Basin. There was no use in Hampton going farther. He could not cross the St. Lawrence to the island of Montreal without the boats Wilkinson was to bring, and there were no supplies to feed his army should he stay where he was or go into camp at Chateauguay Basin and wait his coming. A council was held when the officers unanimously agreed there was no other alternative than to return to their camp on the American side. On the 28th tents were struck and Hampton, by slow marches and without being followed, returned to his camp at Four Corners to await developments. It was no resistance he met, no bugle-blowing in the woods or flourishing of swords behind abattis, that caused Hampton to go back the way he came, but Wilkinson's failure to appear at the trysting-place. Subsequent events justified Hampton, for a fortnight elapsed after he left the Chateauguay before Wilkinson began his descent of the St. Lawrence, and even had all gone well with him he could not have reached the Basin, the place where Hampton was to be in waiting, before the middle of November, a date when floating ice appears on the St. Lawrence, and frost makes living in tents impossible.

While the conquest of Canada made the American revolution possible, that revolution was the surprising cause of preventing Canada reverting to what it had been. Under the conditions of the Quebec Act, and the policy that prevented immigration, it would have become a priestly preserve, expanding with increase of population. What prevented that fate was the abrupt rush of a host of fleeing men, women, and children seeking refuge beneath Canada's forests from the hate and cruelty of the victorious Republicans. It was the coming of the United Empire Loyalists that saved

Canada west of the Ottawa from the doom that has overtaken Quebec. These new-comers were energetic, and the appearance of a chain of settlements on the bank of the Upper St. Lawrence and Niagara river and along the north shore of Lake Ontario compelled the home authorities not only to provide for their maintenance, but also to give them some form of government. Here, again, in framing a constitution to meet the new conditions forced upon them, they blundered. They knew it was impossible to ask people who had fled from the tyranny of the new Republic to live under the conditions provided by the Quebec Act and that a new arrangement must be made. Unlooked for circumstances had arisen that called for another constitutional change. How did the Imperial Ministers meet it? By seizing the opportunity to repeal the Quebec Act and giving to Canada a form of government that would apply equally to every acre of it? That is what statesmen would have done, but the men in office, when it came to Canadian affairs, were not statesmen—they were opportunists, and snatched at any plan that would tide them over the difficulty. A constitution was called for that would make Canada a unit, which would recognize neither race nor creed. Instead of that, they decided to divide Canada according to the origin of its inhabitants, and issued their fiat to create two provinces—one French, the other English—Lower and Upper Canada. So far as practicable, the policy of segregation, of two laws, and two systems of administration, was to be tried. This is the policy which, half a century afterwards, Lord Durham deplored and endeavored to correct. It was too late; the evil was not in his day to be remedied, and the union that could have been easily effected in 1791 failed in 1841. Pitt professed to see in the arrangement of two provinces a means of averting strife between French and English, for each would have their own territory and their own legislature. In this Fox did not concur. Instead of providing for the separation of the two races, he urged, it was "desirable they should coalesce into one body, and "that the different distinctions be extinguished." Outside the circle of officials, the bill was opposed by the entire English population of Quebec. They were few in number, but the commerce and manufactures of the province were in their hands. They had had cause to complain of the rule of the majority, and, therefore, were the more solicitous they should not be left to its exclusive control. In the influx of English into the country west of the Ottawa they saw protectors and were solicitous that Quebec should not be detached from the rest of Canada and created into a province. They held meetings, drafted memorials, and one of their number, Adam Lymburger, was deputed to appear in London and represent their views. He was given a hearing at the bar of the House of Commons, and read an intolerably tedious protest against the proposed measure. Amid his cloud of inconsecutive sentences he made one point clear, that the English settlers desired the repeal of the Quebec Act in toto and a new constitution for the whole country, which would recognize no distinctions as to race or creed; to use his own words, "a new and com- "plete constitution, unclogged and unembarrassed "with any laws prior to" the conquest. He spoke to the wind. The bill erecting two provinces, Upper and Lower Canada, was passed, and another step taken in fostering the French regime under the British flag.

The Canada Act.

The Canada Act provided for a modified system of self-government. There was to be a lower house, whose members were to be elected by the people, and a council composed of Crown nominees. The device was a compromise between self-government and autocratic rule. A remarkable feature of the Act, and of which slight notice has been taken in any of our histories, is that it made the Church of England the

Established Church of both provinces. After declaring that the provision in the Act of 1774, ordering "that "the clergy of the Church of Rome in the Province "of Quebec might hold, receive, and enjoy their accus- "tomed dues" from their members, the Act went on to authorize the Governor-in-Council to erect Church of England rectories within every township, or parish, of Lower Canada, and to pay the rectors' salaries out of the sale of waste lands to be allotted for that purpose, or from any tithes that may be collected. The Governor-in-Council was to have the presentation to these rectories under the same conditions as exist in England. To prevent any obstacle being placed in the way of carrying out these provisions by the Quebec Assembly, it was provided that any Act of the legislature regarding them must be submitted to the Imperial Parliament before receiving the royal assent. The object of this clause, and of the one confining the constituting of rectories and of presentations to them to the governor, is obvious—to block any attempt by the French-Canadian members of the Assembly in carrying out the purposes of the Act. One-third of the Canada Act is devoted to the constituting of the Church of England as the Established Church. It would be correct to describe the Act as one establishing a modified system of self-government and the Church of England in Canada. The Act furnishes incontrovertible proof that, a generation after the conquest and sixteen years after adopting the Quebec Act, the British Government regarded the Church of Rome in Quebec as an alien organization, having no inherent rights, and none beyond those it had conferred upon it, with a declared intention of making the Church of England the established church of Quebec. That the purpose of the Act was not realized does not affect the proof it supplies of the legal standing of the priesthood in Quebec in 1791, or of the intention at that date of the government.

How the Act Worked in Quebec.

The Act was a failure in more regards than its provision to establish the Church of England. Its device to rule by means of an assembly elected by the people, and a council nominated by the Crown, the council having a veto on the acts of the assembly, was foredoomed, for it could not work. The assembly was democratic, the presumed mouthpiece of the people, the other autocratic, representing the governor and his officials. It was inevitable the two should clash, especially in Quebec, where the assembly was French and the council English. Ere long both legislatures were openly antagonistic. In Upper Canada the cause of strife was constitutional; in Lower Canada, where only a handful of educated men knew anything of constitutional government, the cause was race and creed. In Upper Canada, the members of the council were largely of the class who had been Crown officials in the thirteen colonies, and who brought with them to Canada their ideas of privilege, fees, and nepotism, and who treated the members of the Lower House as inferiors, tinctured with republican notions of equality, and who needed the firm hand of a master. That, with the growth of the country, there should be a revolt against the assumptions of such a petty oligarchy was to be expected. Conditions were entirely different in Quebec. To the habitant the proposal of an approach towards self-government was an entire novelty, something he could not comprehend. In no regard had the French kings been so exacting as in seeing that the people should have no voice in public affairs—their duty was to obey, that of the King to govern. Of this the instructions from France to successive governors give ample proof. To such an extreme was this spirit of absolutism carried, that, as already noted, the people were denied a voice even in municipal matters. When Frontenac summoned a meeting of citizens for municipal purposes in the church of the Jesuits at Quebec, he was not only censured by the King, but advised to see that the town councillors he proposed be appointed by the Crown and not by the citizens of Quebec. The instruction, sent in 1685, "It is of very great consequence that the "people should not be left at liberty to speak their "minds," was carried into every domain—that of church, parish and state. Thus trained for generations, the habitant had come to look for the governance of everything outside his farm being conducted by those who claimed to be set above him, and anything approaching the right of free speech, free assembly, and free action he could not imagine. Of voting he knew nothing, and did not take kindly to the innovation. When called upon to vote for a representative in the Assembly, he had his suspicions that it was a trap to do him harm. The farmers of whole parishes refused to vote, and in others the feeling was carried to the extent of forcibly preventing those who wished. However elected, legally or not, members reported from each county. They were, apart from a few farmers, the big men of their parish, seigniors or their sons, notaries or lawyers if French: merchants if English. When the House opened the question of language necessarily had to be settled. The supposition that the use of French as an official language was provided for in the Act of 1791 is erroneous. There is not a word in it about language. English was the sole official language, and all the first Assembly could do was to agree on the permissive use of French in its debates and journals. The debate as to language arose in choosing a Speaker, and the remarks of one of the members have been preserved. Mr. Panet said: "I "will explain my mind on the necessity of the Speaker "we are about to choose should possess and speak "equally well the two languages. In which ought he "to address the governors—is it in the English or 'French language? To solve the question, I ask "whether this colony is or is not an English colony?

"What is the language of the sovereign and of the "legislature from whom we hold the constitution "which assembles us to-day? What is the general "language of the Empire? What is that of one part "of our fellow-citizens? What will that of the other "and that of the whole province be at a certain epoch? "I am a Canadian, the son of a Frenchman—my nat- "ural tongue is French; for, thanks to the ever-sub- "sisting division between the Canadian and English "since the cession of the country, I have been able to "procure a little knowledge of that of the latter—my "testimony will not, therefore, be questioned. It is, "then, my opinion, that there is an absolute necessity "that the Canadians, in course of time, adopt the Eng- "lish language, as the only means of dissipating the "repugnance and suspicions which the difference of "language would keep up between two peoples united "by circumstances and necessitated to live together; "but in the expectation of the accomplishment of "that happy revolution, I think it is but decent that "the Speaker on whom we may fix our choice, be one "who can express himself in English when he addresses 'himself to the representative of our sovereign." A Speaker who knew both languages was chosen.

The House was not in session a week until the incompatibility of the two elements became apparent. The English-speaking members assumed airs of superiority to which neither their numbers nor ability gave them a claim, while the French regarded them with suspicion and banded themselves together for mutual defence. Under the most favorable conditions it would have been difficult to get the two elements to work in harmony; unfortunately, conditions were not favorable. War was going on between the Indian tribes of the southwest and the Americans. The authorities at Washington accused the British of secretly fomenting the strife. We know now, with the confidential correspondence between the Governor of Canada and the Imperial authorities before us, how false that charge

was, how sincerely anxious the British were to keep
on good terms with the American Government, and
how Lord Dorchester and his subordinates exerted
themselves to avoid even the appearance of offence.
They, however, could not control individual Frenchmen, whose traditional alliance with the warring tribes
and dislike of their English-speaking foes led them to
assist the Indians in battling with the United States
forces. Men suspected of acting thus were among the
members of the Assembly, and their presence was
resented by the English members. A second and worse
cause was the firm belief of the English that there was
danger of Canada being reconquered by France. From
the hour of its cession and for over a quarter of a century afterwards, that fear was dominant in the minds
of the minority. That a French fleet would appear
some morning in the St. Lawrence, land an army, and,
assisted by the habitants, win Canada again for
France, was a recurring dread whenever there was a
prospect of war with that country. There was always
a cry of wolf, of emissaries at work with French gold
to seduce the habitants from their allegiance, of plots
afoot to recapture Quebec, of officers disguised as
civilians coming from France. When the Assembly
met, relations between France and Britain were
strained. The French revolution had broken out, party
feeling was red-hot, and it was plain to all, that only
Pitt's great influence kept the two nations from flying
at each others throat. Just when national feeling
was glowing intensely, when English were English and
French were French, with a meaning never before
known, the Assembly met. They could not unite. The
English professed to see on its benches Frenchmen
who were aliens, who were there to plot and scheme to
overturn British rule, and unjustly imputing to every
Frenchman the crimes that were being perpetrated
and acclaimed in Paris. The French members, forced
by prudence to suppress their resentment outwardly,
were as flatly hostile. They insisted not merely in

using French in debate, many could not do otherwise, knowing no English, but in introducing bills in French, and in fixing the quorum at such a figure as made it impossible for the English members to be in a majority at any sitting. The governor, Dorchester, would not submit to bills being sent to him for his assent in French, much less agree to the statutes being printed in that language, and asked the Imperial authorities as to whether he should take a bill laid before him in a foreign tongue. The instruction came back from London, that bills in French must be put into English before being submitted to him.

When each ship that cast anchor off Cape Diamond brought tidings of worse and worse excesses in France, when every institution, however venerable from age or association with all that men reverence, was being overthrown, when scaffolds were daily drenched with blood, and every land was crowded with fugitives from the rule of Robespierre, came the announcement that France had declared war against Britain. The handful of English on the banks of the St. Lawrence realized their danger, and proceeded to take steps for defence. The governor ordered a levy of the militia. It was the second effort to call the habitants to arms under the British flag. It was a paltry contingent he asked, 2,000 men. It was found impossible to make the levy. Disaffection found expression in riots and passive resistance. The English banded themselves in loyal associations, and the government, having suspended the Habeas Corpus Act, was active in arresting suspected persons. This was to be expected under the circumstances, but it had the effect of hurrying the two races into direct antagonism and of interrupting the slowly healing process that had been going on before the ill-advised Act of 1791 was adopted. The French now had a mouthpiece and a rallying point in the new Assembly, and used their new power to obstruct the measures the governor thought necessary. All this was natural. They would have been less than

men had they not yearned to get back under their
own nation: they would have been less than Frenchmen had the blood not run faster in their veins as
they heard of those victories of the French Republic
that promised the displacing of English rule in Canada. Natural as all this was, Dorchester and his executive could not swerve from the line of conduct the
victory of Wolfe had made incumbent upon them.
Sedition was sternly dealt with by imprisonment and
expulsion from the country, and all possible steps
taken in preparation of invasion or a rising. It was
a critical time, and only the victories won by the
British fleet saved Canada from invasion.

Unlike the period of the American revolution, the
priests gave no trouble. The horrible treatment of
their fellow-priests in France overcame alike their
bigotry and their nativism, and they clung to British
rule as their only safety. It was the seigniors who
were the thorn. The prosperity that had come to
Quebec as the result of British rule had multiplied
their receipts from the increasing number of their
censitaires and the introduction of lumbering. They
were no longer the beggarly idlers who sought charity
from the British Government. The opening of the
Assembly was their opportunity. They became members and were in their element in conducting intrigues
to embarrass the authorities. Many had maintained
correspondence with their family relatives in France,
several had visited France: all were Anglophobes of
an implacable type, yet deceitful and plausible towards
the English. Fortunately for Lord Dorchester, they
had lost their influence over the censitaires. The habitants had never liked them, and what respect they
still showed was a survival of the fear implanted under
the old regime. They openly complained of their re-
morseless exactions. Under French rule they could
appeal to the advocate-general to keep the seigniors
within bounds: now there was no restraining hand,
and the habitants were clamant in their demand that

a law be passed to protect them. The government favored such a law, but in an Assembly where the seigniors had so much influence, its passage was impossible. The weakness that left the seigniors their feudal privileges is to be ranked among the causes which have produced the political difficulties which confront the Dominion.

The Habitant Changes.

The development of the habitant is an interesting study. Under the old rule he could hardly be called a farmer, for his income depended more on his employment by the fur-traders than on what he raised from his land. Then his time was not his own. At any moment he was liable to be called out to serve as a soldier. In making forays on the English settlements and in repelling Indian attacks much of his time was taken up. There was no encouragement for steady industry, and as a matter of fact the work on the homestead was left largely to his wife and children. The habitant as we find him to-day, in an economical sense, is the product of English rule. It was under Murray, Carleton, Haldimand the transformation took place. He lost his military character, he lost the irregular habits of those engaged in the fur-trade, he lost the attribute of shiftlessness, of laziness, which intendants and visitors spoke of as a marked feature in his character, and he became, for the first time in his history, a farmer. Dwelling in the midst of his family those domestic virtues were unfolded which form so beautiful a feature in the habitant home, while his limited earnings taught him his distinguishing thrift, for which there was no encouragement during the period when a commissary of the King could empty his barn. Between the habitant of the time of Louis XV. and of George III. the resemblance is slight. And this habitant, created under English rule, is incomparably the finest type of the French people. In solid worth—honesty, industry, kindly disposition, politeness—he commands respect, and if the cause was removed which has kept him unprogressive, he would astonish those who decry him, for the habitant and his children are naturally bright and have the capacity to take foremost place among the peoples of this continent. It is true their intellectual bears no proportion to their emotional and perceptive development, for they have been designedly kept in ignorance to serve the purposes of priest and politician. When the false lights of prejudice no longer distort the vision, when the bandages which have arrested his mental growth have been torn away, when the habitant sees and thinks for himself, there will be a renaissance in Quebec which will compel the wonder and admiration of the world. Those who speak disparagingly of the habitant are ignorant of the qualities which lie latent within him awaiting the touch of the spirit of Truth to spring into life.

Misrepresentations of English Rule.

The character of English rule from the conquest to the approach made to self-government in 1791 is persistently misrepresented. One of the stock pictures of St. Jean Baptiste day pulpit and platform orators, is that of the French people at the Conquest, deserted, helpless, despairing, revived by the appearance among them of their adored pastors, who, holding aloft the cross, summoned them to save their nationality by rallying around them. The people did so, and the priests protected them from the designs of the invader, defeated his efforts, and brought them in triumph to this hour—it was the priests who did it all, saved their language, their nationality, their faith; trust in them for the future by continuing to give them implicit obedience.

These appeals at the midsummer celebration are heightened by all the arts which the priests know how to use with effect. Following the service, conducted with all the pomp and solemnity available, the orator,

with a background that appeals to the senses, rich in
color and design, begins by picturing the past under
the French regime, which he embellishes with deeds
and glories which are drawn from imagination, and
then when he comes to Canada passing under the British he adroitly draws a veil to hide pretended horrors.
Remember, he asks, who it was, when Jean Baptiste
was crushed by calamity, sunk in despair, without a
gleam of hope, he lay dying from injuries inflicted by
the Protestant invader—I call upon you to remember
who it was that came to him, and daring the wrath of
the stranger, lifted his head, whispered a message of
courage in his ear, healed his hurts, taught him to
cherish his language and his faith, and finally so inspired him with holy courage that he stood up before
his conqueror and demanded his rights! All you French-
Canadians possess is due to the priests. It was they
who came to your rescue in the hour of danger and
saved you to be a nation, and here the orator pauses,
crosses his hands upon his breast and bows his head,
to intimate it is to men like him they are in debt.
This representation that the British oppressed the
habitants, sought to rob them of their faith and language, is a deliberate perversion of what took place
after the conquest. The instructions given by Lord
Egremont to General Amherst when he invaded Canada in 1761 were, that he was to make every exertion
to attach the French settlers and to prevent their
being ill-treated or annoyed in any way: to offer the
royal protection to all alike with laudable gentleness.
The instructions to Murray, Carleton, Haldimand were
of similar tenor—they were to win the French by
kindness to be loyal subjects of the King. It is a gross
reflection on these men who carried Canada through a
dangerous period, it is base ingratitude for all the
benefits they bestowed on the King's new subjects, to
hold them up as bigoted tyrants who persecuted and
robbed. The pictures now drawn by the priests and
by those who curry for their support, of Canada after

the conquest, is of course to magnify their office and
to incline the French-Canadians to blinder obedience.
It is the same policy they follow in Ireland, in Poland,
in the Catholic provinces of Germany. The nationalities differ, the course pursued by the priests is the
same, to pervert facts to make their people believe
they have been their saviors. There was cause in
Catholic countries in Europe brought under Protestant
rulers for complaint of persecution; in Canada there
was none. Let those who insinuate otherwise, produce
evidence to bear them out. There never was a conquered people so left to themselves, so tenderly treated,
so helped to repair the losses of war. This being true,
it is provoking to hear the priests of Quebec claiming
to be the representatives of those who preserved and
nourished the French-Canadians at the period when
their allegiance was changed, and posing as their saviors. What is the record of these men who impute brutality, fanaticism, and persecution to British rule? In the
days of New France, when Louis was king, what was
the conduct of the priests? Do not the official records
of those times kept by Catholics, prove beyond all contradiction, that they insisted on the government prosecuting every Protestant who appeared, demanded that
Protestant sailors be not permitted to sing their hymns
in port, that Protestant merchants be not allowed to
stay the winter months in Canada, hunted the holds of
ships as they dropped anchor at Quebec for Protestants as if they were vermin, and when they caught
any thrust them into prison, put them to the rack, and
got the civil authorities to slay them? Do the priests
of to-day condemn this in their predecessors? Would
they not do the same if they dared? These are the
men who prate about bigotry and heap odium on the
British rulers who so petted the French-Canadians,
conceded so much of what they asked, deferred so
much to their prejudices, that they have created
trouble for their successors. These are the men who,
in order to add to their hold on their followers do their

bent to perpetuate divisions on the lines of race and creed, seeking in this new land, where each man has the chance of making a fresh start in life, to maintain medieval barriers between the sections of our population. Let those who have been misled into believing that the priests at the conquest rendered the services claimed by them, turn to the records of that period and satisfy themselves. One priest of that time, not foreseeing how capital would be made by his brethren a century later out of the happenings of his day, has left his testimony. He who soon after became Bishop Plessis, in a sermon delivered in the cathedral at Quebec, 27th June, 1794, said: "The disorders which pre-
"vailed in this colony (before the Conquest) ascended
"to heaven, crying vengeance and provoking the
"wrath of the Almighty. . . . God visited our
"country with the horrors of war. . . . It spread
"the severest grief among all Christian families.
"They all lamented their own unfortunate lot, and
"that they could not live where the kingdom of God
"was threatened with destruction. Our conquerors
"were looked upon with jealousy and suspicion, and
"inspired only apprehension. People could not per-
"suade themselves that strangers to our soil, to our
"language, our laws and usages, and our worship,
"would ever be capable of restoring to Canada what
"it had lost by a change of master. Generous nation!
"which has strongly demonstrated how unfounded
"were those prejudices; industrious nation! which has
"contributed to the development of those sources of
"wealth which existed in the bosom of the country;
"exemplary nation! which in times of trouble teaches
"to the world in what consists that liberty to which
"all men aspire and among whom so few knew its just
"limits; kind hearted nation! which has received with
"so much humanity the most faithful subjects most
"cruelly driven from the kingdom to which we form-
"erly belonged; beneficent nation! which every day
"gives to Canada new proofs of liberality. No, no!

"you are not our enemies, nor of our properties which
"are protected by your laws, nor of our holy religion
"which you respect. Forgive, then, this early mis-
"conception of a people who had not before the honor
"of being acquainted with you; and if, after having
"learned the subversion of the government and the
"destruction of the true worship in France, after hav-
"ing enjoyed for thirty-five years the mildness of
"your sway, there are some amongst us so blind or
"ill-intentioned, as to entertain the same suspicions,
"and inspire the people with the criminal desire of
"returning to their former masters, do not impute to
"the whole people what is the vice of a small number."

Eleven years later, Denaut, who succeeded Plessis as bishop, in a letter to King George, refers to the prodigious advance of the province "Since Canada "happily passed to the Crown of Great Britain."

CHAPTER V.

Quebec Thrown Open to Immigrants

It will be recalled that the policy of Lord North, and it was endorsed by his political opponents, was to keep Canada sealed against emigrants. To soldiers who had served their time and who wished to stay in Canada grants of land were given, mostly on the north shore of the St. Lawrence below Quebec; to all others no encouragement was given to acquire land. It was the appearance of U. E. Loyalists and the necessity of providing for them that shattered the illusions of the home authorities regarding emigration to Canada. The drift of that remarkable movement was towards Ontario, yet streamlets trickled into Quebec. Men with their families, who had been robbed of everything by the successful Republicans, came in ships to Quebec and pleaded for assistance. Most of them were forwarded to the Lunenburg district, but, commencing in 1792, a few were granted lots in Quebec, and they at once set to work to clear them. The tidings which travellers west of Montreal brought of the growth of thriving settlements, showed what was possible in Quebec, and encouragement began to be given to the people of the British isles to come over. From a policy of exclusion the Quebec authorities rushed to the other extreme. After refusing land grants for a generation, they now began to dispense them without discretion. Creatures who had official influence sought and obtained vast areas, ranging from 40,000 acres downwards. The first grant was made in 1795, and in the next fifteen years over two million acres were ceded to men who had not the remotest intention of cultivating the land, but sought its possession in the expectation of selling it to those who would. It was the first of the long series of land-grabs that have lasted to our own time, and the most harmful. The evil effects of this locking up of land in the hands of those who held it in order to sell, were long felt, and discouraged emigrants remaining in Quebec. Had the land been granted only to those who would clear and cultivate it, a large English-speaking population would have been planted in Quebec. When the new-comer found there were no free lots, that the land he yearned for had been conceded to some official or political favorite, who asked a price for it, he passed onwards to Ontario. The course of Canada's governments, from first to last, in dealing with its great heritage of virgin land, has been criminal. It trammelled the development of all the Provinces, it blasted that of Quebec.

Emigrant Ships.

When the first ship came whose main purpose was the conveyance of emigrants cannot be ascertained. In 1817, the year when immigration assumed such proportion that a record of it was begun, vessels arrived with from 300 to 400, which indicates the tide had set in several years before that date. From 1790 ships landed families and groups of families who found homes in Quebec, but a steady stream of immigrants did not set towards the St. Lawrence until 1815, and high flood was not reached until 1820. The years 1823 and 1824 were wet and cold, and where the people in the United Kingdom depended mostly on the potato they suffered from actual want. There was a rush to get away and ships bound for the St. Lawrence were packed. These poor people were land-hungry and, on landing at Quebec, their first quest was to get lots.

The front ranges of the parishes along the great river were held by the habitants. The unoccupied land that lay behind the French settlements was subject to rent, a word they had learned to dread. Back of the seigniories there were vast expanses of wild land, which, had it been given out in free lots, would speedily have been taken up. The Government, however, had conceded it to placemen, who asked prices which the newcomers, whose capital lay in their sturdy arms and undaunted courage, could not pay. The obstacle presented by seigniorial rents was seized on by the majority who controlled the legislature to prevent those who came from the British isles finding homes in Quebec. The governor, Lord Dorchester, seeing the obstruction seigniorial tenure presented to the settlement of the province, proposed that not only all unsurveyed land be granted in free and common soccage, but that power be given seigniors to so convert their unconceded lands.

The Fight Over Seigniorial Tenure.

The French members strenuously opposed these proposals, demanding parish low and seigniorial tenure be made universal. One of their arguments was, that free and common soccage tenure of land was conducive to Republicanism! However, the governor had power enough to make that tenure the rule outside the seigniories, and no Crown lands were conceded after 1796 except in free and common soccage. That did not settle the question. Notaries continued to draw deeds in the old form, and proprietors of ceded wild land claimed the privileges of seigniors. In resisting the change, the majority in the Assembly did not express the desires of the habitants, who were a unit for the abolition of the feudal tenure. They complained that while the seigniors exacted rents beyond what the law allowed, they did not maintain mills, that they refused to sell the best lands, keeping them for their timber, that they inserted a clause in deeds of sale reserving the timber on the lots, and that, owing to the rise in values, the fines, when they wished to sell, were made excessive. They wished to become absolute owners of their farms, and supported the proposed change in the law. Composed largely of seigniors and members influenced by them, the Assembly was deaf to the demands of the habitants, who, ignorant of modes of procedure and incapable of combination, were unable to bring the power they possessed to bear. The more insistent the demand that seigniorial rights be abolished, the more resolute the Assembly became in making it a matter of patriotism to resist. Seigniorial tenure was French, meant French ascendancy and autonomy, and the exclusion from the land of the English. A London merchant, Alexander Ellice, had bought the most western of the seigniories on the south shore of the St. Lawrence with the view of settling it with Scotch emigrants. On his son Edward inheriting the property he exerted himself to have the tenure changed, so that he could sell lots in free and common soccage. His will was potent in the official circle at Quebec, and a bill was submitted in 1822 to empower any seignior to do so who wished. It was thrown out by the Assembly. Supported by petitions from the habitants, the bill was introduced anew in 1825, and was again strangled. Seeing it was hopeless to obtain legislation in Quebec, the authorities did the next best, they got an Act passed by the Imperial Parliament declaring that all lands in Quebec outside the seigniories were of English tenure. Here again, a great opportunity was lost by the Imperial authorities to abolish the French tenure, which remained to blight the prospects of the habitants for another quarter of a century. The passage of this Act was made a grievance by the French members of the Assembly. One of its leaders, Viger, declared "the tenures bill caused the greatest "discontent, because it destroyed at once the system "which we considered extended to the whole Pro-"vince, and which had been acted upon ever since the "conquest."

It is proper to note that had Quebec continued under France, the seigniorial system would have been abolished, for its rulers had come to perceive what a blight it was in a new country. Louis XV. refused to make grants of that nature, and steps were begun to re-unite unsettled seigniories to the public domain. When Cape Breton came to be settled its lands were held en routure.

How the New Settlers Were Used.

The placing of all unconceded land outside French law benefitted the settlements along the United States frontier, for immigrants sought them out. So long as these settlements were weak and struggling, and separated from the parishes by an almost impenetrable belt of forest, little heed was paid them by the French leaders, but the opening of the Craig road and the knowledge that they were growing and prosperous developed unsleeping hostility. Every recommendation of the governors to assist them was ignored, and when it was suggested the newcomers had a right to be represented in the legislature the French members would not hear of it. Quebec was for the French alone. The language used in the Assembly was that these English-speaking farmers were "strangers and intruders," who were not to be recognized in any way. The motive in opposing change of tenure and refusing to recognize the Eastern Townships settlers was the same that led the Assembly in 1823 to reject a proposal to unite with Upper Canada, as expressed by its leaders, namely, that it would endanger the peculiar laws and institutions of the French. In a joint letter of Papineau and Neilson it was hinted the newcomers should unite with Upper Canada.

The open and persistent hostility of the French leaders in the Assembly towards the English-speaking settlements was consistent from their point of view. Their ardent desire was to preserve Quebec for their own people. Secretly, for it was dangerous to avow it, they cherished the hope of its becoming a French Republic. In all this they did exactly what Englishmen would have done placed in a like position. If open to blame, it was that in seeking ends that spoke of love of race and country, they covered their purpose by hypocritical professions of loyalty to the British Crown and Constitution. No greater stickler for British rights ever appeared than Papineau, yet what he demanded for the habitant he refused to the English farmers. The sight of men protesting they were deprived of the privileges that were theirs under the British constitution, while working to restore French domination, was not edifying, and yet that is the sum and substance of the course pursued by the Assembly until its days were ended by the rebellion.

The adoption of the Tenures Act drew a sharp line of demarcation between parish and township, silencing all questions as to the nature of the tenure of the land lying outside the seigniories, and confirming the belief of the settlers in the townships that French law did not run within their bounds. The words of the Hon. J. W. Horton, one of the oldest of the township settlers, when examined by the House of Commons in 1825 were literally true, "English law prevailed throughout the Pro-"vince of Quebec between 1763 and 1774, and, so far "as regards the townships, has never been repealed."

The Men Who Pulled the Wires.

To all appearance it was Papineau and Viger who led the opposition to changing the tenure of the land and in denying the English farmers their constitutional rights as British subjects but, in reality, it was the priests who instructed them what to do, and gave them the support which made their opposition formidable. Their motive was selfish—one of self-interest. In 1821 the Assembly adopted a resolution in favor of extending the seigniorial system to all lands within the Province of Quebec. Onlookers saw in their action merely an expression of nativism. The resolution was urged by the priests, embodied their wish, and secured their effective influence. The Quebec Act distinctly specified that their right to tax did not go beyond the parishes in existence at the date of the Act. Therefore, the priests not only exerted themselves to defeat the movement to abolish the old tenure, pulling every wire and playing on every prejudice to attain their end, which was not only to maintain the seigniorial system where established, but to enwrap in it every acre in the province. To the hurt of the habitant they opposed the abolition of feudal tenure, fooling him by cries of patriotism, and did not relax their opposition until, thirty years later, statutes passed by subservient politicians enabled them to defy the prohibitive provision of the Quebec Act as to levying their dues on lands held in free and common soccage.

CHAPTER VI.

Development of the Nationalist Idea

Excepting Craig, the governors between the departure of Dorchester and the coming of Dalhousie were no credit to the English name. Their greed was excelled only by their pettiness of mind. A great man can wield despotic power to benefit those over whom he is set, a weak one will descend to acts so despicable that resentment is colored with disgust. It has to be admitted the period of their rule was trying. The French revolution had done in Quebec what the American revolution had failed to bring about—it had brought into being a band of Republicans, men who were enthusiastic in their belief that merely changing the form of government would transform everything. Their ardent minds yearned to make Quebec a Republic, and in this they were encouraged by the French Minister at Washington. Something like the clandestine communication between the exiled Stuarts and the Scottish Jacobites was opened by these French-Canadian Republicans with Genet and his successors, who encouraged them with promises and some money. Of more importance was the knowledge that the Americans along the frontier were ready to flock over at the first intimation of the red flag being unfurled. Had Washington, who was then President, given the slightest encouragement there would have been a second invasion by the valley of the Richelieu. After the revolution came the rise of Napoleon. It is impossible in our day to realize the dazzling effect his victories had on the French mind. Although far removed from the scene of his triumphs, and imperfectly informed of them, the French-Canadians exulted in him, looking upon him as the hero of their race. Spontaneously the belief grew in their hearts that he would be their deliverer, that part of his invincible army was sure to cross the seas to Canada. While the French were intoxicated with the achievements of that marvellous soldier and eager to welcome his legions, the English were as decided in their detestation of him, their hatred being unjustly extended to the French people. What approach had been effected between French and English during the rule of Murray and Carleton was obliterated by distrust and hatred. The ruling class of Quebec and Montreal looked on the French as traitors at heart, ready to side with the tyrant who was menacing the existence of England, and, unfortunately, by their haughty bearing and their high-handed acts in averting the danger they supposed existed, intensified the Anglophobe sentiment. Whoever would know the temper of these times, let him read the records of the Assembly and the despatches of the Governors. The squabbles over trifles, the irritating attitude of the Assembly, the mean tyrannies of the official class, were the straws that indicated the tense feeling that divided the two races. If an exception be attempted in the case of Craig, it can only be on the score that, unlike his predecessors and successors, he was not self-seeking, and had a sincere desire to advance the interests of the Province. Yet the well-meaning old soldier, who tried to rule a Province as he had done his regiment, did more to estrange the contending nationalities than all the others. The party that had been formed before he came, on the platform of our religion, our language, our laws, our usages, was consolidated by the course he pursued. Henceforth the majority in the Assembly had one object in view, to gain the government of Quebec for themselves.

Perhaps the most foolish means to which the governors resorted, to defeat a purpose that was palpable, was their endeavor to enlist the priesthood on their side. The attitude to be taken by Protestant rulers towards the priests is so plain that there is no excuse for their going wrong. As the ministers of a section of their fellowmen, they are entitled to the same protection as is extended to other clergymen. To go further, is to place themselves in a false position. The Protestant ruler who looks upon the priests as a depositary of political power, and negotiates with them in order to obtain their support, is a party to an immoral proceeding, for two reasons. First, he is a traitor to those principles the term Protestant represents; second, he does wrong to the priests in asking them to use their spiritual power to advance temporal ends. Yet of this crime against the body politic, this sin against God, every governor, save Dalhousie and Craig, before the union, was guilty. Since the union, when personal gave way to representative government, every party leader stands equally convicted, for, to this hour, it has been their policy to win the influence of the priesthood to their side. In no other way could such effective aid be obtained for the time being: in no other way is the price of aid so pernicious to the welfare of the people. It is a simple statement of acknowledged facts, that in all such negotiations, whether either a governor, a leader of a party, or an ordinary politician approached cure, bishop, or ablegate, the ecclesiastic exacted in return some concession to the organization of which he is a member. They could not do otherwise. In accepting orders they sank their individuality, merging their interests in those of the greatest of all close corporations, becoming its passive agents, looking to its advancement as the purpose of their lives, and always remembering that, while they would pass away, the organization, whose creatures they are, would exist after them, and therefore, ever to have an eye to plan for its supremacy, however remote the realization of the plan might be. The men of the world who came asking for their favor had only a temporary purpose to serve, and cared not for those who were to come after them so long as their personal ends were met. The advantages they craved and obtained perished with them. Not so with the black robes with whom they had dealings. The favors got in return for those the priests gave were not for themselves, but for their organization, and were permanent. The ruler or the politician had a momentary, a selfish purpose to serve: the priest looked solely to the aggrandizement of the vast system in whose hand he was a staff. The early history of Canada exemplifies this as that of no other country, and does so because it is a solitary instance of a large Catholic population being ruled for four score years by a handful of Protestants, and when the non-Catholics did come to outnumber the Catholics, the latter, from their coherence, continued to hold the balance of power. The records I have now to quote tell one story—of the extremity of politicians being made the opportunity of the priests, of how they have grown in power and prerogative through the subserviency of politicians who made alliance with them to promote their individual interests or those of their party. How great the concessions have been only those can realize who compare what the priests were in the days of Murray and Carleton with what they are now. Then they were dependent on the will of the civil magistrate: to-day they dictate their desires to cabinets and legislatures.

Like too many Englishmen who find themselves in a new country, Sir Guy Carleton desired to reproduce the institutions of the country he left without considering difference in circumstances. England had an Established Church, therefore Canada ought to have one. That a Church could be maintained without tithes was, to the ruling class of the reign of George Third as inconceivable as that the Crown should not nominate bishops and present to benefices. For lack of members there was no Anglican Church to establish, so for half a century each succeeding governor tried to mould the Church of Rome to suit his ideas. One after another labored under the notion that it was possible to form the same relation between that Church in Quebec and the Crown, as existed between the Crown and the Anglican Body in England. Sir Guy would have only Canadian-born priests, have them licensed and presented to a parish by the King's representative, who was also to have a veto on the choice of a bishop, and on their presentation, cure and bishop alike must take the oath as to the King's supremacy. In making the priests dependent upon the Crown, the early governors saw a guarantee for the permanence of British possession. The priests humored the idea, for if the Crown placed itself in such close relationship to them they perceived a means of regaining the status they had under the French kings, and after events proved their shrewdness. They never exerted their influence to help a governor without securing an advantage for their order.

Carleton was insistent that the priests should be Canadian born and educated, because he looked upon the priests who had come from France with suspicion. The danger of his time was the re-conquest of Canada, and he regarded the French priests as spies, as agents of King Louis, plotting to overthrow the existing state of affairs. To get rid of them was his purpose, and in this he was aided by the jealousy that existed between the French and the Canadian priests. The former despised the latter for their illiteracy and rusticity; the Canadians, resenting these airs of superiority, assisted the governor in finding excuses for furnishing them with passage on board the first ship bound for France, and he, before long, got what he planned, a native-born and home-educated priesthood. What was the result of this meddling with the internal management of an ecclesiastical society? The governor came under obligation to the priests, and the first price exacted was including in the Quebec Act their old authority to tax and tithe. That was the forerunner of a hundred similar bargains. Whenever governor or politician approached priest or bishop to get support, the price paid has been at the expense of the country at large. Had Carleton not sought the aid of the priesthood, the Quebec Act would not have included Article 5. In the subsequent period, when the danger to the continuance of British rule came from within, not from without, governors and their advisers again relied on the priests for help, who were their spies, reporting what was going on among the disaffected, each recurring obligation involving some fresh concession.

For half a century after the conquest the priesthood were dependent on the goodwill of the State. The newly-appointed bishop did not exercise his functions until he waited on the governor, obtained his approval of his appointment, and had taken the oath of allegiance; he could not erect parishes and the highest legal authority was against him in presenting to parishes without obtaining the governor's leave. The language of the royal instructions was definite, "that "no person whatsoever is to have holy orders con- "ferred upon him or to have the care of souls, without "a license first and obtained from the governor." The principle to guide the governors in dealing with the priests was laid down in these words: "A toleration "of the free exercise of their religion, but not the pow- "ers and privileges of it as an Established Church." In consideration of political services, irregularities in matters of patronage were winked at, and to bind the bishop to the service of the British Government a yearly salary from the Imperial treasury was allowed him. Contrast Bishop Denaut, ready to adopt a scheme that would have given the governor a voice in the temporal management of his diocese, with Archbishop Bourget, placing the State beneath the heel of the priest, and the extent of the change in the condition and spirit of Quebec ecclesiastics, that took place within sixty years, will be realized.

The breaking out of the war of 1812 came opportunely for the priesthood. The new danger caused the executive to seek their assistance, and the plan devised by Craig, to bring the priests under direct control of the governor, was abandoned. The yearly allowance from the Imperial treasury of $1,000 to Bishop Plessis was raised to $5,000, and, what he valued more than the additional money, the warrant for his salary, in 1813, was no longer made out in favor of "the superintendent of the Romish Church," for the existence of a bishop had not hitherto been officially recognized, but in favor of "the Roman Catholic bishop of Quebec," and so giving him, for the first time since the conquest, a legal status as such. Reduced to choosing between the rule of the American Republic and that of Britain the priests had no hesitation in deciding for the latter, so that Prevost's blandishments were superfluous. Indeed, they neither on this nor any previous occasion rendered any service to the Crown of special moment. The claim that it was due to the priests that Canada did not join in the American revolution, that the madness of the French uprising against monarchy did not spread to Quebec, that they prevented an invasion during Napoleon's reign, that they held back the habitants from assisting the Americans in the war of 1812, will not bear examination. In each instance they acted as their own interests required and without regard to the advantage of Britain. In each of the four opportunities the French-Canadians had to rise against Britain, it was obvious the priests were going to profit more by remaining under British rule than in passing under that of Robespierre, of Napoleon, or of the United States. Under such conditions it was easy to pose as the friends of Britain and to accept money and legal concessions for pretended services. Two instances of toleration of this period are often quoted—the use of the Recollet and Jesuit churches for Protestant worship in Montreal and Quebec. These would indeed have been notable instances of toleration had these chapels belonged to the

Recollets or the Jesuits. The properties in question belonged to the British Government, having been confiscated at the conquest, provision being made for the maintenance of the surviving members, who lingered around the old buildings until their death. In Protestants having placed at their disposal by the governor for the purpose of worship rooms in buildings whose title was vested in the Crown, there was nothing remarkable, and a present of candles to the old men in charge was a kindly compliment.

With the close of the war of 1812 came a change in the tone of the bishop and his assistants. The conciliatory, submissive attitude faded, replaced by a gradually increasing haughtiness. Concessions ceased to be humbly prayed for, they were demanded, and the arrogance which ended in making the priesthood dictator in temporal affairs began to appear. This was due partly to Prevost's policy of flattering and fawning, but more to the influence of those French priests who fled to Canada from the horrors of the revolution. They were given a cordial welcome as objects of pity by the authorities, who made provision for their living in comfort while in exile. Such of them as were Sulpicians were granted an allowance out of the revenues of the seigniory of Montreal. These foreign priests, the product of the worst period of Bourbonism, with inflated notions of the superiority of their order, and contempt for the common people, infected the native clergy with new notions of their importance—told them they were imposed upon by their English masters, who could not dispense with their support. It was advice to be expected from priests who had influenced the counsels of France under successive kings, and whose lives and spirit had aided in provoking the greatest national convulsion Europe has known. Their influence in Quebec was malign.

While those who held the reins of government at Quebec labored under the delusion that the priests could be made their instruments, they, with stupid fatuity, strove to fasten on Canada a church establishment similar to that of England. Grants of public money were made to pay salaries to a bishop and clergy, a cathedral was built at Quebec, and a chapter contemplated, and it was looked upon as feasible to levy tithes upon all Protestants until such time as the land set aside as clergy reserves should yield an income. Had these plans been carried out, the strange spectacle would have been presented of a Province having two sets of clergymen supervised by the State, and both subsidized out of the public purse.

A vivid conception of the ecclesiastical situation before the war of 1812 is obtained from a memorial by Bishop Mountain to the Imperial authorities. He complained that Plessis, coadjutor of Denaut, had assumed the title of Bishop of Quebec, in defiance of the King's patent which gave him (Mountain) that title, and was claiming a pre-eminence that was never contemplated nor intended, by styling himself "Mon-"signeur Sa Grandeur, Reverendissime et illustris-"sime," and did so by virtue of a bull from the Pope. He had extended his episcopal authority over Nova Scotia, New Brunswick, what is now Ontario, and had been appointing priests, including French emigrant priests, to parishes, which was expressly against the King's regulation that no person should be given a parish without a license from the governor. Bishop Mountain gave warning that while he would not wish to see the Roman Catholics deprived of any privileges necessary to their worship, he could not hide from himself the belief that unless the gradual extension of priestly authority were checked, the Roman Catholic religion would be to all intents and purposes the established religion of the country, and would be raised to a pre-eminence that was never contemplated nor intended. Lord Hobart, then in charge of the colonies, in reply to this complaint, advised Governor Milnes to notify Plessis of the "impropriety of his assuming new "titles or the exercise of any additional powers." Attorney-General Sewell had interviews with Plessis, and of two of these, reports have been preserved. Sewell did his best to impress Plessis with the fact that the King was the head of the State, and that the bishop could exercise no more temporal power than the King conferred upon him. With his spiritual jurisdiction the government had no desire to interfere, but in all other matters he was under British, not French or papal law. Plessis resented this, asking, Did not canon law obtain? No, answered Sewell, you are under the laws administered by the King's courts. Plessis was told he could not order a tax; he could not even fix the fees for baptisms, marriages, and funerals. These charges were to be regulated entirely by the people of each parish. The bishop expressed a desire to control expenditures upon the building and repairing of churches and parsonages. The Attorney-General replied that these were civil matters; that the people had to do with them, and that all contestations respecting them were cognizable, not in Roman, but in the King's courts. Plessis then demanded authority over the schools. The reply was, "This is impossible." He also wanted to be empowered to erect parishes. The Attorney-General answered that the parishes were certainly ecclesiastical divisions; but inasmuch as civil authority ran concurrent with ecclesiastical authority in the parishes the Crown could not concede the right to create parishes to any bishop, whether Protestant or Catholic. What Attorney-General of our times would take the stand Sewell did in these memorable interviews?

With the restoration of peace in 1814 the obstructive tactics of the Assembly grew increasingly offensive to the executive. Given a representative Assembly French and Catholic, and a nominated Council English and Protestant, what other result could there be than strife? The bills that originated in the Assembly the Council vetoed; those the Council sent down were rejected. There was no intermediary to bring the two together, for there was no Cabinet, no Ministers responsible to the Assembly for the measures introduced, or for the conduct of business. The Assembly was independent of the Council and the Council of the Assembly, and each regarded the other as its enemy. Then, back of both, was an executive council, responsible to neither and having a veto power over both.

Is it wise to give self-government to a people who may use it in endeavors to free themselves from their allegiance to the nation that bestows the boon? The history of Quebec answers No. The well-meant gift of the Imperial Government of an elementary form of representative institutions worked out badly for the people intended to be benefited, and led to endless complications and difficulties to the British authorities. I confess I shrink from the task of outlining the events which ended in the rebellion of '37-'38, for to him who desires to think well not only of his countrymen, but of the French who had been, by the rude force of war, entrusted to their care, in the events between Craig's administration and that of Colborne, there is little that is creditable to either nationality. However, in tracing the causes which have led to the stamping out of the English-speaking settlements, an outline of the events of this period cannot be avoided.

For the detestable struggle which came into being at the organizing of the first Assembly, but which did not become palpable until 1800, nor acute until about 1820, the Act of 1791 is responsible. It was a half-hearted measure. Had it handed over the government of Quebec to representatives of the majority of its inhabitants, that would have meant the loss of the Province to the Crown, for it would have been speedily converted into a French Republic. That was foreseen by Pitt, and a compromise made. The French were given a voice in the government, but to a nominated council, and to the governor and his executive council was entrusted a reserve power to enable them to preserve the Province to the Crown. This arrangement could not fail to breed trouble. The French, zealous in seeking their independence, were constantly

The Tragedy of Quebec.   141

thwarted by the council and the executive, until governor and council came to be distrusted and hated by the French.

The period between the peace of 1814 and 1837 is commonly spoken of as a struggle for constitutional liberty, and gratitude expressed to Papineau and his colleagues for the part they played. Men, who ought to know better, are still heard repeating: We are enjoying what they fought for. If we were enjoying what Papineau and his associates fought for, we would be living in a French Republic. The confusion of ideas regarding the period in question is extraordinary. Because the French professed a zeal for constitutional forms, they were fighting for the freedom Britons love: because the English of those days opposed them, they were the abettors of tyranny. Why be misled by names and cries? Is it conceivable that Papineau was the representative of freedom, and Dalhousie of despotism? Is it not more consonant with fact and common-sense, to say Papineau plotted to overthrow British rule and Dalhousie resisted to maintain it? It is nothing new to seek treasonable ends under the cloak of zeal for the British constitution. In these days we see, in Ireland and India, the leaders in movements to break the Imperial tie using that device. Given a body of men eager to change rulers, entrusted with legislative powers by the government they are opposed to, how could they undermine that government except under constitutional forms? Force being out of the question, Papineau and his party had to keep within the letter of the law. The end they had in view was the overthrow of British rule, which was, from their standpoint, a patriotic undertaking. To achieve their purpose, they had the legislative powers conceded to them by the Acts of 1774 and 1791, and they used them skilfully and persistently. In the Assembly their course was the simple one of obstruction. Whatever the governor asked, they refused—when they dared; whatever the Council enacted affecting their cause, they rejected.

Necessarily they had to do all this on constitutional lines, and so it came they had to use British parliamentary terms and procedure in their efforts to overthrow British institutions. They sought to kill English rule in Quebec with the weapon the British Government had confidingly put into their hand. To illustrate how they worked take the one prominent grievance of the French members, that they were denied the distribution of the Crown revenue—meaning thereby the annual grant allotted by the home authorities for the payment of the salaries of officials. In the Assembly debates no disguise was made as to the motive for the demand—that it would place in the hands of the French members the power to take away the salaries of the English-speaking officials, who, as a result, would have to resign, when they would fill the vacancies from among their own number. Successive governors perceived what the Assembly sought, and rejected their oft-repeated demand. The demand of the Assembly was perfectly constitutional, and its refusal just as unconstitutional. The dispute, however, was not academic, it was one of fact. Those who made the demand sought, under the cloak of zeal for constitutional government, to deal a fatal blow to British rule, and those who denied the demand acted according to the dictate of self-preservation. Because the legislature made a constitutional demand it did not follow its members had a constitutional end in view. Their motive has to be considered. Take another instance. The Assembly demanded that the Crown lands be entrusted to their charge. What was their motive? They did not conceal it. They wanted to stop the flow of English-speaking settlers into the townships. Did Dalhousie act as a tyrant or as a true servant of the government he represented, when he put his foot down, and said "No," with emphasis, he would keep the control of the waste lands in the hands of the executive and go on inducing English-speaking immigrants to take up their abode in Quebec? It was the same with a score of other nominal constitutional grievances. It was a violation of British constitutional precedent for Craig, and, after him, Dalhousie, to carry on the government by means of loans from the military chest, yet they had either to do so or quit their residences and take the first ship for England. Look under the surface of the political agitation of these times, blow away the smoke about constitutional grievances, and there will be seen an ably led and energetic majority using any pretence and any catchword to attain the object of their desire —Quebec for the French—and a pitiably small minority striving to preserve Quebec as a British possession. Both were right from their own standpoint. Nothing was more natural than that the French should use the power given them by the Act of 1791 to endeavor to drive the English out. They only did what the English would have done had they been in their place. On the other hand, how could the officials entrusted by the Crown with the preservation of Canada to Britain, do otherwise than they did in thwarting the efforts of the French? Wolfe's victory placed both in a false position. Under the pretence of zeal for the British constitution the French sought to overthrow British rule, while those in office had to break constitutional law to defeat them.

When appeals were made by the Assembly to the Imperial Parliament regarding the high-handed acts of governors in conducting the affairs of the Province without their consent, it was impossible for the home authorities to justify the King's representatives; their conduct was plainly unconstitutional, yet they acknowledged that force of circumstances justified their irregularities, that, had they not overridden the will of the Assembly, British ascendancy would have been undermined. Dalhousie may be represented in two lights—as a dictator, putting under his feet the constitution in order to tyrannize the French, or as a patriot, who dared to break the letter of the law to keep the British flag flying from Cape Diamond.

Until within a year or so of the rebellion, I know

of no evidence that the French leaders intended resorting to force. They believed they could attain their purpose by so embarrassing the executive that British government would become impossible, and the Province be abandoned to themselves. Their course was shaped to bring about a deadlock—a crisis, when the English executive would have to confess inability to longer conduct public affairs and hand over the reins to them. Every obstacle they could devise was placed in the way of successive governors and their advisers, and no artifice left untried to make them odious in the eyes of the habitants. Grievances were hatched by the dozen. Whoever had a complaint to make against an English-speaking official was invited to lay it before the Assembly, and payment promised for his loss of time in doing so. Even the judges were not exempt. They were described as minions of the governor, who gave judgment according to his instructions and not according to law. The crown of all their grievances, was the complaint that the Assembly was denied power to organize a court which would try and sentence the officials they impeached. For thirty years the Assembly and the executive were in open strife, with brief periods of truce, as during Prevost and Kempt's terms of office. One side demanding, the other refusing, the one thwarting the other, and all the while the two races drifting farther apart. The origin of the distrust which still exists between French and English is a continuance of the feeling of this unhappy period, for the evidence goes to show that until the fatal gift of a legislative Assembly there was no open enmity between the two races.

The Members of the Assembly.

The sort of members who made up that Assembly should be understood. The pall of ignorance that overhung the parishes when they passed under British rule had in no degree been lifted. In 1801 a well-meant attempt was made to establish a system of elementary schools. It was defeated by the priests.

Unless given control of the schools they would prevent their people attending them, and so the plan failed. The revenue derived from the Jesuit estates was available for such a purpose, and that from the seigniory of Montreal could also be brought in, so that there was no financial difficulty in giving the Province a school system. The obstacle in the way of teaching the children of the habitants to read and write was the priests, who took the stand that the education of their people must be left in their hands. To this the British authorities would not consent, and up to 1845, so far as education was concerned, the parishes were as Vaudreuil had left them.

The Habitant.

The habitant's childlike ignorance of the world outside his own Province, his utter unconsciousness of the nature of public affairs, excited the surprise of every visitor. There was no cause for surprise. For generations he had been confined to a secluded part of the world, outside the community of other nations; with the one country to the south of him, that bordered his own, he had been prevented, by brutal penalties, from having intercourse. What he knew of other countries and peoples was what his priest chose to tell him or what he heard from some stray soldier of Old France. For centuries he and his fathers had been taught they were the creatures of their King, that it was their duty to obey him and give their services whenever he called upon them. Of self-government they had no conception. Of the British constitution they knew less than of the Roman decretals. It was the King's province to govern, that of the priest to tell them what to believe. Take such a people, confined to a hermit corner of the earth, trained generation after generation by priest and ruler to blind obedience to throne and church, and it is no matter for surprise that an acute observer so late as 1840 found the ignorance and credulity of the habitant unbounded, so that he had ceased to wonder they became the victims of the agitators who stirred up rebellion. Lieut-Governor Milnes described the habitants as industrious, peaceable, and well-disposed, but liable to be misled by artful and designing men, and there has never ceased a succession of designing men trying to elevate themselves into office by playing on the prejudices of the peasantry of Quebec. The marvel is that, brought up during the French regime under a system of repression, the habitant retained his brightness of apprehension, his liveliness of spirit. Only the happy genius of a superior race preserved him from sinking into the apathy, the sullenness of the Russian serf. To offer to a people so long hemmed in from the world around, in whose natures had been ingrained the lesson that they were born to be ruled, the splendid boon of self-government was folly, for they neither comprehended it nor knew how to use it. The few educated men in the Province, however, saw in it an unlooked for opportunity to obtain a voice in the government of the Province, and the priests a means of benefitting themselves. In the first Assembly were a few of the habitant class but they were incapable of taking part. Had it been otherwise, had an Assembly of habitants been constituted, with their ingrained deference for authority, the governors might possibly have been able to make the Act of 1791 workable. Instead of habitants, the House was largely made up of lawyers and notaries, with an occasional physician, or seignior. The habitants having no political opinions, no conception, in fact, of representative government, the educated members took them in hand to instill in their minds the views they wished them to hold. The political speech after mass became an institution, and hearing no other views, and unable to read, the habitants believed what was told them in those Sunday orations. Here the English were at a disadvantage. They had no class equivalent to that which composed the majority of the Assembly, and the few among them capable of going on the platform were ignorant of French. The consequence was that for nigh forty years a propaganda hostile to British interests was carried on in the parishes without check. The English, although they knew what was going on, were unable to have their side of the case represented; sometimes found it difficult even to find seats for officers of the Crown, such as the Attorney-General, in the Assembly.

Clerical Colleges.

It may be remarked that to this day the habitants have never been represented in Parliament by members chosen from their ranks, though the same cause, lack of sufficiently educated men among them, does not now exist. They are still, as in the days of Craig and Dalhousie, represented by deputies drawn from the professional class, and the Dominion has the views of that class thrust upon it as the voice of Quebec. The representatives of Quebec, in the Senate and in the House of Commons, are of a class distinct and widely different from their constituents, a class of which no other Province has its counterpart—men educated in clerical colleges and who, no matter what profession they choose, expect to figure in public life. It is from this select class the habitants receive their political teaching. This fact, that the parliamentary representatives of the habitants have always been and are to this day, drawn from a distinct caste, is not given the weight it deserves. The word caste is used advisedly. A bright boy appears. The priest advises his being sent to college. The college indicated is peculiar to Quebec, and has not its counterpart elsewhere. In every diocese one or more is to be found. They receive boys who, in other parts, would be in elementary schools—boys of 12 years and upwards, the only matriculation required that they can read and write. These colleges are conventual, the boy being cut off, so far as practicable, from the outside world. The letters received for him are first read by the priest in charge, and so are the letters he wishes to mail. The books he brings with him are examined, he is allowed to buy none, without consent, and if he is found reading book or paper not approved he is disciplined. A system of espionage, even while at play, destroys individuality, and the boy, insensibly, is forced into the mould the priests desire. The colleges being residential, broken only by the summer vacation, cut off from outside intercourse, taught by priests, directed by priests, constantly associated with priests, the lad imbibes their views. The first object of these colleges, as is stated in their announcements, is to make the student a good Catholic. Catechism stands foremost in a course of study which is not of the nature to develop the mind by broadening it, nor are the books allowed to be read calculated to expand it by conveying knowledge from every quarter. For eight years the studies are in the classics and the philosophy that has come down from Aquinas. The cheapness of these colleges is astonishing, rarely averaging over $12 a month for board and tuition, explains the large attendance. It is a growing custom for these colleges to have what they call a commercial course, which lasts three years less than the classical, yet even in that course catechism stands first and Latin is imperative. Whichever course the boy goes through, he leaves college a new being. He is no longer a habitant boy; he no longer means to labor with his hands; his ambition is to scheme to get into the inner circle where power and wealth are to be got. He faces the battle of life with an apprehension sharpened by prolonged study of scholastic philosophy, with a careful training in rhetoric, and, above all, with an implicit faith in the authority of his church. None are more acute in analysis, none more ready or eloquent in speech than the average graduate of these clerical institutions, yet none more narrow, taught to measure by the standard of creed, and none in whom the noble thirst for truth, seeking to gratify it untrammelled and uncoerced, is less manifest. They seek to be notaries, physicians, lawyers, and to become such they are still kept under clerical direction, for Laval, which monopolizes law and medicine, is an integral part of the Catholic

Church. A select number enter the ministry, a growing number seek employment in business vocations; it is almost unheard that any go back to the plow. The alumni of these priestly colleges that dot the province are as distinct from the class from which they sprung as the noblesse of old France were from the common people. They are members of a caste, created and moulded by their Church to serve its ends. In the present parliament at Ottawa out of 54 French-Canadians who have seats in it 50 were educated in these clerical colleges, and it is through the students she sends from these seminaries Rome rules Quebec, and may, as she is now doing, continue to rule the Dominion. The people of the other provinces, who take it for granted the educated men of Quebec are like those with whom they are familiar make a dangerous mistake: while an occasional one may have broken free from the encrustations of his college life, the rest are the agents of their Church, intent on advancing its interests, which they hold above and far beyond those of the nation or its people. Failure to recognize this class, who, having spent eight or more years of their youth in the shade of monastic halls, pass into public offices, to occupy seats in the legislatures, to be Ministers of the Crown, to be heads of departments, to preside on the bench of justice, has led to dangerous misconceptions.

It was during the period when Lord Dalhousie was Governor-General that this class, intermediate between the habitants and the priests, came into prominence by their instilling in the minds of the people the spirit of revolt against England. The ground of their argument was, that as they were the children of the soil, Quebec belonged exclusively to the French-Canadians, who were therefore wrongfully deprived of their own. The governor and his subordinates were depicted as brutal tyrants, who hated everything French and Catholic, who were trampling on the laws in order to plunder and oppress, and these assertions were supported by alleged acts that were always misrepresented, many without a semblance of truth. The object the habitant was counselled to keep in view was the downfall of this corrupt and tyrannical administration, to be replaced by la nation Canadienne, whose purpose would be to preserve the religion, language, laws, and usages, which they made them believe were threatened with immediate destruction. To overthrow this system of tyranny, the habitants were assured, from their being in an overwhelming majority, was easy of accomplishment. The habitants were told Britain was in her decrepitude, that her strength on this continent had become so feeble that all that was needed was a united and simultaneous rush to pluck up every vestige of English rule, and place the children of the soil in power. The habitants believed this, and the belief strengthened with time, until smashed by the experience of the rising in 1837. Against the many unfortunate results that flowed from that revolt, there was, at least, one good effect: it shattered the delusion that had overspread the parishes, that the strength of Britain had become so contemptible that they ran no risk in defying it.

The French Leaders.

In their leaders the French had the advantage. The English had no men to compare in ability, fertility of resource, or persistence with Viger, Cuvillier, and Papineau. The last dominated. Justice has not been done that remarkable man. To dismiss him as a demagogue who played on the string of racial hate, is to misrepresent him. He stands the foremost man of his race in intellect and independence of thought. Had he not made the mistake of consenting to an armed rising, he would have led in the emancipation of the habitant from the despotism of the priests. In him was centred the aspiration of a French-Canadian Republic, and let the English-Canadian put himself in Papineau's place and see if he can blame him. It was no compliment to his political sagacity to suppose that such a Republic was possible—it was to his honor as a Frenchman that he should have striven to regain what his fathers had lost. As a sincere believer in the Republican form of government, the administration at Quebec was objectionable to him as representing royalty. His views he thus expressed: "The people "of this country are preparing themselves for a future "state of political existence, which I trust will be "neither a monarchy nor an aristocracy. I hope "Providence has not in view for my country a future "so dark as that it should be the means of planting "royalty in America, near a country so grand as the "United States. I hope the time has gone by when "Europe could give monarchies to America, but, on "the contrary, the time is approaching when America "shall give republics to Europe."

The English Officials.

There was little in the conduct of the ruling class of his early days to recommend royalty. Several of the governors reflected no honor on the throne they represented, and were surrounded by a clique of officeholders who for greed, indolence, superciliousness, and ignorant contempt of the French, deserved much of what Papineau said of them. Worse than all, there was dishonesty in handling the public monies. The term "bureaucrat" represented to the mind of the habitant for many a year all that was bad. No one who has English blood in his veins can look on certain of the officials and judges of the period preceding the union of 1841 without a feeling of shame. The gentlemen who at their dinner-tables befuddled what brains they had by drinking confusion to Papineau and the French would have served their King and their race by giving Papineau no occasion for the complaints about them he was constantly sending to London. Their private characters did not command the respect of the French, who watched them with envious eyes: there was less in their conduct of public affairs to commend to them English rule. In the movement looking to Quebec's independence, the French had some assistance from the English population. There then appeared the forerunners of a type of politician the Dominion knows well, who thought they could use French influence for their personal advancement, of whom Stuart is an example. Then there were men who had been radicals in the Old Country, and who resented the high-handed acts and dishonesty of those in office in Quebec, siding with Papineau on this score, of whom Neilson was prominent. The number of these English-speaking sympathizers was minute, however, compared with those who wished to see Quebec made a State of the American Union. Up to about 1830 the English-speaking population of the province was largely composed of native-born Americans, and, in Montreal, especially, there was a wealthy colony of them. Firm in the belief that an independent French Republic would be found impossible, the Americans supported Papineau, in the expectation that the result of the agitation he headed would be annexation. The most prominent man in this coterie was Nelson.

English Mercantile and Farming Class.

While the official class were no honor to the Crown there were two sections of the English who did the land of their origin credit. There was, first, the mercantile. Merchants from the Thames, the Mersey, and the Clyde developed a trade that, by 1820, each spring whitened the St. Lawrence with the sails of hundreds of ships, and rose from nothing to be counted by millions of dollars. The second were the immigrants who sought out land, enriching the country not only by their labor, but more by their example in introducing among the French a higher type of farming. It was the Montreal merchants and the Ulster and Scottish farmers who preserved Quebec to Britain in 1837-38. The wealth and influence of the first, and the sturdy resistance of the second, were rocks that could not be swept aside.

Treatment of the English Farmers.

The growth of the English settlements along the frontier was such that, in 1825, it was computed their assessable property outvalued that of the parishes between them and the St. Lawrence, yet progressive and important as they had become, the advantages of governmental institutions were denied them. The Assembly persisted in treating them as trespassers who were not to be recognized. Their petitions for aid to open roads, for registry offices, for courts, were ignored. Most striking of all refusals was that of representation. The patriots who were declaiming as to their inherent rights from being British subjects, who were constantly quoting authors on the constitution, and who grew eloquent over the examples of Hampden and Russell, peremptorily refused to grant representatives to the new settlements. Governor after governor pointed out the injustice thus done, but in vain. No more English-speaking members were wanted in the Assembly. When, for very shame's sake, and when it became advisable to keep up appearances with the Imperial Government, representation was tendered, it was done in a way that would give the votes of the new members no weight. In 1823 the Assembly offered to allot five members to the Eastern Townships on condition that the number of French members be increased by a score. The council declined the magnanimous offer, and the townships continued to be unrepresented. This in itself proves the hollowness of the pretension that the movement headed by Papineau was to redress constitutional grievances. No violation of the principle of self-government is comparable to denying an important section of the population a voice in the government. The men who were denouncing a succession of governors as tyrants who were depriving them of their constitutional rights, were at the very time refusing representation to 80,000 residents of the province. For what reason? Because they were ignorant, because they were disloyal? Not at all: the reverse was the truth. The franchise was denied these eighty thousand of thrifty, intelligent, well-living people because, if representatives from them were admitted to the Assembly, their presence would hinder the plan of making Quebec a nation Canadienne. In a British colony, a large body of people were denied representation simply because they were not French. The settlers expressed this truth in a petition to the Crown, that representation in the Assembly would have been given them "had not their "language and descent been British."

Courts and Registry Offices Refused.

Of more immediate importance was the denial to them of the institutions necessary for the preservation of the rights of person and property. They could get no courts. The consequence was, that an unscrupulous man who wished to wrong another could institute an action in Quebec, Three Rivers, or Montreal, and force the defendant either to make a journey through the forest of a hundred miles or more, or submit to judgment by default. If he chose to brave the cost and fatigue of the journey he found, on entering the court, that his case would be tried according to French law, probably by a French judge. No complaint was more reasonable than that of the French, after the conquest, that they were made subject to laws with which they were unacquainted, and tried in a language they did not understand, and it had more weight in inducing members of the House of Commons to vote for restoring the custom of Paris than anything else. The sons of the people who made that complaint, and who had rejoiced when a British parliament set aside English law to meet their views, showed not the slightest compunction in refusing to right an exactly similar wrong. The English settlers complained of being made "subject to French laws of which they know "nothing, compiled in a language with which they are "unacquainted," and those who controlled the Assembly mocked their complaint. The very Act which revived French law specified that it "should not ex-"tend to lands granted in free and common soccage." In defiance of that condition, on which the French had obtained their request in 1774, the French, fifty years afterwards, did their utmost to force French law and the French language on the settlers of the townships. The mercy the French had asked and obtained they would not show.

Of all the French laws the English settlers were most vexed by was that which gave force to a mortgage passed before a notary without making it of public record. A settler would buy a lot of land, receive a deed, go on and improve the land, to be suddenly surprised by a stranger claiming possession, producing a mortgage executed before a notary living in a distant parish. Scores of immigrants lost their little capital and a year or more of hard work in this way. The demand of the English was, that registry offices be established, where all hypothecs be recorded, so that a search would show whether a clear deed was being obtained. This request was stoutly resisted as an innovation on French law, and it was several years before authority was obtained to establish a registry office at Sherbrooke, and mortgages not recorded held to be obligations without privilege.

Nationalist Obstructions.

The perplexity of each succeeding governor as to how to carry on the business of the province kept increasing. Having control of the provincial revenue, the Assembly used their power to make government impossible. They withheld the salaries of those in public employ, even the pitiful allowances to the teachers in the English settlements, and refused grants for roads and bridges, immigration and the administration of justice. That government be carried on, and the public credit maintained, governors had to draw on the Crown, and their doing so was made a fresh grievance by the Assembly, and so recorded in its journal.

Those who judge of these times by the conditions of to-day wonder at Papineau's belief that he could wrest independence by constitutional means. There is no comparison between the situation of eighty years ago and that which exists. Ontario was just struggling into existence, a string of thin settlements along its water fronts, whose existence was dependent on the use of the St. Lawrence as their channel of supply and export. Its population was not half of that of Quebec, and its political influence in London was almost nil. When Canada was mentioned in the House of Commons, it was Quebec that loomed before the minds of members, and of Quebec and her affairs these members had come to be heartily sick. To get rid of perplexing problems of race and creed, of incessant complaints, agitations, and demands, many members were ready to vote to let Quebec go her own way. Then, there was the financial consideration. Quebec had been a drain on the Imperial treasury from its first occupation. Instead of lessening, the votes asked yearly for Quebec kept growing, and to Britain, at that time, suffering from bad trade and financial depression, stoppage of this expenditure was of vital consequence. In the House of Commons, Huskisson, well qualified to speak from having been Secretary for the Colonies, recognized the gravity of the situation in his reply to those who favored abandoning Quebec. He would not have done so, had they not been influential in number and position. He tacitly acknowledged it would save much trouble to let Quebec go, but asked could they do so in justice to those of their fellow-subjects of English speech, who were faithful to their allegiance and whose good conduct gave them a claim to the protection of Britain? Here lay the crux of the difficulty—to yield to the demands of the Assembly for complete control of the Province of Quebec meant the abandonment of the English settlers, whose quiet, prosperous, and con-

tented condition stood out so markedly against the
restless clamor of the French agitators, who were using
constitutional cries to overthrow the constitution, and
affecting a zeal for the Crown to get into a position
that would enable them to kick it into the St. Lawrence. Supposing Dalhousie had recognized the election of Papineau as Speaker, that he had consented to
the Assembly having entire control of the civil service
and judiciary, that he had given up control of the
Crown lands and the Crown funds, transferring both
to the Assembly, that he had promised to veto no
measure passed by a two-thirds majority, and undertaken that the Imperial Parliament pass no bill affecting Quebec without the Assembly's concurrence, what
would have resulted? Would Quebec to-day be even
nominally British, or, more momentous consideration,
would that vast territory that lies west of it, and to
which Quebec is the gateway, be British? Would
Papineau and his confreres, who denied representation to the English settlements of Quebec, who withheld from them all the institutions that secure property and public order, who opposed building roads
that would give them access to the St. Lawrence, who
placed every possible obstacle in the way of immigration from the United Kingdom, and of the land being
granted to others than their own countrymen, have
taken the steps that have led to the making of Ontario
and the great provinces west of it? Strange to say,
the men who preserved Canada as the seat on the
North American continent of British institutions, it is
the fashion to adjudge as arbitrary, overriders of the
constitution, while their opponents are lauded as
patriots, and are spoken of as the authors of the liberties we enjoy. Consideration of the intentions of the
party represented by Papineau and of the class represented by Dalhousie will correct many grievous mistakes in the popular mind regarding Quebec history.
The one aimed at the formation of la nation Canadienne, the other sought to reproduce on Canadian

soil all that was good in Britain. The great service rendered by what was known up to 1840 as the British party in Quebec, in rendering possible the Canada we know, will yet be acknowledged.

Dalhousie's Policy.

There were governors who fancied if the leading agitators were got rid of peace would be restored to the province. Dalhousie was not one of them. The noisy group in the Assembly were vexing him beyond endurance, but he perceived their inspiration and their strength were drawn from the priesthood. A word from the priests at election time would have deprived the leaders of their seats and turned the tide of sentiment in the parishes. That word was not spoken, for the priests saw the agitation was serving a double purpose, isolating the habitants from the Protestants and, in the end, would secure great advantages to themselves. Dalhousie was resolute in his determination that they should be disappointed, that he would show them their lurking behind the scene and blowing the bellows that was fanning rebellion instead of resulting to their profit would strip them of the favors they had already obtained. His plan was to bring back the priests to the same position as they held in the days of Louis XV. It is of first importance, he wrote the Imperial Government, to bring them to respect the prerogative of the King. A loose rein has been given them, which they have used to strengthen their power. They act as independent of the Crown. Let the King take up the reins and exercise his prerogative in the disposal of ecclesiastical patronage, as the King of France did most peremptorily up to the day when Canada was surrendered to the British arms. Repeated appeals of this nature brought from London no authority to Dalhousie to re-establish the old order, which he assuredly would have done, for he was a man not to be trifled with and cared nothing for the threats and pretensions of sacerdotalism. Had he been given a free hand, there would have been no rebellion, no Lord Durham, and no state church to perplex the Dominion.

Seeking a Remedy.

Abandonment of Quebec being barred, the home authorities had to consider what device they should adopt to end the deadlock between the Assembly and the Executive. The most plausible suggestion was that the island of Montreal be annexed to Ontario, thus freeing its exports from the dues Quebec levied by giving it a seaport. Another proposal was, that the island of Montreal and all of Quebec that lies south and west of it, including the Eastern Townships, be formed into a new province. A third suggestion was, that Bonaventure and Gaspe be given to New Brunswick, and the Magdalen Islands to Prince Edward Island. These proposals were based on the principle that the divisive courses of Quebec could be controlled either by the presence of a majority of English, or made harmless by hiving the French by themselves. These devices were cowardly attempts to get round a difficult situation, and the adoption of any one of them would have merely postponed the impending crash.

The crisis was not due to the French-Canadians being denied the rights of British subjects, but to their seeking to be other than British subjects. Had they been content with the rights and privileges of British subjects, they would have lived as quietly as the settlers of Bedford and Huntingdon. It was their strivings to erase all England had effected that was the cause of trouble. The straightforward course, therefore, was to grapple with the situation by repealing the Quebec and Canada Acts, thus wiping out all special privileges and making the province again a Crown colony; reducing the priests to an equality with the ministers of other churches, no pretension to exceptional treatment being recognized; organizing a thorough system of secular education in every parish, and awaiting the time when the habitants would be capable of being entrusted with self-governing institutions. The deputation sent by the Assembly to England in 1828 laid before the House of Commons petitions signed by eighty-seven thousand against union with Ontario. Out of that number seventy-six thousand signed by making a mark. That one palpable fact, speaking more forcibly from the table of the House, where the petition lay, than words could of the ignorance that prevailed, ought to have convinced parliament of the state of affairs that prevailed in Quebec—a solid mass of ignorant people, dominated by their priests, and, with their connivance, left to be manipulated by agitators. The debate that ensued showed Ministers the bill they had prepared to join Quebec to Ontario would not carry. The agitation over the first reform bill was then at white heat, and with the air full of shouts for constitutional rights and for the abolition of hereditary abuses, it was useless to attempt to convince the Opposition that Dalhousie's course was justified by the conditions he had to face. The bill was not submitted. Had it become law it would have improved the situation.

Papineau Breaks With the Priests.

Events were now allowed to drift, and speedily brought about an open rupture between the Assembly and the Executive. The leaders of the Assembly became defiant, the governors resolute in resisting, confident that, if a rising were attempted, it would fail. Their confidence was not based on the military force available, for it was small, but on an understanding that had been come to with the head of the priesthood. Bishop Plessis encouraged and aided the movement headed by Papineau, but his successor discovered that, in the interests of the priests, a change of policy was desirable. There was, owing to increase of population, need for the appointment of more bishops. The governor asked what he should do. The reply he received from London was to refuse to permit another bishop, as likely to make the situation worse. The despatch went on to say that division is too strongly exemplified at this moment to leave any doubt of the extent to which it might be carried by the existence of two bishops. More serious than refusal to appoint a bishop for Montreal, were clauses in the union bill for putting into force the slumbering power of the Crown in nominating the bishop and presenting cures to parishes. Back of all this, he had information of a proposal to carry into effect the confiscation of the seigniory of the island of Montreal, and use its funds for the Crown. Bishop Poenet was alarmed. What was the cause of la nation Canadienne compared with the interests of the priests? The class of which he was head came first. The governor was approached, the bishop seeing an opportunity for making a bargain. If the government would agree to leave the seigniory of Montreal in the hands of the seminary of St. Sulpice, if it would give its consent to the appointment of a bishop for Montreal, if it would give civil powers to new canonical parishes, if it would drop the clauses in the drafted Union Act about the Crown nominating bishops and presenting cures, if it would erect the dioceses into corporations, the priests would abandon Papineau and give their support to maintain British authority. An understanding between the bishop and the governor was arrived at. The change of attitude of the priests was quickly perceived by Papineau. They had encouraged him in the agitation so long as it suited them, and now they had made a bargain at his expense and that of his associates. He resented the betrayal with all the ardor of his enthusiastic temperament. The bureaucrats, he now told his followers, were not the only class to be dealt with. When the English were got rid of, there were black gowns to be clipped and there were tithes to be reduced.

The Demands of the Nationalists.

In 1831, when a petition from the Assembly was

presented to him, Lord Sherbrooke asked if they had
included all their grievances, was there not something
behind they were concealing; would they not be candid
and tell him all? The something they were concealing it was not yet time to avow, but what that something was had become palpable to the most unobservant. It was asked that all revenues, no matter how
derived, be placed in the hands of the Assembly, that
it have control of all officials, including judges, that
the management of the militia be given over to it by
the governor, with the crowning proposal that the
governor be no longer appointed by the King, but
elected directly by the people of the province or their
representatives. Complete severance from Britain was
wanted, and in a province where the overwhelming
majority of the inhabitants were French, that meant
a French government. Would it be just to the thousands of English-speaking farmers who had settled in
the province, or to the merchants who had invested
their capital in its trade, to abandon them to the rule
of such a government? Would it be just to the
people of Ontario, and to the territory west of it, to
place the only outlet they had to the Atlantic under
the control of such a government? When the issue
had become thus clear, many who had hitherto sided
with the Nationalists fell out. The first to drop away
were the few English-speaking radicals who had supported Papineau. Neilson, the Scotch printer, who
had, to the serious injury of his business, stood by
him through thick and thin, now convinced that it
was not constitutional reform that had animated Papineau, but separation from Britain, withdrew from
him. The Irish Roman Catholics, having no wish to
live in a French Republic, refused their countenance
any longer. French business men in the cities, foreseeing loss of property, signed loyal addresses.

Acting under instructions from England every governor after Dalhousie strove to win over the disaffected. Abuses in administration were remedied, every

request compatible with a continuance of British rule complied with. Kempt, a childish, simple-minded man, despite all he did to propitiate, declared when the Assembly was in session he felt as if sitting on a barrel of gunpowder. Papineau was offered a seat in the council that he might see it was not the assemblage of tyrants he described to the habitants. Aylmer openly curried favor with the bishop.

The Parish System Extended.

Increase of population had compelled the old parishes to be divided in order that no cure have a flock too large to minister to. The habitants of these new parishes could not understand how, in secular affairs, they were held to be inhabitants of the old parish, and there was confusion in title deeds and business misunderstandings. To end this Aylmer agreed to what his predecessors refused, who, indeed, had challenged the right of the bishop to erect even canonical parishes. A bill was submitted to the Assembly to legalize these new parishes for civil purposes. The bill contained no provision for parishes that might in future be erected by the bishop, it simply dealt with the parishes that were in existence at the date of its passage, and when the commissioners had defined the new parishes, and they were proclaimed civil parishes, the Act expired. Despite this limitation, the measure had a deep bearing on future legislation, inasmuch as it made British law an accompaniment of ecclesiastical power, the civil giving force and efficacy to the ecclesiastical, the combination that has wrought woeful harm.

The British party considered the policy of conciliation had been carried too far, and were loud in denouncing the governors, whom they blamed for currying to the priests and to Papineau. That party included a sprinkling of as blatant blusterers as ever embarrassed a government. They had a monopoly of all loyalty, and knew just what ought to be done. The British bayonet, sir, and the hangman's rope was their prescription, and so these loud-voiced men went on from day to day disgracing the English name, making the situation worse, and the task of the governor of the day more difficult. Behind these blusterers stood the solid worth of the township farmers and the mercantile class, the true British party, silent yet ready, patient yet resolute.

Open Revolt.

It is of the nature of all agitations, that when they attain a certain degree of impetus, the leaders lose control, and instead of guiding are driven. It was so with Papineau. He had to go on. Casting aside all pretences about zeal for the constitution, he formally repudiated allegiance to Britain and declared his intention of forming an independent state, to be under the protection of the great Republic to the south. In order to strike the nation of shopkeepers in what he supposed was their vital part, the use of all goods of British make was to be shunned, and not a sixpence was to go from French-Canadian pockets to England. The Irish boycott was thus anticipated by seventy years. Only goods made in Canada, or that had been smuggled from the States, were to be bought. The smuggling of goods from the United States was declared to be perfectly honorable. Statutes passed by the Imperial Parliament, such as the tenures bill, were declared of non-effect. Steps were taken to organize local courts with judges elected by the people, a military organization was outlined, and a tax was levied to pay expenses, under the name of Papineau tribute. All this was possible everywhere outside the townships, and the creation of an independent government went on without hindrance in the parishes, which were exclusively French. The meetings were held on Sunday at the church doors after mass, and were so enthusiastic and unanimous that the habitants believed their purpose was achieved, and all that was needed was a combined effort, on a set day, to drive out the

English bureaucrats. It was an anxious time for those in office at Quebec and Montreal, and had it not been for the secret understanding with the bishops there would have been more cause for anxiety, but their aid was better than a reinforcement of a dozen regiments. Of what was passing in the parishes the authorities had full and accurate information from the priests, so that where danger menaced they knew how to meet it. A secret rising was now as impossible as a united one, and without a united rising there was not a ghost of success.

The Rebellion of 1837-8.

Though Papineau knew the priests had turned against him, so confident was he that the province was under his control he gave little weight to what they might do, and continued in the belief that, once he gave the signal, there would be simultaneous risings from Gaspe to Soulanges. He gave the signal. There was a sputtering response from a few localities only, and these confined to the vicinity of Montreal. More striking proof of the influence of the priests cannot be found. Here was a man who, for a generation, had been to the French-Canadians the embodiment of their patriotic aspirations, who had been swayed in thousands by his eloquence, who had been wrought by him to a pitch of enthusiastic fervor they have never since reached, yet, when the black robes passed the order, they turned their backs upon Papineau and paid no heed to his call. Outside of half a dozen parishes there was not a ripple of excitement: the entire Quebec district slept in unbroken placidity. Bowed to the earth by chagrin, baffled in the aspirations of a lifetime by the priests, Papineau fled to the United States. To add to the bitterness of his cup, there was an episode which showed him what might have been. The priest of St. Eustache was a rare exception to his class, for he was a Frenchman first, a Catholic afterwards. He dared to disobey the command of his bishop, rallied his people, and led them in fight. Had other priests done likewise, Papineau would have been the first President of the Republic of Quebec, for Colborne, in the face of a general rising, would have been helpless. He had only 5,000 soldiers to grapple with 400,000 people. When, after eight years' exile, Papineau returned, he had no use for the priests. At a great age, with death approaching, he rejected all suggestions to call in one. Their treason to his cause he could neither forget nor forgive.

The Government, believing all danger was past, dealt leniently with the defeated. After a brief term in jail, even leaders were allowed to go home. The anxiety on the part of the authorities to conciliate, to let bygones be bygones, was so apparent that the ignorant among the disaffected attributed their course to fear and weakness. A number of those who had been pardoned at once began to plot for a second rising. In this they were encouraged by their compatriots who had fled to the United States, and who, received with open arms by the Americans, sent word they would get substantial support from their new-found friends. On the American side of the frontier, from Ogdensburg to Derby Line, a secret society was organized to assist with men and arms a second rebellion. The secret was so well kept that the authorities were unaware of what was going on until the eve of the outbreak, which had been fixed for the 3rd of November, 1838. On the evening of that day, on the south side of the St. Lawrence, the habitants who were in the plot assembled in groups and began a house-to-house visitation of the English-speaking farmers. Doors were burst in and the men of the family, often found in bed, taken prisoners and marched to some chosen central point. Not all were taken prisoners; a Yorkshireman, who resisted, was murdered. Next morning the habitants formed columns to advance on the English settlements too large to be dealt with by surprise. The rising, however, was not general, and was confined to the territory lying west of Lake Champlain and between it and the St. Lawrence, where the English-speaking settlers were mostly Scotch or Ulster Irish, and who rallied at once to meet the advancing habitants, who hesitated, fell back, and instead of attacking, took up the defensive. There were isolated skirmishes, invariably ending in the flight of the deluded habitants. The chief stand was made where the Richelieu issues from Lake Champlain. There the habitants gathered, awaiting the arrival of the body of Americans who had promised to come and help them. When scarce three-score had come, and they were waiting for the arrival of more, a combined body of Irish Protestants and Catholics, with a few Scotch, appeared, and at once charged them. The habitants and their American sympathizers fled across the border, which was close behind them, leaving nine dead. Their best showing was made at a small village north of where this skirmish took place. There several hundred habitants assembled and had everything their own way for nigh a week. A constitution was adopted, the State of Lower Canada was duly proclaimed as a free and independent Republic, with Dr. Nelson as interim president. There was a great parade when the flag of the new Republic, white with two blue stars, was hoisted on the village flagpole, and saluted amid shouts and firing of muskets. Two officers from old France drilled the habitants, who were armed with rifles that came from the United States. Hearing that a body of English-speaking farmers were posted in a stone church not far distant, it was resolved to rout them and then capture St. Johns. Out from Lacolle marched 1,200 habitants, of whom at least 800 had muskets, the others pikes. Unawed by the approaching host, the 60 men who had crowded inside the little Methodist church, and the 150 behind such cover as the graveyard afforded, prepared to fight. A memorable struggle ensued. For two hours the little band held their own, when, hearing a report of an approaching reinforcement, panic seized the habitants, and they fled.

The second rebellion was over. I have narrated its leading features at some length, because it was put down by the English-speaking farmers, unaided by regular troops. Those who hold the rebellion in Quebec of 1837-8 was a struggle for constitutional freedom, have to account for Scotch radicals, many of whom had fled to Canada to escape prosecution, having been foremost in fighting the habitants. As Lord Sydenham wrote in 1840, the people of Ontario "quarrelled for realities, for political opinions, but in "Quebec there is no such thing as political opinion— "they have only one feeling, a hatred of race." The rebellion was the climax of a prolonged effort by the French to regain control of a province which had once been theirs, which had been taken from them by violence, and to establish it as an independent Republic. It was that, and nothing else.

The Bargain with the Priests.

The terms on which the priests agreed with the British authorities to assist in defeating Papineau and his associates included recognition of the division of the province into two dioceses, Quebec and Montreal, with Lartigue as bishop of Montreal, bestowing on the bishops authority to create new parishes and rearrange old ones, and to give to the Sulpicians the three seigniories they owned before the conquest. Sir John Colborne honorably carried out the bargain. An order-in-council recognized the new bishop, and ordinances were passed giving the power regarding parishes and conveying the seigniories to the Sulpicians. By a special Act of the Imperial Parliament the governor and council were empowered to enact any legislation necessary to carry on the business of the country; Durham made slight use of the Act, nothing more than was absolutely required. On the other hand, Colborne, or rather those behind him, took advantage of the opportunity to enact a mass of legislation, much of it

of an admirable nature, and all remarkably well
drafted. There was a limitation, however, to these
Acts, adopted by a small and irresponsible body of
councillors. They only held good to the end of 1842,
by which time it was expected the new Legislature
would be organized, and which would ratify these
ordinances.

At the conquest, a question that had to be settled
was: What is to be done with monastic institutions?
The course adopted by General Amherst, on his occupying Montreal, was that followed by the Imperial
authorities for three-quarters of a century. The nuns
were left as they were. The property of the male
orders was taken possession of by the Crown, provision
being made for the maintenance of those dispossessed
until their death. The rule was promptly applied to
the Jesuits and Recollets, but with forbearance to the
Sulpicians, as being a teaching body, and therefore
useful to carry out Carleton's plan of a native clergy.
All three were forbidden to receive novices, or to re-
inforce their number from abroad, so that governors
considered it merely a question of time when the last
of those under vows would die, when the Crown would
enter quietly into full possession of their property.
This is what happened with the Jesuits and Recollets.
The Sulpicians were saved from the same fate by the
French revolution. Among the refugees were members of the mother-house in Paris. Pitying their plight,
they were permitted by the governor to find a home
with the aged survivors of the order in Montreal.
These also would have become extinct, and the Crown
entered into possession of its long-deferred heritage,
had not a second revolution rent France. The Sulpicians, alarmed by the rising in 1830, a second time
fled from Paris to Montreal, and were again permitted
to take up their abode in the pleasant buildings at
Montreal. All this was illegal. The Sulpician order
had been prohibited by an Imperial law; the members
representing it in Canada were now of French birth

and citizenship and therefore could not legally hold real estate. All the same, these priests of old France, expelled from their native land, given a home out of pity for their misfortunes, no sooner were fairly settled than they claimed to be owners of what legally belonged to their benefactors. To make that out, they would have had to prove that there was such a thing in English law as right of succession in monastic orders, which it would be absurd to try, so they sought their end by other means. They made friends with the agitators, and got them to take up their cause. How this came about needs a word of explanation. When Amherst took possession of Montreal it was chiefly a miserable collection of log houses, worth less than the buildings of the church which towered above them. All told, when the English passed inside its walls, Montreal had not three thousand inhabitants. The island was only cleared in patches, few settlers being located north of the mountain. The Sulpicians were seigniors of the island of Montreal, and drew its rents, which were small. The coming of British rule made a marvellous change. The paltry town, whose chief characteristic was its monastic institutions, became commercial. Its trade grew by leaps and bounds. It was the same outside the town limits. The crash of falling trees was heard, clearances were made, and the influence of Scotch farming began to tell in the productiveness of crops. All this prosperity enhanced the value of the island as a seigniory, and the revenue of a few hundred dollars a year grew into tens of thousands. A lawyer of the time who investigated the Seminary's affairs, reported that the fines on sales of property put into the priests' pockets the assessed value of the city every forty years. When governors had difficulty in meeting payment of current expenses, owing to the Assembly refusing to vote supplies, it was proposed the government complete the transfer of the property of the Sulpicians, and, by using its revenue for civil service salaries, become independent of the Assembly. Papineau, who cared naught for the Sulpicians, saw the danger to his cause of such a move, and prevented it by making their case his own, and he fiercely denounced all attempts to disturb the Sulpicians. He measured not the selfishness nor the ingratitude of ecclesiastics. When they had profited by his exertions in the abandonment of the plan contemplated, and saw the opportunity of making friends with the government by betraying the cause Papineau represented, they did so. The price agreed on, was confirming the Sulpicians in the property they occupied. The influence of the priests was suddenly thrown against Papineau and his followers, and every movement revealed to the authorities, with the result already recorded. So highly did Sir John Colborne estimate the services of the Sulpician priests, that he hurried to fulfil his part of the bargain. The echoes of the rebellion had not subsided, Montreal jail was still filled with untried prisoners, when he got an ordinance-in-council passed vesting in them absolutely the estates they claimed. This ordinance the home authorities disallowed as outside the powers of the council. However, when the first union parliament met in 1841, among the bills it passed was one conveying to the Sulpicians the property they coveted. It was valuable then, it is incomparably more valuable to-day. The advent of Protestants in Quebec, while it ended its days as a purely Papal preserve, enriched the priests who resented their appearance. The skill and enterprise of Protestants have made the island of Montreal the richest spot in Canada, and every square foot of it worth more than an acre was when under French rule. Out of the increase of values the priests of St. Sulpice have reaped what they never earned, and are the richest corporation in the Dominion. The treasure heaps, accumulated by monks and nuns out of the unearned increment due to the trade of Protestants in town and city, form a factor in supplying the money needed in the removal of Protestants from the rural sections.

Ready as the Legislature was to ratify the transfer of the three seigniories to the Sulpicians, they balked at re-enacting the ordinance regarding parishes.

CHAPTER VII.

Before and after Confederation

The rebellion destroyed the form of government provided by the Canada Act, and placed the province in the same condition as it was at the Conquest, under military rule. The Imperial authorities for the third time were given a free hand as to what the government of Quebec should be. It was an unlooked for opportunity to write a new constitution on a clean sheet, profiting by the errors of the past—avoiding the mistakes which eighty years' experience had made manifest. This was realized at London and Lord Durham was appointed to go and study the problem of Quebec's future government on the spot and report what was best to be done. Lord Durham spent about a year in Canada, and the result of what he saw and learned was a report which is esteemed for its grasp of the principles of popular government and the admirable form in which he expressed his views. The Act of 1841, uniting Ontario and Quebec, is generally spoken of as the result of Lord Durham's advice. This is not correct. His report shows that he was convinced the difficulties in carrying on the government of Quebec arose from allowing in the past privileges inconsistent with British institutions, and his advice was that Quebec be brought into harmony with the rest of the Empire. As a means of bringing this about he favored Quebec's union with Ontario. He wanted a complete fusion—a merging of the people of the two Provinces into one, with one law and one administration of law, no discrimination to be allowed on account of faith or origin, but an effort to be :made, so far as legislation could effect it, of assimilation by the effacing of all differences. This was the kernel of his plan. It was rejected by the framers of the Act of 1841, who left the custom of Paris untouched and continued the priests in all their privileges. Once again did the authorities in London miss an opportunity to convert Quebec into a genuine portion of the British Empire. Instead, they left it with all the elements that had caused disquiet and rebellion in the past, and which, assuredly, would give rise to like disasters in the future. The foreign substances in the body politic of the Province of Quebec, which, for three generations, had induced feverish restlessness, were left, and a cure attempted by moving the refractory one into a larger room and linking him to a peaceable member of the Empire. All the statesmanlike suggestions of Lord Durham were ignored, and the only one partially acted upon was to unite Quebec with Ontario in a joint legislature. It was a forced union, resented alike by French and English. The French, knowing its purpose was to keep them in check, naturally detested it; the English of Ontario did not like an alien people having a voice in ruling them. The first meeting of the members was like a mixture of oil and water—together yet apart. That meeting took place in Kingston, the city identified with Sir John Macdonald, and to him the gathering was one of lively interest. He sketched that first meeting in his after years—the French members clustered in a group apart, sullen, suspicious of every proposal made, resenting all approaches, standing on the defensive: the English-speaking members careless of their presence, if not contemptuous. He made friends with the solid French contingent, sore from recent defeat and forced into a union it was their constant study to break. When, three years later, Macdonald became a member of the

Assembly, he began the plan he had contemplated, of
getting into power through an alliance with them.
Others besides him saw the opportunity, which was,
indeed, apparent. In any deliberative gathering where
votes tell, a sufficient number of members who stand
aloof from their fellows and are fixed upon one purpose, can, eventually, win control. The Ontario members were split into factions, the English-speaking members from Quebec voted with whoever controlled the
patronage, so it came the solid French phalanx soon
held the balance of power. In it, after the first election, there was an appearance of division. Remembering the cause of the collapse of the rebellion, many
young men who had taken part in it argued the priest
ought to have no voice in politics, and their views,
advocated in two papers, L'Avenir and Le Pays, provoked those who differed into preaching absolute submission to the clergy. The one was styled in reproach
at first, for it was the appellation of the revolutionists
of France, by the name rouge, the others came to be
known as bleus. As this difference about the priests
has disappeared, the rouge of our day vying with the
bleu in doing their will, it does not concern the situation of the Protestant minority. What does concern
that minority is, that as a consequence of the prolonged agitation that ended in rebellion, the idea was
firmly ingrained in the minds of the habitants that
Quebec was theirs by right and all others were intruders. Each session of the new legislature made it more
plain, that the very object which the union of the two
Provinces was designed to bring about—control of the
priest-directed element—had been lost, and the union
as a remedy for the evil it was designed to cure, was
a disastrous failure. The parliamentary history of
Canada between 1841 and 1867 is, in essence, a narrative of how, step by step, Quebec obtained dominance.
The first notable advance was in 1845, when a petition
to the Imperial Government was carried, asking that
French be authorized as an official language. No notice
was taken of the request. In 1848, when the re-elec-

tion of Sir Allan McNab was proposed as Speaker of
the Assembly, Robt. Baldwin objected, because McNab
did not speak English. He nominated A. N. Morin,
Lafontaine seconded, and McNab was rejected. Still
the Imperial Government refused to recognize French
as an official language of the House, but, on representations made the following year, it gave its consent and
so amended the Union Act. This was only one of several changes the French members obtained by bargaining with their English colleagues. The supremacy of
Quebec, however, was not absolute until Sir John Macdonald and Cartier took office on the understanding
that no bill affecting Quebec should become law unless
supported by a majority of its members. Such a basis
of action destroyed the principle of the Act of 1841.

The Parish System Extended.

The priesthood now saw their opportunity to obtain
the power they had long desired, but had despaired
of getting, and which they certainly never would have
got but for the union of 1841. The Quebec Act of 1774
confined the parish system to the seigniories. The territory within which it should exist was thus definitely
fixed. Wherever land was held in fief, the priest could
tax and tithe. The moment he crossed the boundary-
line of a seigniory into land held in free and common
soccage, he could claim no more privilege than a Methodist preacher. This was galling to the priests, who
desired to throw the net of the parish system over
every acre of Quebec. The seigniories had become
overcrowded, the land had been divided and subdivided until the majority of the habitants were in
poverty, yet they were in sight of unconceded lands
into which their priests would not incite them to go
because they would be free of the parish system. Lord
Sydenham, in the summer of 1840, made a three days'
trip up the valley of the Richelieu. Writing a friend
he remarks: "The counties bordering the Richelieu
"were formerly the garden of Lower Canada, the soil
"rich to a degree, but they are now used up completely
"by the abominable mode of cultivation pursued by

"the habitants, and present a melancholy picture; the
"population rapidly increasing, and the people un-
"willing to quit their neighborhood and settle on new
"lands until actually starved out." The Act of William IV. related solely to parishes in the seigniories;
the ordinance passed by the Council after the rebellion
failed to be ratified by the legislature. A second attempt was made in 1843, but the bill was killed in
committee. Three years later the priests had it again
submitted, and again it was not reported to the House.
In 1849 it reappeared, but was dropped in its initial
stage. It was not until Baldwin and Lafontaine were
in office that the bill was hurried through its several
stages without attracting attention. It not merely declared the ordinance of 1839 valid, but added to its
provisions. What was glaringly illegal, it ignored the
fact that the ordinance was dead, from not being ratified by the legislature within the prescribed delay of
two years, and in confirming all proceedings that had
been taken under it up to the adoption of the new Act.
The Act received the governor's assent on the 10th of
August, 1850, so that for nine years the bishops had
been erecting parishes illegally. It is right to place
the responsibility of the existence of the parish system
in Quebec where it belongs. It was Baldwin and his
Ontario followers who restored it and gave it new life.

The priests got more than legislative aid in extending the parish system. They obtained for the first
time, legal authority for their organizations. Monastic orders by the dozen received acts of incorporation,
followed by grants from the public treasury and the
public domain, under the guise of charity and education. Among these bills was one fraught with disastrous consequences. It was an innocent appearing
bill, professing to incorporate a new college in Montreal. Just a bill to add to the educational facilities of
that growing city, declared its promoters, and none of
the Ontario members had wit enough to inquire who
the persons were who asked to be incorporated. They
were Jesuits, proscribed by law, and who, in this cun-

ning manner, regained, after the lapse of ninety years, a legal footing in Canada. But for the passage of that bill, incorporating St. Mary's College, the Jesuits might never have obtained legal recognition in Canada. When, in 1887, the Federal parliament was asked to incorporate the Jesuit Society, many members revolted at the proposal. Sir John Thompson, then Minister of Justice, declared the bill was merely a form, for it only recognized what the legislature had done in 1854. By granting a charter to St. Mary's College in 1854 Canada incorporated its faculty, who were Jesuits. He was, asked, Why do they now need further incorporation? and answered evasively. The act he supported covered an even deeper design than the innocent appearing act of 1854.

A Special Privilege is a General Wrong.

In any country where there is a privileged class, it necessarily follows there must be a class that is discriminated against. There is no escaping this social law. Whatever is given to a favored portion of the population, places those who are outside of it at a corresponding disadvantage. It is a self-apparent axiom, that in any country where there is not equality of rights, there is no true freedom, for some class must be suffering wrong. To give privileges to a select few, is to do injustice to the many. Of all forms of inequality the most objectionable is singling out a particular church for special favors, because doing so is not merely repugnant to our innate sense of justice, but offends the conscience. In the session of 1841 and those that followed, the members of Ontario had an opportunity of vindicating the great principle upon which freedom rests, by building a system of government which would have given equal rights. Instead of doing so, they were false to the principles which they professed, and, for the sake of personal or party advantage, sold their principles to secure the votes of members who held their mandate from their priests. In the history of self-governing countries, there is nothing more disgraceful than the course pursued by Ontario's representatives from 1841 to 1867.

With the Conquest the priests entered a condition of sufferance; their next step was a power to be propitiated for the sake of the favors they could bestow. They now blossomed into supremacy. During the last seventeen years of the union the priests got whatever they sought and in Quebec they were buttressed by statutes and enriched by government donations of land and money by the votes of Ontario members. One member realized the extent of the evil, but failed to perceive its cure. The remedy of George Brown, representation by population, was the old delusion in a new guise, that the difficulty that arose from Quebec could be overcome by force of numbers, instead of plucking that difficulty out by the roots. Had representation by population been adopted it would have failed, for it would have been found that, from their solidarity, the Quebec members would still have held the balance of power, and continued to rule Ontario. The lakelet may absorb a river, but will be governed by its ebb and flow and its waters be dyed by it. Only a sea can assimilate what rolls into its bosom, and there is no prospect that the population of the Dominion will ever be so large or of such a character that it will neutralize priestly influence. Those who say there is no call for present action; if we wait until the Northwest attain its growth; the many members it will send to Ottawa will dispose of the difficulties arising from Quebec; may realize they are mistaken if they study the experience of the past. In 1841 it was confidently asserted the introduction of Ontario members would raise an impassable barrier to the influence that was making Quebec a Papal state. They did not. When Confederation was brought about, George Brown and his followers exultantly proclaimed clericalism in politics had received its deathblow. It did not: it is the most potent force to-day in our politics.

Double Majority Tried.

The danger to the state, caused by the existence of a numerous organization of priests seeking supreme control, has to be faced squarely, and the sooner, there will be the less friction. Had Brown traced the wrongs he deplored to their source, he would have applied himself to effecting in Quebec what he helped to do in a measure in Ontario, namely, to bring about complete separation of Church and State. Instead, he spent his strength in advocating an increase in the number of members for Ontario, which was no remedy, for there was no probability of the new members being any more resolute in grappling with clericalism than those then sitting. The government was carried on with daily increasing difficulty, and by adopting the miserable devices of shifty politicians. Sandfield MacDonald's remedy, double majority, was the act of a coward, who, instead of facing a difficulty, evades it. The members of each province were to decide bills affecting their respective provinces, and when there was not a majority of the members concerned in favor of such a bill, it was to be dropped, even if a majority of the united house was in its favor. When a crucial case arose, MacDonald showed the cloven foot. The priests pressed for Separate Schools in Ontario. It was a bill that concerned Ontario alone, and therefore, according to the rule under which the House was acting, should have been left to the Ontario members to decide. On a division being called it was found a majority of the Ontario members had voted against the bill, but a large majority of the Quebec members were for it. In consistency with his rule of double majority the Premier should have withdrawn the bill. Instead of doing so, MacDonald refused to apply his own principle to the bill, and Separate Schools were forced on Ontario by the votes of the Quebec members. No greater calamity has befallen Ontario.

At the core of all wrong there is an antidote.

Wherever any selfish interest moulds a legislature to its will, whether a combination of manufacturers, railway projectors, or a church, the members it wins to its support become corrupt. The Ontario members who did violence to their convictions by acting with the Quebec majority, lowered their moral standard and became self-seekers. Sir John Macdonald, though the most careless of men about his own pecuniary advantage, knew how to win support by exercising the potent lever of self-interest. Whether in the bar-room of the House, slapping members on the back, joking and telling lewd stories, or on the floor replying to grave arguments with gestures, quirks, and jeers that raised the laugh, he was master of his following. Cartier seconded him effectively by using the Quebec votes as a bludgeon to defeat opposition. When in his peculiar, rasping voice the order was heard: Call in de members, discussion ended.

On the floor of the House, at a session in Kingston, Brown declared thirty-five of the Quebec members did not, from imperfect knowledge of English, know what was being done, and that they voted blindly as Cartier ordered them. Each election saw a larger proportion who had mastered English, without decreasing their servility to Cartier. All went swimmingly until the venality of members turned the moral sense of Ontario against the Macdonald-Cartier combination, and its candidates could not secure re-election. Then there was a deadlock—the end of the union of 1841 had come. There was no questioning as to the cause of the deadlock, it was admittedly the thrusting of the will of the priests of Quebec on Ontario. To take steps that, for the future, they should have no hand in the government of the country would have been the remedy of statesmen. The party politicians to whom the solving of the difficulty fell were intent alone on getting the machinery of the state again in motion— the Conservatives to enjoy a new lease of office, the Liberals, long shut out, eager for a coalition, that they might share in honors and patronage. For several weeks George Brown had it in his power to force on the electorate a decision as to separation of Church and State: instead he paltered with the greatest tactician Canada has known, and was circumvented.

Confederation.

There was in progress at the time a conference of representatives of the Maritime Provinces to merge their three legislatures into one. Sir John suggested a larger union, that Quebec and Ontario be included. The idea fascinated both Conservatives and Liberals, and was agreed to. It was only when the form of the new government came to be considered differences arose. In 1866 the experience of the American Republic was fresh in the minds of all. The two great lessons that war taught were, first, the impossibility of having a stable government where a moral evil exists; second, the danger of divided authority. Had slavery not existed there would have been no war in 1861: had the Federal Government been stronger, it could have nipped the revolt in the bud. The latter fact had deeply impressed Sir John Macdonald and he was for a strong central authority, and that could only be assured by having a legislative union. In this he had the support of his English-speaking followers, while Cartier and his colleagues would not hear of it. They had long conferences with their bishops, and the ultimatum delivered was, whatever the other provinces might do, Quebec must have a government of her own. They insisted, writes one who knew of what passed at these secret meetings, "that the Catholics of Quebec "must be conceded the right to govern themselves by "truly Catholic laws." Sir John Macdonald stood out for a legislative union, with guarantees to Quebec, until he saw that was impossible. The demand of the priests for provincial autonomy appealed to the office-hunters of both parties. Why should each province not preserve its integrity, with their multiplicity of offices, and add to them the patronage of the central government that is to be created? Instead of the provincial governments being blotted out, with their lieutenant-governors, cabinet ministers, members and departmental officials, they will all continue, and to them will be added the positions that the Federal system will bring into existence. This appeal to cupidity and love of distinction was irresistible, and Cartier found so many allies among the Protestant politicians for retaining the autonomy of the provinces that Macdonald had to acquiesce, and the draft of a constitution on that basis was prepared. Sir John Macdonald and those who shared his views, comforted themselves with the belief that such a complex and expensive system would not work, and that it would eventually be abandoned for legislative union, giving to each province a magnified type of county council to attend to purely local matters and its own public works. At the consecration of a new church at St. Johns, Que., Cartier presented a copy of the proposed constitution to Bishop Bourget, who received it with the injunction that no further steps be taken until he reported. He considered it with his confreres, and finally sent it to the propaganda at Rome, which returned it with its endorsation. A constitution relating to British colonies had to receive the Papal stamp before it went before the legislatures of the people affected. The constitution withheld from the direct vote of the people of Canada was sent abroad for a foreigner to consider! The French-Canadian already quoted from states, "Had it not been for Quebec there would have been no "provincial legislatures, as all the other provinces, "except Quebec, being Protestant in majority, one "parliament would have been sufficient for all. Que-"bec dictated the constitution of 1867."

In proof that this is a correct statement, it is well to quote the testimony of Sir John Macdonald. There are many so-called "Fathers of Confederation": he alone is entitled to whatever honor the name confers.

It was his fertility of resource, his astuteness in seeing what was possible with the conditions that existed, his dexterity in handling the sort of men he had to work with, that effected the passage of the B.N.A. Act. In 1872 there was a long debate in the House of Commons over Mr. Costigan's motion that the Act of the New Brunswick Legislature regarding separate schools be disallowed. During the discussion Sir John declared, "I believe we might have had a legislative union in-"stead of a Federal union if it had not been for the "Province of Quebec. They insisted on a legislature "having the power to act as they pleased. The Lower "Canadians drew themselves up and said, If the con-"stitution were not so drawn up as to give them the "power to protect beyond a doubt their institutions, "their religion, their language, and their laws, in "which they had so great pride, they would never con-"sent to a union, and if we had not agreed to that, we "should not now have had the Dominion of Canada."

It was agreed to copy the American system, to substitute a Federal for the existing legislative union. Ontario and Quebec were to separate, each to be autonomous and self-governing as regards local affairs, with a Federal House to deal with matters common to them and the other provinces who had agreed to join. That the old difficulty would spring up in course of time under the new system was self-apparent, but it would not be in the day of the framers of the constitution of 1867 and a future generation could grapple with it.

The Quebec Minority.

There were no compunctions as to leaving the English-speaking people of Quebec to the rule of the majority. Protests from the minority against their abandonment were treated as the expressions of bigots. It was represented on behalf of the Quebec majority that there was nothing to fear, that the Protestants would be the objects of their most considerate care. McGee scouted the idea that the Protestant minority would be in any way injured. He declared they would be the pets of the majority, the spoiled children of the new Dominion, that they would be smothered with kindness. Others, whom such gush did not blind, thought the minority could not suffer with a preponderating Protestant influence in the Federal House, while there were many who looked on Confederation as a temporary stage, bound to quickly end in a legislative union. The representatives of the minority gave little opposition. Party allegiance constrained a number to silence; others were bribed by promises of office. Besides, there was a great hullabaloo about loyalty, which blinded many. It was loyal to support the proposed Act of Confederation—loyal to break the solid colonial connection which insured Canada being one and inseparable with the Motherland! Those who opposed Confederation were denounced as annexationists at heart, a singular charge, seeing the main principle of the new constitution was copied from the Republic. There were protests from isolated bodies of electors in the Eastern Townships; no notice was taken of them.

Separate Schools Fastened on Ontario.

The one danger in the eyes of many Protestants in Quebec was the educational. Their cry was, Make our schools secure and we will support Confederation. Sir A. T. Galt assured them he would meet their views by getting a clause added to the constitution that the schools of the Quebec minority would be continued as they were, and that should any complaint arise of invasion of this provision appeal could be made to the Federal parliament. The submission of this amendment to the delegates who were deliberating on the constitution gave the Ontario priests an opportunity of gaining what they were eagerly seeking, but had despaired of obtaining. The constitution, as drafted, placed education in the hands of the legislatures of the several provinces. This was exactly what the priests desired as regards Quebec, for it put its schools in their hands. Their attitude towards the rest of

Canada was different. For instance, the Ontario legislature would be largely made up of Protestants and they did not wish it should control the schools. The plan that suited them in Quebec they did not want elsewhere: what they demanded for the Quebec legislature, leaving the schools in its grasp, they wanted withheld from all the rest of Canada. They knew that the separate school system had been fastened on Ontario against her will, and they dreaded its repeal, now that Ontario was going to get self-government in the matter of education. Galt's proposed amendment came to them as a providential intervention, for they saw how they could use it as a lever to keep the Ontario legislature from repealing the Separate School Act. Cartier was the mouthpiece of the priests. He said to his fellow-delegates, If we concede this amendment of Galt's to the minority in Quebec, we must have the same security for the schools of the minority in Ontario. That sounded fair to the unreflecting, and it would have been just had the schools of the two minorities been of the same character, but they were utterly unlike.

The Schools of the Quebec Minority.	The Schools of the Ontario Minority
Were the the schools of the people, controlled by the people and in whose management no Church had a voice;	Were the schools of the Church of Rome, controlled by its clergy and designed for the children of its members;
Their chief purpose was the imparting of secular knowledge;	Their chief purpose was imparting the doctrines of the Church of Rome and training the scholars in its ritual;
The end they aimed at was to prepare the children to be useful citizens;	The end aimed at being to ensure the scholars would be Roman Catholics, secular knowledge had a secondary and much inferior place;
Their schools were open to Jew and Gentile, the only requirement of parents being, Do you desire your child to learn to read, write and count?	Confessional Schools which only parents who wished their children to be Roman Catholics would patronize.

The purposes of the two classes of schools were as different as day is from night. The one sought to make intelligent citizens, moulding Canadians into a broad brotherhood; the prime purpose of the other, to perpetuate and strengthen religious divisions and the rule of the priests. Yet those schools, so dissimilar in character, management, and the ends they were designed to accomplish, the one the schools of the people, the other the schools of a caste, Cartier and Langevin insisted were exactly on the same footing, and whatever guarantee was conceded to the schools of the Quebec minority must be extended to the schools of the Ontario minority. The effrontery of the claim, that the schools of the two minorities were in the same category, was palpable, yet neither Sir John Macdonald nor George Brown objected. They gave in to the monstrous demand of the priests. Galt's clause was amended as asked by Cartier, thereby placing the Quebec minority in the ignominious position of holding their free and non-sectarian schools dependent on Ontario's legislature continuing confessional schools. Not only that, but by the same stroke, Ontario was robbed of that free control of education which the constitution as first drafted gave her as a right. In all Canada's history there is no more iniquitous transaction. The non-Catholics of Quebec prayed for protection against the possibility of having their free, open, non-sectarian schools changed into confessional schools. It was a reasonable request and ought to have been granted without condition. The priests took advantage of the circumstances under which the non-Catholics of Quebec found themselves and exacted a price for what they were entitled to as a right, by having inserted in the Act of Confederation that the tenure of their schools should be dependent upon the continuance of confessional schools in another province—if the legislature of Ontario abolished separate schools, the schools of the Quebec minority would be abolished also, and parents be left to the unhappy choice of keeping them at home or of sending their children to schools taught by nuns and brothers. The existence of the public school in Quebec was made dependent upon the life of the priest-school in Ontario. The Quebec minority was wronged and so were the people of Ontario by the shameful intrigue by which they have fastened on them, for all time, so far as the B. N. A. Act can do it, the Separate Schools that had been, in the first place, imposed upon them by Quebec votes. Galt ought to have withdrawn the clause he submitted when he heard the price on which it alone would be passed. Those who speak of the framers of Confederation as statesmen may take this as one instance of several, of what poor creatures their political idols were when faced by the priests.

The Passage of the B. N. A. Act.

That the provinces could have continued much longer distinct was impossible. With separate tariffs, no method to promote intercourse between themselves, no means to combine in making representations abroad on questions jointly affecting them, or to unite in the redeeming of the Northwest from savagery, a union of the provinces had to come. The pity is, it should have been accomplished at the time and with the object it immediately served. A constitutional deadlock had arisen between Quebec and Ontario, caused by the clashing of Church and State. The remedy, the removal of all semblance of connection between the two, the politicians of the day would not face. They evaded the difficulty for the time being, by resorting to a union of all the provinces. Confederation was supported by the leaders of the two parties in Quebec and Ontario as a device to leave the connection between Church and State as it was, partially releasing Ontario from the grip of the priests while strengthening their hold on Quebec. Confederation prolonged the life of an evil, the meddling of the priests with the Government of the country; an evil which ought to have been dealt with in 1866, and which, assuredly, will yet have to be dealt with, for it is inconceivable that a free people will continue to submit to their government being subject to the influence of any church; that cardinal, archbishop or ablegate has to be consulted, and his views deferred to when a question comes before parliament in which the priests claim a voice. The right of the people to have their affairs managed by a parliament and administered by an executive, free from clerical dictation, is self-apparent. In copying the American plan of union, the framers of the Act of 1867 did not base it upon equal rights. An article forbidding the Federal Parliament and the legislatures to give preference to any church would have ensured peace and permanence. The United States constitution carefully avoided the subject of negro slavery; doing so resulted in the greatest civil war the world has known. Those who drafted the Act of Confederation as carefully refrained from touching the supremacy of the priest. A generation to come will know the consequences. The commercial advantages of Confederation have been great, so great that they have blinded people to the fact that it was a cowardly evasion of performing a plain duty. The British North America Act carries in it the seeds of future trouble. Its adoption simply postponed an inevitable conflict.

The parliamentary debate on Confederation was, strictly speaking, not a debate. The resolutions for Confederation were placed before the members to be adopted as they stood. Where amendment was forbidden it was absurd to debate. The sole advantage of summoning the House was giving the framers of the resolutions an opportunity for explanation. Those who were against the resolutions were free to state their objections without hope of changing a single word in them. Adopting a new constitution without receiving a mandate at a general election was bad, but calling parliament to consider it without the power to amend was a farce. Few of the speeches contained in the bulky volume which professes to report the doings of the session were delivered. Members wrote what they would like to go on record, and, after speaking a short time, passed their MS. to the reporters. In the discussion over a measure they were incompetent to amend, one true voice was raised. Col. Haultain, member for Peterboro', asked whether it was just to ignore the aversion of the Protestants residing in the townships of Quebec to Confederation, because it would place them at the mercy of an intolerant priesthood. Their suspicions and fears found confirmation in the encyclical letter of the Pope which had been just promulgated. In the syllabus, which accompanied it, of errors to be condemned, was "that emigrants to "Catholic countries should have freedom of worship." He who spoke thus is the head of the controlling influence in Quebec, and the fears, therefore, of the minority were not unreasonable, when called upon to put themselves into the power of the priesthood, for, to them, that was what Confederation meant. The Colonel was jeered by members who had declined committing themselves to the support of Confederation until the scheme had been submitted to the Pope and received his approval. The petition to the Imperial authorities to pass the Act of Confederation was carried by 91 to 33.

Confederation Gave Quebec What Papineau Sought.

Confederation bestowed on Quebec substantially what Papineau had sought. She became an independent, self-governing Province, having a legislature of her own, her own civil service, her own cabinet, her own governor. In every regard, outside of inter-provincial relations, she was her own mistress. The concessions dazzled her public men, who proceeded as if the glories with which their imaginations had invested New France were to be revived. An imitation of the court of Frontenac was established at Spencerwood, the Lieutenant-Governor was styled His Excellency, and there were pretensions heard and ceremonies witnessed that bespoke exultation and satisfaction. To the minority there was also a revival of epithets long unheard, and the distinction of rebellion times between the children of the soil and intruders was again drawn. The assumptions of the laity were not to be compared, however, with those of the priests. Confederation had restored to them greater plenitude of power than they had enjoyed when Louis was King, and they used it to the full. Sir A. T. Galt, quickly realizing the mistake he had made in supporting Confederation, in a pamphlet summarized the dangers which menaced the minority, instancing the assertion of ecclesiastical over civil authority, clerical interference with elections, placing the ban on free speech and on the press, that divine assistance in teaching whatever touches on faith and morals descends from the Pope to bishops, priests, and religieuses. As a politician he had been shocked by a united condemnation on the part of the bishops of Liberalism, by priests being upheld in contested elections who had denounced individuals as guilty of a grave sin in voting for candidates who had not received their approval, and especially by a judge laying down as law that as priests belonged to a spiritual order they were above civil law and beyond the jurisdiction of the courts. There were decisions recognizing canon law, and burial was refused in the parish cemetery to the body of a man because he had been a member of a society which had declared for the principle of religious toleration. Public men made it their boast, that their obedience to the bishops was implicit and unreserved, and, in pleading before electors, held this up as a claim for support, rival candidates competing on the hustings in deprecating each other's loyalty to the bishops. It was a period of distressful explanations by Liberals and of exultant boastings by Conservatives. A new style of journalism was developed, which was happily characterized as more Catholic than the Pope. In this period of reactionary effervescence the Castors rose into prominence. A sign of the times was the annotator of the Quebec statutes putting in the marginal notes "the decrees of the Pope are binding." A bill was submitted to the legislature to place in all courts of justice a large crucifix. To swear a witness he was to "lift his right "hand in front of the crucifix and place his left hand "on the book of the evangelists." The bill was in a fair way to pass, having got its second reading, when the outrage on conscience, in compelling Protestants to take oath in such a way, became apparent to the Ministers, who caused Mr. Lemieux to withdraw his bill.

The Demands of the Priests.

An important part of the duty of every legislature is to make provision for the relief of those who are mentally or physically unfit to care for themselves. The priests demanded that the lunatic asylums, reformatories and refuges, hitherto controlled by government, be handed over to them, and their demand was complied with. They were at once placed in charge of monks and nuns, who reject interference by the legislature, for, by virtue of their vows and ordination, nuns and monks, professing to be of a heavenly class, do not recognize the superintendence of laymen, though most persistent in seeking larger grants of money and lands. Institutions, which had been public, thus became sectarian and no longer accountable to the representatives of the people. If there be one distinguishing feature of self-government it is, that public money shall be controlled by the men in whose hands they place the spending of it. A legislature that divests itself of this high duty by handing over the money of the taxpayers en bloc to a select body of men to allot and spend, ceases to be independent and self-governing: it becomes the servant of the caste· to whom it has surrendered its powers. But the priests were not satisfied with the transference of the benevolent institutions of the province; they aimed higher—they demanded the sole control of its schools. They accomplished this by subtle changes in the wording

of the Education Act. In reconstructing the Council
of Public Instruction it was provided that all the
bishops should be members, and when they did not
attend they had the power to name a substitute. As
this privilege of appointing an alternate was not given
to the lay members, the result was that the bishops
were always in the majority. Thus the educational
system, by one fell swoop, was given into the hands
of the priests, the legislature divesting itself of what
it defines in the Act as part of the civil service; handing
over to ecclesiastics this important function, with
control of the expenditure of the public money for
school and college. How complete was the transference
was speedily illustrated. The government introduced
a bill to facilitate the working of the Education
Act. It was a simple measure of departmental detail.
The Archbishop of Quebec sent for the Premier, expressed
his disapproval and indignation at its being
introduced without consulting him. The bill was
hastily dropped, and the promise made, which is still
observed, that no measure affecting education shall
be introduced without being first submitted to him
and obtaining his approval.

The Jesuit Estates Act.

Could a more striking instance be given of a legislature
calling itself British surrendering its sovereign
and exclusive right to make laws to an irresponsible
caste? It was thought at the time there could not,
but, in 1888, the subserviency of deBoucherville was
eclipsed. No priest wrought so persistently to bring
Quebec under ecclesiastical rule as Bishop Bourget.
To assist in doing so he determined to invite the
Jesuits. The statute proscribing that order had not
been repealed, but the bishop trusted to the spirit of
the times that it would not be enforced. He invited
the General of the Jesuits to renew the tradition of
his order in Canada, who, after inquiry, agreed, and,
in 1842, sent six fathers. These six priests, after sur-

veying the field, proceeded to take steps to found a college, which resulted in the rearing of a large building in Montreal. Whoever cares to look over a parliamentary guide will see how many members, both at Ottawa and Quebec, received their training in St. Mary's College, Loyola College, or the branch at Quebec, and will realize how deeply, through the men imbued with its principles in those chosen seats, Jesuitism influences our politics, and shapes the destinies of the Dominion. These newly-arrived Jesuits and their successors described to their pupils the confiscation of the Jesuit estates by King George, at the conquest, as an act of spoliation, and claimed that compensation ought to be made. None of the scores of young men who passed through their hands and rose high in the political world dared to propose that the Jesuits be compensated for the act of a British administration until Mercier appeared. Visiting Rome he made a proposition to the General of the Order of Jesus, which he afterwards submitted to the Pope, who ratified it. On the assembling of the legislature Mercier introduced a resolution to pay out of the public funds $460,000 as compensation to the order for the estates the Crown had declared public property more than a century before, together with a portion of the seigniory of Laprairie. In effect, this was equivalent to saying the British Government had been guilty of robbery, and the Catholics of Quebec having got the power into their own hands, were now going to make restitution. Never before did a legislature calling itself British so insult the Crown to which it paid lip-allegiance. There were members who staggered at the proposal. Mercier, before the vote was taken, asked the Catholic members to remember their allegiance was first to the head of their church, that the Pope had approved of the resolution before them, that the ecclesiastical authorities said the legislature were holding property that did not belong to them, and if they did not make restitution the members of the government and of the legislature would find themselves subject to certain spiritual penalties. To the Protestant members his menace took another form. If any of them dared to oppose the motion they would not be re-elected. He would remind them of the fact that French-Canadians held the balance of power in the counties they represented, and they would crush, by their votes, any member who opposed the measure.

The resolution was adopted, and the bill founded upon it passed. To none of the guarantees for the rights of the minority, which he got inserted in the Act of Confederation, did Sir A. T. Galt attach the same weight as that of appeal to the Federal Parliament, which he described as their real palladium. It was now to be tested. The principle involved there was no mistaking—was it lawful for the Quebec Legislature to pass a bill whose preamble recognized the Pope's authority; was it lawful for the Quebec Legislature to tax Protestants to make a present to the Jesuit Society? An appeal was made to Ottawa to veto what had been done at Quebec. The appeal was rejected by 188 to 13. The money was paid to the Jesuits and the land transferred, and the delusion about guarantees shattered.

CHAPTER VIII.

The Supplanting of the English-speaking Farmers

Supposing a number of men, ambitious of obtaining power over their fellows, organized themselves into an oath-bound society, and, further supposing, in carrying out their plans, they found it required the driving away of people who were hostile to them, would not their first move be to get control of the land? Possession of the soil means sovereignty. Villages and towns may decay and become effete, but the soil remains, and to whoever the men who plow and reap pay allegiance, will be the actual, though they may not be the nominal, rulers. The priests having got a legislature that was their creature, were absolute in every part of Quebec except in those sections where the land had been grants of the British Crown. To exercise the same domination over that land as they did in the old seigniories was their purpose. The assault was first upon the Eastern Townships, and the priests thrust into them two wedges to effect their purpose, the parish system and separate schools. Bring these free townships under parish law and the English-speaking farmers will not want to stay; deprive them of their public schools and reduce them to the alternative of sending their children to confessional schools, and they will be compelled to go. In the days of Louis XIV. brute force would have been used—

subtler and as effective means were found in perversions of the law. The crude idea, that the remotest approach to persecution was resorted to, is to be swept aside. The priests, relentless as Dominic in seeking ascendency, carried out their purpose in a different way. Concealing their design, plausible in explanations of their coming into the townships, voluble in praise of toleration, and effusive in their expressions of good-feeling towards their separated brethren, they set to work.

The obstacles they had to overcome were such as to any other class of men would have been insuperable. Here was a body of English-speaking farmers spread over eleven counties, who had held the land for sixty years and more, who had completed their social and municipal organization, and developed a characteristic individuality. The Protestants were largely massed in six counties. Stanstead, Sherbrooke, Waterloo, Missisquoi, Brome, Huntingdon, and in these counties in 1867, the year when Quebec passed under the rule of a Catholic legislature, the Protestants numbered 56,600, the Catholics 25,583, mostly employees of the English. With a clear majority of 31,000 the Protestants felt secure. They were passing rich as riches go in rural Canada, prosperous and aggressive, wielding a political influence not in proportion to their numbers but of their wealth and intelligence.

The design of the priests was, that this self-confident, self-reliant and enterprising people should be brought under a pressure that would constrain them to leave their fields and homes to be occupied by French-Canadians. That a farm papulation could be so supplanted seemed incredible, and those who suggested such a design being entertained were laughed at.

Out of a population of eighty-two thousand in 1867 thirty-one thousand was a sweeping majority, and appearances pointed to its increase, for each summer saw the number enlarged by immigrants from Britain. Left alone, these counties in another generation would have counted a hundred thousand Protestants. But they were not left alone. The Legislature, sitting at Quebec, was working hand-in-glove with the priests to work their downfall, and how far that has been accomplished let the census of 1911 tell:—

    Catholics .... 174,004.
    Protestants .... 57,926.

    Majority of Catholics 116,078

Thus in forty-six years a majority of thirty-one thousand Protestants had been changed into a Catholic majority of one hundred and sixteen thousand! Since the days of the Dragonnades has there been such an extraordinary displacement of Protestants from their homes and native land? How, in the face of these official figures, can any man have the conscience to assert Home Rule has been a grand success in Quebec, and, having wrought no injury to Protestants, Ulster need not dread a Dublin parliament? When Quebec was separated from Ontario all six counties had a Protestant majority. Only one, Brome, is in that position to-day, and its majority of 9,652 forty-six years ago has fallen to 3,318, and grows smaller each year. Of all six Stanstead was the most largely Protestant. Within its bounds it counted only 2,100 Catholics in 1867; to-day it has over 11,000, and they dominate. Were I to take up the other five counties more striking instances could be given. There are instances of not a single Protestant family being left in a township. The clerical newspapers boast openly of the "peaceable conquest" by the priests of the Eastern Townships, the Protestant stronghold of Quebec, and with reason, for it is a conquest without parallel.

How Was That Conquest Effected?

The answer can be given in less than a dozen words —By carving the townships into parishes and destroying their public schools. The Legislature aided. The wave of exuberant national feeling that swept the French-Canadians on the adoption of Confederation, led to a system of government colonizing and repatriation. Large sections of the Eastern Townships were set apart and given in free lots to families from the northern settlements. It was hoped that thus the drift to New England factories would be stayed, and agents were sent to Maine and Massachusetts to induce those who had gone to come back. Colonization and repatriation was the cry, and larger and larger government grants of money were demanded to make roads and fit the free lots for the settlers to start on easy terms. Much of that money was spent in the Eastern Townships. The priests made the selections and led the colonists. When the Papal Zouaves returned from their futile errand to prevent Italian unity, they were rewarded by a huge block of land in the English county of Compton, the name of Piopolis being bestowed on the settlement. In the heart of Protestant settlements, where there never had been a resident priest, missions were established which grew into congregations, and these soon became large enough to warrant the mission being erected into a parish, and before Confederation had been in force 25 years the townships were cut up into parishes. In the pamphlet by Sir A. T. Galt, already referred to, he expressed his astonishment at the change which had overtaken the townships and at the rapidity with which it had been effected. Writing only nine years after Confederation, he pointed out that in only two of the constituencies always regarded as English could a candidate be elected independent of the Catholic vote. His alarm was shared by others.

In self-defence, leading men of Sherbrooke moved to encourage immigrants from the British Isles. How the attempt fared, may be judged by the experience of a company that had an option on a large tract of land in Compton. They applied for an Act of Incorporation. The Premier, Chapleau, told their representative the bill would not be allowed to pass unless the company consented to select Frenchmen as half of their prospective settlers. The completeness of the change was as notable as the quietness with which it had been wrought. Confederation had not been in force for a generation until the net of the parish system had been cast over the townships, and costly churches, convents, colleges dotted its landscapes, in every case the most prominent sites being chosen. The presence of moles in the dykes of Holland is not revealed until they have honeycombed them and the fields that depended on their protection are submerged.

It is often said, that the change was a natural one, and not due to the priests—that the English would have left anyway.

From all purely farming countries there must necessarily be a constant passing-away of youth. To get farms young men have to go where land is still to be had free or at a cheap rate. Then there is always a class eager for change, ready to abandon the homestead and go where they believe conditions are better. Account also must be taken of the drift from the country to the city. These causes explain many departures from the townships, but after allowing for them, there is the undeniable fact that a large proportion of the changes were not due to them.

It is well to note that comparison with the drift from Ontario rural counties does not apply to Quebec. The depopulation of Western Ontario was owing to the opening of the Northwest. That of Quebec began twenty years before the Ontario movement.

The Parish System.

As already stated, the priests used two levers to drive out Protestants from the townships, the parish system and separate schools.

The parish system came first. This book has been written in vain if it has not demonstrated that the extension of that system to the townships is a tyrannical invasion of free territory, a defiance of royal proclamation and imperial statute; in one word, a usurpation. Consider what that system means to the English farmer. So long as a farm is owned by a Protestant the priest can levy no tithe; his trustees no building-tax. The moment it is sold to a Catholic, the priest draws tithe and the churchwardens levy taxes.

See the motive here held out, apart from any religious or national consideration, to get the Protestant pushed aside. The patents issued by the Crown for the lands held in the townships read thus:

"Victoria, by the grace of God, of the United King-
"dom of Great Britain and Ireland, Queen, . . .
"have granted to John Doe the parcel of land herein
"described . . . to have and to hold . . . .
"forever in free and common soccage, for fealty only,
"in like manner as lands are holden in free and com-
"mon soccage in that part of Great Britain called
"England."

These deeds were signed for the Queen by the governor then in office, and they read the same from the time of George III. If language means anything, surely these deeds are conveyances to the farmer on the same conditions as if the land was situated in England. Is land in England subject to be taxed by the Roman Catholic priesthood? If not, how can it be in the townships of Quebec? Is the transfer from the Crown not clear as to there being no ulterior condition? Can it be pretended, that the sovereign ever recognized that the priests of Quebec had a latent claim by which, some day, they could tithe and tax? Was the grant made to the settler with a servitude to Rome, or as a free grant from a British sovereign to a British subject? Who ever considers the matter solely from reading the deeds by which the Crown granted, or sold, the farms in the townships of Quebec, can come to no other conclusion than that it was free land with no encumbrance or servitude. That was undeniably the intention of the British Government, for, in the Act of 1774, which restored French law within the seigniories, it is expressely stated:

"Nothing in this Act contained shall extend, or be "construed to extend, to any lands that have been, or "hereafter shall be granted by his Majesty, his heirs "'and successors, to be holden in free and common "soccage."

This law has never been repealed, and stands as much in force to-day as any other section of the Quebec Act. If that section is not valid, is not now the law of the land, then neither is section 8, which the priests consider the legal bulwark of their privileges. There never was a clearer case of defiance of an Imperial statute than the erecting of parishes in the townships. When the agitation led by Papineau reached the point that the Imperial Parliament appointed a select committee to take evidence as to the alleged grievances, Viger was called and gave testimony as to the working of the Tenures Act, which formed part of his complaint. The committee, which included several eminent lawyers, in their report, spoke thus on this head:

"To the provision in the Act of 1774, providing that "in all matters of controversy relating to property "and civil rights . . . be determined agreeably to "the laws and customs of Lower Canada, there is a "marked exception to this concession of French law, "namely, 'that it shall not apply to lands which had "been or should be granted in free and common soc- "cage.'"

The report was adopted by the House of Commons. It proves that, fifty-four years after the Quebec Act was passed, when the townships had been erected and many of them thickly populated, the Imperial Parliament placed the interpretation on the Quebec Act that section eight no more applied to them than it did to Ontario. John J. McCord was appointed a Judge for the Townships in 1842, and from his close association with them knew their condition and circumstances thoroughly. In the spring of 1854 a case was brought before him, by the priest of Milton, in the St. Hyacinthe circuit court, of a habitant, a Catholic, who refused to pay tithes because his farm was township, not fief land, that his tenure was free and common soccage, not seigniorial. The Judge upheld the plea. The only authority for tithes, said Judge McCord, was the Quebec Act, which restricted them to seigniorial land. The conclusion of the judge was, that such being "the "present state of law of the country, and there "being a positive prohibition to the extension of the "right of tithes to land held in free and common soc-"cage, I am bound to maintain" defendant's plea. The law is the same now as in 1854, but the judges are not the same. That summer the legislature passed the Act abolishing clergy reserves, because of the reason that it is "desirable to remove all semblance of "connection between Church and State." This merely reaffirmed the declaration of the Rectories Act, which laid down legal equality among all religious denominations, both in Upper and Lower Canada. The statutes of the united Province have other passages of like nature. Thus in Vic. 14-15, regarding the Catholic diocese of Montreal, a section reads: "Nothing in this "Act shall be construed to extend, or in any manner "confer, any spiritual jurisdiction or ecclesiastical "rights whatsoever upon any bishop or other ecclesi-"astical person."

In the townships were a few Irish Catholic congregations, who had supported their priests and built their churches by voluntary contributions. On being required to pay tithe and building-tax they resisted. Their appeals to the courts were futile: on proof being led that their farms formed part of a parish proclaimed by the Lieutenant-Governor, judgment was given against them. Eventually these parishes were reduced to the level of those surrounding them, by the bishops substituting French priests for their Irish pastors.

Seeing section 9 of the Quebec Act has not been repealed, and no statute can be quoted repealing it, how comes it that the priests could extend the parish system to the townships? How comes it that she is levying her tributes on a single acre outside fief lands? As well ask: How did they go on exercising the powers given them by the ordinance of 1839 during nine years after it had lapsed? Holding the balance of political influence, public men dare not challenge what they do: judges receive their interpretation of the law from their confessors. There has been so far only one Doutre and one McCord.

The Sectarian School.

First the parish system, next the sectarian school, has been the means of ejecting the Protestant farmer. The one is based on the other. Had Sir A. T. Galt, when acting as representative of the Quebec minority in the framing of Confederation, instead of asking guarantees for schools, simply demanded that the parish system be confined to the limits defined in the Quebec Act, the farmers in the townships would have been comparatively safe, for, if in them Rome could not levy taxes to build churches and parsonages and tithes to support priests, it would have had no more interest to bring its forces to bear in expelling the Protestant farmers from the townships of Quebec than it has in meddling with the farmers across the line in Vermont and New York State. One fact the experience of the Eastern Townships has established— the Anglo-Saxon farmer will remain in no country where he is discriminated against. It is different with the business man. He goes where trade and manufactures yield the largest profit. The English-speaking population on the island of Montreal grows and will continue to grow. Of Protestant farmers, each census will count fewer, yet these farmers have an equal claim to the Province with the French and Catholic farmers. Quebec is the native country of the Protestant farmer, it has been the home of his family for several generations, and from their labor in creating that home by carving it out of the primeval forest. Tens of thousands of them know no other country: Quebec to them is their native land, which they desire to live in, and, if need should arise, would die for. The townships are the creation of English-speaking Protestants, what they are, they made them; they were their architects and builders, and by Crown and Imperial Parliament, were secured in the townships as their inheritance, their chosen seat in the Province of Quebec.

In referring to the part schools bear in driving out the Protestant farmers of Quebec it is essential that the two meanings attached to the term "elementary education" be kept in mind. Non-Catholics understand by it the imparting to children of the rudiments of that knowledge which is necessary for their success in life. The priests understand by the term instruction in the doctrine, ritual, and liturgy of the Church of Rome. If to this has been added reading, writing, arithmetic, it has been in deference to the agitation which, in our day, is represented by Godfroi Langlois. To find the school the priests design their people should have, go to the back parishes, where you see a young girl devoting her time to get her scholars memorize the catechism and recite the order of prayers. Her salary is a mockery, sometimes as low as $100, rarely $200, yet considering her qualifications, her youth, and what she has to teach, it is not so inadequate as it seems. When the priest speaks of an elementary school he means a confessional school—a place where the child will be prepared for first communion. When a Protestant speaks of an elementary school, he means a place where his children will be taught the three R.'s. The distinction between the two is as plain as the difference is wide. The purpose and end of the public school is to impart the elements of secular education to the children of the nation, to fuse them into a common citizenship, and make them loyal to the government. The purpose and end of the separate school system is to divide the children, to hive those whose parents are Catholics, to keep them apart from other children, to bring them up as a distinct caste, whose first allegiance is not to Canada, but the Pope. On the community the effect of the separate school is divisive: to the unity of the State it is destructive. There is no comparison between the common school system and that of separate schools, for they differ as dark from light. The common school has an open door, inviting youth of all creeds and races to enter and learn what every citizen ought to know; the separate school has a screen before its door, which admits only those who can go through its meshes, and the first purpose of whose teaching is to make bigots. The one is inclusive, broad, progressive; the other is exclusive, narrow, reactionary.

Origin of Separate Schools.

How confessional schools were introduced into Quebec remains to be told. In 1801 the Imperial Government took steps to establish a system of schools. When the co-operation of Bishop Plessis was asked he refused—the priests demanded their kind of schools, to which the governor would not consent—they must take the schools as designed by the government or do without. They preferred to do without: they would have confessional schools or none. The government's offer had a different reception in the Townships, whose farmers organized schools, often at their sole expense, for public aid was erratic and trifling. Between 1820 and 1841 several educational Acts were passed, with grants per scholar; one provided for half the cost of new schoolhouses. Not one of these Acts recognized difference in creed; they provided for public schools and none other. Sydenham was extremely anxious to have the children of the habitants educated, and induced his Ministers to submit an Act, at the first meeting of the united legislature, to establish public schools in both Provinces. The Quebec members objected, asking Catholic schools. Instead of standing by their measure the government weakly consented to refer the Act to a committee, which inserted a declaratory clause giving permission to Catholics to dissent and form schools of their own. This permission applied to both Provinces. As regards the Quebec parishes the Act was inoperative. Conferences with the bishops followed, ending in submitting the Act of 1844, which forms the basis of all subsequent school legislation. It made distinct provision for sectarian schools. In Quebec the Act failed from an unlooked for cause. It authorized a compulsory tax to maintain schools. This the habitants resented, and attempts to levy rates resulted in a ferment of stubborn opposition with, in some localities, deeds of violence. The Act had to be modified in this regard, without, however, leading to the establishment of a general system of schools in the parishes. So late as 1853 there were municipalities whose ratepayers boasted no school tax had ever been collected. The planting of schools among the habitants is, therefore, comparatively recent. The organizing of the schools fell to their priests, and as has been stated, they made them adjuncts of their church. From the earliest period, the preparation of children for first communion in Quebec has been by means of repetition. Someone, commonly the mother, repeated the catechism and prayers from memory, and their words the little ones stored away as they listened. The introduction of schools was seized to do this work of preparation, and their main purpose to this day in the back parishes is to fit the scholars for their first communion. After ten years of age, few of the boys attend. These schools are as much a part of the Papal system as its convents. They do for the ordinary child what the college does for the select few—train them to implicit faith in and obedience to the priests. To parallel them with schools whose purpose is to teach the three R's and to enlarge the intellect by storing it with information, is to confound two essentially different institutions. Both are named schools but they are not alike.

Intelligent Catholics are quite aware of the defects of Quebec's educational system. That they make no effort to bring about reform is due to their worship of tradition and their fear of incurring the censure of the priests. There have been exceptional men who, provoked by conditions forced daily upon them, have spoken out, and what they have said reveals what thousands think and would say were it prudent. The boldest of these utterances was that of Senator Poirier, because it was made in the presence of a great array of priests. He pointed out that French-Canadians were not occupying the positions to which they justly aspired because they had not received the education that would have fitted them to fill those positions, and went on to prove his statement by citing undeniable instances. Archbishop Bruchesi rose when the Senator sat down and said significantly, "Were I asked by the Senator to give him absolution, I would do so with a few remarks, certain advice, and—a penance." There is the rod that keeps the laity silent —for speaking the truth in public—a penance. The shade of the confessional appals the boldest.

When the Act of 1844 began to be enforced, there were schools in every English-speaking settlement. In farming communities the support available for schools is limited. Children cannot be expected to walk over two miles to school, and that radius gives, where farms range from one to two hundred acres, an average of one school to every twenty families. This physical obstacle to a rural population keeping up more than one school has not been taken into account by those who framed our educational laws. Plant a second school in a district, and one or other has to go out of existence, for there are only sufficient families to support one. A priest goes into a school district in the townships and commands the few Catholic families to dissent and form a separate school. The loss of their rates impairs the revenue of the old school, and, as time passes, whenever a farm comes for sale, by some unseen direction a Catholic buyer is brought, so the revenue grows smaller until the point is reached that it is insufficient, and the door of the old school-house closes for the last time. The townships of Quebec had a system of schools as old as their settlement and as non-sectarian as those of Ontario. They have been undermined and destroyed by the innovation of confessional schools. It has been officially stated that four hundred have gone out of existence. The beginning of every school year sees more doors unopened. No matter under what pretence separate schools are introduced into farming sections, the result is to destroy the original schools. It is different in towns and cities, where sufficient support can be got for both. In the country, where there can only be a limited number of families to the square mile, the priest, when he starts a separate school, does so with the design of breaking down the one in existence. In their invasion of the English-speaking townships the priests planned to destroy the schools of their founders, and they are killing them slowly and surely.

The statistics given in the government reports do not confirm this, for, according to them, the decrease of non-Catholic schools has not been large. These statistics lump together the number of such schools in villages, towns, and cities, with those in the rural parts. There is no column for the little red schoolhouse. The number of elementary non-Catholic schools has increased largely in Montreal and in manufacturing towns and villages, and that increase conceals the loss of such schools in the rural sections. Then, again, the government statistics do not show how long the

schools remain open during the teaching term. A
member of the legislature asked for a special return
on this head, and when it was brought down it showed
that for the scholastic year 1907-8 out of 835 rural
schools 100 did not open from inability to get a
teacher for the salary the ratepayers were able to
offer; two hundred were kept open with difficulty, having only from five to eight scholars, and 300 had less
than a dozen. Only one-quarter were open for the full
scholastic year of ten months; nearly 30 per cent.
of them were open for only seven months or less, and
89 of them were open for five months or less. In the
county of Huntingdon the scholars in ten years fell off
700 in number. These statistics indicate that the ratepayers, upon whom fell the support of these schools,
were so few that they were able to keep them open for
a few months only, which means that three out of four
were inefficient. The case is made worse from the added statement that 459 had teachers without diplomas.
In a typical township, having seven non-Catholic
school-houses, which, forty years ago were crowded,
there were 94 scholars—an average of 14. The school
that had the largest attendance had 17, the smallest 6.
A school with less than ten pupils, and open four
months in the year, is better than none at all, and that
is all that can be said of half of the rural schools in the
Province of Quebec attended by the children of parents who are not Roman Catholics. In the year 1905 of
these weak schools, 66 closed forever. The inefficiency of the education they impart is illustrated by the
fact that out of every 100 who have attended them, 92
scholars have to be content with what little they have
learned, 4 get one or more terms at a model school, 3
at an academy, and 1 goes to a university. And what
of those sections where the non-Catholics are unable
to keep open a school for even four months in the
year? The children in these sections are growing up
illiterates. Already there are respectable families in
these sections whose younger members cannot sign

their names, because the schools they would have gone to were shut by the priests. Everybody has met the man who affects to be an oracle in politics, who boasts he is not narrow minded, who despises the bigots who are always introducing subjects that cause heart-burning in a mixed community, and who considers it only fair Catholics should have their own schools. Men who use such language abound in and out of parliament. In doing what they consider justice to the Catholics, they do not reflect they are perpetrating the cruelest wrong on those who are not Catholics, that they are destroying their schools and dooming their children to ignorance. Place this fact down as incontrovertible, that in rural districts there is support for one school only, and whoever advocates separate schools robs those who cannot attend them of the means of getting an education.

Protestants Forced to Support Catholic Schools.

The demand of the priests is, that the taxes paid by their people shall go to the support of confessional schools and none other—that to take them to maintain even non-sectarian schools is a violation of conscience. They insist that the school tax be divided according to the creed of the tax-payers. The rule is a bad one, but when a legislature adopts it, provision should be made that it be impartially carried out. Whatever money is paid by a Catholic should go to confessional schools, whatever by a non-Catholic to public schools. If it be a dreadful sin in Catholics to pay a tax to maintain a public school, how much greater must be the outrage upon the conscience of Protestants to force them to keep up confessional schools? Singular to say, the priests only recognize conscientious convictions in their own people: that Protestants have any they seem to disbelieve; at any rate, they trample upon them in this matter of school support. The bulk of the commerce and manufactures of the Province of Quebec is in the hands of Protestants; blot them out and Quebec

would be one of the poorest countries in the world.
The visitor to Montreal who approaches it by the
Lachine canal cannot fail to be impressed by the
factories that line its banks and the abounding evidence of manufacturing industry so far as his eye can
reach. Coming to the harbor he sees a long line of
monster steamships. Turning to the business streets he
is impressed by the massive buildings that house banks
and those other institutions that trade and commerce
require, and when he seeks the residential part of the
city he views the palaces where live the men who control these institutions and who own the factories that
darken the lower part of the city with their smoke.
Ninety out of a hundred of these men are Protestants:
of the remaining ten, Jews form a large part. Under
the rule laid down by the priests the taxes levied on
the properties of these wealthy Jews and Protestants
ought to go to maintain public schools. They do not;
the greater part goes to confessional schools, to schools
taught by nuns and monks, to enrich convents and
other monastic institutions. If the money filched out
of the the pockets of Protestants was devoted solely to
public schools, there would have to be a treble tax
levied on Catholic city ratepayers. Seeing the
principle of the statute is, that the school tax be
divided according to the creed of those who pay it,
how is this done? It is accomplished by a legal
quibble in this way. A Protestant owns a factory. So
long as he holds it in his own name, or in the name of a
partnership, his rates go to the public school. The
moment, however, the factory comes to be owned by an
incorporated company, a new method is applied. Keeping in mind the principle of the statute, that the tax is
to be allotted according to the creed of those who pay
it, it would be supposed the school tax of establishments owned by incorporated companies would be
divided according to the number of shares held by the
Protestants and Catholics as they appear on their
stock books. That would not suit the priests, for a

Catholic shareholder is a rarity, so, as regards incorporated companies, they varied the law by enacting that its school tax be divided in proportion to the number of Catholic and Protestant children in the district in which the property of the companies is situated. Mark how the priests can change their cry to suit their own purposes. In the rural districts they preach that it is persecution to take the tax of a Catholic for other than a confessional school, but in city or town it is quite right to compel Protestants to pay taxes to maintain Catholic schools. In the country the taxes must be divided according to the creed of those who pay them, but when it comes to shareholders in the great incorporated companies of Montreal and other manufacturing centres, the school taxes are not apportioned according to the creed of the shareholders, but of the creed of those who live around their places of business! What difference can incorporating those who manage a factory make in their creeds? Can an act of parliament, whose sole object is facilitating the carrying on of business, change the spiritual status of a man? A Protestant has established, by individual effort and investing of his own money, a large mill. To facilitate carrying it on he incorporates his business under Dominion or Provincial act. Is he less of a Protestant because of his having done so? Yet, by so doing, he loses the right to designate where the school tax levied on his factory shall go, and his taxes are taken to maintain schools whose teachings he condemns. The tenderness of the priests for rights of conscience where the dollars are to be exacted from Catholics, contrasts strangely with their total disregard for the rights of conscience when dollars can be filched by law from the pockets of Protestants. If it be a monstrous wrong to make Catholics contribute towards non-sectarian schools, it must be a much greater wrong to compel Protestants to maintain Catholic schools. If the conscience of the Catholic is outraged by his helping to keep up a non-sectarian, a neutral, school, what shall be said of the outrage of forcing Jews and Protestants to support nuns and friars under the name of education? The priests cannot endure neutral schools, but a neutral panel to provide them with the taxes of Jews and Protestants is an admirable device. Of late there has been a general movement among mercantile firms to become incorporated companies. By the change the greater part of their school tax goes to the Catholic schools. It is within the truth to say that of the capital of these companies nineteen-twentieths is that of Protestants. Catholic firms, where possible, avoid incorporation, and the amount of rates from companies composed of Catholics is a negligible quantity. An estimate, prepared by one who investigated the subject, gives a million dollars yearly as the amount taken from Protestants for the support of Catholic schools. That is excessive, but the amount has nothing to do with the principle at stake, which is, that Protestants having investments in banking and insurance companies, commercial and manufacturing enterprises, are compelled by law to support Catholic schools in the Province of Quebec. An ingenious evasion by Catholics of the law governing incorporation, is to name one of the corporation proprietor of the real estate, and from him the company leases.

There are two grounds upon which this mode of dividing the school tax of companies is defended. One is, that as it applies equally to Protestant and Catholic, it cannot be unjust. Were it a tax for a public purpose, involving no moral element, that would be sufficient justification. Seeing it is a tax to bolster sectarian education, it fails. Does anybody suppose for a moment, that were the majority of corporations composed of Catholics the priests would have ever suggested dividing the taxes drawn from them in the way that is done? The second argument advanced is, that the tax is just, because although the proprietors of the great industrial concerns in the Province of Quebec are

Protostants they are interested in the education of their employees. Certainly they are interested in seeing that they get a secular education, and would not object were their taxes used to give them such an education, but it is of the brutality of bigotry for the priests to confiscate the school taxes levied on incorporated companies to secure the teaching of the doctrines of their church. In Quebec the government prescribes Catholic schools as the schools of the Province, and then uses various devices to seize the money of Protestants and Jews to pay for their upkeep. First of all, the State assumed a function that did not legitimately belong to it in designating a certain denomination as the favored church of the Province and then went further by coercing those who disown that sect and its teaching, to pay to support it. Each dollar levied in taxation or taken from the public treasury for the support of any church or for the teaching of its creed in any school, is not merely tyrannical, it is a violation of the rights of conscience. The priests declaim against taking the taxes of Catholics to maintain public schools in Ontario and Manitoba as an outrage that cries to heaven for redress, but in Quebec, these same men get the law so shaped that a considerable part of the taxes levied on the real estate, incomes, and capital of Protestants shall go to maintain schools in which are daily taught doctrines abhorrent to them. A mark of a true church must be honesty. Is it honest to demand exemption in the Dominion for Catholics from supporting non-sectarian schools on the score of conscience, and then cunningly plunder Protestants in the Province of Quebec to maintain Catholic schools? Have Protestants no consciences to be respected? Each session we hear members at Ottawa dwelling on the fairness of allowing Catholics in the Northwest to retain their tax for support of separate schools: these very members uphold the law in Quebec which seizes the bulk of the tax levied on the real estate, incomes, and capital of Protestants to maintain schools taught by nuns and friars, and strenuously resist a change in that law. I care not who the politicians are who pose as statesmen, I care not who the prelates are who rustle in gorgeous robes and profess to speak as representatives of Christ, I declare their seizing the money of Protestants to maintain their institutions to be more than intolerance, it is robbery.

The Coming of the Jews.

The influx of Jews into Montreal is going to bring this question to the front. Their appearance raised the point to which school panel their taxes should go. As the priests would have nothing to do with their children, the legislature enacted that for school purposes Jews were to be classed as Protestants! Half of the scholars in Montreal schools under the charge of the Protestant board are Hebrew, yet a Jew is never appointed by the Government to sit on that board, nor can a young woman whose father is a Jew qualify to be a teacher. No people can be expected to long endure such injustice. The remedy proposed, that the Jews have schools of their own, would be to endorse and perpetuate the sectarian principle, but it is impracticable. Give the Jews separate schools and a separate board of management, and a like favor could not be denied to those who profess allegiance to the Greek church, and the adherents of that church in Montreal are yearly increasing. If all are to have schools of the creed they profess, what would remain but confusion and the reign of illiteracy? There is only one solution, the public school, which has no sectarian bias, and which Protestant and Hebrew, Greek and Armenian, can support—the school that unifies and does not divide, the school whose purpose is to elevate the children to an equal plane of citizenship, and, leaving the creed of each child alone, strives to impart a knowledge of those duties they owe to society and to the State when they grow to be men and women, and that school is the public school. It is satisfactory to know that the Dominion has no more ardent supporters of complete separation of Church and State than the Jews.

The air is full of plans to save the English-speaking farmers of Quebec their few remaining schools. In 1906 the Protestant Committee of the Council of Public Instruction adopted a motion asking the legislature to levy a small tax on the assessable property of Protestants. It was shown that in that year such property amounted to one hundred and thirty million dollars, and that a tax of five cents on the hundred dollars would yield $65,000, which would be sufficient to save the schools that were slowly dying. The proposed tax was abominable, being based on the principle that ought to be eliminated, of recognizing creed in public affairs. Rescue the rates levied on Protestants for the support of Catholic schools, place them in a general fund, and there will be no need to call for aid from the benevolent, for an increased grant from the government, or for the levying of a special tax on real estate owned by Protestants.

Present Condition of the Quebec Townships.

The early days of the townships were full of hope. Each morning work was begun in joyous expectation of plans to be realized. There was activity, progress, life. Periodically there was exultation over what had been achieved: neighbor meeting neighbor to review results, encouraging one another to attempt greater things. The pages in which Bouchette tells of his successive visits to the townships and of their marvellous advancement give a thrill of delight to the reader. A brighter morning no new country could have. How different the picture of to-day! In a few centres there is much industrial activity: Sherbrooke and Granby hum with the revolving wheels of mill and factory, around which cluster the tenements of workers. These are apart from the rural population, and it is with the English-speaking farmer I am concerned. Let us see how he has fared. Here is a concession on which, a few decades ago, in each home was heard the kindly speech of the Lowland Scot; here another where Highlanders predominated; another where Irish Catholics and Protestants dwelt in neighborly helpfulness; another where neatness and taste told of its dwellers being of New England descent. To-day approach one of those homes, and with polite gesture madam gives you to understand she does not speak English. Here is the school the first settlers erected, and which they and their successors kept open with no small denial. Draw near to it and you hear the scholars in their play calling to one another in French. The descendants of the men who cleared these fields of forest and brought them into cultivation have disappeared. The meeting-house where they met for worship stands there on a knoll, with broken windows, and boarded door, dropping to decay. The surrounding acre where they buried their dead, is a mass of weeds, which defy approach to read the lettering on the stones discerned through the tangle of vegetation. Once in the course of years there is a funeral: a corpse comes by train from some far-distant State, that of one who was once a settler and yearned to rest with her kindred. A vanished race: why did they go? Because the pledged word of a British King and the statute enacted by a British Parliament, were broken and set aside by Canadian politicians in obedience to the priests who helped them to office. These acres were meant by the King and Parliament of England to be free land: the blight of servitude to a church is now upon them.

The situation of the few families who cling to a decaying township settlement is painful. They have seen neighbor after neighbor leave, and French Catholic families take their place. The people they visited and who visited them are in the United States, for of those who have left the townships the large majority sought the Republic instead of our Northwest, as if from an instinctive fear that no part of Canada is safe from the power that expelled them. The lack of social intercourse presses on the wife and children; the lack of neighborly helpfulness on the father. A feeling of isolation and loneliness creeps upon them. It is with difficulty services in the church are maintained: were it not for help from home mission funds its door would be closed. A day comes when there are too few families to maintain the school. The father sees the new Catholic one within sight of his door. Will he send his children to it? What is the daily routine of that school? Learning the prayers and ritual, so that the children may be able to follow the service on Sunday; learning the catechism, with such questions as these:

"What is the Church Jesus Christ has established?
"It is the Catholic, apostolic, and Roman Church.

"Can one be saved outside of the Catholic, apostolic, and Roman Church?
"No, out of the church there is no salvation.

"What then must one think of all those sects which are separated from the Catholic Church?
"One must consider them as so many human institutions, and as false religions, which only lead men into error and which cannot lead them to God."

These the questions of a primary class. Take a specimen of those in the more advanced:

"Do you believe that the Holy Church, Catholic and "Apostolic, is the only true Church, in which but one "baptism is given, and a true remission of all sins?
"I do believe.

"Do you reject and anathematize all heresies against this Holy Catholic Church?
"I anathematize them.

"Who is the visible head of the Church?

"The Pope, who is Christ's vicar on earth and the "supreme visible head of the Church.

"Can the Pope, as head of the Church, teach false "doctrine?

"No, the Pope is an infallible teacher of all doctrines "concerning faith and morals, which he defines, as "pastor and teacher of all Christians."

This is the catechism which forms the staple of the course of study with more or less of the three R's during the intervals between it and prayers. The teacher assures the father his children will not be asked to join in catechism or prayers, but he knows from experience they will be involuntarily fixed in their memories by daily hearing. I know an Orangeman, unable from distance to send his children to a public school, who allowed them to attend the confessional school on an adjoining lot. Everyone of them, from the constant iteration in their hearing, could repeat the little catechism. Then the day comes when the priest is to visit the school, and the scholars join in preparing and decorating the little shrine. The text-books are Catholic, the whole atmosphere of the school is Catholic. The farmer cannot in conscience send his little ones to it, and so the French-Canadian, who has been wanting his farm, gets it, and, a week after he is in possession, a priest comes to see the new acquisition of his church, for it has a joint proprietorship with the habitant in its acres. For the first time a priest drives up the lane lined by maples which the grandfather of the dispossessed Protestant planted, and levies tithes on the yield of fields his great-grandparents redeemed from the wilderness, and which four generations of Protestants have ploughed.

It has to be observed that the English-speaking farmer finds no fault with the language of the confessional school being French. The desire among the township farmers is that their children should speak both languages, and were the school non-sectarian the father in the foregoing paragraph would have no hesitation in sending his children to it. He is well aware from experience that, in Quebec, it is a great advantage to know both languages, and that advantage he would have each member of his family possess. No ridiculous notion that the language taught in the school can supersede the language of the family prevents his patronizing it; as well tell him that were the language taught in the school Latin his children would drop their mother tongue for the speech of Cicero. His objection to the confessional school is not that its language is French, but that the subjects taught within its walls are those dictated by the priests to ensure the scholars being subservient to their rule and to engrain in their minds a life-long prejudice against Protestants.

Where the English Sinned.

When the stream of emigration from the United Kingdom set in a century ago, it was so marvellous that any portion of it should have been diverted to the back country of Quebec, that he who weighs all the conditions of those times traces the hand of design—that God would have in Quebec a people who would bear testimony to his truth. Hundreds of families who sailed from the Old Land purposing to settle in Ontario, were, by what seemed to them accidental happenings, diverted from their intention and remained in Quebec. Of the many first settlers I have conversed with, not one in twenty said they crossed the Atlantic with the intention of remaining in Quebec. Was there no purpose in this? Are the settlements of Ulstermen and of Lowland Scots that rose in the midst of the all-pervading forest to be regarded in no other light than that which the economist views them? The fundamental truth of Christianity is the individuality of man in his relation to God. Each of us stands accused before Him, and for our reconciliation there is no provision for a human intermediary. No fellow-being can step between the soul and its Maker: no organization speak or act for Him. In every age and in every country there have been men who professed to be the deputies, the representatives on earth, of God; assuming to speak for Him and asserting the efficacy of their services as intermediaries in saving souls. In no other part of the continent was there more need than in Quebec for a body of men and women to bear witness by their lives that no fellow-mortal can stand between the soul and God, teaching the twin truth of the individual responsibility and of the spiritual independence of man. The settlers, so strangely guided to Quebec, knew this great truth, but hid it in their materialism, their eager seeking after what the world can give, and the example they ought to have set was lost in their inconsistent lives, their utter indifference to the eternal welfare of the people whose eyes were upon them. It was their duty to be lights, to be witness-bearers to the sovereignty of Christ and the all-sufficiency of his intercession, yet, if by naught else than their neglect of associating together to fan the flame of piety, and the meanness of their contributions to sustain Gospel ordinances, they disgraced, and finally blasted the cause they were called to recommend. Had they realized the grandeur of their opportunity, had they been faithful to their duty, would they have been abandoned to those who, from their first coming, plotted against them? The Protestants of Quebec had presented to them an opening to do a grand work. They threw it away, and as a people they have been thrown away. Will the remnant consider where their fathers failed and earnestly set their faces to redeeming the past? If they are to hold their own, it must be by a great spiritual revival among themselves. They have been sinned against, wantonly and cruelly, but they also have sinned by not living up to the knowledge they possessed.

The Townships Have Been Robbed of Their Autonomy.

A favorite topic with our politicians is, that the content of the French-Canadians is due to Britain's securing to them their autonomy. During the Boer War Sir Wilfred Laurier visited England, and kept repeating with eloquent iteration that the secret of binding alien peoples to the English Crown is to copy what has been done in Quebec, thrusting the advice on British statesmen that to solve the situation in South Africa they should grant the Boers the fullest autonomy. What of the hypocrisy of talking thus and at the very time being a party to the crushing of the autonomy of the Eastern Townships, robbing its Protestant settlers of their rights as British subjects, winking at the violation of laws in order to make their situation unendurable, and so drive them forth to seek equal rights in another Province—too often under another flag? Judged by their acts, it is seen there are men who in clamoring for autonomy really seek the power to supplant those who do not think as they do. These Townships' farmers, as fine a yeomanry as the sun ever shone upon, the influence and services of whose fathers in hours of danger saved Canada to Britain, are being ousted by a class in whose mouths autonomy, self-government, constitutional rights, are being constantly repeated—inspiring words when they mean power to benefit the people, sinister, hypocritical words when they mean dragging a people under the rule of the priests. The victims of priestly designs in Quebec ask for no exceptional treatment. What they do ask is, that they be rescued from the schemes and stratagems of the priests, and that they be rendered powerless to hurt them by being placed on the same level as other ministers. Is that an unreasonable demand? The shame is, that in a British colony British subjects should have to prefer such a demand.*

---

*As illustrating how the English have been driven out of certain districts this incident is given by a lady who was being driven to a house of a friend by a French-Canadian boy. The lady was a native of the district, but had been away for a few years. She was not recognized in her own early home. She spoke French fluently and the boy assumed that the passenger was one of his own people. The lady asked about this farm and the other farm formerly occupied by English-speaking yeomen. The boy answered in French, giving the names of the French-Canadian successors to the English-speaking farmers. Then as they passed a few farms still cultivated by their English-speaking owners, the boy said: "We will soon have the rest of them out of here." The lady was the daughter of an Irish Roman Catholic family. She was of the boy's creed, but not of his race, and had no sympathy with the racial ambitions that speak even out of the mouths of babes and sucklings. Alluding to the incident when speaking with Protestant neighbors near her own home, the lady said in English: "The little wretch, I would have liked to have cuffed his ears."

CHAPTER IX.

Canon Law

To the majority of the people of Canada the term Canon Law has no definite meaning. Even in Quebec it is only of late years what it is has come to be realized, attention having been drawn to it by frequent annulment of marriages. In Quebec, Canon Law is a reality, outside of that province it is still a name. What Canon Law is may be explained in a few words. The priests, claiming they form a complete society, with authority given them by Christ to rule mankind in all their relations, have a code of laws and courts of their own to enforce them. Canon Law is an elaborate and minute code, regulating everything pertaining to life and morals, applied by a fixed course of procedure, with voluminous commentaries, and administered by courts appointed by the bishops. This code of laws is left in abeyance where Protestants are in the majority, and in these sections the priests appear as ministers of a purely religious system. Where conditions are favorable, however, Canon Law is put into practice, and the priests in addition to their spiritual duties, assume functions that, elsewhere, pertain to the courts and to the legislature. The scope of that law and the methods of its administration can be best illustrated by relating how it has been enforced in cases relating to marriage, burial, the press, private judgment, the action of municipal councils, and the school.

Marriage.

A couple were married in the parish church of St. Johns. It proved an unhappy union, and the man asked the priest to have it dissolved on the ground that he and his wife were second cousins, a fact of which the girl was ignorant at time of marriage. The priest suggested the marriage could be made regular by a dispensation from the bishop, which would be granted on payment of a certain sum of money as alms. The husband rejected the suggestion, the marriage was declared null by the Archbishop of Montreal, and the man married another woman. Another resident of the diocese of Montreal, Oliver Lachapelle, applied for a dispensation to marry his second cousin, and obtained it. Tiring of her, he asked the marriage be annulled on the ground that they were first cousins. He had represented to the priest who married them that they were second cousins, in order to save paying the larger amount, $100, the price of a dispensation to marry first cousins. The marriage was annulled; the woman hid herself in a nunnery. A French-Canadian couple presented themselves before a Protestant minister in Montreal to be married. They had a license and he united them. Six years afterwards, four children being then born, the man, who was secretary to the Lieutenant-Governor, asked the Archbishop of Quebec to declare the marriage null. His ecclesiastical court heard the parties and rendered a decision, to this effect, that the ceremony by a Protestant minister was not binding, separated the couple, and declared them free to form anew the matrimonial tie. The woman was deserted. Two young French-Canadians, both on a visit to Europe, met in Paris, became enamored of each other, and decided to return to Canada as man and wife. They went to the British embassy, where the civil contract was made, and then proceeded to the Church of St. Sulpice, where Abbe Jobin married them. On their return to Canada they found they were not congenial, and both desired separation. The court of the Archbishop of Montreal declared the ceremony performed by the Paris priest was not binding, because neither the young man nor the young woman belonged to the parish of St. Sulpice in Paris, and had no dispensation from their ordinary, the bishop of Montreal, to be married outside his jurisdiction. A couple were married in St. Bridget's Church, Montreal, in 1903. In 1911 the husband asked their marriage be declared null because they were related in the third and fourth degree of consanguinity. The ecclesiastical court granted the petition. The simplicity of the method of having the judgment of the priest-court being given practical effect by the King's court is admirable. A lawyer appears in open court before a judge and asks to file a document that reads thus:

Archbishop's Palace, Montreal, November 3rd, 1911.
Re the marriage case of Meunier vs. Blanchet.

Mrs. Anna Meunier,
   20 McGregor street, Montreal.

Madam,—

I am directed to announce to you that His Grace, the Archbishop of Montreal, has pronounced a sentence of nullity of marriage in the case that you have submitted.

Yours very truly,
EMILE ROY,
Chancellor.

Imagine the feelings of a woman on receiving such a notice from men whom she was taught from her childhood are the representatives of Christ!

The judge accepts the bishop's decree, declares the marriage civilly null, and the man leaves the court free to repudiate any liability for the maintenance of the woman whom he pledged to succor until death parted them, and to contract a marriage with some one else. Sometimes, so rarely that only a few cases are on record, the woman revolts at being got rid of in such fashion and asks a Superior Court judge to protect her. Such a case was that of Malvina Lapatie, who was married to a man, named Napoleon Tremblay, in 1904 by the parish priest. In 1910 the husband asked that he be released because he was a fourth cousin of his wife. The bishop of St. Hyacinthe issued his decree, declaring the marriage null. Tremblay next applied to the Superior Court at Sorel, to give the decree civil effect. The wife opposed, and it was proved she was ignorant, at the time of the ceremony, that she was related to her husband and that their common ancestor was dead over a century, that he lived in 1780. It was also proved that by paying $7 the husband could have got a dispensation from the bishop authorizing their marriage, and that it was still in his power to apply for a dispensation and again go through the marriage ceremony. Her lawyer pleaded if Tremblay had not heart enough and honor enough to do this, the judge should not consider he had any standing before the Court. Judge Bruneau, while acknowledging the force of this, in an elaborate judgment, declared he had no choice but to confirm the bishop's decree. The wife appealed to a higher court, which confirmed the finding of the lower, one judge, a Protestant, dissenting. Friends enabled her to carry the case to England, where, after being heard, the Privy Council held that further proof as to what the law of Quebec is was needed before giving a decision, and ordered the case to be reargued.

To further illustrate how the priests act a case may be cited where judgment was obtained by default. Mrs. Meloche was notified her husband had applied to have their marriage declared null on the ground of their being third cousins, and that, unless she appeared at the palace of Archbishop Bruchesi on 11 October, 1904, she would be declared in contumacy and the tribunal would pronounce sentence. The woman by advice of her lawyer, did not attend. A decree annulling the marriage issued, and when fyled in court was given civil effect, the bench having accepted the ruling of Justice Papineau as axiomatic, that "Marriage in the Roman Catholic Church is a sacra- "ment and a religious bond over which the Superior "Court has no jurisdiction." How many marriages have been annulled cannot be ascertained, but they are numerous. In the rural parishes marriages have been going on between relatives for generations, so that a family cannot be found that is not related to several. With accurate registers of baptisms and marriages available, evidence can be got when couples wish to separate.

There are other causes accepted by the priests for quashing marriages. For instance, George Normandin, a French-Canadian, was married in Detroit, to Emma F. Williams. For the reason that the marriage ceremony was performed by a Protestant minister, Archbishop Bruchesi declared there was no union, and Justice Bruneau gave effect to his decision, which opened the way to divorce for couples who had been married in the Republic by Protestant clergymen and who desired to be separated. A case, however, with no foreign element came before the courts. On the evening of July 14, 1908, a young couple called at the residence of the Rev. Wm. Timberlake, a Methodist minister of Montreal, and desired him to marry them. The man produced the license under authority of the Lieutenant-Governor and both were of age. Seeing no reason why he should not comply with the request Mr. Timberlake married them. The following year the husband, having regretted their marriage, applied to Archbishop Bruchesi to declare it null because the ceremony was performed by a Protestant minister. On November 12, 1909, a decree was handed him, which he filed in court with a motion to have it given civil effect. There being no opposition, the court complied, and the man left the court free from any legal liability to maintain his wife, and to marry some other woman.

Shortly afterwards a lawyer appeared on behalf of
Mrs. Hebert, who asked that the judgment be reconsidered, on the ground that she had been prevented
from putting in an appearance through deception and
threats. She pled for the reopening of the case, not
only on her own behalf but of the child, a daughter,
who had been born, and who, unless the court quashed
the judgment it had given by default, would be
branded as illegitimate. Judge Charbonneau, Feb. 21,
1912, in an elaborate judgment, which took him an
hour-and-a-half to read, upheld the marriage as valid,
and declared the decree of the Archbishop to have no
civil effect. This, considering the judge is French and
a Catholic, astounded the public, and it was expected
the Archbishop would appeal. Instead, the husband
went before a judge and gave notice he would not
proceed further, alleging lack of money as his reason.
The subtlety of the move was apparent, his desisting
would prevent the case going to England and judgment being rendered there as to the validity of canon
law. By this time, widespread interest had been
aroused and the necessity was recognized for an
authoritative decision as to whether a court of priests
could annul marriages. The point was a purely civil
one, but, unfortunately, it was treated by the public
at large in its sectarian aspect, and there was much
declamation in Protestant pulpits about the Papal
decree ne temere, and many wild assertions as to what
the Federal Government should do.

The Move for a Dominion Marriage Law.

When Parliament opened a private member had a
bill ready that provided that every marriage performed by an authorized person shall everywhere be
deemed valid, irrespective of the faith of the persons
married or of the celebrant. The bill was challenged
by those opposed to it on the point, what does the
B.N.A. Act mean by solemnization of a marriage? There
was a marked lack of sincerity among the supporters

of the bill, who declaimed in a style obviously intended for their constituents, for each one of them knew that the passage of the bill by the Commons meant their party being turned out of office. The first and last duty of a Dominion premier is to keep his party in power, and to this unwritten law Sir Robert Borden was obedient. To pass this bill, which flew in the face of numerous decisions of the Quebec courts, was equivalent to restoring Sir Wilfrid Laurier to office. He moved in amendment, that the bill do not now pass, but that a stated case on the points raised by it be referred to the Supreme Court to find out what were the powers of the Dominion Parliament. Five judges heard the argument on the questions submitted. Of these two were essential—was the Dominion Parliament competent to pass the Lancaster bill? Was any marriage, by regularly qualified minister, in the Province of Quebec legal? The court held the bill was beyond the authority of the Dominion Parliament to enact, as to the second question the judges divided according to creed. The two Catholics held a Protestant minister could not marry two Catholics in Quebec; the three Protestants, that he could. The arguments of the counsel brought out the pretensions of the priests that they were absolute in all matters concerning marriage and above parliament. This unsatisfactory finding, which decided nothing beyond that Mr. Lancaster's bill was so crudely drawn that it could not meet the evil it was intended to cure, quickened the desire to have a pronouncement by England. Security for costs was demanded by the defence. There was hesitation in subscribing, when the Orange Association came forward and lodged $5,000 to ascertain from the Empire's highest court whether a marriage performed by a Protestant minister is valid. Judgment has not yet been rendered.

The Law That is Called For.

In the multitude of words and contradictory statements the root of the matter was lost sight of. Let the reader keep steadily in mind, that marriage is a contract, and as a contract, affecting not only the two persons who make it, but prospective children and the inheritance of property, it is imperative the contract be made of public record. To provide such a record is the duty of the state, and necessarily, it must define who are eligible to contract marriage, and make sure they enter into it understandingly and of their free will. With their signing and the registration of the contract, the duty of the State ends. The parties to it may, and it is desirable they should, add the sanction of the denomination of which they are members, by a religious ceremony. The confusion of mind that prevails, that marriage depends on the religious ceremony and not on the mutual agreement of the parties to the contract, explains much of the uncertainty regarding what is a legal marriage in Canada and the deciding upon a remedy for an acknowledged evil. When a union contracted in one province is declared to be no marriage in another, when a marriage by a Protestant minister is set aside by a court of priests, when marriages are declared to be no marriages at all because of conditions and circumstances that the priests have devised, and which they assert to be of vital consequence, it is imperative that the situation be ended by the Dominion Government defining by statute what shall be a legal marriage for all Canada. To make that law effective it must ordain that in every municipality it shall have an officer, who must be a layman, to keep a register of marriages, and that only such marriages as are recorded by him shall be legal. Of the competency of the Dominion Government to enact such a law there is no question, and by passing such a law it would only be doing what has been done by the governments of Italy, France, Great Britain, and other countries, and its adoption would settle the situation in Canada. The Federal Government has no power to dictate what ceremonies shall solemnize marriage, but under Sec. 91 of the B. N. A. Act, it is given authority to define the status, which implies enacting the necessary regulations. The line of demarcation is definite—to the State belongs the marriage in so far as it is a civil contract, to the churches the ceremonies with which it be solemnized. No church has a right to interfere with the State in what it enacts as to marriage as a civil contract; the State none to dictate what the churches may do in the light of its being a union ordained by God.

A couple desirous of being married may have a religious ceremony or none, may discard vows and ring, but they must observe those requirements of the State designed to perfect a legal contract binding on both. It is wasted effort to argue about Papal decrees or what privileges any church may claim. These are beside the question of the right of parliament to define and make secure the most important contract of our social life and to ensure its permanent record. Had the premier and his ministers held that, as marriage was, in the first place, a civil contract, they were not going to be dragged into controversy over its religious aspect, they would have submitted a measure providing for civil marriage over the breadth of our land. If the Dominion has not reached the point in self-government that would enable it to declare positively what is a valid marriage, what is a binding contract in every province, in Quebec equally with British Columbia, then it is only the creature of the Supreme Court and the slave of any religious body that defies its authority. For the protection of wronged women, for the succor of innocent children, for clearing doubts as to succession, it is imperative that a civil marriage law be enacted at once. No reform can come before the defining and establishing beyond all question, of that institution on which the homes of our country are built. The politicians who will not pass such a law for fear of what the priests may do to them or their party, are cowards and traitors to home and womanhood.

Write it down, that whatever else the Parliament at Ottawa may do, it is its imperative duty to provide at once, a system for the registration of marriages as civil contracts. That, and that alone, will give a death blow to priestly usurpations and throw a shield over innocent women and children.

Canon Law and Burial.

Canon law enacts that every child baptized by a priest is placed in the care of the church, which cannot lose her hold over the person unless he makes a formal act of apostasy. Here is a case that shows how canon law works in this regard. In the township of Franklin, county of Huntingdon, an aged woman was committed to mother-earth in a Protestant burial-place. One of the King's judges was asked for an order to raise the body and re-inter it in a Roman Catholic cemetery. Reputable witnesses testified the woman had not been in a Catholic church for two score years, that in her latter days she gratefully received the ministrations of the Anglican rector, who had conducted the funeral, committing the body of the poor old woman to its kindred dust until the day of judgment with the most impressive of all burial services, that of the Church of England. All was urged in vain against the fact that her baptism by a priest was on record and that there was no proof in writing that she had made a formal act of apostasy. The judge granted the order, the body was exhumed, conveyed to the parish cemetery, and buried by a priest. Here is another illustration. A husband died a Catholic. His widow, a Protestant, anxious that he be buried where she could be laid, when her time came, beside him, for they were deeply attached to one another, sought to bury him in the general cemetery. She was warned that if she did so, the body would rest no longer in its grave than was required to get an order of court to raise it and re-inter it in the Catholic burial place. There has been no definite decision as to who has the first voice as to the disposal of the dead. The nearest being one between a widow and her late husband's relations, where the judge decided the widow's choice between two cemeteries. was to be preferred. All the parties to the case being Catholics, the case does not govern where one or other is Protestant. The priests declare they come before the nearest of kin, before widow or parent, brother or child, and in this the courts of Quebec uphold them. Thus backed, the interference of the priests on deaths occurring in households which are in part Protestant causes unspeakably distressing scenes. People naturally kind become changed when they believe they are doing the will of their church, and, in the name of religion, become cruel and relentless. A recent instance is that of Hormidas Lafond, who had been a Protestant for over twenty years and died a member in full communion of the Presbyterian church. Of the mission congregation at Belle Riviere he was a member of its board of managers and its treasurer. He died May 21, 1914. His brother, a resident of Montreal, an educated gentleman, came to attend the funeral, accompanied by two French Presbyterian clergymen, who were to conduct the service. Other relatives had resolved he should be buried in the Catholic cemetery and gathered in a crowd as the service was about to begin. Their spokesman produced an opinion from a lawyer, who is also M.P. for the county, to the effect that as all the relatives of the deceased, with the exception of his brother, were Catholics, they had the legal right to say where the burial should be. To avoid an affray over the possession of the corpse, the two Presbyterian clergymen advised the few Protestants present should leave the house. The excited crowd took possession of the coffin and, carrying it to the Catholic cemetery, buried it in the corner set apart for suicides, heretics, and unbaptized infants. The brother appealed to the court, and on proof being made that Lafond had expressly asked that he be buried in the Protestant graveyard, Judge Robidoux issued an order to transfer the body.

Canon Law and the Press.

These are instances to show how canon law affects individuals and families. In the devising of these laws laymen had no part. They were framed by the priests to strengthen their power and exalt themselves above the laity. In applying them the priesthood supplies prosecutors, counsel for the defence, and judges. Civil courts may be asked to put the decisions rendered into effect, but are allowed no power to change them. Where the priests are in a position to apply their laws to communities, freedom of the press becomes a name, for they are used to prevent newspapers from saying anything likely to injure the priests in public estimation. To show how this is done, a few instances will suffice. In Montreal there was a weekly newspaper called the Canada Revue. It had a staff of contributors eminent in their way, all Catholics, and the majority of them Nationalists. The paper had its circulation among the higher class of French-Canadians. In 1892 articles appeared in it calling upon the archbishop to protect the homes of Montreal against immoral priests, that scandals had been going on for over fifteen years without effective effort to end them. The archbishop issued a mandement acknowledging the guilt of one priest and calling on the people to do penance for the scandal done the church. This letter was followed by a combined pastoral from all the bishops, which also acknowledged there had been scandals among the priests, but denounced the newspapers that had alluded to them, claiming they did not concern the laity. The words of the bishops' letter are:

"Doubtless abuses may creep in, in spite of the "great precaution used by the enlightened prudence of "the church, but it is to us, her chiefs and her head "pastors, to Us alone that it belongs to repress and

"punish those lamentable and exceptional errors. . . .
"The church, dear brethren, has it chiefs, legitimately
"appointed, the same as has the family and society.
"Who these chiefs are, their names, their talents, and
"their qualities, matters little. In the eyes of faith
"they are the depositaries of the authority of God
"himself and the lieutenants of Jesus Christ. When
"our Lord said to his apostles, 'As my Father has sent
"me, I send you; go ye, therefore, and teach all
"nations,' he gave his power and his mission to the
"bishops; he appointed all the bishops, and all the
"priests chosen and ordained by them, to continue for-
"ever his work and his teachings. In a word, he
"created in his church different privileges and differ-
"ent rights; its members were divided into two classes
"perfectly distinct—the priests and the laymen, a
"division corresponding to the two elements of the
"social body, the authorities and the people, the rulers
"and the ruled. In the case of the human family, is
"one of the sons entitled to command and censure the
"father? In the state, are the simple citizens called
"to enact laws and render judgments? In the army,
"is it the private soldiers who dictate the plan of
"campaign, and order the charge or the retreat? No.
"More especially is this true in the case of the church.
"It behooves the bishops only, whom the Holy Ghost
"has established, to direct the church. It does not
"belong to the faithful, however good Catholics they
"may be, or pretend to be, to trace for the bishops
"a line of conduct, much less to pass judgment upon
"or to censure them. In everything concerning piety,
"morals, or discipline, the priests are in no way sub-
"jected to the opinion of men, and have no lessons to
"receive from those over whom God has appointed
"them judges and pastors."

The rule here laid down, that laymen had no right to comment upon the conduct of priests, was succeeded by a letter from the Archbishop of Montreal formally condemning the Revue and a country newspaper.

The sentence is contained in these words:
"Having invoked the holy name of God, we con-
"demn, by virtue of Our Authority, the two publi-
"cations printed in our diocese, to wit, the Canada
"Revue and the Echo des Deux-Montagnes, and forbid,
"pending further order, all the faithful under penalty
"of refusal of the Sacraments, to print, to put or to
"keep on sale, to distribute, to read, to receive or have
"in possession, these two dangerous journals, or to
"work for them or encourage them in any manner
"whatever."

The result of this order was the immediate "strangling"—so its publisher expressed it—of the country paper. The Revue tried to make a fight, and continued to be issued at an increasing weekly loss. Published by a company, a delegation of shareholders was sent to interview the archbishop with a view to his modifying his attitude towards it. He frankly acknowledged The Revue had not offended in doctrine, but it had in discipline, by exposing the conduct of priests, and demanded complete and unconditional submission. This the conductors of the paper were not prepared to give, as it meant an acknowledgment they had done wrong in exposing the guilty priests. The interdict was therefore continued; contributors severed their connection with The Revue, subscribers returned their copies, merchants withdrew their advertisements, newsagents would not keep it on sale. A profitable business was changed into a losing one with certainty before its owners of having to give it up. To determine whether the priests could thus ruin a legitimate enterprise they sued the archbishop for $10,000 damages. The case was heard by one of the youngest members of the Bench, a product of the Jesuit college. The point at issue was simple. Had a man, no matter what his title or position, what pretensions he assumed, or what divine authority he claimed, the right in a British colony to punish a newspaper otherwise than by an action-at-law? Instead of grappling with that question, Judge Doherty set up such men-of-straw as, Was the archbishop's order libellous? If it was, was it not privileged? Was the issuing of the letter not within the right of the archbishop? And, then, laboriously knocked them down, by assuming that the archbishop was a superior person, who had the morals of the community in his keeping. Judge Doherty dismissed the action, with all costs against The Revue. In the eyes of British law the archbishop stood no higher than any other man, and he had no more the keeping of morals in his charge than the editor of a newspaper. If anybody was aggrieved by what The Revue said, it was the priests whose conduct it exposed. They entered no action against it, but the archbishop wreaked their revenge on the editors by a proceeding unknown to English law. The publishers of The Revue carried the case to the Court of Review. The appeal was heard by two English-speaking judges and one French. Chief Justice Tait substantially followed the argument of Judge Doherty, ruling the archbishop, in consequence of his office, was a privileged person, and that any act of his "according to canon law and the rules of the "church," was binding upon Catholics. Judge Taschereau took the same view—the archbishop in condemning The Revue had acted within the just and lawful exercise of his authority and power. Judge Archibald dissented, considering the pretensions of the archbishop had no authority in either French or English law. He had ruined a lawful business without any form of law whatever, had done what no British court or functionary has power to do, suppressed a newspaper without trial and without compensation. The publishers desired to carry the case to England, but there was no adequate response to their appeal for help to meet the costs, and so The Revue disappeared, leaving the archbishop victorious. Other papers that have been interdicted have met a like end except in a few cases where the publishers made unconditional submission and did penance.

As bringing out a few new points the case of L'Electeur, of Quebec, may be described. During the general election of 1896 it had reported numerous instances of priests intimidating their people, under spiritual penalties, from the pulpit, in the confessional, and in presence of others, what candidates they were to support. It was not pretended these reports were erroneous. A remarkable petition from the Liberal members of the Quebec legislature, 26 in number, assured the Pope that:

"In a number of counties, in the election of June, "1896, the clergy went so far as to say that the elec- "tors could not vote for Liberal candidates without "involving their conscience, committing a serious fault, "and incurring refusal of the sacraments."

The petitioners asked the Pope to send a legate to abate the injury before the coming election of 1897. That L'Electeur was only reporting what was true is undeniable. The Bishop of Chicoutimi, in whose diocese the priests went to the greatest extremes, resented these newspaper reports and issued a letter to be read from every pulpit. The bishop said:

"The church has been constituted by its divine "founder a perfect society by itself, independent and "distinct of the civil society. The bishops have been "established by the Holy Ghost to erect that society "called the Church of God. Therefore they have, in "their respective districts, the triple power, legisla- "tive, judicial, and coercive—the power to teach, "command and judge. Such powers, of course, are "subordinate to the authority of the chief of the "church, who alone possesses the plenitude of apos- "tolic power. All the priests and the faithful owe "docility and obedience to the bishops. It is to them, "as well as to his apostles, that Jesus Christ said, Who "obeys you obeys me: who despises you despises me."

Proceeding from this assertion of his divine authority, the bishop tells of the existence of a school of journalists who deride the spiritual power of the bishops, "who claim that the bishops are not infallible, "and, consequently, people are free to accept or reject "their directions in affairs of conscience."

Among these bad journalists is L'Electeur, of the city of Quebec, and warns it he will not "hesitate to "interdict the reading of it under special penalty."

In reply to this pastoral letter L'Electeur pleaded politics and elections were outside the sphere of the church. The bishops, for others had joined in the issue, replied through their leading theologian, "that "the church has the right to authoritatively determine "what is and what is not within her competence, and "the State is bound to abide by her decision." The publisher yielded, and on his unreserved submission was permitted to continue his newspaper on changing its name.

Other instances could be given. The latest and most peculiar is that of Le Pays. Its editor was Godfroi Langlois, one of Montreal's representatives in the Quebec legislature, a man of ability and unresting energy. Although a pronounced Nationalist, he could not be persuaded that the priests are the guardians of the institutions cherished by French-Canadians. On the contrary, he held they were the means of keeping Quebec from attaining the high destiny it might reach, attributing the ignorance and backwardness that prevailed in the rural parishes to their influence. That the French-Canadian might equal the Anglo-Saxon in the race of life, he advocated taking the schools from under the control of the priesthood, and placing them under a member of the government, who would be responsible to the legislature alone. Minor reforms were uniform and free text-books, the abolition of fees, so that no parent could plead poverty as a reason for not sending his children to school, and, especially, compulsory attendance. The priests were stunned at the bare proposal of taking public instruction out of

their hands. The climax came in July, 1912, when a
great convention of delegates from St. Jean Baptiste
societies met at Quebec. Mr. Langlois ridiculed the
importance attached to the saint and his "little sheep"
while weightier matters were ignored, and condemned
the resolution declaring any except Catholics ineligible
to be members of St. Jean Baptiste societies. He said
that "places French-speaking Protestants under the
"ban of our race, and makes the state decree that you
"cannot be French-Canadian unless you are a Catho-
"lic." The priests tried to deprive Mr. Langlois of
his seat in the legislature and failed, for the division
he represented is largely composed of foreigners, many
of them Jews. Archbishop Bruchesi, in a pastoral
letter, June 30, 1912, warned him that if he persisted
in the line he was pursuing his paper would be placed
under the ban. Mr. Langlois made no change, and
the threat was put into effect. The last Sunday of
September, 1913, a letter from Archbishop Bruchesi
was read from the altar of every church in the diocese
of Montreal, interdicting the faithful from reading
Le Pays, as it was the enemy of "our old religious and
national traditions." Mr. Langlois protested that he
was a sincere Catholic and had never allowed a line to
appear in his paper against the doctrines of his church,
but he would assert his right to discuss any secular
question, and would continue to advocate educational
reforms, including the appointment of a minister of
education. Asked what he would do touching the
interdict on his paper, Mr. Langlois replied, "I am
"determined to face the music if the friends of Le
"Pays and the partizans of liberty of speech will stand
"by me and give their aid." He did find friends, but
they were more free in words than dollars, and he
speedily realized that no paper under the ban can be
self-supporting in Quebec. However, as the breaking
down of Le Pays threatened to be tedious, a shorter
method was adopted to get rid of it and its editor.
The government created a new office, a representative

of Quebec at Brussels, and appointed Mr. Langlois, who gladly accepted. In this adroit manner the agitator for educational reform and his editorials were got rid of.

Canon Law and Private Judgment.

The ban has not been confined to newspapers; books and pamphlets have been placed under it. The most notable instance was that of the Hon. L. O. David's book, entitled, "The Canadian Clergy, their Mission and their Work." The writer's object was to uphold the proposition, that the priests ought to confine themselves to the spiritual domain, and as his reason for so saying he quoted from history to show that whenever they meddled with secular affairs it was to their own hurt and that of the province. Starting by laying down "that bishops and priests are men subject to "error" he went on to point out how, in his view, they erred in 1837 and at each subsequent crisis when French nationality was in jeopardy. Professedly a devout Catholic, Senator David deplored this, blaming the mistaken course of the priests to ignorance of public sentiment. "The truth," he declares, "reaches "them (the priests) with difficulty through the fumes "of the incense which envelops them," and he warned them to awake from their sleep of false security and escape the storm which menaced them by leaving politics alone. The little book, which was issued in September, 1896, was condemned by the bishops in a joint pastoral in January following. After stating the book had been submitted to the Holy Office at Rome and been formally condemned "with the approval of the sovereign pontiff," the rule is laid down that no layman "has authority to judge, condemn, or approve of "doctrines or writings. . . . It is, by your bishops "and the priests, who are united with them, that you "are to receive the teachings of the Holy See . . . to "be with the Pope you must not be in opposition to "the bishops," and the direction of the bishops was

that whoever had a copy of Mr. David's book was to
destroy it at once or hand it over to his confessor.
This was the command of the Pope to the bishops
"whom he orders you to obey as you would Jesus
"Christ." How would the author take this condemnation? His book was a vindication of the right of private judgment in politics, denying the priests the
authority they exercised in driving "men from the
"church who wish to exercise freely their rights as
"citizens . . . believing themselves in a better posi-
"tion than the priests to choose the best mode of
"action. . . . Men living in the world and seeing
"what is going on, hearing what is said, have the right
"to give advice to the clergy, or rather to point out
"the dangers which threaten not only their influence
"but that of religion. They are right to fear that their
"children may not be Catholics if the priests do not
"understand that the salvation of souls is worth more
"than the salvation of a party." When the first
blast of condemnation reached him, Mr. David said:
"When I wrote the little book I had no idea of the
"storm I was raising. I thought I was doing the
"clergy a service in speaking out the thoughts that
"I could not drive from my mind. After the last
"general election I noticed a growing feeling against
"clerical interference in politics, and simply gave it
"publication. They may condemn me; they may
"excommunicate me. I cannot help that, but I shall
"still remain a Catholic—that is my religion, and they
"cannot take my faith from me. I thought when I
"wrote my book that, as a British subject, I had a
"perfect right to do so. If not, there is something
"wrong, for I feel that, as a French-Canadian and a
"Catholic, I should have the same rights in politics as
"my English-speaking brethren."

The sentiments of his book were the expressions
of his sincere conviction that each elector has the right
of private judgment in selecting the candidate for

whom he shall cast his vote. This the Pope declared an error. The Archbishop of Montreal expressed the rule that governs the elector in these words:
"In our days, because of the representative sys-
"tem which obtains in the civilized world, and which
"places the election of those entrusted with authority
"in the hands of majorities and multitudes, the Pope
"often encounters opposition to the liberty of the
"church . . . whether in public life or by the voice
"of the press, the Sovereign Pontiff gives as a rule
"to follow, the direction which will be given by the
"Vatican and by the bishops."

Mr. David was given an opportunity to justify the claim of his co-religionists to poll their votes free from priestly dictation, to act as citizens of a self-governing State, but he proved unequal; he had no desire to be a martyr; he wilted under the condemnation of a clique of his fellow-mortals who blasphemously claimed the inerrancy of divinity, and doing violence to the reason God had given him, made a humiliating submission, and ordered the destruction of all unsold copies of his book. Such the heroic spirit of the historian of Les Patriotes de 1837-8.

Canon Law and Municipalities.

The domain of ecclesiastical law is not confined to the fields that have been touched upon. It extends to all the concerns of life, and if not applied to all in practice, it is because conditions at present are not favorable. It is well to mention another. The unit of territory in Ontario is the township: in Quebec it is the parish. The township is purely secular, the parish combines the ecclesiastical with the secular. The parish has for its centre a church, municipal attributes being added. Since Confederation the bishops have had an unrestricted hand in erecting parishes; they issue their decree and all Catholics within its limits are liable to pay the tax levied to build a church and a house for the priest. As a con-

sequence of what the bishop has done, the parish
becomes also a distinct municipality, electing a mayor
and councillors. In the days of the French regime the
secular affairs of the parish were in the hands of
laymen, the fabrique, as it was called, being similar
to the vestry and churchwardens of England. Nominally this is still the case, the old forms are observed,
but are merely a cover for the will of the priest who
directs. The power of the bishops to erect new
parishes is more often injurious to Catholics than
Protestants. The bishop decides on dividing a parish,
which means the people in the new one will have to
build a church, which may cost anywhere between
twenty thousand and a hundred thousand dollars. The
disjoined habitants object; they were taxed to build
the church they are ordered to leave, and shrink from
being taxed to raise another. In the old time they
would have had a voice in the proposed change, for,
previous to Confederation, it was undisputed that no
change could be made in the boundaries of a parish
without the consent of a majority of its ratepayers.
The bishops, however, ignore the statute and proceed
according to canon law. What happened in the diocese of St. Hyacinthe in 1892 will illustrate what is
going on all over Quebec. The bishop formed a new
parish by taking parts of three old ones. The people
included in the new parish of St. Pierre de Verone
protested against being wrenched from their old
parishes, and appealed to Rome. Mr. Mercier, the
same who afterwards became Premier, crossed to Italy
to argue their case, and left Rome persuaded he had
won. Soon after his return to Canada came the decision, signed by Cardinal Ledochowski, sustaining the
action of Bishop Moreau in every point. The people,
by refusing to accept the Italian verdict, put themselves in the position of excommunicated Catholics.
They persisted in their opposition, one of their number, Julien Campbell, a French-Scot, taking out a test
action for $20,000 damages against the bishop for de-

priving him of his rights as a parishioner of St. Damien, one of the three sub-divided parishes. The main point in the plea of the bishop was, that his action was in accord with canon law, which "is beyond "the competence and jurisdiction of the civil courts "of this country." In his reply to the bishop's plea, Mr. Mercier laid down these principles:

"That the ordinances of the bishops, even when "they are purely disciplinary and have only canonical "effects, as falsely claimed by the defendant in his "said demurrer, do not escape, in this country, the "control of the courts, which may quash, annul and "lay them aside:

"That there are no privileged classes in this country, "and that the bishops are amenable to the laws like "everybody else;

"That a bishop must answer before the courts for "his acts and his writings, like anybody else, even if "these acts and writings were, as the defendant claims "they are in this case, purely canonical and discip-"linary, if they injure and damage others;

"That it is absurd to pretend, as the defendant "does, that a person disturbed in the exercise of "religious and civil rights by a Roman Catholic bishop, "has no other recourse but before the ecclesiastical "superior of that bishop;

"That this proposition is the denial of all religious "and civil liberty recognized by law in this country "and that upheld by our country, and that these "Roman Catholic bishops can exercise their power in "Canada only within the limits and in the manner and "form prescribed by law."

While the case was before the court an incident happened that brings out the peculiarities of Quebec life. A resident of the new parish, an aged habitant, fell sick, and desired the last rites. The priest of his old parish, St. Damien, was sent for, who refused to come, as the dying man belonged to the new parish, and must send for its priest. This the sick man would

not do, and the priest of an adjoining parish was asked
to come. He responded, heard the old man's confession but refused the last rites, as the man was one of
those who supported the suit against the bishop. The
difficulty was evaded by sending for a priest who was
unattached to a parish. The court decided in favor of
Bishop Moreau.

The forming of a new parish means the bringing
into being of a new municipality, involving political,
financial, municipal and social changes—it may be a
hiving of electors for party purposes, or bringing in
more farms on which to levy taxes to pay a church
debt, with the incurring of which the owners of them
had nothing to do. Protestant ratepayers have no
desire to interfere with any bishop in erecting new
parishes for church and school purposes, but as his act
involves a new municipality, they do object, considering it high-handed that any priest should, at his will,
transfer them from one municipality to another. A
decree for a new parish having been issued in the
county of St. Jean, 69 Protestants signed a petition to
the court against it. Judge Tellier ruled their names
could not be counted, and this decision was upheld by
the Court of Appeal, which also confirmed his ruling
that ecclesiastical authorities (the bishops) are not
subject to the jurisdiction of the civil courts. A
more flagrant case was that of Ste. Barbe. On the
south bank of the St. Lawrence was a small settlement,
which dates back to 1820, composed of Scotch farmers.
One day an official visited each house demanding payment of a rate levied by the municipal council of the
parish of Ste. Barbe. The Scotsmen were amazed,
for they knew nothing of the proceedings that had
been going on by which the Bishop of Montreal had
sub-divided St. Anicet to make a new parish, his commissioners completing his work by also making it a
civil parish. Notices of what was being done had
been given, but as the law only requires these notices
to be posted on the Catholic church door the Protest-

ant farmers knew not of them. A prolonged attempt was made to undo what the bishop had done. It was pled that, whatever powers the bishop might have in the seigniories in erecting parishes, they did not extend to municipalities where the land is held on English tenure. The Protestant farmers in the new made parish objected to being wrenched from their old municipality as an injury to their pecuniary interests and placing them subject to a majority with whom they were not in accord. The fight was long and bitter. The Protestant farmers had no objection to Ste. Barbe being an ecclesiastical parish, but strenuously opposed its being also a municipality—the priests insisted it should be a municipal as well as an ecclesiastical parish, and the judge, before whom an appeal was taken, upheld them. After being beaten in the courts and in the legislature, the Protestants had to submit, the parish being established beyond dispute in 1886. It had then eleven Protestant farmers, by far the largest proprietors and taxpayers: in 1908 it had two. The oldest Scotch settlement in the county of Huntingdon was blotted out.

Canon Law and City Taxes.

It would be tedious to follow canon law in all its applications, some of which are surprising. Thus, when it was proposed in the city council of Montreal that the real estate of the different denominations should not be allowed to go wholly untaxed, the archbishop issued a mandement to be read from the altar, censuring the aldermen who supported the change, and advising the ratepayers at the next election to give their votes for men who are well disposed towards the priesthood. The archbishop based his command on the claim "that ecclesiastical property is, according to "canonical law, which is recognized by our legislation, "exempt from taxation." Thus threatened, the Montreal councillors dropped their proposed reform.

Canon Law and Canonical Courts.

In following this narrative of the working of canon law, the sympathies of the reader have been drawn to the persons who have suffered from it, but their wrongs must not be allowed to divert his attention from the stupendous revelation that, apart from the King's courts, there exists in Quebec a judicial organization, with a full code of laws, a minute code of procedure, and stated courts. The claim of this judicial system is, that it is superior to all secular courts, that its laws are above those enacted by parliament, and that its decisions go before those delivered by laymen. It is difficult for British-born people to comprehend a judicial system other than that built up by parliament, of laws other than those enacted by parliament, of decisions which do not come from the King's courts. Yet in Quebec there are dual laws, those promulgated in Italy and those framed by British legislatures, and where they conflict the foreign laws prevail. There are also dual courts, and the deliverances of those of the priesthood override those of the lay-judges. To many it will be inconceivable that in a British province there should be two standards of law, two administrations of law, and, when judgments clash, that of the foreign court prevails. Is it not the very essence of the British constitution that those who live under it shall be subject to no laws enacted by a foreign power, and be amenable to no court that does not derive its sole authority from that constitution? Forget the theological aspect of the case, forget the creed of the men who expound and administer canon law, and look at the situation from a purely secular standpoint and ask, Does not what these priests propose for the Dominion, and have already succeeded to a considerable degree in bringing into operation in Quebec, mean the destruction of British institutions? Can two governments exist together, one claiming to be divine, the other to draw its authority from the people? Must not one or

other give way—which is it to be, the Papal or the
British? Can two systems of law, two courts, two
standards of right and wrong, two claimants to obedience continue to exist in the same community? As
well ask what would become of the ship that has two
captains or the army with two commanders. One or
other must be deposed. Are British subjects to be
amenable not solely to the statutes enacted by their
representatives, but also to a pretended higher law?
The answer to these questions is not to be evaded by
saying canonical decrees concern spiritual matters
alone. Is strangling the press a spiritual matter; is
dictating to electors the candidate for whom they are
to vote a spiritual matter? It is also urged canon law
only affects Catholics. Go tell this to the Protestant
girl who has her marriage to a Catholic declared no
marriage, and is sent forth to the world branded as a
concubine and her children as bastards. Is it nothing
to non-Catholics to have the laws relating to baptism,
marriage, and burial dictated by the priesthood? Our
social state so binds us together, that no wrong can be
done to the Catholic which the Protestant entirely
escapes. Even were it not so, has the Catholic no claim
on his fellows that he shall stand in the full liberty
which British freedom implies? The existing state
of affairs in Quebec is a menace to British institutions
in every Province from Nova Scotia to British Columbia, and if Canada is to be British in reality as it is in
name, this state of affairs has to be reformed. Politicians may wriggle as they please, cry out against
bigots, firebrands, and extremists, talk about the beauty
of toleration and mutual forbearance, prophesy that if
we only keep quiet all will come right, but let them
answer this: Can two judicial systems, so directly opposite as the Papal and British, develop together—must
not the one that is to survive smother the other? In
Quebec we know which of the two is being slowly and
surely smothered. Two systems of jurisprudence, two

authorities claiming allegiance, cannot exist side by side.

Incapable Legislators.

In new countries, government largely falls into the hands of men incapable of discharging their duties. The forms and names are there, but not ability to use them worthily. Members of legislatures are called statesmen who in the Old Land would be classed with pot-house politicians. Ignorance and stupidity can be excused as inevitable where a country is newly settled and the choice of representatives is limited, but not the greed which perverts colonial governments into mediums of benefiting supporters: expenditure on public works used to keep the party in power in office, the civil service degraded into filling offices with incapable partizans. Worse than all, the national domain, given in trust for future generations, plundered and, along with huge grants from the public treasury handed over to gangs of projectors who combine to raid it under pretence of securing great enterprises, while the levying of revenue is adjusted to enrich one class by the impoverishment of another. All these crimes against the people are not comparable for a moment to those committed by the heads of successive administrations in aiding a caste of ecclesiastics to plant a system of government in the heart of that we have derived from the Mother Country. That is Treason; the others were robberies. High-sounding pretences of being Empire builders and of cherishing ideals of Imperialism only add hypocrisy to their offence.

The call to every true Briton is to vindicate the right of self-government, to root out the interference of foreign emissaries in the ruling of our country, and to make good the boast that our allegiance is alone due to the executive that derives its powers from the people. There is a clashing of the two contending systems heard every session at Ottawa and in our legislatures. If the British cause is to be maintained that clashing will increase and thunder over the land. He is a coward who would waver in his determination to uphold the cause of equal rights and a government independent of clerical control, because it will result in the destruction of the existing political parties and the injury of personal interests.

Canon Law is Placed Above British Law.

The term "the British constitution" is vague in the sense that it is not a written document, but one feature of that constitution is not open to question—that its underlying principle is government by the people. It was to establish that principle a succession of patriotic men wrought since the days of Elizabeth, until it became embodied not simply in precedents, declarations and statutes, but in the organization of the government—in extending the powers of the House of Commons, in restricting those of the House of Lords and of the sovereign. Britons are free in that they rule themselves, that the laws are made by men whom they elect, and that the government of the day is responsible to them—that if the people do not approve of their actions, of the course they are pursuing, they can compel the ministers to resign and put others in their place. No other government in the world, not even that of the United States, is so sensitive to public opinion, or so quickly responsive to the popular will. The government may be right or it may be wrong, but it is the people's government, and it is the voice of the people that is supreme. To tell the inhabitants of England and Scotland that in one of their colonies a totally different system of government prevails—a colony where the people do not rule, but where the laws that are obeyed are laws made in Rome by a caste of clergymen whose head is a foreigner—will sound incredible. Read the following extract from a pastoral letter of the Archbishop of Quebec, February 2, 1882, and judge if what is here set down is not true:

"At times the Roman pontiff defines the impre-"scriptible laws of morality, and his decisions, as those "relating to dogma, are irrefragable. . . . The "holy church is also a kingdom . . . a visible "society, which all must join under pain of eternal "damnation. The church requires a visible head in "whom is reflected the majesty of her invisible Head. " . . . The spiritual royalty of the Roman pontiff "has a vigorous claim to our respect and to our obedi-"ence. . . . And as the Son of God exercises his "pontificate and speaks his word by the ministry of "his priests . . . the duty of every true Catholic "is to obey this tutelary authority. . . . We "ordain that this solemn decree be frequently incul-"cated to the faithful of this Province, that all may "know the sovereign pontiff, the legitimate successor "of Peter . . . has full authority to enact on faith, "morals, and discipline, decrees which all are bound "to obey both in mind and heart."

The formula laid down is definite. The one Church of Christ on earth is the Church of Rome, the head of that church is Christ's representative on earth, his domain is the world, his commands are as those of God. These commands are in part embodied in canon law and demand absolute obedience. In Quebec they receive, as has been seen from the cases quoted, unquestioning submission even from His Majesty's judges. So far as I can learn there has not been an instance of a decree of an ecclesiastical court having been quashed by a Quebec court. A lawyer stands up before a judge and tells him he holds in his hands a decree of the bishop in-such-and-such-a-case, and the judge, whether Protestant or Catholic, ratifies it as a mere matter of form, and so gives the decree of the priest-court civil effect. Let it be declared by a bishop, that a matter falls under canon law and the effect is the same as when a Polynesian priest pronounces the word taboo —it is taken out of the ordinary sphere, is above civil functionaries, above British law, something which permits of no appeal, no discussion or amendment, is simply to be implicitly obeyed.

The practical application of canon law is to deny to those affected by it the benefits of British law— freedom of speech and of the press vanishes, statutes are superseded by canons, our highest parliament denied the right to regulate so vital a concern to society at large as marriage, and allegiance to the State superseded by obedience to a caste of men who claim to be imbued with a divine essence which places them above criticism and makes questioning of their acts sacrilege. Is the demand, that there shall be only one law in Canada, and that British, unreasonable? A few years ago Canon Law had no civil force, it is now superior to the King's courts.

CHAPTER X.

It is a Papal, not a French Quebec that Menaces the Dominion

Convinced of the danger to the Dominion arising from the state of affairs that exists in Quebec, the question comes, What can be done to avert it? Can the Federal Parliament interfere with what is considered to be provincial rights? Nay, more, can what the priests claim to be prescriptive rights be set aside? On this latter head it is advisable to have a clear understanding before taking up the other. Are there not vested interests coming down from the days of Louis XIV., which form an insurmountable barrier to the Dominion Parliament stripping the priests of Quebec of whatever is hurtful to Canada as a nation—privileges that clash with the rights of the people and of the other Provinces, privileges that irritate and prolong strife? In foregoing chapters several of the pretensions of the priesthood of Quebec have been brought to the test of historical facts—such as that their privileges were secured to them in the treaty of Paris, that the Quebec Act gives them authority to levy church dues on every acre of the Province of Quebec, that it was through their influence Canada was preserved to Britain during the American revolution and again during the War of 1812. There remains another, namely, that the organization, powers, and attributes they now possess are theirs by prescriptive right, for they were theirs during the French period. This claim I wish to compare with the records preserved in the archives of France. In the past it has been the habit of the people of the other Provinces to take for granted as true the assumptions of the Quebec priests. Claims founded on fact is one thing; claims founded on pretension quite another. Sacerdotal pomp, the affected airs of superior beings, the assertion they represent Christ, have gone far in imposing upon the public mind. When the age, the power, the wealth, the assumptions of the Church of Rome are considered, this is not to be wondered at. The prestige of the centuries is hers, and outside of heathendom and its twin, Mohamedanism, no other single organization numbers so many million votaries. Her emissaries hover around every court, and there is no country where her influence is unknown. Widespread and potent as are her secular successes they become insignificant when compared with her spiritual claims, for these are, that she is the sole channel of God's truth, and that her ministers are the exclusive agents of Christ's grace to man. Through the haze of incense, shimmering in purple and scarlet, white and gold, is seen that carved structure which affects to be a symbol of Calvary, and the mortal-man on its steps is affecting to repeat the sacrifice which Christ made once and for all time on the hill that witnessed the world's shame and was the starting-point of the world's hope. To challenge the truth of statements made by men who say they represent Christ, to sweep aside their attitudes of haughty command, their elaborate ceremonies, their gorgeous robes, the triumphant music, the homage of the multitudes who fall on their knees before them, is not easy, for these are of the things that dazzle the imagination and darken the understanding. Set aside all this, free the mind from the witchery of the past, the glamor of the present, strip these priests of their robes of lace and silk, take them from their self-erected pedestals, and having done so test their assertions as you would those of laymen. The point to be examined coldly and critically is their claim that they inherited from the French regime the extraordinary and exclusive privileges they enjoy in Quebec. Before doing so, it is well to have a knowledge of the results of these privileges which have been brought about in town and country.

The Habitant at Home.

To the visitor who travels through the parishes of Quebec for the first time, the outstanding feature is the size and number of conventual buildings. In villages, that are a cluster of one-storey houses, he sees a church large enough and costly enough for a city, and nearby massive structures where, he is told, certain orders of brothers or sisters dwell. Whatever route the visitor chooses, road, steamboat, or rail, he meets men and women in uniform that tells of their being members of some clerical order, and in whatever direction he turns his gaze the gleam of a cross is discerned, while the tinkle of convent-bell or the boom of the big church bell breaks on his hearing from dawn to sunset. Passing along the road he is startled by coming on a cross by the wayside, accompanied by emblems of the tortures of the Saviour of the world. Each house he enters, no matter how humble, has symbols of Christ's humiliation and pictures of saints. These are only appearances, yet, like the faint vapor that rises from the summit of an isle of the Indian Ocean, they indicate the unseen, the strange fire that burns beneath. It takes patience and close observation to ascertain the nature of the pervading influence which enthralls this quiet community, and the knowledge of it comes by slow degrees. As it does, the visitor's prepossessions are dissipated. He thought of them as French, as jealously preserving the customs and traditions of the country whence came their forefathers. He finds they know nothing of France, that France has become merely a name, and that neither in spirit nor sympathy have they anything in common with the France of to-day. There is little reading, few newspapers, and fewer books. The books are devotional, the newspapers are frivolous and sensational as to secular affairs, devotedly clerical when political or social subjects are referred to. In conversation he finds certain topics are tabooed, and that on many vital subjects there is no independence of word or thought. While politely treated, he comes to feel that under the cover of the courtesy with which he is addressed lurks a strange mingling of pity and suspicion. The belief has been deeply impressed upon the people among whom he sojourns, that Protestants are not religious, that their pretended faith is a mere negation, which was invented by Luther, and Luther was inspired by the devil. Taught thus, they pity him as one of the lost. This fundamental fact, that the great body of the population of Quebec are firmly grounded in the belief that Protestants have no religion, and that, if they persevere in rejecting the aid of the priests they are lost, affects more than their personal bearing in coming in contact with non-Catholics, it shapes their politics, colors their opinions of whatever is happening near or far. How has this been brought about? The visitor watches the classes of the elementary school, examines its text-books, and sees how carefully the scholars have impressed upon their infant minds everything the priests desire they should believe, and how they are kept in ignorance of everything they wish withheld. From the wayside school he turns to the college and marks the art of the procrustean beds where the pupils, robbed of their intellectual individuality, and their higher sentiments, are forced into the narrow mould of their priestly preceptors. From the college to the convent is a step, and here, amid surface accomplishments, the future women of the Province are imbued with belief in the infallibility of the Church of Rome and the duty of unquestioning obedience to its priests. Passing from these institutions, where the minds and wills of the youth are thus shaped, the observer no longer wonders at the influence the priests exercise, the moulding of the youth of a great Province lies entirely in their hands. Talk of passive obedience to Kings. Here is the reality of which Charles I. and his son James dreamt. Talk of espionage. Here in actual service is such a system as Fouche never conceived. In the presbytery and the buildings around it is the intellect that thinks for the community, the will that holds and directs its will, the tongue that commands, the eye that sees every detail of their daily lives, the ear to which comes the tattle and the innermost secrets of the dwellers beneath the roofs of each house in the parish. The atmosphere thus created is not national, it is ecclesiastical: it is not French, it is Papal. It is a population trained to do the will and advance the interests of the Church of Rome. True the priests exhort the people to be French, and nothing but French. That is merely part of their system to keep them under their thumb. Were the habitants of any other origin they would use the same cry—were they Irish they would tell them to be Irish and nothing else; were they Germans or Poles they would get like advice. In their speaking English, especially in their learning to read English, the priests see danger, and so they reiterate the precept that they are to be first Catholic then French, and that on their continuing to be Catholic depends their being French, and they are made to believe that the priests are the sole surety of their nationality and their language; that if they leave their Church they lose everything. No pains are spared to keep them isolated from Protestants. The partition-wall is maintained so high that practically there is no social intercourse, no intimate relation permitted. Here, again, the dividing-line is creed, not race, for if the English-speaking neighbor becomes Catholic the priest encourages the freest intercourse. The longer the visitor stays and the more intimate he becomes with the people, the more conscious he is of the all-pervading influence of the priests, how they dominate every concern of daily life, how every interest is made subservient to their interest, how every prejudice is fostered that aids their plans, every cry raised that will bind their followers. It may be said all this is true of rural Quebec alone. Let the visitor leave. He is now treading the streets of the city of Quebec. Mark those colossal buildings behind whose barred windows and sentinelled gates are monks, and nuns, and novices by the hundred. At every step he meets a many uniformed procession. The legislature is in session; he goes to its place of meeting, and, standing in the corridor, watches the ever-shifting crowd. Here, again, priests mingle in the throng: if there be a measure that interests them they are in committee-room and in the galleries of the House. He calls on members of the cabinet; in their ante-rooms he finds priests or meets them leaving his private room, and wherever they go observes how their opinions are deferred to, their requests granted. Attending the meeting of the city council he finds like obsequiousness to the requests that come from the archbishop's palace. The Church of Rome owns a third of the real estate of the city, and, therefore, ought to be its largest taxpayer. It pays no tax, yet is insistent on being granted favors at the expense of those who do.

Standing whether in country or city, in presence of conditions so extraordinary, so utterly opposite to what prevail in every other Province, two questions press for answer:

1. How has this come about?

2. Is not the existence of such conditions in a Province that elects sixty-five members of the House of Commons, a menace to the Dominion's continuing to be British in reality, and to its people enjoying free institutions?

Conditions not a Survival of French Rule.

If you ask a Roman Catholic he assures you what you see is a survival of the French period, that the French, under British rule, in their love of Romanism, have preserved it in every detail as their fathers knew it before the Conquest. Is this true? Is it really so, that the Church of Rome, as it exists to-day in Quebec, is only enjoying the privileges, immunities, and prerogatives it did before Canada became a British possession? This question has a most important bearing on what course our rulers should take with regard to the priesthood of Quebec. If it can be proved that they are only enjoying what was their use-and-wont under the French kings, respect for vested privileges makes the reformer hesitate. On the other hand, if it can be demonstrated beyond all question from official records of the French period, that the priests were held in New France subordinate to the State, that they were denied the privilege of being autonomous, that even the details of conventual life and of pastoral work were regulated by the civil magistrate, the question assumes an entirely different aspect, for the reformer knows he has to deal not with privileges inherited from the French period, but with privileges that have had their origin while Quebec has been under the British Crown. He who would hesitate about uprooting institutions that came from another regime, hoary with three centuries, has no hesitation whatever in manfully grappling with them when he has ascertained he has been grossly deceived.

As to what really was the status of the priesthood in Quebec during the rule of the French Kings, there can be no better testimony—indeed, no other testimony—than that of these Kings. In the voluminous archives these Kings left, we have minute details of all they did and ordered in their governing New France. What is the evidence of these State-papers on the question under consideration? To begin, what was the attitude of Louis XIV., and of Louis XV. towards the religious orders of New France? Instead of summarizing what they contain and citing references, I give literal quotations from the edicts, despatches and letters of those two Kings to the governors, intendants, and bishops of Quebec.

No public question can be more delicate than whether the parliament of Canada would be justified in overseeing convents, with the view of protecting their inmates and securing the public welfare. Ninety-nine out of every hundred would stand aghast at such proposed legislation; half our population would call it sacrilege. What did the French Kings think about regulating nuns and nunneries? Listen to what they said:

May, 1671—In answer to the question respecting the vows to be taken by the Sisters of the Congregation de Ville Marie, and by Les Hospitaliers, it was not the King's intention in granting Letters Patent to these sisters to make real nuns of them. According to all authorities, and the practice in the first times of the Church, and to the royal statutes, the liberty of the King's subjects belonged to the King and not to the Church. The King can grant or refuse the founding of a religious community, the privilege of assuming vows, etc. His permission once granted, the religious authority alone has the right to judge as to whether the person asking to take such vows possesses the necessary disposition to find holiness therein. The daughters of La Congregation having been established to live a secular life only, cannot, without permission from the King, change their status and their rule of life by imposing upon themselves the obligation of taking vows, whether simple or solemn.

April 10, 1684—The King gives 500 livres, and sends out three women to teach the squaws to knit and spin. This money is not to be entrusted to the Ursulines.

May 5, 1700—To the bishop: Multiplicity of religious establishments has a bad effect. The King will tolerate the establishment of the Ursulines at Three Rivers, but will not give letters patent. Regrets to learn that, on his own authority, the bishop has taken Sisters from the Hotel Dieu, and given them the direction of the General Hospital. Must send them back to the Hotel Dieu, it being the wish of the King that his hospitals shall be governed by administrators under his own control. His Majesty will not allow the Sisters of the Hotel Dieu to make a convent of the General Hospital. His Majesty sees with regret the multiplication of establishments for religious of both sexes.

May 11, 1701—The King consents to the establishment of the nuns of the Hotel Dieu at the General Hospital, but their number must never exceed eight. Will give letters patent to the Ursulines of Three Rivers, if their revenue admit of it, but the number of nuns shall be limited.

June 1, 1701—The King requires, if he is to continue his gratuities to the religious communities in Canada, annual certified statements of their fixed and casual revenues, of their expenses and liabilities; otherwise he will suppress their gratuities, as he cannot consent that they should be used for superfluous embellishments.

May 3, 1702—The King will not make any more grants to the communities, which are already too powerful.

June 17, 1705—You do well not to allow the establishment of communities which have no letters patent, as well as other undertakings of the Church people.

May 6, 1707—His Majesty desires to be more fully informed in relation to the establishment of the Sisters de la Congregation. In any case he is not to allow them to be cloistered, for then they would be a burden, instead of being useful. His Majesty is informed that

The Hospitalers of Montreal take simple vows, wear a uniform habit, etc. They are to leave off the habit. Insists specially on the execution of his orders in this matter. Will not be pleased if he does not carry them out to the letter. His Majesty is absolutely opposed to the hospital service being performed by persons wearing a uniform habit, and who have taken vows, whether simple or solemn, this being a charitable institution established for the relief of the public.

June 30, 1707—The King will continue his gratuity to the hospital, Montreal, but on the express condition that the persons in charge shall not take vows, shall have no statutes, no uniform habit and shall not call themselves Brothers. Should they act otherwise, the establishment is to be suppressed.

July 12, 1707—His Majesty is quite willing to continue to grant to Les Hospitaliers of Montreal the gratuity he has heretofore allowed them, but they are not to take any vows, or wear uniform habits, or assume the name of Brothers. There are already too many communities and convents in Canada. If they do not observe and adhere strictly to these conditions, they are to be dismissed.

Nov. 12, 1707—The King cannot permit the Sisters of La Congregation to be cloistered, their usefulness would be much impaired thereby.

June 6, 1708—The King is well pleased with the services being rendered to education by the nuns established at Ile St. Laurent, but if they take vows, they must be forbidden to do so. The King will never suffer it. His Majesty has refused the request of the Superior of l'Hospital General, to allow an increase of the number of sisters in the service.

Nov. 12, 1708—Report to the King: The Hospital Brothers have conformed to His Majesty's orders. They have laid aside their bands, girdles, and uniform habits.

May 10, 1710—To the bishop: His Majesty has considered the petitions of the Sisters of La Congregation de Quebec and of the Hospitaliers of Montreal, as well as his (the Bishop's) letter in support of their request. Is surprised at so much persistence. Their letters patent were granted on the express condition that they should make no vows. His Majesty adheres to it and begs that he, Mgr., conform to it.

May 23, 1710—The members of La Congregation de Ville Marie have asked permission to retain their simple vows. The King refuses to make any change in his orders in this matter.

March 14, 1714—The King cannot permit the Hospitalieres of Quebec and Three Rivers to increase their number, any such increase being most prejudicial to the country.

May 5, 1716—Letters patent from the King giving power to increase by four the number of the nuns in the General Hospital at Quebec. (The number had been previously fixed at 10, with two lay sisters.)

June 7, 1720—To the bishop: The General Hospital at Quebec must admit invalid soldiers, and take the benefit of their half-pay. Grants request for an addition of 10 nuns, on condition that they be furnished with dowers.

February 12, 1748—His Majesty does not wish the General Hospital of Montreal to be turned into a community of women. There are already too many of them.

Royal Ordinance of 1743—No religious community shall exist or be formed without Royal permission and letters patent; the property such communities might hold was solely and exclusively that designated in the letters patent, and that it could not be added to either by gift, purchase or otherwise, without Royal Letters of permission. Notaries are forbidden to make or receive for the benefit of communities any deed, until after the production of letters permissive, and a decree ordering registration, whereof special mention is to be made in the said deeds under pain of nullity.

May 21, 1743—To the bishop: The King encloses a memorandum which shows the advantage of suppressing one religious community in Canada (the Charron Brothers).

January 18, 1748—The King has been graciously pleased to grant the request of the Hospitaliers of Quebec to admit into their community the four ladies named (daughters of officers), each with a dowry of 1,500 livres, but the King will not allow them to make further proposals of the nature in favor of no matter whom. It is to be hoped, for the purpose of reducing the number of religious communities, the Hospitaliers and the nuns of the General Hospital will be amalgamated.

When the British took possession of Canada there were only four companies of nuns—those of the Hotel Dieu, of the Congregation, the Ursulines, the Hospitaliers; the total number about 150. Of male orders there were the Recollets, the Jesuits, the Seminarists, and the Hospitaliers, in all less than one hundred. The monastic system as found in Quebec to-day had no existence in New France. The visitor to Quebec, on seeing the massive blocks of buildings owned by monks and nuns, thinks he sees a survival of the time when Canada was under French rule. He sees nothing of the kind. Had Quebec continued under France neither those buildings nor those who live in them would be there; buildings and inmates are monuments of British toleration, of the weakness of governors and of unprincipled politicians. So far from being antique, few of these buildings date farther back than 1841. Orders whom Louis XIV. and Louis XV. forbade setting foot in Quebec have crowded in within the past seventy years.

The Kings named ruled not only the monastic orders

with a rod of iron, but exacted humiliating submission from bishop and priest. In proof, take these passages from their instructions to viceroys and intendants:

March 27, 1665—Instruction to Talon before he left Paris: Those who have made the most faithful and disinterested reports have always said that the Jesuits have assumed an authority to which they were not entitled. In order to maintain it they secured the appointment of M. de Laval as Bishop, as one entirely dependent upon them; in fact, they have also nominated the governors, and used every means to obtain the cancelling of the appointment of those who were not wholly devoted to their interests. You must study the situation and so act that the spiritual authority shall be subordinate to the temporal.

May 5, 1669—You must act most prudently with regard to the Bishop, or rather the Jesuits; as the country becomes more densely peopled, it will be easier to render the Royal authority paramount over that of the church. Meantime, you may, by setting cleverly about it, prevent, without causing rupture, any ambitious enterprises they may undertake.

May 17, 1669—You must maintain a good understanding with the ecclesiastical authorities, work for the establishment of the Recollets, and protect the Sulpicians, in order to moderate the authority assumed by the Jesuits.

June 13, 1673—Will send out two Recollet priests, and a like number every year, in order to counterbalance the excessive authority of the Jesuits. The Bishop (Laval) is not disposed to return to Canada this year. Unlike the ordinary clergy, the Jesuits do not appear to wish to attract the Indians to live with the French and become civilized. You must strive, in concert with the Recollets, to work a change in this matter.

April 16, 1676—You must with prudence take the necessary measures to prevent the ecclesiastical power from encroaching in any respect upon the temporal, which it is somewhat inclined to do.

June 4, 1695—You must not permit the ecclesiastics to meddle with things temporal, nor must you fail to consult with them in private before exercising your authority; on the other hand, you must be very careful not to interfere in purely ecclesiastical matters.

May 27, 1669—You are to watch carefully over the interests of religion, and give every possible aid and encouragement to the missionaries, the Bishop and the parish priests, but must see that they do not encroach upon the civil power.

May 28, 1712—The King has informed the Bishop that for the collection of the tithes he must employ other means than the refusal of absolution and of the Sacrament at Easter.

The proof is overwhelming that the Kings of France acted on the same principle in Canada as they did at home—that in every sphere of the Church except that of faith the King was supreme. The principle laid down by the French Kings was that the Pope was subject to the canons of the church universal, that the rule of Kings was not to be interfered with by the Pope, that in temporal concerns the church has no voice. These articles of the Gallican church, the despatches that came from Versailles instructed their viceroys to maintain in Quebec.

April 15, 1676—You must see that the usual public prayers for the king are said in all churches. It is his purpose to preserve his own rights and those of the Gallican Church.

April 16, 1676—You must maintain the King's authority firmly in all that relates to military matters, and support the privileges of the Crown, and of the Gallican Church.

Following out the principle that the King was supreme in the temporalities of the Church, Laval and his successors were not allowed a free hand in managing their clergy. Laval wanted the priests to be at his absolute disposal, to be moved hither and thither as he willed: the King repeats his orders time and again that priests were to be fixtures in their parishes. Presentation to benefices and the nomination of the bishop were the King's prerogative. The Crown would not even allow the bishop to erect parishes. In 1717 the bishop petitioned that the erection and dismemberment of parishes may be left to his decision. Back came the answer from Paris:

"In the erection and dismemberment of parishes "the Governor, the Intendant, and the Bishop, shall "act conjointly, subject to ratification by the King."

One of the claims of the clergy of Quebec is that they are exempt from municipal taxation, which they base on an alleged immunity derived from the French regime. Even where a rate has been levied for providing improvements unknown during that regime, such as waterworks and sewage, convents have claimed exemption from paying their share, and judges have upheld them. Now, what was the custom under the French King? The bishop petitioned the King to instruct the intendant to exempt the Hotels Dieu of Montreal, Quebec and Three Rivers from statute labor and public rates, to remit the tax on the salt they used, and grant them the privilege to sell meat during Lent. The petition was put under the table. The decree ordering a wall to be built round Montreal specifies that it shall be built at the expense of the inhabitants, at the rate of 6,000 livres a year, of which 2,000 shall be paid by the Seminary and the remainder by the other religious communities and the settlers. Among those included in this assessment were the Jesuits, who asked for a reduction in their amount. They did not get it. The Jesuits of Montreal paid municipal taxes under Louis XV · they pay none under King George V. Even cures were not exempt. An

order of June, 1754, lays it down that only those priests
who have no real estate are to be excused from supplying pickets for the fortifications at Quebec, and,
under date May 21, 1743, the King writes the bishop:
"You should look into the question whether it is
"advisable to exempt the religious communities from
"paying tithes." They had been formally exempted
by the King's order in 1682, but now he suggests they
pay them out of their abundance, for these communities were now flourishing.

What Do These Facts Prove?

When Canada was French, the King ruled the church.
He not only appointed its bishops, its deans, its canons,
but kept the priests subordinate to him by paying part
of their salaries, erected parishes, regulated the religious communities, fixing their number, prescribing
their vows, their duties, their dress, and exacted from
their real estate taxes for local purposes. Over and
above all, the interference of the clergy in civil affairs
was sharply resented, and they were confined to their
purely spiritual duties. The official orders that came
from Paris were that the kings wanted no more monks
and nuns in Canada than were needed in hospitals.
They would have none who had taken perpetual vows,
none who would not engage in nursing the sick, caring
for the aged and helpless, or in teaching the Indians.
The evidence is consistent and repeated for over a
century, that monks and nuns who were to remain immured in cloisters, spending their time in prayer, meditation and penance, were not to be permitted admission
into New France. The few convents authorized were
ruled not by the bishop or their superiors, but by the
King. This control was carried so far that neither
bishop nor superior could take in new members: the
King fixed their numbers, their location, and even their
dress. The King of France wanted to plant in America
a French colony but not a Papal one—he was to be its

sole ruler, not the priests. The narrative of events given explains how the situation has come to be reversed, until, to-day the priesthood and not the State is supreme. The change has been wrought by the army of men and women who were taken from their families in their youth, and in seclusion from the outer world, prisoners to all intents and purposes, had their individuality obliterated and were disciplined into one mould. With that point reached, and fit for service, they were oath-bound to obey implicitly the commands of their superiors, who, with wealth beyond estimate, independent of law, with the Quebec legislature their creature, and the Federal Government standing in awe of them from their holding the balance of power in parliament, these ecclesiastics have about completed their design of becoming the permanent controlling political force of the Dominion. Had the British continued the policy of the Kings of France towards the priests there would have been no tragedy of Quebec. When Wolfe scaled the heights of Abraham, the priests enjoyed no such privileges, made no pretension to such powers as the priests of to-day. Those who assert differently belong to a class who have a selfish interest in making the electors of Canada believe them, and who are using a pious invention to bolster their claims to immunities and privileges no French King permitted, for, with an absolutism equal to their own, and linked to greater power, the Kings of France, for 150 years, kept the priests of Canada subject to their will. After them, for 80 years, the governors, from Murray to Colborne, gave no encouragement to monastic institutions, which grew fewer, the male orders being suppressed with the exception of the Sulpicians and Seminarists. It was not until the union of Quebec with Ontario, when politicians competed for the support of the priests, that representatives of foreign orders appeared in the lobbies of the legislature, claiming recognition, and receiving acts of incorporation, accompanied, not infrequently, with public assistance in some form. Thus it went on until Confederation, when a fresh impetus was given to the influx of monks and nuns. Of late years the action of the French Government in suppressing monastic institutions has sent increased instalments, including several orders whose rule, in mortifying the body, is repugnant to humanity, from including practices of self-torture. Since Confederation, acts of incorporation have been granted by the Quebec legislature to fully forty new orders of monks and nuns, half the number since the new ecclesiastical laws began to be put into force in France. Twenty-five distinct orders of men, with over 3,000 members, have their headquarters in the Province of Quebec, and sixty-five of women, with considerably over ten thousand nuns. The number of convents and other monastic buildings exceed six hundred. To this has to be added the scores of convents established in the Northwest, which are offshoots of the orders in Quebec, financed and officered by them, directed and controlled, and, no matter though thousands of miles away, are one with the parent society. These innocent appearing convents and stations in the Northwest are little bits of Quebec. They are planted on the prairie or by sub-Arctic rivers in the expectation that they will lead to the reproduction of other Quebecs. To the members of monastic orders have to be added 2,500 priests, making a total approaching twenty thousand under vows. Adding novices and postulants greatly swells that number.

The Legal Pretences of the Priests.

The four authorities on which the priests base their title to the privileges they exercise are:

A. Prescriptive right, that what they claim was theirs during the French regime;

B. The articles of capitulation and of the Treaty of Paris;

C. The Quebec Act;

D. The British North America Act.

1. All the records of the past disprove the claim that the priests enjoyed, during the period when the French Kings ruled, the privileges they claim.

2. Examination of the articles of capitulation, of the treaty of Paris, and of the royal instructions to governors, show they do not give even a color to the claims of the priests.

3. If the priests base their claims on the Quebec Act, then they must be content for the future with what it gave them and make reparation for their violation of article 8. It is not for men who have deliberately and flagrantly broken one part of a statute to invoke another part. At the best, the Quebec Act is merely a statute, and statutes can be amended or repealed.

4. The B. N. A. Act covers only a minute part of the privileges exercised, and it can be changed at the will of the people. It has been amended several times, on the last occasion at the instance of Quebec in order that it might draw more money from the Federal chest.

There is no legal obstacle in the way of stripping the priesthood of Quebec of every one of their special privileges, and that they know such to be the case they show by their Herculean efforts to keep the Dominion in political thraldom. So long as they rule at Ottawa they are safe.

The Priest in Quebec and His Fellow Elsewhere.

The course pursued by the priests is governed by the locality where they are. Their attitude is different in Quebec, where they have indisputed sway, from what it is when surrounded by Protestants. Those who form an opinion of the Church of Rome in Quebec by the priests they meet in Ontario and the Western Provinces are judging by the freshly-planted and well-trimmed sapling at their door of the full-grown tree in Quebec, which they have not seen. The demeanor, the pretensions of the priests in the East and in the West

are not comparable. Take, for instance, their relation
to politics. In the other Provinces the priests, in a
quiet way, influence their people; in Quebec they have
to be obeyed. The assumption of supreme authority is
the same in all the Provinces, but where Protestants
are in the majority it is concealed, it is veiled, it is left
as a latent force to be called into activity when the
time comes that will permit of its being brought into
operation. In Quebec no prudential cause for reserve
exists, the cloak is thrown aside, and the claim of the
priesthood to supreme rule becomes active and
absolute.

Of the French members sent to Ottawa, delightful in
manners, well dressed, trained to speak and acquit
themselves in public with ease, it is rare to find one
who has not attended a church college. The priests
have completely in their hands the education of the
professional class, a secular college is unknown, and
from the lawyers, notaries, physicians they have trained the electors to select their representatives. Properly
speaking, the Quebec delegation to Ottawa does not
represent the people; they are the product of an educational system peculiar to Quebec, are the prepared
representatives of the priests, agents to carry out
their wishes, and when their interests are to be defended or extended Liberal and Conservative vote as
one man. They do not sit as free agents, for if they
dared to act as such they would not be re-elected. No
Dominion Cabinet is formed without considering the
wishes of the bishops, and no Minister retains his
portfolio who becomes objectionable to them: no
lawyer made a judge for Quebec or the Supreme Court
who is not approved by them. Can a department at
Ottawa be named where their influence is unknown?
In parliament their representatives act on the rule that
the way to obtain and hold power is to take advantage
of divisions among the Protestants. Oscar Dunn thus
defines that course:—

"It is our duty whether in Provincial or Dominion

"politics to remember that our only hope, and our only
"safety, lies in being prompt to make alliances with
"the English factions. By uniting our forces and our
"votes at Ottawa we can always manage to secure the
"balance of power.... We must be French-Canadians
"first, Liberals or Conservatives afterwards."

For French-Canadians read Catholics, as Dunn recognized no other kind of French-Canadians. Another adds these words: —

"With sixty-five members voting as a unit in the
"Commons of Canada, any politician of common
"intellect can control the destinies of the Dominion
"of Canada."

What Papal Quebec is Doing.

Keeping it well in mind that it is not a French but a Papal Quebec with which the Dominion has to deal, let it be asked, What is this Papal Quebec, with its great army of monks, nuns, and priests, doing? I have described their obtaining possession of the Eastern Townships, that in them Protestants are fast melting away. Is that all? Will this great army be content with Quebec? The answer could be given in extracts from sermons and pastoral letters. It will save space to take the summary of one of the ablest Jesuits, Father Hamon. In his hand-book on missions, those of New England in particular, he says the movement, begun over forty years ago, to extend the parish system over the Eastern Townships had a larger design than merely expelling their Protestant farmers; it was a necessary step towards the conquest of New England for his church. In the manufacturing centres of Maine, New Hampshire, and Massachusetts are hundreds of thousands of French-Canadians, who are separated from their compatriots on the St. Lawrence by a belt of Protestants. Remove the belt and the two branches of Catholics will become one, and what then? I quote the Father's words:

"See what will happen when the French-Canadian

"race shall have completely occupied the space
"relatively restricted and found between the south
"shore of the St. Lawrence and the American bound-
"ary, that which we call the Eastern Townships. It
"will not probably take more than another generation
"to acomplish this work. Then the grand invasion (of
"the Republic) will commence. . . . When the French-
"Canadians shall have arrived in mass at the Ameri-
"can boundary line, they will find more than half a
"million of their compatriots awaiting them . . . who
"have the Canadian parish organized as absolutely as
"in Quebec, and are very decided, while discharging
"their duties loyally as citizens, to remain, every-
"where Roman Catholic and French.
"   . . . The French-Canadians in the United States
"will soon be too numerous and influential for any
"political party, whatever it might wish to do, to dare
"to dispute their privileges. . . . According to Bishop
"de Goesbriand, the French-Canadians are fulfilling a
"providential mission, they compete on their part for
"the pacific conquest of New England in the name of
"religion. When the collisions occasioned by the
"strife of the struggle for the installation of parishes
"and of district schools shall have calmed, ... they
"will rally with Catholics of other nationalities around
"the cross to defend or regain their common rights.
"This will assure to the Roman Catholic Church a
"magnificent position in New England, which was the
"cradle, and remained for a great while the citadel of
"American Protestantism. . . . The American union
"is too big to be managed successfully. It is within
"the range of the possible that there will be a break-
"up when Quebec, New Brunswick, Maine, New Hamp-
"shire, Massachusetts, Rhode Island, and, possibly,
"Eastern Ontario, will constitute a distinct republic
"giving a spirit and character to the new republic."

This idea of Hamon's that there will be a disrup-
tion of the United States, and that in the formation

of its north-eastern section into a new republic, the priesthood will dominate, is not peculiar to him. It is common to many. Bishop Lafleche, of Three Rivers, wrote:

"In the more or less distant future, and for causes "already apparent, the American republic will be "divided into several independent States, and it is "not improbable that a portion of this last republic "will seek annexation to Canada."

In speculating on the future of Quebec clerical writers see only two alternatives—independence or annexation. None have a word in favor of Britain. Hamon's remarks are worth quoting:

"Two suppositions seem possible: either the Pro-"vince of Quebec will one day have its autonomy, and "will become an independent nation, or else it will be "annexed to the United States. Independence or an-"nexation—these are the two possible hypotheses. "Independent, the Province of Quebec would have all "the haughtiness and ambition of a young nation, its "people high-spirited, daring, proud of being, at least, "the master of their destinies. . . . Annexation would "immediately weld together two fractions of the same people, separated at the present time by a political frontier. Instead of being 400,000 the French-Can-"adians in the United States would form with those of "Quebec a compact whole of two million souls."

It will be noted that Eastern Ontario is counted upon to form part of the confidently expected great Catholic Republic. The conquest of Eastern Ontario is now going on, with an advance guard to stake out the Northwest. Just as Frontenac established a chain of forts from Kingston to the Mississippi to take possession of the heart of the continent for France, so Rome has established settlements of French-Canadians from Ottawa to lake Nipissing to control the future avenue by water to the Northwest. Ponder over these words of one of the shrewdest priests who ever lived in Quebec and see how the extension by the Federal Government of Quebec's northern boundary from the height of land to the Hudson Bay, and next the request of the Grand Trunk Company to extend its line from North Bay to the Pacific was seized to secure the construction of a railway through northern Ontario and Quebec, fall in with the plan of the bishops. Protestant members of parliament, who voted for both, regarding the extension of boundary of no great moment, viewing the change of the line of railway as a mere commercial consideration, may now learn how they were aiding in carrying out designs that were formed in secret conclave.

The priests, at present, have the shaping of the course of the Ship of State. They have got this masterful position by playing on the natural feeling of the habitants in favor of their language and customs. That feeling the priests have nursed and intensified. They have used every means, they have lost no opportunity to impress them with the belief that absolute submission to their priests is the only possible means of preserving their language and customs. Nobody is assailing the French language nor troubling themselves about French customs, but as children are frightened to stay in bed by bugaboo stories, the habitants are driven into compliance with the designs of the priesthood by the invention that there are enemies who seek to destroy their language and customs, but who will be unable to do so while they maintain their priests as their defenders. That in this twentieth century, on a continent the very air of which is democratic, a body of men are laboring to bring about the creation of a Papal nation sounds incredible, yet here we have the words of the priests themselves that that is what they are striving for.

CHAPTER XI.

Nationalism and Nationalists

In the course of the narrative of Quebec's doings since the Conquest, the reader has been kept informed of the aspirations of the French-Canadians for separation from Great Britain. The desire took varied forms. Following the Conquest it was to drive out the English and restore connection with France. The American revolution evoked the purpose of forming an independent State under the protectorate of the new republic. The French revolution put an end to all inclination to be re-united with France, and for the next forty years connection with the United States was looked to by the patriots. The collapse of the rebellion of 1837 together with the forced union with Ontario induced a reaction towards clericalism and more ardent nationalism. For the following score of years there was strife between those inclined towards annexation and the priests, who vehemently opposed it. Difference of opinion on this point gradually extended to others, until the Rouges became distinctly anticlerical. In a platform set forth by Eric Dorion were such planks as separation of church and state, abolition of tithes, secular schools. This exasperated the priests who waged a war of extermination, the more unrelenting as the old Gallicanism was being supplanted by Ultramontanism as expounded by the newly imported Jesuits. A group of fearless and intellectual young men, with such leaders as the Dorions,

Joseph Doutre, R. Laflamme, L. A. Dessaulles, waged an unequal contest which could have only one ending, the extinction of the Rouges. Though writers like Buies continued for several years afterwards to sound its familiar war cries, Liberalism, in the sense it is used in France, disappeared with the stoppage of Le Pays. The Liberals who now appeared were of the English type, and we have them still, experiencing difficulty in reconciling the principles of Macaulay, Bright, and Gladstone with conformity to an ecclesiastical autocracy. Exercising an iron censorship of the press, the priests henceforth had the moulding of public opinion in their own hands, and the craving for an independent Quebec now assumed an exclusively Catholic character. Suggestions of union with either France or the United States were discarded and what was looked forward to was a great nation that would be French in speech and Catholic in creed. How this idea developed and came to be crystallized in its present form is an interesting study. The result, however, is alone of importance, and that is that this dream of a great French and Catholic nation has got a hold on a majority of the people. Commercial interests, the advantage of working with political parties to get office and grants of public money, causes many strange twistings, affirmations and denials, explanations that do not explain, hypocritical professions of loyalty and of tolerance, while underneath is the steady look towards the time when the English in Quebec will have to submit to be part of the great Catholic nation that is to be a power on the American continent. Tardivel embodies the attitude of the clergy in these sentences.

"For many years past French Canadians have had "no cause to complain of British rule, which with us "is far more theoretical than real. As a matter of fact "we govern ourselves very much as we please. . . . "Patriotic French-Canadians are striving to build up "on the banks of the St. Lawrence a new France, "which, when the providential hour arrives, shall be-

"come an independent nation. . . . Our aspiration is "to found a nation which shall profess the Catholic "faith and speak the French language." The prevalent notion is misleading, that Bourassa is the author of the Nationalist creed and that with his disappearance it will die out. He only picked up what existed long before his day and by his energy has given it more prominence. In the letter Cardinal Taschereau sent to the Pope in 1866, asking if it was lawful for Catholics to support the B. N. A. Act, seeing it made provision for divorce, he wrote—We French-Canadians "shall "advance with a firm and certain step towards the "accomplishment of our destiny, which is, without "doubt, the formation of a great Catholic nation in the "St. Lawrence valley." This hope dates back still further and was common after Ultramontanism got a footing in Canada, that just as soon as Quebec grew strong enough under British protection, it would break away from the Empire and become independent as a Catholic State. The watchword of present-day Nationalism is French Catholic supremacy in the Dominion. That is what Nationalism stands for and nothing else.

All French-Canadians are not Nationalists, there are thousands of them who have no sympathy with Nationalism, men who know what clericalism leads to and do not want Quebec to be like the South American States; men who would compel the priests to confine themselves to their spiritual duties and resent their interference in politics; men who consider it of vital importance that Quebec should apply itself to its development intellectually and commercially, and give up dreams of forming a separate nation that cannot be realized; men who are convinced and sincerely believe that government on British principles is a hundredfold preferable to a government inspired and guided by the priesthood; men who desire a united Canada on the basis that the people shall rule and not the priests. The number who think thus is increasing, and they are the hope of that future Quebec which will cease to look backwards, not seeking isolation, not clinging to wornout ideals and naming it patriotism, but unite with the other peoples of the Dominion in building up a nation that will give opportunity to every man to earn a living without discrimination as to creed or origin. Against Nationalism, with its harking back to theocratic rule, let us set constitutional government as developed by the Motherland, and against the narrowness that would give a priestly caste influence to shape Canada's destiny, let us set the sovereignty of the people—the wideness that gives to all equal rights and knows naught of special privileges.

Nationalism is no theory. In practice, we see these days how it hinders giving assistance to the British Government and how it resists every approach to drawing the bonds of union closer between the members of the Empire. A peculiar feature of the Nationalist cult is its contempt for Britain—its belief that she is decadent, and will before long be so weak that she will be unable, even if desirous, to resist Quebec's breaking away. Instead of the war being proof to the Nationalists of the virility of Britain, a revelation of its vast resources, they affect to believe it will be the means of leaving her exhausted, and sink into becoming a second-rate Power while France will take the supreme position in Europe. This sentence by Lavergne embodies the Nationalist expectations: "When we shall be sufficiently numerous and strong "the Franco-American race will wing its flight, inde- "pendent and unmixed, to play in the new world the "glorious and sublime role played in Europe by France." The Nationalist reverses the general belief, that had not Britain intervened France would have been crushed, for he affirms that it is France's alliance that has saved Britain from destruction, and that it is to French arms the victory will be due.

The term Nationalist implies a man striving for another government than that he lives under. In Quebec it indicates one who is satisfied with the government of the province but who desires to change the federal government by bringing it into harmony with that of Quebec. In what regard is the Dominion at large not in harmony with Quebec? The answer is obvious— Quebec is obedient to the priesthood, the governments of the other provinces are not; a clerical government has been firmly established in Quebec; we will exert our influence to bring all Canada responsive to clerical control. To that end the extension of Quebec is necessary, and the spreading of its people into adjoining territory with corresponding increase in number of representatives at Ottawa has been a marvel. The policy of isolation persistently followed for 150 years has put in the hands of the priesthood two million people who obey them and are the instrument by which they are resolved to win supremacy over all Canada, realizing the condition the bishops laid down in their pastoral at Confederation. "It is not the church that "is comprised in the State—it is the State that is com- "prised in the church." Properly speaking, the Nationalist movement is not political, it is ecclesiastical. The idea as to when this Catholic nation is to be is vague; there is no hurry about it. So long as the present immunity lasts, the bishops do not desire the severance of the tie with Britain, for they look on the influence of its government as security for the privileges of their church. Only the other day a Nationalist leader declared he wanted no change, but if there was a vital attack on Quebec, independence would be forthwith declared. It either displays simplicity of knowledge or confidence in the counteracting effect of the Catholic population in the West, that no doubt is ever expressed that opposition to an independent nation at the mouth of the St. Lawrence would come from those whose produce must have an outlet to the Atlantic. The opposition of Ontario is looked on as sure, never that of the provinces west of it.

The end of the war will bring a clash with the Nationalist spirit. An unavoidable result of the war will be a readjustment of the relation between the Mother Country and her dependencies. On no question are the Nationalists more agreed, than that the bond between Canada and Britain is not to be strengthened. The Imperialist aspirations, which find freest expression in Toronto, and have sympathizers everywhere, will be resisted. That congress which is looked forward to, of representatives from every land over which the Union Jack floats joining to frame a basis of Imperialistic union, will have no whole-hearted support from Quebec.

Nationalism has produced a type of Canadian unknown thirty years ago, who shouts French when he knows he who asks him a question speaks only English, telephones in French, demands what he wants in French, persists in using his mother-tongue as an instrument to humiliate his English neighbor. Then there is a new air of superiority to make the English feel they are unwelcome intruders. When a Canadian of this sort is elected a representative he makes himself a nuisance in parliament. He lies in wait for fancied slights and omissions, yelling "En Francais," demands "une sou" be stamped on coppers, and French words on postage stamps; is loud in denouncing appointments of English to office and asking that more salary be paid to some official in his county. At the late session a resolution was spoken of, that all officials who draw salaries of $2,000 a year or over be required to speak both languages, and Mr. Boulay advanced the further claim that appointments be in proportion to population, ignoring what is obvious, that if any rule be followed other than fitness for the duties of office it ought to be according to the amount of revenue derived from the French and from the English-speaking sections of the population. The chief element in the position of an official is his salary, and justice to those who pay the greater part of it ought to be considered. The mailbag dropped in a French village is a slim affair; the bag at an English village of the same population is a heavy one, yet the postoffice department is overloaded with French clerks. The English of Montreal pay three-fourths of its revenue yet are served by French officials. With the rule that appointments be in proportion to the revenue derived, Mr. Boulay would find Rimouski's claim would be small indeed.

The idea fostered by the Nationalists, that the French-speaking people occupy a superior position to the English, and their insistent exhortation to boldly claim their alleged rights, is widening the cleavage between the two peoples. It is dangerous to foster in the minds of a section of our population that they are not receiving their due, that they are discriminated against, that they have wrongs that call for redress, and yet that is what the entire Nationalist press is daily and weekly doing seconded by the exertions of the Nationalist members at Quebec and Ottawa.

The underlying idea of Nationalism is that the French have rights and privileges peculiar to themselves and which are not shared by others. The daily exhortations of their newspapers is, that they assert themselves and enter more fully into the enjoyment of those alleged rights and privileges. It is dangerous talk, ominous of serious trouble in the coming years. The Canadian who is discontented with his status as a British subject and who is preparing the way to replace the Union Jack with another flag, is a rebel. Nationalists repudiate being disloyal. They do not, many of them, realize it, but they are breeding a rebellion.

CHAPTER XII.

The War of French Priests on Ontario's Independence

That distinguished Jesuit, Father Hamon, in his book descriptive of French-Canadian missions, spoke of Eastern Ontario being included in that Catholic republic for which he and his fellows were laboring. Here is his reference to Eastern Ontario:
"None of the obstacles met have checked the settle-
"ment of the valley of the Ottawa and of the Province
"of Ontario. And yet, for the French-Canadian, is
"not Ontario a country different from theirs, both in
"religion and language, and even in politics, in that, at
"least, which relates to local interests? In spite of
"these difficulties, in spite of a tenacious English ele-
"ment, hostile to the invasion and seeking by all possi-
"ble means to prevent it, the French-Canadian pushes
"toward the end for which he set out. The French-
"Canadians infiltrate themselves everywhere in those
"counties of Ontario which divide it from the Pro-
"vince of Quebec, and continue bravely to march to-
"ward the West. The policy of the Church is to
"guide the movement, plan and forward settlement,
"establish the parish system, the parochial school, and
"the religious and national societies; then, to watch
"and wait for providential developments, that she may
"mass and lead the people for the effective overthrow
"of Protestant error and paganism. . . . . The
"French-Canadian race is God's chosen people to save

"North America and to restore its population to the "bosom of the Church of Rome. Is this a dream? No, "it is more; it is an everyday issue."

This was written in 1891 and what has been accomplished in the years since is proof that the priests have been persistent in carrying out their design to conquer Ontario. Their campaign to do so started fifty years ago, when habitants began to cross the Ottawa in noticeable numbers to take up land. It was not a case of over-population on the Quebec side pushing across the river for existence. The newcomers were largely from a distance, many from lower St. Lawrence parishes, and had been recruited by the priests and led by them to their new locations. The Ontario Government granted lots on easy terms and helped by giving employment in making roads. There was no need of the habitants moving into Ontario. There was good land to be had free in the St. John Valley and other districts in Quebec which had been set aside for colonization, coupled with liberal inducement from the government. The fact of their being diverted from their own province and passing in a steady stream into Ontario confirms the statement that the priests had settled on a plan of campaign to bring that province under their control. In studying that remarkable migration, whoever fails to keep in mind what Father Hamon tells, will be unable to account for people, deeply attached to their own province, wrenching themselves from hereditary surroundings, ignoring the offers of their own government, and journeying into a country where they knew a majority of the inhabitants spoke neither their language nor professed their creed. The people of Ontario were slow to realize the purpose of the invasion. For years they looked upon it as a genuine colonization movement, failing to recognize that it was due to the far-sighted policy of the master-minds who were guiding those habitants to settle where they did. Thirty years ago Methodist circuit riders sounded the alarm, that on the upper

Ottawa and the lakes to which it gives access the foundations of a second Quebec were being laid. No attention was paid to them; it was easy to class them as bigots. Had the habitants come into that region voluntarily no objection could be made. They were doing a good work in extending the settlement of the country and making what had been a waste productive. There were no finer cavalry in the world than those in the army of Louis XIV: as soldiers they deserved admiration, but when heading the Dragonades to circumvent the Huguenots, little can be said for them and much less for Lachaise and his fellow Jesuits who used them as their tools. To tell us these habitants who flocked into Northern Ontario are industrious, simple and kindly does not affect the fact that they were brought where they are with the design to subjugate Ontario to the will of the priests. Regard for the habitant does not blind us to the plans of those of whom they are the unwitting agents.

No Respect for Ontario's Laws.

The newcomers totally ignored the fact that they had come into another province and the priests encouraged them in their belief that they had brought the laws and institutions of Quebec along with them. Under the guidance of their religious advisers they proceeded to establish, as Father Hamon states, "the "parish system, the parochial school, and the religious "and national societies." This quiet defiance of the Ontario Government, this intimation that they were a separate people and not amenable to its rule, explains the trouble that subsequently followed.

Confederation ended the union that had existed for nigh 30 years between Upper and Lower Canada, and with the severance of that union Ontario, in its relationship to Quebec, became as separate as Nova Scotia or British Columbia. It made its own laws and developed its own institutions. English and English only was recognized as its language, and with the single exception of recognition of separate schools there was complete severance of church and state. On whoever sought to become inhabitants of Ontario it was incumbent they should obey its laws and observe whatever regulations were of a public nature. The priests, as the sequel has revealed, brought these people to carry out their deep-laid design of assimilating Ontario with Quebec, grafting on its soil the French parish system and bringing about the declaring of French as an official language. There are other methods of conquering a country than by brute force. The victory the priests had obtained in the Eastern Townships, by enforcing conditions under which the English-speaking farmers would not live, they were going to repeat in Ontario.

Compel English Farmers to Leave.

All who took part in this, to appearance, peaceable invasion of Northern Ontario were not in poor circumstances. There were habitants who owned live stock and had some money. These were assigned to buy out English-speaking farmers, money being lent them. Thus the settlements began to spread until they reached as far as Glengarry. The first intimation that could not be set aside by the educational authorities came from Irish Catholics, who complained that their children were untaught because the French had taken possession of their schools. Later the Scotch Catholics in the rear of Glengarry said likewise. The schools they had founded had been taken out of their hands and French teachers installed. The Mail, of Toronto, sent a reporter to investigate. His letters told of schools that were similar to those in the Quebec parishes, where catechism was taught and prayers recited twice a day, and little else. English-speaking farmers, unable to get their children educated, were selling out and moving away. Glengarry furnished the first instance of seeking redress by law, and succeeded in securing a decision that English must be the teaching language of their school. Irish Catholics followed the example of their Highland co-religionists. In every instance, and in the appeal to the higher court, the judges declared English was the language ordained by the Ontario statutes. When it was tried to carry these decisions into effect there was resistance. When an inspector entered a school to find out whether the instructions of the Department of Education and the decisions of the courts were being observed, the scholars left their seats, and, led by the teacher, walked out, or on its being known he was in the neighborhood the schools were deserted and the doors locked.

Dr. Merchant's Report.

Before taking action to end this incipient rebellion Premier Whitney desired full information, and appointed the chief inspector, Dr. Merchant, to make a thorough inquiry. This was done, the doctor taking over a year to collect information by personally visiting every accessible school. He found there were, in 1911, no fewer than 187 Catholic schools in which French was the teaching language. The attendance was irregular, and the 10,000 on the rolls did not comprise the school population. Fully half of the teachers were natives of Quebec and incompetent. Twenty-eight had no certificate of any kind, and 48 had only temporary certificates. The special purpose of the investigation being to ascertain if English was taught, careful tests were used. English is the teaching language of Ontario, yet Dr. Merchant found it was ignored, that the schools, with a few exceptions, were French and nothing else. Twenty-two of the teachers who were drawing their salaries from Toronto could not speak English, 18 could speak a little, but not enough to teach that language: only a few were capable of teaching English, in an imperfect fashion. The teaching language of the schools was French, that is arithmetic, geography, history were taught in French, and that was the language in which the teachers gave all their directions—it was the language of the school. Where lessons were given in English it was an extra subject, as if it were Latin, and was taught by rote, the scholars repeating words of whose meaning they had no idea. Even judged as French schools they were found woefully lacking in efficiency, a large proportion of the children leaving them with inadequate equipment to meet the demands of life. So declares Dr. Merchant who, as a French-speaking Canadian, had no prejudice in the matter. In conversation with the schoolmams he found the belief was common that the regulations of the Ontario Department of Education do not apply to French Catholics, and that they were under no obligation to teach English. This feeling extended to a few teachers of the public schools in the section examined, where the Catholic catechism was being taught during school hours.

Sir James Whitney's Decision.

With this authentic information before them, that the law making English the language of its schools, was being defied, what was the Ontario Government to do? Extremists replied: Enforce the law to the letter. Premier Whitney pointed out that justice called for forbearance. His predecessors in office were to blame in not checking the violation of the laws of the province at the start. They had winked at the coming into being of French schools and at their defiance of the regulations of the Department of Education. They had, as a result, grown greatly in number. What Mowat could easily have done in maintaining Ontario as an English-speaking province was now difficult. Premier Whitney and his ministers, while determined to uphold the law that English was the teaching language of Ontario's schools, were just as resolute in doing justice to all. The boys and girls attending those schools had to be considered.

The French-Canadians who had been fetched into

Ontario had no claim upon its government other than what pertained to them like the rest of the people. Having voluntarily come into Ontario, they were under the jurisdiction of its laws, and the law of Ontario in regulating schools is, that English is their teaching language. The talk of the agitators in assuming that French-Canadians have a special claim in Ontario in the matter of language has not an atom of foundation in either law or common sense: in settling there they assumed the responsibility of obeying its laws. Had Sir James Whitney kept by the letter of those laws, he would have turned out from the schools in question all teachers who had no diplomas and all incapable of teaching English, and required that the Ontario curriculum of studies be strictly observed for the future. That, while legally justifiable, would have been an injury to the children of the settlements, and Sir James kept them in his mind—he wanted them to be educated and not grow up illiterate. He decided that the children who knew only French would be allowed to take the lessons they had been receiving until they passed the First Form. The returns showed that would be, on the average, when they were nine years of age. Up to then they would be taught in French; taught not alone to read and spell it, but to write it. When qualified to pass to the Second Form they would be required to take a daily lesson in English. Mark how considerate the Whitney Government was—not until the child had the opportunity of learning to read and write in its native tongue would it be required to learn English.

Regulation 17.

On the suggestion of Dr. Merchant regulation 17 was adopted. It reads: "Where necessary in the "case of French-speaking pupils, French may be used "as the language of instruction and communication; "but such use of French shall not be continued beyond "Form I., excepting that, on the approval of the Chief

"Inspector, it may also be used as the language of "instruction and communication in the case of pupils "beyond Form I. who are unable to speak and understand the English language."

While firm in requiring that each child have the opportunity to learn English, the regulation was considerate of its claim to be able to read and write its mother-tongue. In one word, Regulation 17 established bilingual schools. But the priests did not want bilingual teaching—they did not want English taught at all, they wanted none other school than prevailed, the parochial school of Quebec, which they had transplanted bodily into Ontario. Though they kept discreet silence on it for obvious reasons, this regulation was to the priests more obnoxious than 17:

"No teacher shall be granted a certificate to teach "in English-French schools who does not possess a "knowledge of the English language sufficient to teach "the public and separate school course. No teacher "shall remain in office or be appointed in any of said "schools who does not possess a knowledge of the "English language sufficient to teach the public and "separate school course of study."

This swept the schools the priests had fostered outside those entitled to government aid. It would not do for them to say they objected to English being taught, for, in public, they pretended they wished it, while in practice they smothered it.

The Priests Concoct a Plea.

To go before the public they must object on another score, so they proclaimed they wanted bilingual schools, where the children would be taught both English and French, and it was because of their seeking such schools that the Ontario Government was persecuting them! To those who knew the facts this assertion was monstrous in its untruthfulness. The priests had established 187 schools, and in not a score of them was there the slightest pretence to teach English, and for the best of reasons, that the teachers they had provided for these schools did not know English. Yet these were the schools which the priests are now holding up to the people of Canada as bilingual! Solemnly declaring their hearts' desire is to do justice to both languages and that the Ontario Government will not allow them to do so, these men provided forty teachers who knew no English and the rest of them only imperfectly. The bilingual schools organized by the priests were a joke. On each one might be chalked on the door: Here English is taught by a schoolmam who does not know English.

Sir James Whitney's Motive.

In seeking that the French-Canadians who had come to make their homes in Ontario should learn English, Sir James Whitney was doing them a great kindness. English is the language of a continent of 110 million people. The French-Canadian who cannot speak English has his life's activities confined to a province of two million inhabitants. Ability to speak English ends his confinement to a pent-up Utica and opens to him all the advantages and prospects of advancement which a wide continent affords. In January, 1916, a deputation from the Montreal Trades Council had an interview with Premier Gouin. He was told that all the good positions are held by Protestants because of the imperfect education of French-Canadians in the rural districts, to which is added the handicap of inability to speak English. No injury done the habitants equals that visited on the tens of thousands of them who have gone to the New England States. With their skill of hand and their facility in learning, they ought to fill the best positions. From lack of elementary education, withheld from them in their native parishes because it suited the purposes of the priests, they far too often fill the commonest and worst-paid callings. Arrogating to themselves the character of their preserver, the priesthood, is the worst enemy of the French people of Canada, for it has used them to advance their own interests heedless of what would be to their advantage. In language, Quebec elementary schools are purely French. Except where the Irish, as in county Pontiac, will not submit, there is not a trace of bilingualism about them. The very priests who are clamoring that Ontario make their schools bilingual would resist to the death a law requiring that their own teach English. What they would not do themselves, they demand Ontario shall do. The priests, who would not hear of a bilingual curriculum for their own schools, cry out persecution when Ontario limits French as the teaching language to the primary form.

A Hypocritical Cry.

There could not be an agitation raised upon a more misleading cry than that which is now convulsing Quebec—a cry for bilingual schools. Those who carry it on plausibly declare they want schools that will teach both languages, and there are tens of thousands who believe them. The priests had a generation to establish bilingual schools in Northern Ontario and they did not—they fetched teachers from Quebec and organized purely French schools. Yet these very men, when Ontario offers to provide the schools they would have us believe they want, cry out persecution! The priests organized French schools, Sir James Whitney insisted on schools that would teach both languages, and because of that his memory is being vilified. It is not uncommon to hear sympathetic people say it is not fair to treat French children as the agitators declare they are being treated. Those who speak thus should inquire into the facts and not credulously accept the falsehoods that are being shouted.

Whoever blows the bellows of creed or race can always get a following in Quebec. The cry that the Orangemen and Free Masons of Ontario were robbing their compatriots in Ontario of their language fanned the habitants to a white heat. It was in vain to assure them the cry was not true, that the facts were all the other way, prejudice swept common sense aside and they hugged the delusion that their fellows were being persecuted. A grievance is dear to many people, and the habitant believed he had got one. When he heard from pulpit and platform, and had read to him from the newspapers, that the people of Ontario were fanatics and bigots, that they were treating French-Canadians worse than the British Government had dared to treat the Boers, that they were trying to chase them back to Quebec, and could only be compared to the Germans who had despoiled the shrines of Belgium, he waxed indignant. The belief was as implicit as it was widely spread, that sacred rights were being violated by the fanatics of Ontario, that French women mounted guard at the doors of their schools to save their children from assaults on their language and their religion.

Sir Lomer Gouin Intervenes.

On the 11th January, 1915, the agitation took a new aspect. The legislature was in session at Quebec. The debate on the address in reply to the Lieut.-Governor's speech had been dragging when the premier, Sir Lomer Gouin, rose to bring it to an end. He had been replying to the criticisms of the Opposition when he abruptly switched off to the Ontario schools. The subject had not been alluded to either in the Lieut.-Governor's speech or during the debate, and was deliberately dragged in by the premier. He regretted the people of Ontario were preventing the teaching of the language of the discoverers of Canada to their children, because Confederation was based on equal rights as to religion and language. ''I ask,'' he said, ''for the ''French language the right to come to the lips of the ''school children of Ontario who wish to learn and ''speak it.'' By pre-arrangement, before the applause with which the premier's declaration had cooled, Mr.

Bullock moved a resolution advising the people of
Ontario to consider the school question on generous
and patriotic lines and with regard to the rights and
privileges of minorities. The resolution was seconded
by Dr. Finnie, put to the house, and declared carried,
no member calling for a division. In our parliamentary history there has been no incident like this—one
province advising another province what it should do
in a matter that the B. N. A. Act expressly assigns to
the exclusive jurisdiction of each province. When
the Quebec Legislature deliberately assumed to criticize the action of the Ontario Legislature and tell its
members what they should do, was there not an invasion of Ontario's independence? Are Ontario's legislators to be dictated to by outsiders? And to be lec-
tured, above all other subjects, on education by a
province that has the poorest apologies for schools in
the Dominion, was the depth of humiliation. Had the
Ontario legislators made reply, they might have asked
Sir Lomer Gouin and his followers how many of Quebec's teachers can speak English, and in how many
of its 6,000 elementary schools in rural parishes is
English taught? But Ontario took no notice of the
insulting resolution, treating it with contempt.

The Agitation Grows.

This action of the Legislature had a great effect in
Quebec. It lifted the agitation to a higher plane by
being made an issue of the province, for it now bore
the stamp of Sir Lomer Gouin and of the legislature.
The direction of the agitation was undertaken by the
French-Canadian Association for Education in Ontario,
with headquarters at Ottawa, which was reinforced by
the Young French-Canadian Catholic Association. At
its congress at Three Rivers, Bishop Cloutier, in the
sermon that began proceedings, blamed the Jews as
well as the Free Masons for the trouble in Ontario.
Dr. Brail, of Laval University, declared the fundamental principle of the Association in regard to edu-

cation was absolute and unquestioning submission to the Roman Catholic Church, and advocated the exclusion altogether of the Government from the sphere of the schools. His advice was embodied in the resolution adopted by the Congress that the Church be the sole director of education to the exclusion of the Government. There was great activity in holding meetings and organizing branches of both associations, one feature being meetings for women addressed by women. The denunciations at these meetings and by the French press, of Ontario and its Government, are to be passed by as the vaporings of people misled by priestly falsehoods.

The Ottawa association advised the school boards of Eastern Ontario to ignore regulation 17. The department at Toronto gave notice that schools which did not obey the regulation would have their grants withheld. The opening of the schools in Ottawa in September brought the crisis. The old commissioners had refused to be supplanted by the board nominated at Toronto, and now went a step further by refusing to yield up the schools. On the day they should open a crowd of women and children took possession of a large school, installed the old teachers, and defied the police to put them out, a bodyguard of women remaining day and night. To get money to pay the teachers an appeal was made to their sympathizers, and meetings to further that end were held. Next, pressure was brought to bear on the Federal Ministers. A deputation of over 2,000 marched to Parliament to submit a petition asking for their intervention to secure the repeal of regulation 17. Sir R. Borden received a deputation, and pointed out that the Dominion Government could not interfere, and suggested that violence and contempt of law would injure their cause. A few hours later the priests launched another demonstration. Drawn in big bob-sleighs a mob of children encircled the building where parliament was in session, waving banners and blowing horns. They were refused admission. The Sunday following this demonstration seven French priests united in a letter to their parishioners advising them not to contribute to the Patriotic Fund, but, instead, to hand in donations to ensure "successful resistance to the tyranny of relent-"less persecutors who wish to transform our schools "into centres of English information." Deputations visited the districts along the Upper Ottawa, counselling resistance to the Ontario authorities and promising aid to pay their teachers. Among those who thus counselled resistance to Ontario's laws were two Senators. The advice not to contribute to the Patriotic Fund was followed by the suggestion to young men not to enlist.

Montreal's Gift.

The Quebec legislature had listened to declarations that of the two civilizations the German was preferable to the British, and made no protest. On the occasion of the effort to raise the Patriotic Fund to twenty million dollars, the Montreal City Council was urged to do something liberal, and reluctantly subscribed $250,000. Alderman Routhier said the majority were not for giving a cent, but were constrained by fear of the English vote. The motion was only passed on adding a rider, that $50,000 be left at the disposal of the council for other benevolent purposes. The consent of the legislature had to be got for such a money grant. On the bill coming before that body an amendment was moved that Montreal be authorized to give $50,000 to the French schools of Ontario. There were difficulties in doing that in so direct a manner, which were evaded by a bill giving power to all municipal councils in the Province of Quebec to vote up to five per cent. of their gross revenue "to funds opened by corpora-"tions or persons for public subscription for patriotic, "national or school purposes within the province or "elsewhere." The author of the bill moved that it be amended by inserting words to give like power to boards of school commissioners. A motion, that the

Montreal council give the entire $300,000 to the French schools in Ontario, was moved by Mr. Lavergne, who declared that not a single cent should leave the province for any war fund until the mothers of French-Canadian children in Ontario were allowed to keep their schools for the instruction of their children in their own language; the quickest way, he added, to get justice would be to boycott, to refuse to buy goods made in Ontario. The Premier explained, while sympathizing with the intention of Mr. Lavergne, his motion would defeat his purpose. Mr. Gault could not see why the business men of Montreal should be asked to pay a tax to something outside the province. On the vote being taken seven voted with Lavergne. The Premier said he had been asked to impose a special tax on the Province for the Patriotic Fund, but had declined, preferring to leave it to the municipal councils to subscribe. The leader of the Opposition pointed out that the bill was unconstitutional in proposing to expend money in another province, and also injudicious, as it would lead the people of Ontario to believe Quebec had organized to fight their Government. Should Ontario and the other provinces organize in like manner to defend themselves, where will we be? It was criminal to begin such a contest. Mr. Cousineau closed by declaring he was as much in sympathy with the French schools in Ontario as any Canadian in the house, but he was not going to fly in the face of the B. N. A. Act. The bill was passed on a vote of 47 to 3, Mr. Cousineau having only two supporters. By the time the bill reached the upper chamber, there were intimations from Montreal, that if it passed and the city council gave a grant to the French schools, an appeal would be made to the courts. That council had already paid a thousand dollars for these schools, but the amount was too small for an individual ratepayer to take action. The promoters of the bill saw what would be the result of trying to collect a tax off Jews and Protestants for French Catholic schools in another province, and so they changed it to read that Catholic boards of school commissioners could vote grants to the extent of six per cent. of their gross revenue, and in that shape the bill passed.

What Was Said at Ottawa.

At Ottawa several French members repeated what had been said in the Quebec Legislature, that for the altogether inadequate response of their province in recruits and donations to patriotic funds Ontario's treatment of their compatriots was solely to blame, thus these pretended enthusiasts for the French language could find no better excuse for their failure in duty to the nation that is the mother, exemplar, and pillar of the French language being crushed out of existence. The reports of Ontario's liberality in contributions of money and the spectacle of her battalions steaming down the St. Lawrence hastening to the relief of France, were lost on them. They saved their dollars and their lives by throwing the blame for their conduct on Ontario, calling its people bigots, persecutors, worse than Huns. Though the call to fly to the rescue of France was loud and insistent, the advice was passed in a thousand parishes to stay at home and let the English go. For all that, the time will come when to the boasts that it was Jean Baptiste who saved Canada in 1776 and 1812 from the devouring Yankee will be added another, that he saved France in 1916, and with equal truth.

The Agitation Becomes a Religious One.

Outwardly, the agitation up to this point had been conducted on racial lines, the agitators declaring all they asked was that where French scholars were in the majority the teaching language was to be French and that Ontario pay the teachers their salaries. A momentous change was now made by Cardinal Begin, by his authoritatively giving the agitation a religious complexion. Writing Archbishop Bruchesi in an open letter, after assuming that there was no doubt about Ontario's robbing its French settlers of their language, the Cardinal went on to say: "The tongue which "these people want to banish is that which guards "our faith, and which is the instrument of our na- "tional culture." A stimulus to active resistance is contained in the inflammatory suggestion: "Who "knows but a similar attempt might not some day be "levelled even in our own province." In ending his letter the Cardinal gave his official sanction to the agitation in these words: "If, although may God for- "bid, the injustice now suffered by our Ontario "brothers is prolonged, it will be the duty of the "French and Catholic Province of Quebec to support "with its influence and all its resources those who "suffer and those who strive up to the time when full "justice is meted out to them."

Laval is Quebec's university, and its faculty hastened to endorse what the Cardinal had said, and also give to the French in Ontario "encouragement in the "fight which they are carrying on, not only to defend "their language, but also to protect their faith, of "which their language is the vehicle, the interpreter "and the guardian." The Educational Association issued an address to the supporters of the French schools, which in part took the form of a catechism. To the question should French-Canadians accept regulation 17? the answer is "No, because in destroying "our language it will annihilate our race and make "easy the abandonment of our religion."

This difference in the character of the agitation in the two provinces has to be kept in mind—in Ontario the issue is solely one of language: in Quebec it is one of language and creed. Ontario says: To no school that does not teach English will a government grant be paid. Quebec says: We demand for the schools of French settlers in Ontario the same conditions as they enjoyed in Quebec and that the Ontario Government pay their teachers.

The Merits of the Agitation.

The agitation has spread to the remotest parishes of Quebec, and will grow in intensity. It will be fostered and continued so long as it suits the purpose the priests have in view, namely, the extension of the Quebec parish system to every province in the Dominion. That the agitation is based on a flat misrepresentation of facts does not affect its vitality. Few of those who are carried away by it can be reasoned with, for with them it has become a matter of feeling, of sentiment. The priest who, in his discourse, draws a picture of "the wounded" in Ontario, mothers having their children torn from their guidance by the Ontario Government and forced to go to schools to learn English and forget their own tongue and the Holy Roman Catholic religion evokes a prejudice invincible to reason. What though Bishop Fallon defends Ontario's schools and Dean Corbett approves of regulation 17, is not the one Irish and the other Highland Scotch, and both unfriendly to French-Canadian claims? The attitude of the English-speaking people is different. There is the class who look upon the difficulty superciliously and as of a temporary nature. Others dismiss it as due to a few hot-heads on both sides and think when these are sat upon the difficulty will settle itself. A considerable number of French-Canadians saddle the blame on Bishop Fallon and the Irish Catholics of the Ottawa district. The talk of the Superior Person is to get rid of extremists on either side and the Ottawa and Ontario Governments meet in friendly conference and devise a compromise. If that cannot be brought about, let three or four large-visioned men get together with open minds, study the question from its inception up to the present and suggest a policy of reconciliation and mutual understanding. To the Superior Person the problem is beautifully simple, it is to be solved by the heart, not by the head. From many sides there is a call for a truce until the war ends, a condition of the truce being

Ontario's suspending regulation 17. To that proposal there is the objection, that suspending the rule would compromise Ontario before the courts. The English law-lords would be justified in holding that, if the regulation could be suspended at will, it did not involve any fundamental principle of Ontario's constitution. Ontario's contention is, that the violations of her laws, which No. 17 was designed to meet, are so flagrant that no compromise is or can be entertained. Her laws have been set at defiance, and she must either vindicate them or confess she is too weak to grapple with the French priests who mock her.

The Issue Briefly Described.

The issue is so simple that it is within the grasp of everybody who will take the trouble to consider it:

1. The Ontario Government, desirous that every child have an opportunity to receive an elementary education, sets aside yearly a large sum for the support of schools;

2. The conditions to get a share of that grant are that schools have teachers with certificates from an examining board;

3. That English be taught in all schools and that they be subject to inspection to ascertain whether they have complied with the conditions that entitle them to the grant of public money.

These conditions are reasonable. If a school be efficient, it gets a grant: if it is not, no grant is given. Observe, simple as these conditions are, how the priest schools in Northern Ontario violated them:

1. Few of the teachers had certificates of any kind —they came from habitant families without training in teaching;

2. A large proportion of them are incapable of teaching English, for they do not know it;

3. The schools were shut to the government inspector. On seeing him coming the teacher sent the chil-

dren home and locked the door, and this even when the inspector is French and Catholic.

Here comes the vital point. Though these schools do not comply with a single condition of the terms specified by the statutes of Ontario, the priests demand that they shall draw the money grant the same as if they met each one of the three. The department at Toronto specifies that no school shall receive a grant unless the teacher has a certificate. The priests demand cheques for schools with teachers who have none. Then there is the racial difference between the two parties as to what constitutes schools. The department aims at efficiency—the priests at schools that suit their own ends. The department insists on schools that teach French and English, the priests prefer schools that teach French alone. The department has regard for the advancement of the children, the priests place their own interests first. Is the Ontario department to be condemned for refusing its sanction to the spending of public money on so-called schools that are devices to promote the plans of a society of men, who, under the guise of education and religion, are seeking to control Ontario? Is Ontario to be forced either by the Dominion Parliament or by courts of law to help men who seek her political life? Take another instance. The department specifies that English be taught in a school to entitle it to a grant. The priests demand grants for schools in which not a word of English is heard. To be certified that the school is complying with the law, the department requires it to be inspected. The priests spurn inspection, yet hold out their hands for the grant. How can the department do its duty under these circumstances otherwise than by saying to the priests, If you will not meet the conditions of the law you shall get no money? Surely the Ontario Government is not to blame for seeing that the taxes entrusted to it are paid according to the laws of the province! It is not Ontario's conduct that has caused the trouble and turmoil. It is due to the conduct of the priests in glaringly defying Ontario's laws.

Has French Any Claim to Be an Official Language?

The pleas of the priests for acting as they are doing call for examination:

Their chief plea is, that French is on a perfect equality with English from the Atlantic to the Pacific, therefore a school that chooses French as its teaching language has a legal right to the government grant. In support of this plea four reasons are given:

1. That the French having been the original settlers of Canada French is its language. If there be any point to this argument, Iroquois has a better claim than French.

2. That there is a constitutional right, meaning what is contained in the B. N. A. Act. The sole reference to language in the constitution is contained in these paragraphs:

"Either the English or the French language may be "used by any person in the debates of the houses of "parliament of Canada and of the houses of the legis- "lature of Quebec; and both these languages shall be "used in the respective records and journals of those "houses; and either of these languages may be used "by any person in any pleading or process in or issu- "ing from any court of Canada established under this "Act and in or from all or any of the courts of "Quebec.

"The Acts of the parliament of Canada and of the "legislature of Quebec shall be printed and published "in both these languages."

If the constitution meant that French was to be on an equality with English would it not, in so many words, have said so? Instead, it specifies that French shall be legal solely in the Province of Quebec, with permissive use in the federal parliament and in any courts it may establish. The article on which the agitators base their claim is actually one of limitation, for instead of placing French on the same level as English, it localizes French by expressly confining its official use to one province, to the federal courts and houses of parliament, where citizens have the alternative of employing it or English. In all the Dominion outside of Quebec, the Ottawa Parliament, and Federal courts, French is not an official language, and has no legal standing whatever. It is time this was emphatically asserted, not only by Ontario, but by the other provinces. The future peace of Canada requires this. Supposing, however, that French was of equal official authority, what would that have to do with its being the language to be taught in schools outside of Quebec? Have not the provincial governments, that subsidize those schools, the sole right, under the B.N.A. Act, to say how they shall be taught? The assertion set forth by Sir Lomer Gouin, Cardinal Begin, and a host of others, that French, being an official language in one province, makes it an official language in all other provinces, in schools, courts, and legislatures, has only to be stated to realize how fatuous it is. It would mean that all our legislatures would have to be conducted in both languages, all officials have to write and speak both, litigants could be served with documents in either language, that the records of registry offices would be a mixture of French and English, municipal and city councils would have to give both languages a like standing, banks and railways have clerks at their counters who could speak French and English, and merchants prepared to make out invoices in both languages. Put in force the claim of the agitators, that French is an official language, having the same privileges and rights as English, and the whole business of the Dominion would become disorganized; in public matters there would cease to be unity of action; in the most ordinary concerns of life outside their homes people would be at a loss in having no fixed standard of communication, and confusion, destruction of unity and prosperity, ensue.

3. That French should be an official language of Canada because it was the language of discoverers and pioneers, of missionaries and confessors, was spoken by Champlain and Maisonneuve, Breboeuf and Lallemand. This plea deserves a reply of the same kind. The language of Wolfe and Murray was English.

4. There is another plea, so intangible that it can only be indicated, namely, that there is an imprescritible right, derived from God, which entitles the priests to say what the schools shall be. Bishop La Tulipe, at the congress held last February, came nearest giving a comprehensible definition of what is meant than I have seen. He said:

"We are asked to observe the law, but the real law "expresses the Divine Will, not tyranny and oppres-"sion. I felt so keenly about this matter that I went "to Rome and explained it fully to the Holy Father, "who said to me: 'I think exactly as you do.' "

The priests claiming to be the sole interpreters of the divine will, it follows it is for them to say what laws legislators shall enact. That point has been reached in Quebec. Are Ontario and the other provinces going to have the bishops supervise their legislation? Archbishop Bruchesi declares he sees in the French language "the guardian and protector of our faith," consequently to him the divine will has revealed that French must be an official language of Canada!

A Threat.

Mingled with the pleadings and protestations of the agitators there is a threat—if Ontario refuses to withdraw No. 17 we will put the screws on the minority in Quebec. This threat is the background of many of their speeches, all of them based on the misrepresentation that the separate schools of Ontario correspond to the dissentient schools of Quebec. Senator Belcourt, addressing an English audience at the Quebec Canadian Club, said:

"The rights of the minority in the Province of Que-

"bec, with reference to their religious tenets and their "language, have no other and no better foundation "than the same rights of the French or Catholics in the "Province of Ontario. If we are deprived of the right "to use the French language in our schools in the "Province of Ontario, and if that is constitutionally "sound, there is nothing to prevent the Government "of the Province of Quebec from saying that in the "English schools of the Province of Quebec there shall "be no word of English spoken."

Quebec is a part of the British Empire, and British-born natives have in no degree less rights than had they remained in England, Ireland, or Scotland. Their crossing the Atlantic has in no sense impaired their constitutional rights. Among those rights is that of English speech. To assert that the Quebec Government could degrade the legal status of English, or limit its use, is surely the excess of priestly arrogance. Until the Union Jack is hauled down and the banner of the Sacred Heart takes its place, the minority of Quebec will be under no obligation to its Government for the schools they send their children to or what they learn in them. I tell the President of the French-Canadian Educational Association, Cardinal Begin, and all his suffragans, that the English minority do not look upon their residing in Quebec as an act of sufferance on the part of the majority. They are here because they have the best of right to be here, they are British-born and in a British dependency. Nor will they ever consent for a moment to look upon their usage of sending their children to schools not taught by nuns or brothers as a privilege, graciously conceded to them, but as their right as free-born Britons and defy them to touch that right. If they did, their act would call the attention of the Imperial Parliament to the monstrous situation that exists in Quebec—of a British province being ruled by French priests—when steps would be taken to bring Quebec into line with the rest of the Empire. Let no elector of Ontario hesitate for a moment to uphold No.

17 for fear of its provoking retaliation on the Quebec minority.

Dropping No. 17 Would Not End Strife.

To withdraw No. 17 and put in its place the rule asked by the agitators would not bring peace. A separate school has, say, 35 scholars—20 French, 15 Irish. According to the rule laid down, the French having the majority, the teaching language would be French. Where would the Irish children go for an education? In the Green Valley lawsuit, one Highland farmer after another went into the witness-box to testify that since a French teacher had been given control of their school, their children were without means of learning. One took occasion to say that, as he and his Gaelic-speaking neighbors had agreed English should be taught, he did not see why the French should not make a like concession. The more No. 17 is considered in its relation to all parties, the more its wisdom and equity will be recognized.

The campaign being conducted under the name of bilingual schools, many people are misled into supposing that all that is wanted by the agitators is schools that teach both languages. If that was what they sought, they would accept No. 17, for it provides, in the only way practicable, for teaching both. Professing to be in favor of scholars learning English as well as French, the agitators show their insincerity by rejecting a mode of securing that end. It is not bilingual schools they seek: they want French schools, with a curriculum dictated by the priests and free from the interference of the Toronto department, yet drawing salaries from the Ontario treasury. It is no question of language. It is whether schools located in Ontario, and receiving Government aid, shall be controlled by the Ontario Legislature or by French priests.

It Was Not Ontario That Began the Trouble.

The facts in the case show that the trouble originated

in the conspiracy of the French priests to obtain control of Ontario. They planned the invasion of Ontario, and have sedulously nursed it to the present hour. Indeed, since the agitation began, they have been more active than before. Hardly a day passes that some French-Canadian does not join the colonists of New Ontario, not infrequently a car completely filled by them draws up. They have been induced by priests all over Quebec to come, and are met by Bishop La Tulipe or one or other of his priests whose special duty is to receive them and see them settled. No government land agents equal those priests in zeal or skill, and their inspiration is that they are laboring for the great organization of which they are members, looking to the time when it will prevail and dictate to Old Ontario what it is to do. Blind to what is going on, Old Ontario supplies the land, and by recent legislation provides loans for those people who have been brought to subjugate her. It is not Sir James Whitney, his ministers, nor their successors who are to be blamed for the crisis that has arisen, but the French priests who deliberately planned the conquest of Ontario.

The Debate in the House of Commons.

A petition to the Governor-General and his Ministers, praying that they disallow the Act of the Ontario legislature relative to the Ottawa schools, was signed by tens of thousands, not only in the section affected by the Act, but generally throughout Quebec. It was followed and emphasized by a petition in support from Cardinal Begin and the bishops. The delay for disallowance ended on the 28th April, 1916, without the cabinet taking action, so a new move had to be made by those who were guiding the agitation. They clamored for a motion in the house of commons censuring the government for not disallowing the Act. Neither party desired to shoulder the responsibility of introducing such a motion, to which was added the difficulty of framing it so that the Speaker would not rule it out of order. Finally it was agreed the motion should come from the Liberal side and that the draft revised by Sir Wilfrid Laurier be adopted. It declared that subjects of French origin in Ontario complained of having been deprived of having their children taught in their own language, and, therefore, parliament suggest to the Ontario legislature to remove the cause of complaint. The method of bringing the resolution before the house was significant. Introduced by itself members would have been free to vote without compromising their party standing. Instead, it was brought in as an amendment to the motion to go into supply, and consequently was a vote of want of confidence in the government. Members who favored the resolution, yet were averse to turning the government out, were constrained to vote against it, while members who disapproved of the resolution had to choose between supporting it or turning their backs on their leader, Laurier. The objection that the resolution was out of order was overruled by the Speaker and the debate began. It lasted two days. Whether what the resolution asked was or was not outside the jurisdiction of the federal house appealed to the legal mind and much time was spent in discussing that aspect of it. Nearly every speech made in favor of the resolution had in it an appeal to the feelings, and while member after member gushed more or less over the stereotyped phrases, this time of stress and strain, brothers fighting side by side, peace and harmony, they were advocating an amendment which, if carried, meant that the government would have to resign and a general election be held. And what would then be the question before the electors, what the issue on which that election would be fought? It would be purely one of race and creed that might lead to civil war. The members who, with the whine of Pecksniff, posed as conciliators, as pourers of oil on troubled waters, whose whole desire was peace, knew full well, under their hypocritical pretences, they were endangering the welfare not only of Canada but of the Empire. Two speeches were notable contributions to the understanding of the resolution. One was by Sir Wilfrid Laurier, the other by the member for Edmonton, Frank Oliver.

Sir Wilfrid declared he took part in the debate because of an open letter addressed to him by the editor of The Sentinel of Toronto. That letter was an appeal to him to exert his influence to allay the perilous agitation that prevailed among his compatriots. To Mr. Hocken's letter he gave the disingenuous twist, that it was a request to lay his views on bilingual schools before the country, which he would now do.

In response to a call to support the Old Chief by their presence, the house was crowded with sympathizers of the agitation. Sir Wilfrid's opening remarks disconcerted them, for he denounced as erroneous all the statements on which they had been advocating the cause of "the wounded." In the cry of French being an official language outside the limits laid down by the B. N. A. Act he could not join, for it had no warrant. Then he went on to declare each province has the right to prescribe its official language. Ontario, he affirmed, "is an English-speaking province, and will "remain as an English-speaking province." The cry about treaty rights was equally unfounded, and he told his hearers there was not a word about the French language either in the articles of capitulation or in the treaty of Paris. Ontario was being denounced for passing regulation 17, but its legislature in doing so was within its rights, and, therefore, the Borden ministry had acted correctly in refusing to disallow its School Acts. The agitators might well ask, Is this the champion we came to acclaim, who denies that French is co-equal with English as an official language and who justifies Ontario and the federal government. When he gives us away in this style, why does he identify himself with our cause? Because, answered Sir Wilfrid, every child of the French race should have the privilege of education in the language of his father and mother. That regulation 17 provided for such an education he denied, on account of its putting a limit to the use of French as the language of communication between scholar and teacher. To support his assertion he entered into a minute examination of the wording of the Ontario regulations and to quote specialists on the teaching of languages. Much that he said was more suited for a teachers' convention than a deliberative assembly. On the meaning he forced on the word "hitherto" in 17 he has been officially shown to be entirely wrong. His conclusion, that the language of communication even in teaching English should be French, when carried into practice would mean that the Ontario Government was not merely bound to teach each child the language of its father and mother, but to draw its schoolmams from Quebec. How were these concessions to be got? Not by force of law, for even a decision of the privy council would be ineffectual, while federal dictation was not to be thought of. How then? By going to the electors of Ontario and appealing to their sense of justice and fair play. In persuasion and conciliation alone lay Sir Wilfrid's hope of having the French and English languages taught in Ontario and the other English provinces.

Analyzing the speech, which took over two hours to deliver, it will be found its argument can be put into few words. It consists in the affirmation, oft repeated, that every child has a right to be educated in the language of its father and mother. On this assertion Sir Wilfrid built all the claims he set forth. It is obvious the assertion is vague. If he means fathers and mothers have an inherent right to teach their children any language they see fit, nobody will dispute so evident a truth. Or, again, if he means every man and woman has the right to speak any language they choose without interference, everybody will agree with him, for the right of speech is part of our personality. That, however, is not the question before the country nor the question he was debating; if it were, there would be no discord. The question before the country and which awaits settlement is, Whether Ontario is bound to provide schools to teach each child the language of its father and mother? Freedom to speak a language is one thing, to declare that a legislature should provide scholastic media, the means, to teach that language is quite another. The reply of the Ontario legislature is, "Speak as much French as you "please, but you have no right to ask us to teach it in "our schools: you want French schools, you are at full "liberty to provide them at your own cost, but do not "ask us to take the taxes paid by English-speaking "people to do so. We have gone as far as we could "with justice to the taxpayers of Ontario; we have "freely provided schools to teach your children Eng-"lish, with sufficient French to bridge the period when "they will be able to take up English. Further than "that we will not go."

Sir Wilfrid will not accept this answer. He insists Ontario shall provide schools that will give equal facilities to teach French as English, and by schools, he means not only schools of the language of the parents, but of their creed. See how such schools would work out in practice. The rural school is necessarily small, with one room and with a single teacher, who may have 20 or more scholars, ranging from 6 to 16 years of age. She begins with getting the scholars to commit certain prescribed prayers to memory, then catechism, occasionally drill in the meaning of the ritual so as to follow the services when in church. This is the most important duty of the teacher, to make certain that her scholars be good Catholics, and to do so she takes an hour in the forenoon and another in the afternoon. Next she hears them their lessons in reading, spelling, arithmetic, geography, and oversees their writing. All this is to be done in French, for Sir Wilfrid insists it come first. With several classes the school day of six hours has been fully occupied, but the schoolmam's labors are not done. Sir Wilfrid says: "I want every "child in the Province of Ontario to receive the benefit "of an English education," so he expects the poor girl to repeat in English the lessons she has already given in French. She cannot—it is impossible alike for teacher and scholars. At its best, the rural school is capable of imparting lessons in only one langauge and does so imperfectly. To require it to teach two languages is to make it useless. Scores of managers of schools in the English-speaking districts of the Province of Quebec I have known to try to have both languages taught and failed. The scholars got an imperfect knowledge of English and what they caught of French was of no practical benefit. It is a fact not to be controverted, that the most the rural school can do is to give lessons in one language, and when Sir Wilfrid demands that the language of communication between teacher and scholar shall be the child's mother tongue he means it shall be a French school. He would have saved time and his hearers would have grasped his meaning at once, had he merely said he was in favor of the schools in the Temiskaming diocese being restored to the condition in which Mr. Merchant found them. All his talk and that of his fellow-agitators about bilingual schools is designedly misleading. A school that teaches English and gives a suggestion of French is possible: a school that will give the same attention to both languages is an impossibility with the little red school. Schools of higher grade, with two or more teachers, may do so, but it is not these the agitators have in their minds. The words "bilingual schools" are used to deceive, what the agitators are seeking is French schools at the expense of the English. Thousands of French children are learning English by going to English schools, or playing with English companions, men and women by intercourse with English employers, none of the laboring class outside town or city learn it in French schools.

Several times Sir Wilfrid sought to strengthen his plea by asserting the French had a right to have continued the schools they had at the conquest. There was no school system before the conquest, no parish schools that taught the three R's. In Quebec, Three Rivers, and Montreal nuns and priests had classes that gave religious and industrial lessons. Few men of the better classes could read, and fewer still could write. There were no schools at the conquest to be continued. It is reported Sir Wilfrid is to hold meetings in Ontario. When he tells you electors of Ontario he is perfectly fair, that he wants schools that will teach English as well as French, understand this, what he asks is French Catholic schools, and that you pay the cost of them.

A remarkable feature of his speech was his assuming that Ontario was the aggressor. It was Ontario who had provoked the agitation, she was the cause of it, she alone was to blame, and the remedy lay in her hands. Now, the fact is that the trouble originated in a flocking of French families into Northern Ontario, led by priests who had enticed them to leave their own province. What motive had the priests for so acting? What other motive can be suggested than that they had a plan to subjugate Ontario, to bring it under their control and make it another Quebec? For over fifty years the priests had been nursing this conspiracy to destroy the political independence of Ontario. It might have gone on other fifty years had Sir James Whitney not raised his hand and commanded it should stop. Not a word in condemnation of this plot to strangle Ontario's independence, not a word in support of Ontario's contention that whoever comes to live within its borders is bound to accept its laws as he finds them, and has no right to ask exemption from the operation of those laws, much less demand money from the provincial treasury to teach another language than English, or help to plant institutions foreign to and destructive of its own. Sir Wilfrid had not a word to say about these vital points, he passed them over and tried to persuade his hearers the only question before them was one of language and schools and nothing more, just as if whether French children shall be taught English was the sole point at issue. That is a trifling matter in comparison with whether the greatest, most enlightened, most progressive of our provinces shall be brought under the heel of the French priesthood.

Not only did he ignore this palpable conspiracy, but conceals that the agitation he has identified himself with is one of creed. It is merely a gilding of the pill to get the Ontario electors to swallow it to pretend the question before them is one of language and nothing else. This can be conclusively proved. Were the settlers in the diocese of Temiskaming French-speaking Protestants, would there be the same wild resistance to their children being taught English? It is because these settlers are Catholics, and the priests fear teaching their children English will lead to their ceasing to be Catholics, that we have an agitation backed with a threat of civil war. What say the priests who alone can speak with authority on this head? From Cardinal Begin and Archbishop Bruchesi down to the most obscure cure of the most remote parish are they not all declaring it to be indisputable that the agitation is Catholic and is a crusade to extend Catholicism in Ontario? In face of all this, Sir Wilfrid Laurier would have the electors of Ontario believe it is simply a question of language, of teaching children the language of their father and mother. Take creed out of the agitation and it would die to-morrow. It is creed that inspires it and makes it dangerous, and no man knows better than Sir Wilfrid that the issue at stake is Quebec Catholicism and not language.

Like other speakers, Sir Wilfrid laid much stress on Britain recognizing Dutch as an official language in South Africa. There is a difference between the Boers and our agitators for pretended bilingual schools. The Boers fled to Africa from the persecution

of the Spanish inquisition. To them the rule of the
priest is an abomination. They are ready to fraternize
with the English, to learn their language, to inter-
marry, to co-operate in maintaining one allegiance.
In a few generations the Africanders will be a new
race, with one common language and one school. There
is no comparison between them and a people whose
first allegiance is to the priesthood and who are convulsing the Dominion by an agitation to make French
an official language, with the sole purpose of raising
another barrier to their ever becoming part and parcel
of the British nation. Is this not proved to be true by
the response the Boers have given in enlisting to fight
the Germans? Compare what they have done with
Quebec's record. Sir Wilfrid declared, "I ask that
"every child of my own race should receive an Eng-
"lish education." Yet he had not a word of reproach
for the priests who for forty years had been sending
out from schools in the Temiskaming diocese thousands of children who had not been taught a word of
English.

In his peroration Sir Wilfrid intimated that if Ontario would adopt the suggestions he had been advocating, there would spring up a new spirit of affection
and brotherhood between French and English "such
"as has never before been heard of or known since
"the angels themselves brought from heaven the
"divine message of Peace on earth, good will to men."
Has not all the discord and strife that exist on earth
one cause—individuals or combinations of individuals
seeking special benefits, special privileges, at the expense of their fellow-men? Yet here we have a richly
gifted man arguing by the hour in our highest court,
that French priests be given by Ontario a free hand
and grants of public money to segregate their followers and keep them separate by means of exclusive
privileges, and, in arguing thus, he asks us to believe
he is striving to realize the song of the angels!

Sir Wilfrid Laurier occupies a position before the

Dominion different from that of any other of our public men. For nigh twelve years he was its premier, and as such the interests of all the provinces ought to have been equally dear to him. While he was in full control, what did he do to protect Ontario from the conspiracy which was going on to destroy her independence? As a resident of Ottawa he was cognizant of what was going on. Did he make the slightest move to defend Ontario from her priestly assailants? In his book, "The Catholic Church in Canada," Father Alexis says:

"The Diocese of Ottawa, to-day, is without ques-
"tion, after Quebec and Montreal, the most important
"in the Dominion. This ecclesiastical province is es-
"tablished astride of the Ottawa River, extending
"into the two civil provinces of Quebec and Ontario.
"At first sight such an arrangement may seem strange;
"but it becomes plain, and seems providential, when
"we consider the needs to which it responds. In order
"to foster the pacific invasion of Catholic Canadians
"into Protestant Ontario, was it not essential to have
"unity of view in its guidance, and abundance of
"instruments in carrying it out? The wisdom of the
"plan has been proved by its success, since, to-day, the
"counties of Prescott and Russell, the county of
"Nipissing, and the territories of New Ontario are
"completely conquered to our faith, or are in a fair
"way of becoming so."

As first Minister of the Crown, Sir Wilfrid, had he been true to his duty, would have checked that conspiracy. He did nothing; he let it go on. And, now, when the purpose of that conspiracy has become palpable, when the priests, dropping disguise, work in the open, when Ontario gathers up her forces to defend her independence, what does he do? He identifies himself with the agitation and becomes its most plausible exponent. The priests have before this, time and again, used public agitations and even rebellion to extort the privileges they covet, but it is unspeakably deplorable to find a man, eminent from position and talent, falling in behind them. Shall the French priests in their designs on Ontario's independence, be thwarted or shall they triumph? Sir Wilfrid Laurier has answered for himself. He will do nothing to stop the onward sweep of Clericalism towards victory.

Mr. Oliver spoke from the standpoint of a Westerner, of a man familiar with the conditions of that vast territory, which he truly described as the future heart of the Dominion. The resolution they were debating had for its object a change in the law of Ontario, that wherever there were children of the French race they must be taught in their own language. Applying that rule to the Western Provinces, how would it work? They had people from every country in Europe, and if each race was to have schools in its own language, the result would be they would have no school at all. It was only by uniting in schools that would teach one language, and that English, that it was possible for the settlers in the West to have schools, and, added Mr. Oliver, "the re-"sult is that you can travel through those German and "Russian settlements to-day, and you will find that "while the old people cannot speak English, the young "people, both German and Russian, speak English just "as well as you and I do, without an accent." Mr. Oliver went on to state that experience had shown bilingual schools were not practicable in the West, confirming the experience of Quebec, that small country schools can teach but one language. With the sparsity of population that necessarily prevails in the rural sections and the climatic conditions that make regular attendance impossible, it was, from the economic standpoint, utterly impracticable to educate the children in more than one language.

On the 8th of February, Sir Wilfrid Laurier seconded a resolution to extend the term of parliament for one year. In doing so he declared it was necessary because "at a time when the energies of the nation

"should be bent towards one end and one end only,"
"the very thought that there might be an election,"
"with all its concomitant strife and division, was"
"alarming." Now, three months later, the Sir Wilfrid
who shrank from a general election while England was
engaged in mortal combat, had no hesitation in voting
for a resolution designed to compel the Borden Administration to resign and precipitate the country into
a general election. Happily the motion of want of confidence was declared lost by 107 to 60. Every Liberal
from Lake Superior to the Pacific voted against it.
With such a unanimous expression of the sentiment
of Western Canada it was apparent Sir Wilfrid
Laurier had ceased to be leader of the Liberal party.
Ten days later the election of a new legislature for
Quebec took place, when the followers of Sir Lomer
Gouin overwhelmed their opponents. The vote at Ottawa had no effect in this result beyond that the defeat of the resolution added fuel to the zeal of the
agitators, and Quebec lined up to a man against Ontario.

The St. Jean Baptiste Celebration of 1916.

This celebration was looked forward to as a test of
popular sentiment and to give an insight as to future
course of action. The largest of many meetings was
in a Montreal park, where over 12,000 were present.
At Ottawa, a convention sat to consider what should
be done in the event of the appeal to England failing.
All the meetings were alike in the abusive language
used towards the government and people of Ontario.
When the priests started the agitation, the favorite
designation for the inhabitants of Ontario was
"fanatics." On St. Jean Baptiste day the choice of
the orators was "barbarians." Two peculiarities of
the meetings were the assumption that the French-
Canadians are in the right beyond all controversy, because they have the approval of Cardinal Begin and
the clergy, and, second, that their forefathers being

the first to settle in Canada, what they ask must be granted. Speaker after speaker assumed it to be undeniable that the French-Canadians stand on a higher plane than the rest of the people of the Dominion, that they are a people set apart to carry out a divine mission and in fulfilling that destiny no province has a right to raise any obstacle. Whatever they ask, is to be granted. If denied, they are justified in resorting to force. One prominent leader spoke of the re-conquest of Canada by his countrymen being called for. Every allusion to coercing Ontario by the strong hand was cheered. Quebec's attitude towards its Protestant minority was exultantly contrasted with Ontario's treatment of the French-Canadians, each speaker taking it as unquestionable that anything more generous than Quebec's conduct towards Protestants was inconceivable, and Ontario was called on to copy it. No meetings so unanimous, so enthusiastic has Quebec known since Papineau stirred it to its depths. The cries, the gesticulations, the vociferous applause, told, without scanning the tense countenances of the hearers, that they were body and soul in unison with the speakers. There on the platform was a bevy of black robes, smiling furtively at the success of the agitation they originated and are piloting. Posing as ministers of the Prince of Peace, they encourage meetings to foster hatred of Ontario and fan a movement which, when it passes their control, will end in violence. Why? Because they see in the agitation a means of advancing their caste towards the point for which they strive—the political control of Canada. At the Ottawa convention it was unanimously agreed to accept no compromise to their demand that French be an official language and the medium of instruction in all schools wherever French-Canadian scholars form the majority. Should the privy council reject their appeal, the fight would be continued in another form, and reference to the Quebec Legislature undertaking the financing of the agitation evoked wildest applause.

Ontario Has Vital Interests at Stake.

The agitation over the schools has distracted the attention of the people of Ontario from the fundamental danger that threatens them, namely, the invasion of their northern territory by a host recruited, led, and encamped by French priests who look to the time when that host shall have so grown that it will elect sufficient members of the Evanturel type to hold the balance of power in the Ontario Legislature. In 1881, there were 24,223 French-Canadians in the counties of Russell and Prescott; in 1911, there were 42,599, besides 26,000 in the territory north of them—a compact mass transplanted from Quebec, with confessional schools and the parochial system. In 1881, there were 4,188 French-Canadians in Glengarry; in 1911, there were 8,710; in Stormont, in 1881, there were 1,967; in 1911 there were 7.016. Forty years ago, Northern Ontario knew only occasional missionary priests; it has now 25 stationed cures and a bishop, who has a stone cathedral that in size and architecture would be an ornament to any city. Who dare predict a limit to the increase in numbers or extension of this priest-managed colony? Let it be borne in mind that it is planted on the best land there is within Ontario's borders—on the famous Clay Belt, that great stretch of fertile soil that reaches from Pontiac to within reach of Manitoba, and with a greater depth of rich soil than is to be found in the entire Northwest. There is one drawback, June frosts, but these may disappear as the country becomes settled. Here is room for hundreds of townships. Here is the soil that will make this region a granary. Is it to be settled by people with aspirations, habits, and language like those of Old Ontario, strengthening them by their trade, and helping to build up those institutions which have given distinction to Ontario? Quebec priests are pre-empting the Clay Belt. Those who know fear they have coralled it and that it is too late to counteract them. The expectations of Father Hamon are being realized. Ontario has been slumber-

The Tragedy of Quebec.

Quebec has separated herself from the partnership formed by Confederation. She is defiant of its terms and of her sister provinces. She has refused to furnish her quota of men to help the Empire in its direst need, she stands aloof to criticize and misrepresent; in short, in the greatest crisis the Dominion is likely to ever know, she is the rebellious sister, who not only will give no help, but distracts our rulers by making trouble. Do not blame the habitants. Put the blame where it lies, on the shoulders of the priests, who, by working on the sympathies and prejudices of their people, have brought the agitation to the point that the parliament at Ottawa has only two alternatives, to yield to the demands of the priests or else refuse and tell them to do their worst. Had our federal government insisted on Quebec supplying the number of soldiers allotted to her, and had it brought to account the men who blocked enlistment, would the situation have assumed the gravity that confronts the Dominion to-day?

Of all boasting, surely that which declares the English-speaking people of Quebec have no cause for complaint, that they are indulgently treated, is the most audacious. Was the cowardly device of preparing a legal poison-gas that has compelled thousands of Protestant farmers to leave the townships a recognition of their rights? Does laws that have shut the door of hundreds of schoolhouses bespeak tender regard for Protestantism? Is compelling Protestants to pay taxes to maintain Catholic institutions an illustration of tolerance? Does denying Protestants, although the largest taxpayers, representation in the Quebec cabinet, fair, for the minister assigned to them in no sense represents Protestantism? The Quebec minority, while being slowly smothered out of existence, has the added humiliation of such abjects as Bourassa and Lavergne making mouths at them by telling them every right they are entitled to is recognized.

ing, ignorant of the great gift Providence has entrusted to her. Will she now awake and assert her independence, her right to control her own soil, to vindicate her own laws and defeat the plot to entangle her in the thraldom of Quebec?

Ontario's Responsibility and Opportunity.

Is Ontario, the Mother of Provinces, not going to rise to the level of the situation? Is she, who is the leader in all the commercial enterprises that have brought renown to Canada, who has set the standard in arts and agriculture, who has been so potent in every movement tending to moral and social advancement, who, in brief, is the centre of the Dominion's life—is she going to fall down before a conspiracy devised by French priests to absorb her soil, violate her laws, and undermine her independence? She has come to a crisis in her career—a crisis that might have been delayed, but has been sprung upon her unexpectedly—and on how the people of Ontario act turns her future destiny, whether she is to remain a self-governing province or fall under the rule of French clericalism. Every consideration that appeals to the lover of British freedom calls on the electors to unite to repel the secret foe and assert Ontario's independence.

In Canada's career during the past century there have been repeated crises when it was said, Had those who were in power done their duty these difficulties would not have survived to perplex us. Such a crisis Canada now faces. Not a mere passing emergency, not a matter that affects herself alone, has Ontario to decide. The issue that has grown out of this matter of elementary schools is fundamental and admits of no compromise; it is one that is not local but affects the future of the entire Dominion. It is simply: Whether this Canada of ours is to be British, and nothing else than British, or whether it is to be a mongrel land, with two official languages and ruled by a divided authority? Should Ontario knuckle under the demand now made upon her, farewell to the hope of Canada being British. The electors of Ontario have a great responsibility thrown upon their shoulders, but they have also such an opportunity as patriots welcome. No matter who may gnash their teeth at being baffled in their designs upon her independence, no matter what dire threats may be uttered, may the electors of Ontario vindicate their right to make their own laws and maintain over their soil and institutions that sovereignty which is the inheritance of the British-born. Every Canadian has a deep interest in Ontario's answer, for upon it depends whether our country is to have two official languages fastened upon it and its legislatures pass under the lordship of French clericalism.

CHAPTER XIII.

The Peril of Clericalism

We are sinking beneath a power before which the proudest conquerors have grown pale, and by which the nations most devoted to freedom have become enslaved—the power of a foreign priesthood.—Lord Beaconsfield.

No man was ever born into the world without ambition. It might take an ignoble form, but the quality was there—the desire to advance, to rule, to exercise authority. The form it takes is modified by circumstances. It is exemplified alike in the household tyrant who makes his children miserable, and in the crowned despot who grinds millions. All history is studded with instances of men who sought and planned to obtain power, and humanity's woes are largely due to the strivings of those who used the supremacy they won to plunder and oppress. When the desire to attain a commanding position is to help and benefit, aspiration is laudable; when the motive is selfish, it is odious. Between John Bright seeking office that he might reform public evils, and Napoleon looking to his own aggrandizement, there is a wide gulf. With what men of masterful intellect or of exceptional military talent have accomplished, the world is familiar; but it has not recognized that a number of men of mediocre attainments, working together, may acquire in the course of centuries what it took a Charlemagne to achieve in a lifetime. Wherever bands of men have joined together with the thirst to rule, to obtain control, they have won a place for their society which individually they could not have reached. This is especially true where these combinations of men have affected to be ultra-religious. The priesthoods of pagan ages have their counterparts to-day, and from Japan to Italy they are ruling powers. Individually despicable, yet as members of a large society with centuries of tradition behind them, and strong in the experience and methods elaborated during these centuries, they are a formidable force. The man who wishes to have influence over his fellows, to command implicit obedience, to obtain a living he does not earn, can obtain all by uniting with a priesthood.

The Priests of Quebec.

To comprehend what the priesthood is as it exists in Canada, the reader must divest his mind of all theological notions, and look at it not as the repository of a system of religious views, but in its civil, its secular aspect. I know how difficult it is to do this, to set aside all preconceived notions of the priests as religious teachers, as representatives of a system of theology, and to regard them solely as members of a secular society, of a great world-wide corporation, whose aim is to rule their fellowmen. Until able to thus regard them, you can have no correct conception of the danger that confronts the Dominion. Blot out your impression of priests, bishops, and cardinals as clergymen, and regard them as what they really are, members of a complete and highly organized society, whose master aim is to obtain power to rule whatever community in which they are placed. These priests, by years of skilful training, have had impressed upon their minds that they have been selected and set aside to win for their society the government of the world. Fresh from their ordination vows, they start to do what they can to establish the authority of their society as supreme over the rule of all laymen. The laws of their society are to be superior to all other laws, its mandates to go before those of kings and parliaments; the voice of the people to be a meaningless sound in their ears. Their years of training having left no doubt in their minds that the ruling of the people is committed to their hands, they believe that in striving to assert that rule they are only seeking what belongs to them. It is for them to mark out the limits wherein civil rulers are to act, to define what they are to do, and when they have given their orders all that is left for the civil authorities is to carry them into effect. As we find this association of priests in Quebec, we see its members fired by a conception before which the wildest Imperialism pales—of establishing their authority above that of local and Federal legislatures for the governing of Canada. From the experience of Europe we are familiar with despots who, by brute force, have obtained supreme power over the people, but have forgotten that a society may seek to do what individuals have done, and seek their end, not by the mailed fist, but by pretences to divine authority and by political intrigues so craftily carried on that they they do not attract public attention. An Imperial tyrant is bold in his claims and brutally frank in his means of enforcing them. He is palpable to the patriots who would overthrow him, but a body of men bound together with the purpose of dominating the people, using as their means social and political strategy, the influencing of public men, the poisoning of the press, the deceiving of the multitude, are intangible, and the more readily allay suspicion as they act under the garb of piety. No more dangerous combination could attack the liberties of the people than a band of men aiming at supremacy under the guise of a church.

The Habitant Boy Who Becomes a Priest.

Here is a lad, one of a numerous family, who, by means of constant labor, earn a bare subsistence. The boy sees before him no better prospect than that his father had—to buy a farm with borrowed money, spend years in paying the mortgage, and live penuriously. It is the life of the habitants around him and he would like to do better. He sees how the priest of the parish is deferred to, how his word is law, how he lives in a style that seems to his eyes to be affluence. When the bishop comes on his yearly visit, he is met by a procession of habitants a mile long, the bells are rung and decorations appear. It is a high privilege to be introduced to him, do him reverence, and leave a donation with his secretary. In departing the bishop is again escorted until he meets the procession from the next parish. The boy is told the bishop is all-powerful at Quebec, that cabinet ministers and the premier himself drop on their knees to kiss his hand, and whatever he asks of them they are pleased to give. Yet this bishop was once like the boy who watches him, the son of a poor habitant, and so was also the priest of the parish. They escaped hard living by becoming priests: they emerged from being unknown to places of power and prominence. Why should he not do likewise? and his ambition is centred on becoming a member of that society which will change his homespun into gorgeous robes, which will make his father drop on his knees to do him reverence, and give him the influence to dictate to his former neighbors who shall represent them, and to governments what laws they shall pass. By simply becoming a unit in the great secret society of Quebec the son of the habitant is transformed into a dictator. Were the head of one of our political parties to become possessed with the ambition of being a dictator and use all the means in his power to attain his object, the people of Canada would revolt, but a caste of men seeking the like end plan and work without hindrance because they do so in the character of ultra-pietists, asserting they are the sole authorized exponents of the one and only true faith, that the control of the solitary bridge which spans the gulf between earth and heaven has been committed to them by the Lord Jesus. Their claim is, they are extending the Kingdom of God, and millions believe it, when they are really engaged in adding to the strength of their society and preparing for the time when it shall have the supreme voice in the government of Canada. This may be said to be a vain dream of pious visionaries which, in our age, is impossible of fulfilment, were it not for the evidence of their success in the Province of Quebec.

What the Priests Have Accomplished.

1. Kept the French and English two separate peoples and thereby prevented Quebec becoming in reality as it is nominally—British;

2. Driven the English-speaking farmers out of the Townships;

3. Established schools which do not fit youth to act their part in a self-governing country;

4. Got the legislature to be its minister in whatever it desires, and is yearly entrusted by it with the spending of one-third of its income.

5. Established courts that administer foreign laws independent of and above those enacted by parliament;

6. The subserviency of the judges to their demands;

7. The suppression of free speech and of a free press;

8. The tacit acknowledgment by almost the entire Province of Quebec that there is a rule above that of the Crown and to which their first allegiance is due.

The marvellous success of the ecclesiastics in Quebec is their encouragement to assail the other provinces and seek to do in them what they have already done. Whoever claims there is no cause for fear, who denies that Quebec is a menace to the Dominion, that what the priests have accomplished in Quebec they cannot duplicate outside its limits, must demonstrate that these assertions of what they have accomplished in Quebec are fabulous.

Apart from Quebec, is there not evidence to be found in every corner of Canada? Is even British Columbia free from the demands of the priests for exceptional treatment? Are not separate schools and language the burning questions in the Maritime Provinces, in Ontario, and in the Northwest? So the original question asked stands, Is not Quebec a menace to every part of the Dominion? To master the answer to this question, get rid of prepossessions, such as that the first object of the priests is the conversion of Protestants. It is not a spiritual empire they aim at, but a political. They know that to bring the mass of Protestants into their fold is impossible, but it is not impossible, as Quebec has proved, to bring Protestants under their direction. To be the masters of Canada's political life, to dictate to Legislatures and Parliament what they shall do, is the goal aimed at. They have succeeded in Quebec in becoming masters, and from their entrenchment in Quebec they carry on their campaign to subjugate all Canada.

The Measures of Defence Called For.

If Canada is to continue to be a nation of freemen, it is necessary alike to demand that all interference by priests cease, and to repudiate the claim on which they base their pretension to interfere. It intensifies though it does not affect the merits of the situation, that these clerics assume their airs of superiority because of offices bestowed by a foreign power, and that a power repudiated by the Motherland and by a majority of Canadians. Apart from every other consideration, a government influenced by the agents of the Vatican would not be a free government. What sense in boasting of our freedom, in holding up our constitution for other British dependencies to copy, when the controlling power is of foreign inspiration? The British North America Act had to be approved by the Pope before Quebec would accept Confederation. The constitutions of Saskatchewan and Alberta were drafted to suit his representative at Ottawa. The sovereign will of the people has to be vindicated in

Canada—the battle of our fathers against ecclesiastical usurpation has to be fought over again and decided on the virgin soil of Canada. It is monstrous that such a contest should be forced on the people of a new country. It shall be to their everlasting shame if they evade it and do not repeat the victory of their fathers.

It is vexatious, it is passing strange, that difficulties peculiar to continental Europe should embarrass the development of British institutions in our Dominion. The origin of the difficulty is apparent. A bit of medieval Europe, plucked from its native soil, was planted on the banks of the St. Lawrence, and sceptical of the warnings as to its nature, it has been nourished by those who ought to have kept it within bounds, until it has become vigorous enough to overshadow our country. Is it possible that Canada can be dragged under the influences of three centuries ago? It would not be possible did the electors recognize the situation, but when it is considered how the leaders of both our political parties pander to the bishops for their support, how our history is a record of concession after concession made to them, how our Northwest is being dotted with colonies of foreigners—hordes from Austria-Hungary, Poland, Italy, notorious for their subserviency to Rome—he who ardently desires to see Canada British in deed as well as name has solid grounds for the fear that a day may come when, like the governments of Europe in the past, like that of Quebec at this hour, its real rulers will be ecclesiastics. The forms, names, and procedure of constitutionalism go for nothing when its spirit has fled. The bishops can rule as effectively from behind a screen of governors and premiers, senators and members, as ever did Richelieu or Mazarin in their princely ostentation. The danger-centre of the Dominion is Quebec. A French Quebec, free in thought and action, would be no menace to the Dominion; a Papal Quebec is, for it stands for a power that is not working for the common good, but to place the reins of political power in the hands of an ecclesiastical caste. That caste seeks not to exalt our country by strengthening its unity, binding man to man in the bonds of common interests and of a common brotherhood. On the contrary, in order to advance its designs it schemes in every possible way to thrust wedges to keep our people apart.

The Nature of Clericalism.

The call to the electors of Canada is not to defend themselves against a church, but against a society of men who assume the character of a church that they may effect their purpose of attaining supreme power. Do not fly to the Bible and begin quoting texts, do not engage in controversy, but, realizing the fact that a numerous body of men, oath-bound and highly disciplined, are working to bring the Dominion as completely under their control as Quebec is, face the members of that society and do your best to defeat their efforts. We have no quarrel with any church that confines itself to spiritual duties, but a society of men wearing the livery of a church who strive to overthrow constitutional government is to be faced without flinching.

Will the electors of Canada not arouse themselves to assert their manhood—are they going to continue to bow before a society of men who assume to be of different mould from the rest of mankind and pretend to have been given divine authority to govern them? This claim of the priests that they are members of a society to whom God has entrusted the rule of the world, is constantly overlooked. Theologians fly at the doctrines peculiar to Rome and darken the air with futile controversies, the commonalty make them a subject for jokes, while the one important question at issue, the one claim that affects the world's welfare and the liberty of man, is forgotten. That which makes the priesthood a menace to society and to free government, is their pretension that they are God's

The Tragedy of Quebec. 337

representatives, and as such have been given authority to dictate to mankind what they are to believe and do. Wherever there are a sufficient number of men who make this claim and are backed by a sufficient number of followers, it is vain to speak of liberty —of constitutional government, of a free Canada. The people are domineered, kept down, dictated to by a select body of men whose usurped authority is based on a claim of their own device, that they are the chosen and inspired representatives of Christ. If they are what they pretend to be they would be entitled to obedience. What if they are not?

The Claim of Supremacy Over the State.

It is a self-apparent truth, that the peace of no country can be assured which is not governed solely in the interests of its people. When there is planted in the midst of a country a compact body of men and women whose interests are not those of the masses, whose lives are devoted not to furthering the common good but to the upbuilding of an ecclesiastical organization, strife must follow. The spirit of independence instinctive to human nature will not continue to submit to dictation. Necessarily any organization that seeks to establish its rule must work through the ordinary agencies of the social state—the school, the courts, the press, the political convention, parliament —bending them to advance its cause, and laboring persistently through them until its object is attained—the government of the Dominion in accordance with the will of men who pretend to have authority direct from God. The history of Quebec illustrates this, and that province stands as an object lesson to its sisters of what its hierarchy is working to make them. Entrenched in Quebec is an organization that threatens the existence of civil and religious liberty wherever it extends its arms. Shall that organization be left in its plenitude of power to be a menace to the Dominion, or shall it be reduced to a state of harmlessness? Do not take the word of the writer as to the authority the bishops of Quebec claim in interfering with the affairs of the other provinces. Listen to their own words in their pastoral of May, 1896, in defence of their movement to force Separate Schools on Manitoba:

"If the bishops, whose authority issues from God "himself, are the natural judges of all questions which "touch upon the Christian faith and morals; if they "are the acknowledged heads of a perfect condition of "society, sovereign in itself and standing above that "of the State; it follows that it is in their province, "when circumstances render it desirable, not merely to "express generally their views and wishes in regard to "religious matters, but also to indicate to the faithful "the best means of attaining the spiritual ends in "view."

The bishops retaining the deciding of questions touching upon faith and morals, gives them control over all legislation. Let those provinces that think themselves safe, consider this, that the measure of the priests' privileges in Quebec is the standard of their demands in the rest of the Dominion. What they possess in Quebec is the claim of the bishops at this hour in Manitoba and her sister provinces. The great issue that cannot be evaded and the settlement of which is fast becoming imperative, is the disestablishment of the Church of Rome in Quebec. The issue is political, one of self-preservation. It is common to speak as if it were one of race, a misconception fostered by those whose interest it is to have the French-Canadian identify his cause with that of the bishops.

The Claim to Divine Authority.

In the last analysis of the subject, it will be found the political issue that has been forced on the Dominion is simply whether the people or the priests are to rule. Under the pretence that they possess divine authority, the priests claim to be above the people, and to their requirements governments must conform.

With whether they have divine authority or not no British subject requires for a moment to trouble himself. The question so far as Britain is concerned was settled once for all three hundred years ago, by the Act of Supremacy, passed in the days of Queen Elizabeth, which vested the sole control of the government in the estates that represented the people. It is the basis of the British constitution that the people are sovereign and to swerve from that grand principle is treason. This, then, is our answer to the priests: We repudiate your claim to any other voice in the government of the country than what pertains to you as British subjects—with your pretensions to divine authority we have nothing to do, and will not consider.

The call to every Briton is to make a stand on behalf of British institutions, and to take it at once. Any plan of resistance will prove vain that does not comprehend that the menace is confined to the priests, that the French-Canadians are simply used as tools, and that the cry of a French nation is adopted to cover what is really aimed at, a nation subject to and controlled by Papal influence. To Sbarretti what do French-Canadians signify? He would sooner have Italians were they to land in sufficient number and be as obedient as the habitants. Once the people outside Quebec realize the fact that a gigantic movement is in progress to enthrone the rule of priestcraft, they will proceed to deal with the men who shelter themselves under a cloak of divinity.

The Injury Done the French-Canadians.

The Church of Rome is dual: it is a spiritual system, and it is a political system. In the United States it is a spiritual system: in Quebec it is more political than spiritual. The French-Canadian who looks back on the history of his race on this continent will see how his church in its political capacity has been its blight. The intolerance that drove the Huguenots away was the first step in the failure of New France.

The priests backed the Kings of France in keeping the habitants vassals, isolated, and without that education that would have enabled them to hold their own with their neighbors to the south. It is Bourinot who says: "In Canada, as in France, absolutism and centraliza-"tion were the principles on which the government "was conducted." (Constitutional History of Canada, Chap. I.) And it is Parkman who, in concluding his history of New France, declares the French-Canadians "have imposed upon themselves a weight of "ecclesiastical tutelage that finds few equals in the "most Catholic countries of Europe. . . . It is "fatal to mental robustness and moral courage. If "French Canada would fulfil its aspirations it must "cease to be one of the most priest-ridden communities "of the modern world."

What do French-Canadians owe the priests? Who prevented New France prospering as New England prospered? Was it not the priests who prevented the Huguenots becoming settlers? Who defeated Frontenac's plans for founding a great French colony in the valley of the Mississippi? Was it not the priests? Who connived at the rule of men, of whom Bigot is a type, who plundered the people and made the country an easy prey for the invader? Who was it that fostered discontent that they might extort concessions from the English governors for themselves? Who was it that played fast and loose with the Americans at the Revolution? Who was it who patted Papineau on the back and encouraged him to rebel, and then, when they had got all they sought for themselves, betrayed Papineau and his followers? Who was it that traded, after the union of 1841, the French-Canadian vote for concessions to their own associations? Who are they who have absorbed the earnings of the habitants until they have created the richest corporations in the province? Who has kept the habitants illiterate that they might be the more obedient? Who are they who to this hour play with racial and religious passions to obtain the advantages they covet? And above all, who have kept the French-Canadians in an attitude of jealousy, distrust, and dislike towards their Protestant fellow-citizens? The French-Canadian who is truly loyal to his race can only see in the priesthood the enemy of his people, who, with consummate subtlety have kept them in thrall that they might use them to rise on their backs. To only one object have the priests of Quebec been true, the aggrandizement of their order and organization.

What We See in the United States.

The problem that confronts our country being not one of race or language, but of a compact and powerful body of ecclesiastics who would establish their rule as supreme, and who, in seeking that end, use, as they would any other prejudice, appeals to race and language, the question before the electors is, whether they are going to recognize that rule. When the Kings of France, among them he who revoked the Edict of Nantes, earning thereby a special blessing from the Pope, the promise of the eternal praises of the Church, solved the difficulty by placing the State above the Church, why should it be blasphemy for any Catholic to propose what these eminent sons of the Church did? Refer to the extracts from the despatches of those Kings already given, and see how determinedly they kept bishop and priest in check. Yet those Kings who would not permit cloistered convents, would not allow nuns to wear uniforms, resented interference by cure or bishop with secular affairs, were Catholics, the eldest sons of the Church, blessed and honored by the Popes as no other monarchs of their times were. Why raise hands in horror when it is proposed to do in the twentieth century what was accepted by Pope and bishop in the eighteenth? The disestablishment of the Church of Rome in Quebec must come if Canadians are to remain in truth, and not merely in name, a self-governing people. In the United States all churches are equal, none having special privileges. Will any one dare say, because that is so, American Catholics are inferior to the Catholics of Quebec? American Catholics pay no tithes, they build their churches by voluntary contributions, they send their children to the same schools as their neighbors, when a candidate for public office solicits their vote they do not ask whether he is approved by their bishop, no mandements are proclaimed from the altar telling what books and newspapers they must not read, what meetings they must not attend, there is no interference with freedom of speech and press. Because American Catholics profess their faith under such different conditions from those of Quebec, who calls them bad Catholics? What is orthodox south of the boundary line cannot be reprehensible north of it. If French-Canadian Catholics, who have gone to the States, are emancipated from obligations they are held to in Canada, and are still counted among the faithful, why is it wrong to advocate that those on the Quebec side of the border be relieved from a system that may have had its use in feudal times, but is incompatible with the conditions of the twentieth century?

The Conventual System.

English-speaking people have forgotten what the conventual system is. It was so intolerable to our fathers that they utterly destroyed it. Its revival in a sporadic form in Protestant communities is regarded with something of sentimental interest, nuns and monks having a halo cast around them of self-sacrifice which an intimate knowledge of their commonplace characters and shallow natures would dissipate. What is the judgment of every age and every country upon them? There is not a Catholic country to-day, not even Italy, where monastic institutions are not restricted by law, where their accumulations of wealth have not been forfeited for public purposes, and certain orders suppressed. This was done not by Protestants, but by Catholics, and why? Because they were found to be injurious to society and an obstacle to government by the people and for the people. The only countries where convents and monasteries are left undisturbed, and are not regulated by law, are Protestant countries, and, in Canada at least, they are abusing that forbearance in aiding to bring our government under clerical influence. France saw that their suppression was essential for the public good, and enacted laws regarding them which every Catholic country will yet copy. The proposal that these laws of Old France be adopted by Canada will be mocked as preposterous, as unattainable. If they are not enacted on the soil of New France, then Canada will never be wholly free—the influence which rises from the monastic system where, as in Quebec, it is numerous and wealthy, is a potent instrument in the hands of the priests to crush the will of the people and control our public men. The enlightening of the electors as to the true nature of the conditions that exist may be slow, and their realization of the course they should take may be slower still, but as they comprehend the imminence of the danger that threatens them, they will come to see that in such legislation as is here indicated lies preservation from the tyranny that is moving to get them in its grasp.

Separation of Church and State.

May the tragical fate of the English farm settlements of Quebec be a warning to the people of the other provinces, to rise above their local affairs, and grapple with the great issue that is before them, and which the longer it remains unsettled, the more complex and difficult it will become. The union of church and State in Quebec is incompatible with the stability of the Dominion. The existence of that system in one province will be found, as in session after session of late years, a menace to the other provinces and a constant hindrance to the proper working of the Federal

Government. No church can with safety to the public weal be given a preference by the State over other churches, and the State cannot become the servant of any church without conjuring a hundred troubles. Separation of church and State would have saved the English-speaking settlements of Quebec; separation of church and State can alone save the Dominion. To that end, an agitation in favor of amending the B.N.A. Act by inserting an article declaring complete and entire separation between the two is demanded. Nothing less will do. To sever the roots which interlace church and State will take time, and the most effective means of doing that is the adoption of the laws now in force in France with regard to religious associations, making such changes in them as the differing circumstances of Canada require. The evil that threatens, the shaping of the Dominion's destiny to suit a body of ecclesiastics, is too menacing to be dealt with by a feeble hand, and the laws the French people need to secure them in their civil rights cannot be too drastic for us. When these laws were outlined by Gambetta, he was derided by the clerical party as a dreamer of impossibilities. A generation had scarce passed when the voice of France embodied them in statutes which are enforced with an iron hand. What has been done in France can be done in Canada? Shall Canada be a land of equal rights, or is it to continue to endure a caste with its government subservient to that caste?

What is Your Choice?

The foundation stone of Democracy is that the people be self-governing. That the rule of the people be successful it is essential that the electorate be free from outside influence; that no power lurking among them dictate how they or the representatives they elect shall vote. An electorate intelligent and unbiased is necessary to the working of self-governing countries. Universal suffrage does not imply Democracy. If it did, Mexico and the Central American states would be the best governed countries in the world, instead of the worst. On the character of the electorate, their ability to use their private judgment in considering how they shall vote, depends the quality of the government of a country. In Canada, with a disciplined, compact, and powerful society of men who claim, in the name of religion, the supreme direction of its affairs, rule by the people and for the people is impossible. There will be constant clashing between the democratic aspirations of the people and clericalism. There shall be no peace known in Canada until the priest is made to understand he is not different from the ordinary citizen and is compelled to cease from interfering in public affairs. The struggle to vindicate the right of the people to be ruled by themselves and not by a clerical organization may be long and may be fierce, but it cannot be avoided, it must be fought, and on the result depends whether Canada is to be British or Papal.

The call to you, oh, reader, is to throw your influence on the side of rule by the people. Do not try to shirk. Give up calling yourself by a party name and determine you shall vote for the candidate who is to be depended upon to fight Clericalism. Your motive is no narrow one; it is, by destroying privilege, to bestow equality on all. Shall Canada be a land of equal rights, or shall it not? What say you?

CHAPTER XIV.

Is Our Northwest to be British or Papal?

By a great sacrifice Canada was made part of the British Empire. By the thousand her sons laid down their lives in the struggle, and a debt was rolled up that caused the Motherland to stagger in her effort to carry it. There never was another instance where territory was paid for more dearly or won more decisively, than Britain's conquest of Canada. The French king acknowledged that, when, by the treaty of Paris, he renounced his sovereignty over it without reservation and without exacting a single concession in return. Since the Conquest it has been by a struggle against foes within, that Canada has been maintained a part of the Empire to this hour. That it may so continue is the heart-desire of every loyal subject—that, with the coming years, Canada may go on expanding until its vast domain has been redeemed from the wilderness and then, strong in united sentiment, powerful in population and resources, she will be the champion of the Motherland and defy her enemies to assail her. More than this, the loyalist looks for constitutional institutions of the British type being more fully developed here than where hindered by feudal traditions or hereditary interests. What the thirteen American colonies might have done it is open to Canada to do—to cultivate and develop the shoot off the old tree—with this difference, that in place of enmity towards the land where it grew, there shall be forbearance and reverence. Are we to take our stand, that, as Canada has been British in the past, it shall be British in the future—that on this virgin soil those institutions which are the glory of the Mother State—self-government, regard for law and order, equal rights, devoted patriotism—shall be its characteristics? If the answer is Yes, then let us look to it, that there are no conditions to prevent realization of this hope.

One obvious menace to the continuance of Canada as British, is the avalanche of foreigners being shot into our midst—people who know neither our language nor our customs, totally ignorant of the working of constitutional government; people who have escaped from under the heel of despotic rulers and bring with them hatred of law and constituted authority. Are we doing what self-preservation dictates, when we give these foreigners portions of the great heritage of fertile land that Providence has entrusted to our care? Who would invite an alien of objectionable record to become an inmate of his home, a member of his family? Were a man found so foolish, would it be surprising were he, in course of time, displaced by the newcomer and evil wrought among his children? Had the Federal Government retained the ownership of the land, its passing into the hands of undesirable foreigners could be stopped, but our government has not retained the ownership; railway and land companies control millions of acres, and these corporations care nothing for the future status of the country, and, in their greed, rush in settlers regardless of qualification, race, or character. The most now that can be done would be to exact that no foreigner be allowed to vote until he can read and write English.

When the danger of this influx of foreigners is urged, it is the common reply, that we should set to work to convert them into good British subjects. Do those who speak so, ever think of the impossibility of

the task they propose? What could they do if sent
into a settlement of several hundred foreigners, who
do not know even how to live decently, yet bigotedly
attached to their own superstitions, prejudices, and
customs? Are the people who speak so glibly about
moulding this foreign material into loyal subjects of
Britain, willing to go as missionaries into these Northwest settlements? Less than that, do these people contribute to maintain the few devoted men and women
our churches are making such a sacrifice to send to
those settlements? If, when these settlements number only a few hundred thousand foreigners, the people in the eastern Provinces can do so little for them,
what will it be when the foreign element mounts into
millions, and the number in the older Provinces, who
are zealous to do mission work among them, shows no
increase? We already acknowledge that the undesirable
foreign element is so large that it is with difficulty it
can be kept subject to those influences which will make
them desirable citizens and loyal subjects. Unless the
door is closed to their influx, the Northwest will cease
to be, in the real sense of the term, British, and it is
the Northwest that is going to decide what Canada is
to be.

The United States Not An Example.

The experience of the United States is quoted as
proof that we have nothing to fear, that the republic
has assimilated just such hordes. That the American
people have had surprising success is true, but it has
been far from complete success, and the foreign peril
shadows the future of the republic. It has to be
considered the Americans faced the difficulty under
different conditions from ourselves. Before the flood
from continental Europe set in, the people of the
United States were English-speaking, and had settled,
so far as it is possible for all time, that there should
be no connection between Church and State, and that
no other than public schools, free and unsectarian,

should be recognized. Canada faces the problem with none of these advantages. A fifth of our population speaks French, there is a State church dominating our second largest Province, and we have no national school system. Whoever claims that Canada can do what the United States has accomplished in assimilating strange peoples, forgets how Canada is handicapped when she faces the foreigner to make him a British subject. Given a State church within her borders, sectarian schools, and a fifth of her population not speaking English, the United States could not have achieved what they have done with the foreigner. More than that, the United States, in proportion to its population, has not had the same number of aliens to deal with. The percentage of foreign immigrants has been much greater in Canada. What a country with a population that counts by tens of millions might effect, a country that counts its people by units cannot do. Our native leaven is too small for the mass of foreign meal.

Shall Canada continue to be British? That is the question that ought to over-rule all others, and must be settled now, for what is in our power to-day will be impossible a few years hence. It is provoking to reflect that what could have been easily done in 1885 to ensure the Northwest being British, is beyond our grasp now. The task is difficult, but it is not impossible, and should be grappled with at once. The call of patriotism, the call of self-interest and self-preservation, is to make sure that Canada shall, for all time, be British not merely in name, but in fact, and that ought to be the aim of all political effort.

Supposing the loyalists of Canada were awakened to the peril that overhangs them, that they were fully convinced of the importance of uniting in a supreme effort to keep the Northwest British, what would they have to do? I submit there are four essentials—One Language, One School, Severance of Church and State, No Recognition of Race.

Train the Children.

There is no disputing that the hope of doing anything with the foreign element already entrenched on our soil lies in their children. The grown-up foreigner is set in his ways and not to be remoulded, but there is a possibility of making Britons out of his children —inspiring them with our ideas and attaching them to our form of government. In taking the two-score nationalities represented in the Northwest, and fusing them into British subjects, the chief agency must be the school. To do its work there are two indispensable requisites, one language and no discrimination as to creed. If the language is not English, the school is useless as a means of making the boys and girls Britons, and equally useless if the boys and girls are sorted out according to the religious belief of their parents, and given separate tuition. The object sought is unity—dividing on creed, or having any other language than English, is fatal to unity. Ample provision has been made in the Northwest for supporting schools. Should these schools vary with the predominant nationality of each settlement, some Galician, others Russian, a few Polish, with Italian, Greek, Ruthenian, German interspersed, the Northwest will be a conglomerate, a mixture of discordant elements, without cohesion, and with a large part of its population having no regard for the government that gave them their farms and aided them in making a new start in life. Unless it is irrevocably decided now, that the Public Schools of the Northwest are to teach English, and nothing else than English, Canada is not going to continue to be British.

Language is not all. It is necessary that the Public School be inoffensive to the parents whose children go to it, and, to that end, there must be no interference with religious belief. The population of the Northwest is divided as to creed—there are members of the Greek Church and its branches, there are Armenians, Doukhobors, Jews, Protestants, Mormons, Roman

Catholics, and a large number who are not within the pale of any church. All these people have a just claim in asking that their children be not interfered with in spiritual matters, and, therefore, the schools must be colorless as regards creed. In an ideal State, where all the people think alike on religious subjects, a school that combines secular with religious instruction is possible. But the Northwest is not Utopia, and we have to deal with conditions as we find them, and these are a mixed multitude who differ in their religious views. A school for their children is a necessity, and the only basis on which they can unite in having one, is that it will confine itself to secular knowledge, therefore, of necessity, not of choice, the Public School has to be neutral, colorless as to creed.

The Distribution of Patronage.

The impartiality that leads to the Public School being made a common meeting-ground for children of all origins and creeds, ought to be extended to their parents. Both Federal and Provincial Governments should dispense their patronage without regard to nationality or creed. Unless an end is put to office-seekers demanding appointments because of their race or religious belief, the work of assimilation will be defeated, for such a method of filling public offices perpetuates sectionalism. The system of civil public service, which we have made a start in copying from England, has its defects, but it ensures impartiality by making ability the standard. The civil service commissioners take no cognizance of the nationality or belief of applicants for office, but they do of the manner in which they passed their examinations. There are over twenty thousand salaried officials, Federal and Provincial. At the present time it is safe to say three-fourths were appointed because of influences which had nothing to do with their fitness. The principle, which it has been tried to establish at Quebec and Ottawa, that each nationality and creed is entitled

to its proportion of patronage, is destructive of the
purpose to make Canada British. If, for no other
reason than this, the Senate should be changed into
an elective body, and end the scandal of men in every
sense unsuitable being appointed to it on the ground
that they represent some section of the population in
religion or origin.

The principle involved in banishing from the
Public School and the civil service the elements of
creed and race, must apply to all grants of public
money. Taxes being contributed by all citizens, no
part of them should be applied to purposes offensive
to the consciences of any section of the population.
Grants of public money or land to benefit any particular church are at the expense of those who do not
belong to that church, and, therefore, unjust—a cause
of discontent, an element of strife. As in the case of
the school, fair play can alone be shown by giving protection to all denominations but contributing to the
support of none. Where the State is truly neutral, no
offence can be given to the adherents of any religious
body, and it interferes with none so long as they respect the common law. In a mixed population no
other course is possible that will ensure peace.

The difficulty of applying these principles is urged.
If not reduced to practice, and that speedily, the result will be an increasing number of discordant peoples, each demanding special privileges in the matter
of schools, churches, language, and public offices. With
French schools and Russian schools, Galician and
German, the government making laws to suit the
special requirements of the Catholic creed and the
Greek, of the Armenian and the Judaic, and premiers
compelled to study, in making selections for public
positions, the creed and nationality of applicants,
there will be discord and contention, weakness and
corruption, and whatever the Canada might be that
in course of time would be evolved from such chaos,
it certainly would not be British. It is no injustice

to the descendants of people who were brought
under British rule by force majeure, or to people
who voluntarily seek homes in Canada to better themselves, to insist that they comply with conditions that
are obviously imperative to continue Canada as British.
If foreigners do not like the conditions, they need not
immigrate here, and their coming is a tacit consent to
their accepting our conditions. That people fleeing
from the poverty and oppression of continental
Europe should receive free grants of land, share in the
advantages of the enormous expenditure we have
lavished on the Northwest to make it accessible, and
then turn round, demanding their language and creed
be recognized by the State, and our laws modified to
suit their Old World customs, is intolerable. We have
given them much, endured much, are we, in addition,
to pluck the core from the British constitution to suit
their notions? The stand has to be taken that Canada
is British, and whoever seeks to live in it must become
British and be content with the laws and the administration of them that are required to continue Canada
as British. If foreigners are not prepared to recognize English as the language of the State they had no
business to come here; if they want the same privileges given their respective churches as obtained
whence they came, they should have remained where
they were, or gone elsewhere and founded a colony
for themselves. No foreigner has a right to come
among us and attempt to graft upon our institutions
those of the land he left. By virtue of conquest, of
settlement, of sacrifices to make it what it is, Canada
is British, and whoever plans or attempts to make it
anything else is an enemy and to be treated as a traitor
to the common weal. There must be no compromising,
no paltering for the sake of securing temporary peace.
Requests for special favors are to be decisively refused. The time has come when the insolent demands
of foreign interests have to be grappled with or Canada will cease to be British.

1. One language;
2. Public schools;
3. No sectarian grants or laws;
4. Government appointments by merit.

These proposals are reasonable in their simplicity, yet no four could be made which will meet with such obstinate resistance. The opposition will be prompt and bitter, and will start from the Province that most strikingly illustrates the result of their non-enforcement. Had our public men in the past insisted that one language, one school, no sectarian legislation, and no consideration of creed or race in filling offices, were essentials to be maintained, Quebec would not be what it is to-day—the danger-centre to British institutions in the Dominion, the chief obstacle to making Canada what it ought to be. The resistance of the scattered settlements of foreigners in the Northwest to an immediate effort to **unify and assimilate would be** easy to overcome; it is the support they receive from Quebec that makes the undertaking formidable.

ONE LANGUAGE.

No power can prevent people from using in the family or in business whatever language they please. That is a natural right which pertains to the individual, and which must be left to those concerned. The State cannot say you must give up speaking Gaelic, French, German, Russian, or Italian, but its duty is to see that these languages be not recognized as official, that, while exceptions are to be submitted to where the administration of justice or the carrying out of executive orders require their use, they are not on the same plane as English. To facilitate the transaction of business it is necessary to have a standard of value, for it would be a source of confusion and endless difficulty were it lawful to use all manner of foreign coins and keep accounts in foreign currency. Likewise it is essential that one language be decided upon as the medium of communication in all matters outside social intercourse. A polyglot nation would be one of misunderstandings and divisions, and lack the unity that makes for peace and permanence.

The Quebec Congress to Make French an Official Language.

Moves have been made by isolated groups in the Northwest to have their language made the language of their schools, but the most formidable effort is to have French placed on the same plane as English. Quotations from the report of proceedings at the great international congress held in Quebec city during the summer of 1912 will enable the reader to quickly grasp the nature of the agitation to fasten on Canada other languages than English. Far and wide invitations were extended to all who spoke and loved French to attend. Thousands came from all over the continent; it was the largest assemblage of French-speaking people Quebec had known. They came filled with enthusiasm to glorify and deepen their love for the language of their parents, of their childhood, and the choice of their mature years. Seeing the advertised purpose of the congress, French-Canadians who are Protestant desired to take part. The impression abroad, that French Protestants are a negligible quantity, is not correct. Their number is not contemptible, and the encouraging feature is that it is increasing. In Montreal and the city of Quebec, French Protestants form charming circles of their own, for their animating spirit is a fine fraternal feeling which makes them happy socially and in their mutual helpfulness. The vivacity, the courtesy, the regard for others opinions, which makes the French-Canadian so delightful a companion, is enhanced in those French-speaking Protestants by the absence of that reserve, that suspicion in discussing subjects which border on creed that makes the English Protestant fear, in social converse with a Catholic French-Canadian, he is giving unwitting offence. The Baptist,

Methodist, Anglican and Presbyterian schools and colleges have not been at work among the French-Canadians for two generations in vain. French Protestants prove this. In intelligence, business aptitude, and knowledge of books they are the equal of Canada's best society. They have eminent men among them. Do not the brothers Lafleur lead in their respective professions? Are not professors of McGill to be found among them? Are there any more eloquent or impressive in the pulpit? And where can an equal number of French-speaking people be found in Quebec comparable in their ardor in mastering the topics of the day and in keeping abreast with the best books that come from the presses of Paris? Change of creed has not affected their patriotism. They glory in being French-Canadians, so when this congress was announced they desired to be represented. They had as much interest in the French language as anybody could have, and they sent delegates to Quebec. They were peremptorily and decisively refused admission.

Now, if the congress was really what it professed to be, a gathering for the furtherance of the French language, why had those French Protestants its doors slammed in their faces? Does that one act not prove in itself, that the congress was not organized to promote the French language, but to advance the efforts of the priests in their project of establishing Papal supremacy by preventing their people learning English?

There was further proof. Among the delegates from the United States were a number from towns in the State of Maine who had a controversy with their bishop, not over any doctrine, but regarding his administrative acts. It was acknowledged these delegates from Lewiston and Biddeford were good Catholics and true French-Canadians, but they had set up their will against that of their bishop and, therefore, they would not be recognized. Delegates to this pretended congress for the uplift of the French language must not only be Catholics, but Catholics who give implicit obedience to their clergy. This completed the proof, that the congress was not what it professed to be, and that its pretence about language was deceptive.

In its atmosphere and management the congress was a purely clerical meeting, presided over by Mgr. Roy, with bishops and cures as the chief speakers, their subject, the spread and triumph of their church from the Atlantic to the Pacific. Archbishop Langevin struck the keynote that the congress was to insist that the French language was on an equality with English in every province of Canada, and it was their duty to act like men and assert what was theirs. "We recognize," he said, "the right of no one to stop us on the frontier of the Province of Quebec, saying outside of that line you are no longer at home." Father Quinn, French in all except name, called English "a foreign language." Archbishop Bruchesi declared "the Constitution guaranteed the French language and the British flag protects it as it protects our religion, our churches, and our priests."

Bishop Mathieu spoke of the close connection between the French language and the Catholic religion, and "as they guarded their religion so must they guard their language and their schools." He urged that for settlements outside of Quebec nuns be provided, and that Catholic doctors and lawyers be encouraged to go to these Western settlements. Dr. Reaume, then a member of the Ontario Cabinet, endorsed this, saying: "Before we leave this congress we should make a vow to raise and educate our children in the French language, no matter what part of Canada we live in," and this was to be done by State-aided schools. Bourassa was emphatic in asserting that French was an official language not merely in Quebec but in every province of the Dominion. "Two "races," he exclaimed, "the rights of which in "language as in everything else, are equal." Father

Lebel told how, while a missionary in New Ontario, he had promoted the settlement of many parishes along the C. P. R., the Grand Trunk, and the Northern railways, and had founded 14 Catholic schools. In Ontario, out of 106 constituencies, the French, he declared, already had either a large vote or a clear majority in 22.

For three days the congress was in session, and nothing was said that did not fail to emphasize the vital connection between the French language and obedience to the priests. Instead of being a congress to promote the French language, by dwelling on its excellencies, its development and attainments, it was really a gathering to extend priestly supremacy. Among the resolutions adopted was one enjoining that when French-Canadians settled in another province they reproduce the organization of parishes identical with those they had left in Quebec. Whoever reads the proceedings of this congress and takes pains to find out their drift, can come to only one conclusion, that there was no real concern for the French language, per se, in itself, but that the affected zeal and self-assumed championship of that language was merely a cloak to hide its real purpose, namely, to extend and entrench more securely priestly absolutism.

Dual Language Does Not Work Well in Quebec.

The assertion that the system of two languages works well in Quebec is so frequently and positively asserted that many believe the assertion. Such is not the case; the existence of two official languages in Quebec works badly, and is a hindrance to its prosperity. Look at a few instances in proof.

The commerce of Quebec lies in the hands of the minority—blot them out, banks would close, steamships cease running, railway shops disappear, factories shut their doors. The great employers of labor, the directors of gigantic enterprises, the suppliers of capital, are English-speaking. It is from them the

Provincial Government draws most of its revenue, Montreal constituting the milch cow from which the Quebec politicians replenish the province's treasury, yet no consideration of gratitude prevents wanton interference by the Legislature with the English minority in its modes of doing the business that pays their salaries and supplies the funds they spend. Twice has the legislative assembly adopted a bill to compel commercial companies to use French. That these companies, in their own interest, will use French wherever called for is plain, but the proposal is to coerce them, by fines, into using French where they consider there is no need, and an opening is given to lawyers to harass and prey upon them by recovery of prescribed fines. Is there another British dependency where companies, which have received no State aid, are punished for not using another language than English? How would the manufacturers of Toronto like to be dictated to in this manner, yet that is what the recognition in Ontario of French as co-equal with English would bring them. Again, take the use of two languages in court. Here is an illustration. An action is taken out against an English-speaking farmer. The document notifying him of what he is ordered to do is served upon him in French. He is unable to read it, and asks for an English copy. The reply is, that French is an official language in Quebec, and he has no right to ask for a translation: the document served upon him is according to the law of the province. He attends court, all that is said is in French, for, unless the charge against him is criminal, he cannot claim to have the evidence of witnesses repeated in English. All he knows of what is going on is what his lawyer whispers to him. The judge takes the case en delibere, and when he comes to a finding the farmer gets his decision in a long French document. To learn what the judgment is that has been passed on his case, he has to search out some one who can read it to him, perhaps pay for a translation.

Trial of An English Farmer.

Supposing it is a criminal charge upon which the farmer is brought into court, this is what happens: The judge, a Frenchman, having taken his seat, the lawyer who appears for the farmer asks the court for an English-speaking jury. The prosecutor for the crown objects, and that ends the matter, and the jury sworn in is, therefore, a mixed one, half being English-speaking. The crown prosecutor addresses the jury, first in French, then in English. Of what he says to the French half of the jury the farmer understands not a word. The witnesses are now called. There is an interpreter, who repeats what the French witnesses say in English, and what the English witnesses say in French. The translation is often bad, necessarily it is rough-and-ready. The manner and exact expressions of the witnesses are lost to half the jury. The French jurymen get the evidence of the English witnesses as filtered through the translator: the English jurymen that of the French witnesses not as it comes from their lips, but as paraphrased by the translator. It is all slow, tedious, mechanical, but there is not an official who does not desire to have the trial spun out a week or more, for they are paid by the day, and a criminal term in Quebec means found money to them. A disinterested spectator comes to perceive there are two trials going on instead of one —that the farmer is being tried under conditions he understands by his six countrymen, and under conditions he does not comprehend by the six French jurymen. The evidence all in, the addresses to the jury come next. The farmer may be poor, but if he wants to be acquitted, he has to engage two lawyers, one to address the French jurymen, the other the English half of the jury. The crown is likely to have joint-prosecutors, one English, the other French, so that their addresses differ in substance as well as in language. The farmer knows naught of what the French prosecutor is declaring with such vehemence and gesticulation against him. The judge charges the jury in both languages, and there are often discrepancies between his two deliverances. The jury retire to consider their verdict. One half cannot discuss the case with the other half. The Frenchmen talk among themselves and decide on their verdict—the Englishmen do the same. Unless one of the twelve speaks both languages fluently they cannot arrive at an intelligent finding. Such a man is rare, so, in broken English and worse French, a verdict is patched up by the twelve men in order that they may end their confinement and get back to their work and homes. Often it is six against six and, neither giving in, a disagreement is reported and the farmer has to undergo another trial at the succeeding term, generally a year after. This is the travesty of justice that goes on in the Province of Quebec from year to year. The farmer had a right to be tried by twelve of his peers—he was actually tried by six only, and the other six, unconsciously, no doubt, regarded him with the prejudice of race and creed. Behind the judge is the coat of arms, but the farmer has been denied that justice the British coat of arms is supposed to represent, and for him Wolfe died in vain. Had the farmer a right to be tried in the language of the Empire and by his peers, or had he not?

All this is inevitable wherever any language is made legally co-equal with English. Wherever there is variety of speech there must be difficulty and drawbacks in administering justice, but the point is this, Why, in a British country, should the litigant, whose mother tongue is that of the Empire, be made to suffer from those drawbacks? Why should a native of Britain or a descendant of a Briton, be treated in Quebec as a foreigner in a foreign land? Is he not entitled to whatever advantages follow from English being the language of the Empire, and those who speak other tongues be the parties who have to submit to the inconveniences, defects, and delays of procedure by means of interpreters? Surely the English-speaking Canadian is entitled to the preference. Let readers of this who are living in the Western Provinces substitute for the word "French" in the foregoing narrative Russian or Greek, Galician or German, and he will realize what will happen if he does not stand up for English being the sole official language of Canada. English is in process of being tabooed in Quebec, it is year by year being placed at a greater disadvantage, and more and more being treated as a foreign language in its courts, departments, and legislature. May the other provinces take warning of what will surely come to them in course of time if they do not insist on one official language and that the language of the British Empire.

The Separate School Considered.

No self-governing country can afford to have any considerable portion of its people illiterate. The exercise of the franchise makes intelligence imperative. The man who cannot read cannot have an enlightened opinion on any public issue, and, therefore, ought to be adjudged incapable of having a voice in the government of the country. The better educated the electorate, the more widely informed, the safer, more progressive, more stable the government. A despotism cherishes ignorance for it conduces to blind obedience. Intelligence is the breath of a free State, therefore Canada's aim ought to be to have every child given the elements of education. No one will ever be able to say that public schools teach all that is desirable, but it is within our power to see that no child shall fail to be put in possession of the three keys which unlock the doors of knowledge. In assuming a duty necessary to the preservation of a self-governing country it is essential that all the children be dealt with on the same terms, that no family or set of families be given a preference, but all be treated alike. When a parent comes and says, "I want my children taught "the doctrines and ritual of the church I belong to," surely the government ought to have no other reply than that the schools are intended to impart only the elements of secular education, and to add aught else is beyond their purpose and touches subjects with which no government has a right to meddle. To see that Jack and Jenny shall be able to read, to write, to count, to learn something of the resources and institutions of the land they live in, is the duty of the government; to go beyond that, and undertake to give them the training to fit them as members of any church, is not. Is not this the A B C of political principles, of the mutual compact on which all self-governing communities rest? Objectors, who style secular schools infidel, show they have hazy ideas of their own duties, for they would unload upon the government, a composite and purely secular organization, the teaching of spiritual truth, a task which belongs to the parents and their church. No government is capable of imparting spiritual knowledge. The only province that voluntarily attempts it is Quebec. Here, as in language, Quebec is an object-lesson to the other provinces. Its boast is that its schools, from the lowest to the highest, teach religion, and, therefore, are infinitely superior to those of the rest of the Dominion, which are scornfully called "godless."

Separate Schools Are Not Religious.

If by "religion" is meant the imbuing of the infant mind with love to God and man, then the teaching in these schools does not comply with that standard, has no claim to be religious, for their teaching is so uncharitable that the children are made to believe that all mankind outside the **Church of Rome are in a state** of condemnation.. Examine the so-called religious teaching of these schools and it will be found it is not to expand the mind with broad views of the highest of all Truth, or to enrich the affections with the purest conceptions of pity and mercy, but to make bigots, to so cramp the intellect by means of forms and catechism, to smother the natural aspirations of piety by routine prayers, that the children are ensured for life as believers in priestly dogma. There is a short and decisive way of settling the pretence that the scholars of such schools are superior in morals to those from non-sectarian schools, and that is by an appeal to experience. Are those trained in Catholic schools distinguished from their fellows by being less profane, less drunken, less coarse, less immoral, more scrupulous in their respect for the property of others, more benevolent, more active in promoting every agency for the betterment of society? What do the statistics of the police and criminal courts tell? Are the bulk of offenders against law, men and women who have got their education in "godless" or in "religious" schools? To focus the enquiry, take a single instance—that of the Italians. Are the tens of thousands who have come to live among us conspicuous for their observance of the moral law? Yet they never knew of any other creed than the Papal, for centuries upon centuries they have been under the exclusive training of the priests, who had the most ample opportunity of moulding them to their standard. If the training of a people by the priests secures the highest type of manhood, strong in morals, lofty in religious aspirations, bright in intelligence, as the advocates of priest schools are never tired of asserting, how do they explain the Italian as we find him in our communities? Nurtured in the land which is the home and heart of the order of priests, the Italians ought to be superior to the product of godless schools and heretical temples. Are they? Go ask the municipal officials to whom the care of health and decency is committed. Go ask the police, the judges, the superintendents of charitable institutions or hospital physicians, if there is any class who gives them the same trouble? Are the Austrians, the Hungarians, the Poles, models of the Christian graces?

Brought to this simple, practical test, of judging priestly training of the young by the lives presented to us of those who have been subjected to its discipline, the assertion of the priests, that their methods insure a moral and religious people, is seen to have not an atom of evidence to support it. Their claim that they have the one infallible means of curing the ills of society, of doing away with ignorance, crime and dissolute living, is contradicted by the palpable evidence of the peoples they have had in hand for centuries in Europe. The charlatan who vaunts his elixir as a specific for diseases which the medical faculty can only relieve, is on a par with the priest who asserts the separate school will do for the uplift of society what the public school cannot approach. The separate school is not religious in the true sense of the word. It is theological—an instrument to engrain into the child's brain the belief that the priest is the sole exponent of Christian doctrine and that all who do not accept what he teaches, will go to hell. To dwarf and narrow the intellect and to foster spiritual pride, no device in civilized countries equals the separate school. Are the priests to be permitted to seize our public schools, supported at the public cost, and shape them to suit their own ends, by drilling the rising generation in the doctrines and practices of a sect—to pervert a public institution into an instrument to suit a denomination? Visitors to rural Quebec note the evidence that meets them of a country behind the age, and, in part, trace the cause to the inefficiency of the schools, for many cannot read and only few write. In the first requirement of the State, giving the people the elements of secular education, the rural schools of Quebec, more than those of any other of the provinces, have manifestly failed.

The Claim As to Taxes.

A plausible argument of the advocates of separate schools is, that as the government levies a tax for school purposes Catholics are entitled to get back their share. This would be an effective plea if the tax was levied according to creed. Do we pay taxes as Catholics, Presbyterians, Methodists, or Jews, or do we pay them as citizens? Are there separate cash-boxes in the treasuries of our provinces and at Ottawa, labelled with the names of the various churches, into which the taxes are dropped according to the creed of those who pay them? If so, then the members of each denomination might claim what is in their particular box be expended in the way they ask, but as there is no such system, when all taxes go into a general fund, it is foolishness to pretend that any church has a claim upon a particular portion. The government levies taxes for public purposes to be expended on behalf of the people as a whole, therefore, if the State diverts any part of its revenue from public purposes to bestow on any church, it is guilty of a breach of trust. How could the business of the country be conducted were every dollar of revenue credited according to the creed of the person who paid it, and the government pay it out on the same plan? It would be impossible, yet the Baptist, the Methodist, the Presbyterian, the Anglican, has an equal right with the Catholic to make such a demand. For a section of the population to say, Our standing is different from these, they are only pretended churches, ours is the true church, is to raise a question with which the civil magistrate has nothing to do.

When a body of people demand that, because of their religious belief they be treated differently from the common herd, is any government justified in recognizing such a claim? The government that does, violates two principles of the civil contract by asserting, (1) that the State is competent to judge religious beliefs, and (2) to grant special privileges to the church it prefers.

The Principle Involved in Separate Schools.

It is only by people giving, regardless of creed, that schools can be maintained. In an agricultural country like ours, as has been pointed out in Chapter 8, the number of children in the average school district is small, and, at the best, the teacher has few pupils. Introduce the principle that a favored sect is to have its own school, and there can be none for the children of other faiths, and so, just because of the religious belief of their parents, that they do not belong to the sect it favors, the State deprives their children of their right to an elementary education. The government that does this demonstrates its preference for one particular church, and gives it special benefits at the expense of members of all the other churches. There is no escaping the fact, that separate schools imply a State church. Are we in Canada to ignore the experience of Europe on this point? With the record before us of the evils that have flowed from State churches, are we going to fall into the same pit? The argument against separate schools is strong on the ground of expediency, that they defeat the purpose of assimilating the diverse elements of our population and fitting the rising generation for fulfilling the duties called for in a self-governing country, but the argument is tenfold stronger and is conclusive to all lovers of liberty, that such action is an interference by the State with the consciences of its people. In our age there is no saying more readily accepted as undeniable than that it belongs not to the government to dictate what shall be the creed of province or dominion, for it is justly held that religious beliefs are beyond and above the functions of the civil magistrate. Whoever gives his assent to this truth, should, in all consistency, set his face as flint against separate schools, for the two are irreconcilable. If you say the government has no right to enact that a particular church shall be the church of the province in which you live, what right has it to pick out one church and endow it with favors it denies to all other churches? To recognize separate schools, implies the recognition of the right of your government to interfere in spiritual matters. Though he may not think so, the elector who submits to the continuance of separate schools concedes the principle that the State is endowed with the right to judge of spiritual truth, to reward those who come up to the standard it fixes, and to punish those who do not, by placing them under disabilities. Is this not contrary to every conception of liberty of conscience? When the priests unitedly declare it is an essential part of the teaching of the church they represent, that the children of its members be educated apart from the children of other faiths, and demand the government provide separate schools for them, the answer of the State ought to be, that if they will not eat out of the common dish, and drink out of the common cup, they must provide dish and cup at their own cost—that the State would be going outside its jurisdiction to judge creeds and beyond its duty in taking funds contributed by the people as a whole to build partition walls and nourish sectarianism. The government places at the disposal of all a train to transport the children of the nation from ignorance to the realm of secular knowledge, and parents who are so exclusive that they will not send their children into the same car with those of their neighbors, ought to be told they must pay for a Pullman out of their own pockets. Once admit religious belief as constituting a claim for exceptional treatment by the government, and where will these claims end? In Quebec, where this claim has been most fully acknowledged and most fully developed, it does not end with the school. The principle of separation is carried into every public institution. There are not only separate schools and colleges, but separate asylums for the Catholic indigent, the Catholic insane, the Catholic helpless; separate hospitals for the Catholic sick; separate reformatories, and even separate prisons. From the cradle to the grave the government is required to pay towards keeping Catholics by themselves and under the care and control of the priests.

Come to close quarters and ask, Whether this claim of the priests upon the government for exceptional treatment has not two sides? If the conscience of the priest is so tender that he cannot possibly permit the children of his people to attend a secular school, what about the conscience of the Jew or Protestant who sees public money taken to maintain a Catholic school? Have priests alone such tender consciences that the State must bow to them? Is there no assault upon the conscience, when a government takes public money to maintain schools that teach their scholars enmity to those of other creeds? Is not every separate school subsidized out of the public chest an insult to the convictions of every non-Catholic? Were non-Catholics as alive to their convictions and their own self-preservation as the priests, they would not allow a dollar of public money to go to the support of separate schools. The priest with his non possumus should be met with an equally decided reply, that public funds shall not be taken to propagate his creed. Let the priest be given to understand in the most emphatic language, that other citizens have an equal right to have their conscientious beliefs respected.

The Kernel of the Priestly Claim.

When Catholic bishops come before a legislature, they do not speak as citizens, as men on an equality with other subjects, but as superior beings, who come with an authority laymen must obey. Liberty rests upon the principle of the equality before the law of all subjects, that no man possesses inherent rights not shared by his fellows. Because a certain cluster of individuals claim to soar far above the mass, to be in a distinct and sacred class by themselves, are our public men justified in acknowledging their claim? On what principle, on what authority, do the members of our governments recognize that awful claim that the priests are the representatives of Christ, and, therefore, can command our legislatures to use the funds meant for the country as a whole to keep their followers separate and distinct from the rest of the people? Is the money of non-Catholics to be taken to maintain institutions that insult them by proclaiming they are unfit to participate with Catholics in their benefits, that their presence would be contamination? A body of men and women set themselves up to be holier than their neighbors, to be possessors of a spiritual unction shared by nobody else, and forthwith demand that the State recognize their exclusive holiness, and assist by money and statute to keep them a separate people. To yield to the demand is to thrust a knife into the principle upon which Britain's government rests, that all her subjects are equal before the law. Were Canadians awake to a sense of the grandeur of the principle of equal rights for all, exclusive privileges for none, they would see the necessity for bestirring themselves, in order to save the liberty of the country by facing the priests, telling them they shall have all the privileges which are the heritage of every British subject, but not one iota more.

Separate Schools Involve Subjection to Canon Law.

Without being aware of it, electors outside Quebec who proudly think there is no canon law for them and they would like to see the men who would attempt to bring them under it, are all the time obedient to that law wherever a separate school is established and receives support by reason of any statute of their legislature. There is no part of canon law more emphatic than that which declares the bishops shall have control of schools and their teachers, consequently any government that admits that claim acknowledges submission to canon law. To quote the teaching of the Syllabus of 1870 on that head is sufficient to show what is claimed. I quote from the authorized version in the affirmative: "If anyone says that all the direction of "the public schools, in which the youth of a Christian "State receives instruction, Episcopal seminaries "being excepted, can and must be confided to the "hands of the civil authority; . . . let him be "cursed. . . . If anyone says that Catholics can "approve a system of education outside of the Catho- "lic faith, and outside of the authority of the Catholic "Church, and having for its object, or at least for its "main object, only the knowledge of things purely "natural and the interests of the social life on this "earth, let him be cursed."—Articles 45 and 48.

These articles the Archbishop of Quebec, in his pastoral regarding the Syllabus, interpreted thus: "The "church must have admission to the schools, not only "by simple tolerance, but by virtue of its divine mis- "sion. . .they stigmatize as a sacrilegious usurpa- "tion all civil laws concerning the education of the "youth; they say that, by its divine institution, the "church must have to itself alone the direction of "schools, even in what concerns letters and natural "sciences."—Pastoral letter, 31st May, 1870.

This is the claim, reiterated and reiterated in speech, sermon, and mandement—the education of the child is the inalienable care of the priesthood. The Hon. Mr. Bernier, speaking on behalf of the Archbishop of St. Boniface, defined the scope of the priesthood and of the State: "It was the duty of the former to guide "and supervise and of the latter to supply the mater- "ial aid necessary." The clerical organ of the diocese of Montreal, summed up the claim of the priests in a syllogism:

"The formation of the Christian in the child is the "principal work of education;

"The Roman Catholic Church alone has the mission "to form the Christian;

"Parents and teachers are lieutenants representa- "tive of the Roman Catholic Church from the power "conferred upon her by Christ."

There is more involved in this matter of separate schools than people think. The government that yields to the demands of the priests for separate schools, thereby recognizes the validity of canon law and its duty to comply with it. When the demand is made for separate schools it is regarded by the average elector as a matter concerning the education of the children of his Roman Catholic neighbors and nothing more. It means much more, for the demand for separate schools conceals the claim that the government yield obedience to canon law. On this ground, the public conscience of Canadians needs to be enlightened—electors shown that it is not a question of expediency to grant separate schools, but a question that involves their obedience to Papal law and Papal decrees.

A fact, having a significance on the subject, should be noted that only those peoples who are under priestly thrall resist equal laws. Finlanders, Icelanders, Swedes, Norwegians, Danes do not seek separate schools or raise objections to English being the language of the schools.

That in order our Northwest may realize the great future which Nature has designed for it, that millions of free, enlightened and progressive people may fill its homes, it is essential that it be freed from the shackles and weights of class-privileges, that its legislatures have not two measures of law, one for a favored section and another for the people generally, but one law applied equally to all. This requires one school and one language.

The Call of the West.

The unit upon which the Northwest is built is the British farmer. He left the Old Land buoyant with the hope that he would be his own master and be able to make ample provision for those he loved. He and they have had a strenuous period, endured sore privations with patience, looking forward to the better time coming. The settler has struggled to his feet so far that he can think of something else than keeping cold and hunger from his home. The department has granted the petition for a school, and he is glad for the sake of his children. While it is building he hears of a dispute as to the language to be taught. The settler is astounded, for it never entered his mind that Canada was aught but British. There is contention among the foreigners nearby, each wanting his own tongue to be chosen. The priest pays them a visit and orders that the teacher be a Roman Catholic. The settler, more astounded than before, again asks, Is Canada British? An election is in prospect. He gets in touch with his English-speaking neighbors and they agree they will vote for a candidate who thinks as they do. They are on hand on polling day, and when the hour for closing draws nigh they are confident their man leads. While pleased with this prospect, a long string of foreigners appears, led by their headman. They unitedly cast their votes for the candidate who will do what they and their priest want, and he is elected. The Englishmen go to their homes vexed and angry, saying had they known that coming to Canada would place them under the rule of priests and foreigners they would never have left England. When the school is in session the Union Jack floats from its flagstaff. It is hoisted by order of the legislature that has not the courage to enforce the principles for which that flag stands. The settler reads the reports of the proceedings in the legislature of his province and of the parliament at Ottawa, and comes to perceive how the conduct of both is guided so as not to offend the unseen power behind and to which they both truckle. Such are the conditions in scores of settlements. With their existence how will the Northwest develop? British in name but not British in reality. There was once a member of the Dominion Parliament who realized what would be the outcome of these conditions, and to ensure that the Northwest would, in truth and verity, be part and parcel of the British Empire, he advocated it have one school, one language, and one allegiance. He was detested by his own party and mocked by the Opposition for insisting that action be taken. Though not many years have passed since D'Alton McCarthy died, we see how what he foretold has come true and how much strife and heart-burning would have been avoided had his reforms been enacted. Are we, who have not a doubt that British rule stands for what is best for all, to be cowed by bishop, cardinal, or ablegate from establishing on a foundation that cannot be shaken, the mastery of British principles in our glorious Northwest? Our politics have degenerated into mere struggles between the ins and outs. Can we not redeem them from contempt by introducing a commanding issue? The future of the Northwest is trembling in the balance. Are we, who love the Old Land and who glory in being British, going to listen to the call of the West to save it from the thrall of the priest and of the foreigner?

THE END.

Index

AMERICANS—
  Settle in Eastern Townships 12
  Relations with New France 36, 39
  Invade Canada 97
AMHERST—What he granted and what he refused 61
ARGENSON—Refused to shoot a heretic 44
ASSEMBLY, QUEBEC—
  Divided as soon as it met 113
  Disputes with Council 139
  Motive of opposition 141
  Claim crown revenue 142
  Trumps up grievances 144
  Character of Members 146
  Its leaders 150
  Treatment of Eastern Township farmers 153
  Refuses supplies 155
  Last demands 162
AYLMER, GOV. 162

BALDWIN AND LAFONTAINE—Make parishes legal and
    French an official language of Assembly 176-177
BEGIN, CARDINAL—introduces religious cry into bi-
    lingualism 302
BILINGUAL SCHOOL AGITATION 294, 296, 299
  Its issues described 305
BISHOP BRIAND—testimony as to morals 51
BISHOPS GET CONTROL OF QUEBEC 192
BISHOP DE ST. VALLIER—complains of beggars 50
BLEUS AND ROUGES 175
BLUE LAWS OF QUEBEC 46, 48
BOOKS BURNED 49
BOUCHETTE 14
BOUNTIES offered for scalps of Protestants 38
BOURGET—
  Contrasted with Denaut 135, 183
  Brings Jesuits back 193
BRANDY, sale of to Indians 46
BRIAND, BISHOP, on state of society 51
BRITISH party at rebellion 169
BRODEUR, JUSTICE—his misrepresentations 105
BRUCHESI, ARCHBISHOP 208, 242

INDEX.

BROWN, GEORGE 179, 181, 182
BUREAUCRATS 151
BURKE, EDMUND .... et seq 76

CABOT 22
CADILLAC on the priests 46
CALL, THE, of the West 372
CANADA—
    Its discovery 22
    No-man's land 24
    Developed by Huguenots 24
    Held by British 31
    Its three stages under France 31
    Conquest by British 53
    Divided into Upper and Lower Canada 108
CANADA ACT 108
    How it worked 111
CANON LAW—
    On marriage 225
    Burial 226
    The press 236
    Private judgment 243
    Municipalities 245
    Taxes 249
    Its courts 250
    Above British law 253
    Education 370
CARLETON (Lord Dorchester)—
    Evidence as to Quebec Act 76
    Instructions as to French law and the priests . 85
    Scouted rising of Americans 94
    Goes to defend Montreal 96
    Habitants and Indians refuse help 97
    Returns to Quebec 99
    Pursued Americans 101
    Saved Canada to Britain 102
    His opinion of French-Canadians 98, 105
    Efforts to establish Church of England 133
    Dealings with priests 134
CARROLL, FATHER 103
CARTIER, SIR E. 181, 182, 183, 186
CARTIER, JACQUES 22, 32
CASTORS 192
CATECHISM, R. C.—What it teaches 219
CATHOLIC BUILDINGS used for Protestant worship ... 136
CATHOLIC REPUBLIC 278
CHAMPLAIN—
    First visit 25
    His period 32

INDEX.   iii.

CHAPLEAU 200
CHARLES FIRST sells Canada to France 31
CHARLEVOIX compares Canada with New England 50
CHATEAUGUAY, the skirmish of 105
CHURCH OF ENGLAND 110, 126-130
CHURCH OF ROME in Canada has no treaty rights 85
CLAY BELT coralled by priests 326
CLERICALISM—
    The peril of 329
    How it works 335
    Its nature and claims .... 336 and 337
CLERICAL COLLEGES .... 147 and 148
CLOUTIER, BISHOP—his claims as to education 298
CONGRESS about French language 355
CONFESSIONAL schools contrasted with public schools. 205
CONVENTUAL SYSTEM, THE 342
CONQUEST OF CANADA—
    Made separation of U. S. possible 90
    Its effect on Canada 104
    Policy of George Third .... 93 and 94
CORVEE 97
COURTS and registry offices refused E. T. farmers 154
COUREURS DE BOIS 35
COUSINEAU opposed municipal grants to bilingual
    schools 301
CRAIG, GOVERNOR—his policy 130
CRAIG ROAD 13-15
CROWN LAND PATENTS 201
CRUCIFIX BILL 193

DALHOUSIE—
    Efforts to maintain British supremacy 141
    His course justified 142, 143, 157
    His attempts to curb priesthood 158
DAVID, SENATOR, his book 243
DE MONTS 25
DENAUT, BISHOP—letter to George III. 122
DENONVILLE, GOVERNOR—tells King Louis no heretics
    in Canada 45
DE VALLIER, BISHOP—
    Women's dress 46
    Order about tithes 47
DIFFERENCE between concessions by treaty and by
    statute 86
DOUBLE MAJORITY 186
DUPLESSIS, BISHOP 50
DURHAM, LORD 106, 173

INDEX.

EASTERN TOWNSHIPS 13, 14
   Refusal of Representation 158
   Present Condition 217
EDUCATION handed to priests 193
EGREMONT, EARL—testimony as to treaty of Paris ... 66
ELLICE, ALEX. 126
EMIGRATION—
   Its start 15
   Few stayed in Quebec 17
   None desired 78
   Change of policy 123
   Emigrant ships 124
   Opposed by French 127
ENGLISH RULE MISREPRESENTED 213
ENGLISH FARMERS—
   Their treatment 153
   Plan to drive them out 196
   Their deeds to farms clear of all servitudes 201
   Quebec their native land 205
ENGLISH-SPEAKING PEOPLE 152, 205
ENGLAND, CHURCH OF 138
EXPLORERS, difference between French and American. 26

FEAR OF RE-CONQUEST 114
FEUDAL SYSTEM 33
FOREIGNERS
   Influx into Northwest 347
   Difficulty in assimilating 350-353
FOX, CHARLES—
   Opposed Quebec Act 74
   Also the Canada Act 108
FRANKLIN, BENJAMIN 96
FRENCH-CANADIANS have no treaty rights 85
FRENCH KINGS, how they ruled the priests ...... et seq 262
FRENCH LANGUAGE—
   Not mentioned in treaty of Paris 66
   Nor in the Quebec Act 86
   Nor in the Canada Act 112
   Panet's views on 112
   First time made official in legislature 176
   Congress to promote 355
   Claim to be an official language 307
FRENCH PARISHES, conditions in 259
FRENCH M.P.s 275, 302
FRENCH PROTESTANTS—
   Developed Canada 24
   Of to-day 355
FRENCH REPUBLIC, A, for Canada 278
FRENCH REVOLUTION 114

INDEX.

FRONTENAC—
  Opinion of Jesuits 29
  Changes he made 35
  Plans to make France supreme 36
  His recall 36
  His second term 38
  Opinion of priests 49
  Effort to establish municipal council 111

GALT, SIR A. T. 191, 195, 199, 204
GARNEAU 71
GOVERNORS—
  French, their poverty and pride 34
  English 130
  Draw on crown to maintain government 155
  Kempt's remark 163
  Aylmer's concessions 163
  Colborne had few soldiers 166
GOUIN, SIR LOMER 297
G.T.R. PACIFIC 279
GRANTS, public money 352

HABITANTS—
  Their farming 14
  Not allowed to manufacture 39
  Or have horses 40
  Hocquart's describes them 40
  Compelled to be soldiers 41
  Forbidden to leave the province 42
  Treatment by British 54
  Condition at Conquest 56
  Helped American armies 98
  Knew nothing of self-government 111
  Complained of seigniors 116, 125
  Their illiteracy 160
  At home 258
  No respect for Ontario laws 289
  How injured by priests 339
HABITANT BOY who became a priest 331
HALDIMAND 104
HAMON, FATHER 276, 287
HAMPTON, GENERAL 106
HAULTAIN, COLONEL 190
HEROIC PERIOD SO-CALLED 48
HEY, JUDGE 66, 77
HIGHLAND FARMER on language 311
HOCKEN, H. C. 314
HUGUENOTS 24-26, 43, 45

INDEX.

INCAPABLE LEGISLATORS 252
ILLITERATES IN E. T. 210
IMPERIALISM 285
INDIANS refused to serve 97
INTERCOURSE forbidden with outside world 42
IRISH ROMAN CATHOLICS 162, 203
ITALIANS 364

JESUITS—
    Arrival 28
    Secure purchase of Canada 30
    Thwart Frontenac 37
    Persecute Protestants 43
    Their expulsion 169
    Brought back 193
    Get their estates 195
    Under French Kings 268

KERNEL, THE, OF PRIESTLY CLAIM 369

KIRKE CAPTURES CANADA 31
LAFLECHE, BISHOP 278
LANCASTER, E. A. 231
LANGEVIN, SIR H. 187
LANGUAGE 112, 115, 350, 354, 358
L'ELECTEUR 240
LA MOTTE 46
LAPOINTE'S MOTION—
    Debate on 313
    Sir Wilfrid Laurier's speech 314
    His argument, throws blame on Ontario 318
    No censure for Quebec priests invading Ontario..319, 321
    Boers no parallel 319
    F. Oliver's speech 322
    Defeat of motion 323
LA SALLE 46
LAURIER, SIR WILFRID 205, 314
LAVERGNE 283
LAVAL, BISHOP 35, 41, 44, 49, 94
LE PAYS 241
LEGISLATURE OF U. C. AND L. C. 174, 182
LIBERALS, PETITION to Pope of French 240
LOUIS XIV. AND XV. 39, 262
LOWLAND SCOT SETTLER 18
LUNATIC ASYLUMS, etc., handed to be controlled by
    bishops 192
LYMBURNER 109

MACDONALD, SIR JOHN 174, 181-183

INDEX.   vii.

MACDONALD, JOHN SANDFIELD 180
McCARTHY, D'ALTON 374
McCORD, JUDGE 203
McGEE, D'ARCY 184
McNAB, SIR ALLAN 176
MAIL, THE, OF TORONTO 290
MASERES 62, 66
MERCHANT, SCHOOL INSPECTOR 291
MERCIER, HON. 104, 205, 246
MIGNAULT, BATTONIER 70
MILITARISM OF NEW FRANCE 89
MILITIA OF NEW FRANCE 41, 56, 115
MONASTIC ORDERS 169, 177, 253, 267
MONTGOMERY, GENERAL 100
MONTREAL—
    Proposal to annex to Ontario 159
    Its merchants 47
    Its grant to bilingual schools 300
MOUNTAIN, BISHOP 138
MURRAY, GENERAL 66-69, 77, 92

NEILSON, JOHN 152, 162
NAPOLEON 131
NATIONALISTS 161, 280, 282, 285
NEUTRAL PANEL .... 212 and 213
NEW FRANCE 33, 42, 43
NORTH, LORD .... 73 and 74
NORTHWEST, to be Papal or British 346
NOVA SCOTIA 64
NUNS 29, 74, 263

ODELLTOWN, fight at 166
ONTARIO—
    Invaded by French priests 287, 326
    Should vindicate her independence 327
ORDERS, crowding in of foreign 272

PANET, BISHOP 161
PAPAL QUEBEC 276
PAPAL RULE a failure in New France 50
PATRONAGE, how distributed 285, 351
PAPINEAU, LOUIS 13, 128, 141, 150, 152, 160, 163,
                                                      164, 166, 190
PARISH SYSTEM 33, 82, 93, 163, 176, 201
PARIS, TREATY OF 63
PARKMAN 53
PARLIAMENT, IMPERIAL—
    Opposed emigration 78, 147
    Favored abandoning Canada 156

PLESSIS, BISHOP 121, 136, 160, 206
POIRIER, SENATOR 208
POPULATION AT CONQUEST 56
PREVOST, GOVERNOR 136
PRIESTS—
    Status at Conquest 59
    And later 135
    Attitude towards English 94, 118, 120, 128
    At French Revolution 115, 132, 134
    Their Legal Pretences 274
    Their organization 330
    What it has accomplished 333
    Kernel of sacerdotal claim 369
PRESCRIPTIVE RIGHTS, claim to 257
PRESS, the bishops' letter on the 236
PRINTING PRESS, NO, in New France 51
PROCLAMATION of George III. 65
PROTESTANTS, ENGLISH .... 210 and 211
PROTESTANTS, FRENCH 24, 43

QUEBEC ACT, THE .... 72 to 87, 174, 202
QUEBEC, THE ARCHBISHOP 254
QUEBEC MINORITY .... 184 and 185, 220, 221, 309, 325
QUEBEC A U. S. STATE 102
QUEBEC ULTIMATUM, THE 182

REBELLION OF 1837 165
REBELLION OF 1838 .... 166, 286
REGISTRY OFFICES 154, 155
REPRESENTATION BY POPULATION 179
REPUBLICAN PARTY IN QUEBEC 130
REVOLUTION, AMERICAN .... 94 to 105
ROBERVAL 24
REVUE LE CANADA 236
RICHELIEU, CARDINAL 31, 33
ROMANTIC PERIOD ALLEGED 33
ROUGES 281

SEIGNIORS 33, 57, 72, 116
SEIGNIORIAL SYSTEM 123
SEPARATE SCHOOLS 180, 185, 209, 362, 363
    Principle involved in 367
SEPARATION OF CHURCH AND STATE 343
SEWELL, ATTY.-GEN. 139
SHERBROOKE, GOVERNOR 162
SKETCH OF SETTLER 18
STATUS of Church of Rome under French Kings ...262, 272
STATUTES were in English only 115
STE. BARBE 248

INDEX.

ST. EUSTACHE 165
ST. JEAN BAPTISTE Celebration of 1916 323
STATE SUPREME under French Kings 268, 279
STEWART, BISHOP 15
STRENGTH OF Church of Rome 273
SULPICIANS 161, 169
SYDENHAM, LORD 168, 176, 207
SYLLABUS QUOTED 370

TALON 35, 41, 49
TARDIVEL 281
TASCHEREAU, CARDINAL 282
TAXES, Catholic claim to school 365
TESTIMONY to English tolerance 59
TITHES 33, 75, 82
TOWNSHEND, GENERAL 60
TOWNSHEND, THOS. 73
TOWNSHIPS, EASTERN 12, 153
TRADE OF NEW FRANCE 51
TREATY RIGHTS, claims to 64, 69, 85, 87
TRIAL OF English-speaking farmer 360

USE OF Recollet Church 136
UNION OF QUEBEC to Ontario proposed 160
U. E. LOYALISTS 107
U. S. CATHOLICS 341
UPPER CANADA, its rebellion 168

VAUDREUIL 61
VIGER 128
VVIL, DANIEL 44

WEDDERBURN 65, 74
WHITNEY, SIR JAMES 292, 295
WILKINSON, GENERAL 106
WOMEN shipped like cattle to New France 41

YOUNG FRENCH-CANADIAN ASSOCIATION 298

www.ingramcontent.com/pod-product-compliance
Lightning Source LLC
Chambersburg PA
CBHW032023290426
44110CB00012B/647